Webster's Basic Thesaurus

Promotional Sales Books, LLC

How to Use a Thesaurus

If you have never used a thesaurus before, you are in for an unique experience. In some ways, it is like a dictionary, but there are no definitions given. Instead a thesaurus gives you *alternative* words.

First, you will learn the correct spelling of the word. Then, you will be given an extensive selection of choices that you can use instead of the primary word. These are synonyms, and providing a series of similar alternative words is what a thesaurus is all about.

When the first thesaurus was published by Peter Mark Roget, the primary purpose of his book was to provide the reader with synonyms for a word. In addition, his goal was to provide the reader with a tool that would offer a wide range of words that could be used as a substitute to the original concept. His book, however, was somewhat more complicated than this one, since it presented not only the *synonyms*, but *expressions* that were pertinent to the ideas of seventeenth century philosophy and science.

In this thesaurus, the words are presented in alphabetical order, just like a dictionary, to help you quickly find the words you need. However, these are not just synonyms, but the words are presented on the basis of grammatical type—nouns, verbs, adverbs, adjectives, etc. Whether you are a student, a writer, a businessperson, a player of word games, or someone who just enjoys reading, this book will provide you with a wealth of synonyms to increase your word power.

One word of caution: you will note that not all of the words presented as synonyms are completely and identically interchangeable alternatives for the primary word. Instead, by presenting the richness of the language, you will have access to a broader choice of words. Somewhere in those extensive choices you will find those words that can best express your intended meaning.

It is interesting to note that most lexicographers recognize the fact that there are no true synonyms. Although many words may mean the same thing, they each may have slightly different meanings. Something that is odd may be *abnormal* as well as *peculiar*, but these are not the same words. Something odd may also be *uncommon*, and that still does not carry the same meaning. Therefore, as we have mentioned above, choose your words carefully.

In addition, we have also provided you with many foreign words, but those that have come into popular or common usage. These, too, will enhance your writing skills, and provide an often "colorful" alternative to your original word.

Finally, we have taken care to include important and current words and synonyms, but these were purely editorial decisions. You may take exception to the words we have included or excluded. If you don't find the word you are looking for, or don't agree with our selection of choices, we suggest you consult a dictionary, where you will certainly find the words to your liking, and hopefully, those that will satisfy your need.

We hope you **enjoy** (*appreciate, delight in, dig, experience, have, like, make a meal of, own, posses, rejoice in, relish, revel in, savor, take pleasure in, use*) using this thesaurus.

A

abandon *v.* abdicate, cede, desert, desist, discontinue, ditch, drop, evacuate, forgo, forsake, give up, jilt, leave, leave behind, leave in the lurch, quit, relinquish, renounce, repudiate, resign, surrender, waive, withdraw from, yield. *n.* dash, recklessness, unrestraint, wantonness, wildness.

abate *v.* alleviate, appease, attenuate, decline, decrease, deduct, diminish, discount, dwindle, ease, ebb, fade, fall off, lessen, let up, moderate, quell, rebate, reduce, relive, remit, sink, slacken, slow, subside, subtract, taper off, wane, weaken.

abbreviate *v.* abridge, abstract, clip, compress, condense, contract, curtail, cut, digest, epitomize, lessen, reduce, shorten, shrink, summarize, trim, truncate.

abet *v.* aid, assist, back, condone, connive, egg on, encourage, goad, help, incite, promote, prompt, sanction, second, spur, succor, support, sustain, uphold, urge.

ability *v.* adeptness, adroitness, aptitude, capability, capacity, competence, deftness, dexterity, expertise, expertness, facility, faculty, flair, genius, gift, knack, know-how, power, proficiency, qualification, savoir-faire, savvy, skill, strength, talent, touch.

able *adj.* accomplished, adept, adequate, adroit, capable, clever, competent, deft, dexterous, effective, efficient, experienced, expert, fit, fitted, gifted, ingenious, masterful, masterly, powerful, practiced, proficient, qualified, skillful, skilled, strong, talented.

abolish *v.* abrogate, annihilate, annul, blot out, cancel, destroy, do away with, eliminate, end, eradicate, expunge, exterminate, extinguish, invalidate, nullify, obliterate, overthrow, quash, repeal, repudiate, rescind, revoke, stamp out, suppress, terminate, vitiate, void.

about *prep.* adjacent to, around, beside, circa, concerning, encircling, encompassing, in respect to, in the matter of, near, nearby, on, over, re, referring to, regarding, relative to, surrounding, with regard to, with respect to.

above *prep.* atop, before, beyond, exceeding, higher than, in excess of, on top of, over, surpassing, upon. *adv.* aloft, atop, earlier, overhead, supra.

abroad *adv.* about, at large, away, circulating, current, elsewhere, extensively, far, far and wide, forth, in circulation, in foreign parts, out, out-of-doors, outside, overseas, publicly, widely.

absent *adj.* absent-minded, absorbed, abstracted, away, bemused, blank, day-dreaming, distracted, faraway, gone, heedless, inattentive, lacking, missing, not present, oblivious, out, preoccupied, truant, unavailable, unaware, unconscious, vacant, vague, wanting.

absolute *adj.* actual, autocratic, autonomous, complete, decisive, definite, entire, exact, indubitable, omnipotent, perfect, positive, precise, pure, supreme, sure, total, unambiguous, unequivocal, utter.

absolve *v.* acquit, clear, deliver, discharge, emancipate, exculpate, excuse, exempt, exonerate, forgive, free, justify, let off, liberate, loose, pardon, ransom, redeem, release, remit, set free, shrive, vindicate.

abstain *v.* avoid, cease, decline, deny, desist, eschew, forbear, forgo, give up, keep from, refrain, refuse, reject, renounce, resist, shun, stop, swear off, withhold.

abstract *adj.* abstruse, conceptual, generalized, hypothetical, indefinite, philosophical, subtle, theoretical, unrealistic. *n.* abridgment, abstractive, compendium, digest, epitome, résumé, summary, synopsis. *v.* abbreviate, abridge, condense, detach, digest, extract, outline.

absurd *adj.* anomalous, comical, crazy, daft, derisory, fantastic, farcical, foolish, funny, humorous, idiotic, illogical, implausible, incongruous, irrational, laughable, ludicrous, meaningless, nonsensical, paradoxical, pre-posterous, ridiculous, risible, senseless, silly, stupid, unreasonable, untenable.

abundant *adj.* ample, bounteous, bountiful, copious, exuberant, filled, full, generous, in plenty, lavish, luxuriant, overflowing, plenteous, plentiful, prodigal, profuse, rank, rich, superabundant, teeming, uberous, unstinted, well-provided, well-supplied.

abuse *v.* batter, damage, defame, denigrate, disparage, exploit, harm, hurt, injure, insult, libel, malign, maltreat, manhandle, mis-use, molest, oppress, revile, scold, slander, smear, spoil, swear at, take advantage of, upbraid, vilify, violate, vituperate, wrong.

accent *n.* accentuation, articulation, beat, cadence, emphasis, enunciation, force, ictus, inflection, intonation, pitch, pronunciation, pulsation, pulse, rhythm, stress, thesis, timbre, tonality, tone.

accept *v.* abide by, accede, acknowledge, acquiesce, admit, adopt, affirm, agree to, approve, assume, believe, bow to, concur with, cooperate with, get, have, jump at, obtain, receive, recognize, secure, stand, stomach, suffer, swallow, take, take on, tolerate, undertake, wear, yield to.

acceptable *adj.* adequate, admissible, agreeable, all right, conventional, correct, delightful, desirable, done, grateful, gratifying, moderate, passable, pleasant, pleasing, satisfactory, standard, suitable, tolerable, unexceptionable, unobjectionable, welcome.

access *n.* admission, admittance, approach, avenue, course, door, entering, entrance, entrée, entry, gateway, increase, ingress, key, onset, passage, passageway, path, road, upsurge.

accident *n.* blow, calamity, casualty, chance, collision, contingency, contretemps, crash, disaster, fate, fluke, fortuity, fortune, happenstance, hazard, luck, misadventure, miscarriage, mischance, misfortune, mishap, pile-up, serendipity, shunt.

acclaim *v.* announce, applaud, approve, celebrate, cheer, clap, commend, crown, declare, eulogize, exalt, extol, hail, honor, laud, praise, salute, welcome.

accommodate *v.* acclimatize, accustom, adapt, adjust, afford, aid, assist, attune, billet, board, cater for, comply, compose, conform, domicile, entertain, fit, furnish, harbor, harmonize, help, house, lodge, modify, oblige, provide, put up, quarter, reconcile, serve, settle, shelter, supply.

accompany *v.* attend, belong to, chaperon, co-exist, coincide, complement, conduct, consort, convoy, escort, follow, go with, occur with, squire, supplement, usher.

accomplish *v.* achieve, attain, bring about, bring off, carry out, compass, complete, conclude, consummate, discharge, do, effect, effectuate, engineer, execute, finish, fulfil, manage, obtain, perform, produce, realize.

accord *v.* agree, allow, assent, concede, concur, confer, conform, correspond, endow, fit, give, grant, harmonize, jibe, match, present, render, suit, tally, tender, vouchsafe. *n.* accordance, agreement, assent, concert, congruence, correspondence, harmony, rapport, symmetry, sympathy, unanimity, unity.

accordingly *adv.* appropriately, as a result, as requested, consequently, correspondingly, ergo, hence, in accord with, in accordance, in consequence, properly, so, suitably, therefore, thus.

accumulate *v.* accrue, agglomerate, aggregate, amass, assemble, build up, collect, cumulate, gather, grow, hoard, increase, multiply, pile up, stash, stockpile, store.

accurate *adj.* authentic, careful, close, correct, exact, factual, faithful, faultless, just, letter-perfect, mathematical, meticulous, minute, nice, perfect, precise, proper, regular, right, rigorous, scrupulous, sound, spot-on, strict, true, truthful, unerring, veracious, well-aimed, well-directed, well-judged, word-perfect.

accuse *v.* allege, arraign, attaint, attribute, blame, censure, charge, cite, criminate, delate, denounce, impeach, impugn, impute, incrim-inate, indict, inform against, recriminate, tax.

ache *v.* agonize, covet, crave, desire, grieve, hanker, hunger, hurt, itch, long, mourn, need, pain, pine, smart, sorrow, suffer, throb, twinge, yearn. *n.* anguish, craving desire, grief, hunger, hurt, itch, longing, misery, mourning, need, pain, pang, pining, pounding, smart, smarting, soreness, sorrow, suffering, throb, throbbing, yearning.

achieve *v.* accomplish, acquire, attain, bring about, carry out, compass, complete, consummate, do, earn, effect, effectuate, finish, fulfil, gain, get, manage, obtain, perform, procure, produce, reach, realize, score, strike, succeed, win.

acid *adj.* acerbic, acidulous, acrid, astringent, biting, bitter, caustic, corrosive, cutting, harsh, hurtful, ill-natured, incisive, mordant, morose, pungent, sharp, sour, stinging, tart, trenchant, vinegary, vitriolic.

acknowledge *v.* accede, accept, acquiesce, address, admit, affirm, agree to, allow, answer, attest, avouch, concede, confess, confirm, declare, endorse, grant, greet, hail, notice, own, profess, react to, recognize, reply to, respond to, return, salute, vouch for, witness, yield.

acquaint *v.* accustom, advise, announce, apprize, brief, disclose, divulge, enlighten, familiarize, inform, notify, reveal, tell.

acquiesce *v.* accede, accept, agree, allow, approve, assent, comply, concur, conform, consent, defer, give in, submit, yield.

acquire *v.* achieve, amass, appropriate, attain, buy, collect, cop, earn, gain, gather, get, net, obtain, pick up, procure, realize, receive, secure, win.

acquit *v.* absolve, bear, behave, clear, comport, conduct, deliver, discharge, dismiss, exculpate, excuse, exonerate, free, liberate, pay, pay off, perform, release, relieve, repay, reprieve, satisfy, settle, vindicate.

acrid *adj.* acerbic, acid, acrimonious, astringent, biting, bitter, burning, caustic, cutting, harsh, incisive, irritating, malicious, mordant, nasty, pungent, sarcastic, sardonic, sharp, stinging, tart, trenchant, venomous, virulent, vitriolic.

act *n.* accomplishment, achievement, decree, deed, enterprise, feigning, make-believe, maneuver, operation, performance, pose, posture, pretense, stance, undertaking.

action *n.* achievement, act, activity, battle, clash, combat, conflict, contest, deed, encounter, endeavor, energy, engagement, enterprise, exercise, exploit, feat, fight, fighting, force, fray, litigation, motion, move, movement, operation, performance, undertaking, war- fare, work.

active *adj.* acting, activist, alert, animated, assiduous, bustling, busy, diligent, energetic, engaged, enterprising, enthusiastic, forceful, hard-working, industrious, involved, lively, occupied, on the go, on the move, spirited, sprightly, spry, vibrant, vigorous, vital, zealous.

actual *adj.* absolute, authentic, bona fide, certain, concrete, confirmed, current, definite, existent, factual, genuine, indisputable, legitimate, live, living, material, physical, positive, present, real, realistic, substantial, tangible, true, truthful, unquestionable, verified, veritable.

adapt *v.* acclimatize, accommodate, adjust, alter, apply, change, comply, conform, convert, customize, familiarize, fashion, fit, habituate, harmonize, match, metamorphose, modify, prepare, proportion, qualify, refashion, remodel, shape, suit, tailor.

add *v.* adjoin, affix, amplify, annex, append, attach, augment, combine, compute, count, include, join, reckon, subjoin, sum up, superimpose, supplement, tack-on, tote up, total.

adequate *adj.* able, acceptable, capable, commensurate, competent, condign, efficacious, enough, fair, fit, passable, presentable, requisite, respectable, satisfactory, serviceable, sufficient, suitable, tolerable.

adhere *v.* abide by, agree, attach, cement, cleave, cleave to, cling, coalesce, cohere, combine, comply with, fasten, fix, follow, fulfil, glue, heed, hold, hold fast, join, keep, link, maintain, mind, obey, observe, paste, respect, stand by, stick, stick fast, support, unite.

adjust *v.* acclimatize, accommodate, accustom, adapt, alter, arrange, balance,

change, coapt, compose, concert, conform, convert, dispose, fix, harmonize, modify, order, proportion, reconcile, rectify, redress, regulate, remodel, reshape, set, settle, shape, temper, tune.

administer *v.* apply, assign, conduct, contribute, control, direct, dispense, dispose, distribute, execute, give, govern, head, lead, manage, officiate, organize, oversee, perform, provide, regulate, rule, run, superintend, supervise, supply.

admirable *adj.* choice, commendable, creditable, deserving, estimable, excellent, exquisite, fine, laudable, meritorious, praiseworthy, rare, respected, superior, valuable, wonderful, worthy.

admire *v.* adore, applaud, appreciate, approve, esteem, iconize, idolize, laud, praise, prize, respect, revere, value, venerate, worship.

admission *n.* acceptance, access, acknowledgement, affirmation, allowance, concession, declaration, disclosure, divulgence, entrance, entrée, entry, exposé, granting, inclusion, ingress, initiation, introduction, owning, profession, revelation.

admit *v.* accept, acknowledge, adhibit, affirm, agree, allow, allow to enter, avow, concede, confess, declare, disclose, divulge, give access, grant, initiate, introduce, intromit, let, let in, permit, profess, receive, recognize, reveal, take in.

admonish *v.* advise, berate, caution, censure, check, chide, counsel, enjoin, exhort, forewarn, rebuke, reprehend, reprimand, reproach, reprove, scold, upbraid, warn.

adopt *v.* accept, affect, appropriate, approve, assume, back, choose, embrace, endorse, espouse, follow, foster, maintain, ratify, sanction, select, support, take in, take on, take up.

adoration *n.* admiration, esteem, estimation, exaltation, glorification, honor, idolatry, idolization, love, magnification, reverence, veneration, worship.

adore *v.* admire, cherish, dote on, esteem, exalt, glorify, honor, idolatrize, idolize, love, magnify, revere, reverence, venerate, worship.

advantage *n.* account, aid, asset, assistance, benefit, blessing, convenience, dominance, edge, gain, good, help, hold, interest, lead, leverage, precedence, profit, purchase, service, start, superiority, sway, upper-hand, use, usefulness, utility, welfare.

adventure *n.* chance, contingency, enterprise, experience, exploit, hazard, incident, occurrence, risk, speculation, undertaking, venture.

adverse *adj.* antagonistic, conflicting, contrary, counter, counter-productive, detrimental, disadvantageous, hostile, hurtful, injurious, inopportune, negative, opposing, opposite, reluctant, repugnant, unfortunate, unfriendly, unlucky, unwilling.

adversity *n.* affliction, bad luck, blight, calamity, catastrophe, contretemps, disaster, distress, hard times, hardship, ill-fortune, ill-luck, mischance, misery, misfortune, mishap, reverse, sorrow, suffering, trial, tribulation, trouble, woe, wretchedness.

advertise *v.* advise, announce, apprize, blazon, broadcast, bruit, declare, display, flaunt, herald, inform, make known, notify, plug, praise, proclaim, promote, promulgate, publicize, publish, puff, push, tout, trumpet.

advice *n.* admonition, caution, communication, counsel, direction, do's and don'ts, guidance, help, information, injunction, instruction, intelligence, memorandum, notice, notification, opinion, recommendation, suggestion, view, warning, wisdom, word.

advise *v.* acquaint, apprize, bethink, caution, commend, counsel, enjoin, forewarn, guide, inform, instruct, make known, notify, recommend, report, suggest, teach, tell, tutor, urge, warn.

affair *n.* activity, adventure, amour, business, circumstance, concern, connection, episode, event, happening, incident, interest, liaison, matter, occurrence, operation, organization, party, proceeding, project, question, reception, relationship, responsibility, romance, subject, topic, transaction, undertaking.

affect[1] *v.* act on, agitate, alter, apply to, attack, bear upon, change, concern, disturb, grieve, grip, impinge upon, impress, influence, interest, involve, melt, modify, move, overcome, penetrate, pertain to, perturb, prevail over, regard, relate to, seize, soften, stir, strike, sway, touch, transform, trouble, upset.

affect[2] *v.* adopt, aspire to, assume, contrive, counterfeit, fake, feign, imitate, pretend, profess, put on, sham, simulate.

affected *adj.* afflicted, agitated, altered, changed, concerned, damaged, distressed, gripped, hurt, impaired, impressed, influenced, injured, melted, moved, perturbed, smitten, stimulated, stirred, swayed, touched, troubled, upset.

affection *n.* amity, attachment, care, desire, devotion, favor, feeling, fondness, friendliness, good will, inclination, kindness, liking, love, partiality, passion, penchant, predilection, predisposition, proclivity, propensity, regard, tenderness, warmth.

affirm *v.* assert, asseverate, attest, aver, avouch, avow, certify, confirm, corroborate, declare, depose, endorse, maintain, pronounce, ratify, state, swear, testify, witness.

afraid *adj.* aghast, alarmed, anxious, apprehensive, cowardly, diffident, distrustful, faint-hearted, fearful, frightened, intimidated, nervous, regretful, reluctant, scared, sorry, suspicious, timid, timorous, tremulous, unhappy.

after *prep.* afterwards, as a result of, behind, below, following, in consequence of, later, post, subsequent to, subsequently, succeeding, thereafter.

again *adv.* afresh, also, anew, another time, au contraire, besides, conversely, da capo, de integro, de novo, ditto, encore, furthermore, in addition, moreover, on the contrary, on the other hand, once more.

against *prep.* abutting, across, adjacent to, athwart, close up to, confronting, contra, counter to, facing, fronting, hostile to, in contact with, in contrast to, in defiance of, in exchange for, opposed to, opposing, opposite to, resisting, touching, versus.

agent *n.* actor, agency, author, cause, channel, delegate, deputy, emissary, envoy, executor, factor, force, functionary, instrument, intermediary, middleman, mover, negotiator, operative, operator, representative, substitute, surrogate, vehicle, worker.

aggravate *v.* annoy, exacerbate, exaggerate, exasperate, harass, hassle, heighten, incense, increase, inflame, intensify, irk, irritate, magnify, needle, nettle, peeve, pester, provoke, tease, vex, worsen.

aggression *n.* aggressiveness, antagonism, assault, attack, bellicosity, belligerence, combativeness, destructiveness, encroachment, hostility, impingement, incursion, injury, intrusion, invasion, jingoism, militancy, offence, offensive, onslaught, provocation, pugnacity, raid.

agile *adj.* active, acute, adroit, alert, brisk, clever, fleet, flexible, limber, lissome, lithe, lively, mobile, nimble, prompt, quick, quick-witted, sharp, smart, sprightly, spry, supple, swift.

agitate v. alarm, arouse, beat, churn, confuse, convulse, discompose, disconcert, disquiet, distract, disturb, excite, ferment, flurry, fluster, incite, inflame, perturb, rattle, rock, rouse, ruffle, shake, stimulate, stir, toss, trouble, unnerve, unsettle, upset, work up, worry.

agree v. accede, accord, acquiesce, admit, allow, answer, assent, chime, coincide, comply, concede, concord, concur, conform, consent, consort, contract, correspond, cotton, covenant, engage, fit, fix, get on, grant, harmonize, jibe, match, permit, promise, side with, square, suit, yield.

agreement[1] n. acceptance, accord, accordance, compact, compatibility, compliance, concert, conformity, congruence, congruity, correspondence, harmony, resemblance, similarity, suitableness, sympathy, unanimity, union.

agreement[2] n. arrangement, bargain, compact, concordat, contract, covenant, deal, pact, settlement, treaty, understanding.

aid v. abet, accommodate, assist, befriend, ease, encourage, expedite, facilitate, favor, help, oblige, promote, serve, subsidize, succor, support, sustain. n. a leg up, assistance, assistant, benefit, contribution, donation, encouragement, favor, help, helper, patronage, prop, relief, service, sponsorship, subsidy, subvention, succor, support, supporter.

ail v. afflict, annoy, be indisposed, bother, decline, distress, droop, fail, irritate, languish, pain, pine, sicken, trouble, upset, weaken, worry.

aim v. address, aspire, attempt, design, direct, endeavor, head for, intend, plan, point, propose, purpose, resolve, seek, set one's sights on, sight, strive, take aim, target, train, try, want, wish, zero in on. n. ambition, aspiration, course, desire, direction, dream, end, goal, hope, intent, intention, mark, motive, object, objective, plan, purpose, scheme, target, wish.

aimless adj. chance, desultory, directionless, erratic, feckless, frivolous, goalless, haphazard, irresolute, pointless, purposeless, rambling, random, stray, undirected, unguided, unmotivated, unpredictable, vagrant, wayward.

air n. ambience, appearance, atmosphere, aura, breeze, character, demeanor, effect, manner, melody, mood, puff, quality, strain, tune, waft, whiff, wind, zephyr.

aisle n. alleyway, ambulatory, corridor, division, gangway, lane, passage, passageway, path, walkway.

alarm v. agitate, daunt, dismay, distress, frighten, give (someone) a turn, panic, scare, startle, terrify, terrorize, unnerve.

alert adj. active, agile, attentive, brisk, careful, circumspect, heedful, lively, nimble, observant, on the ball, on the lookout, on the qui vive, perceptive, prepared, quick, ready, sharp-eyed, sharp-witted, spirited, sprightly, vigilant, wary, watchful, wide-awake.

alias n. assumed name, false name, nickname, nom de guerre, nom de plume, pen name, pseudonym, soubriquet, stage name.

alive adj. active, alert, animate, animated, awake, breathing, brisk, cheerful, eager, energetic, existent, existing, extant, functioning, having life, in existence, in force, lifelike, live, lively, living, operative, quick, real, spirited, sprightly, spry, subsisting, vibrant, vigorous, vital, vivacious, zestful.

allegiance n. adherence, constancy, devotion, duty, faithfulness, fealty, fidelity, friendship, homage, loyalty, obedience, obligation, support.

allot v. allocate, apportion, appropriate, assign, budget, designate, dispense, distribute, earmark, grant, mete, render, set aside, share out.

allow v. accord, acknowledge, acquiesce, admit, allocate, allot, apportion, approve, assign, authorize, bear, brook, concede, confess, deduct, endure, give, give leave, grant, let, own, permit, provide, put up with, remit, sanction, spare, stand, suffer, tolerate.

almost adv. about, all but, approaching, approximately, as good as, close to, just about, nearing, nearly, not far from, not quite, practically, towards, virtually, well-nigh.

alone adj., adv. abandoned, apart, by itself, by oneself, deserted, desolate, detached, discrete, isolated, just, lonely, lonesome, on one's own, only, peerless, separate, simply, single, single-handed, singular, sole, solitary, unaccompanied, unaided, unassisted, unattended, uncombined, unconnected, unequaled, unescorted, unique, unparalleled, unsurpassed.

also adv. additionally, along with, and, as well, as well as, besides, ditto, further, furthermore, in addition, including, moreover, plus, therewithal, to boot, too.

alter v. adapt, adjust, amend, bushel, castrate, change, convert, diversify, emend, metamorphose, modify, qualify, recast, reform, remodel, reshape, revise, shift, take liberties with, transform, transmute, transpose, turn, vary.

alternate *v.* alter, change, fluctuate, interchange, intersperse, reciprocate, rotate, substitute, take turns, transpose, vary. *adj.* alternating, alternative, another, different, every other, every second, reciprocating, reciprocative, rotating, second, substitute.

alternative *n.* back-up, choice, option, other, preference, recourse, selection, substitute. *adj.* alternate, another, different, fallback, fringe, other, second, substitute, unconventional, unorthodox.

although *conj.* admitting that, albeit, conceding that, even if, even though, granted that, howbeit, notwithstanding, though, while.

altitude *n.* elevation, height, loftiness, stature, tallness.

altogether *adv.* absolutely, all in all, all told, as a whole, collectively, completely, entirely, fully, generally, in all, in general, in sum, in toto, on the whole, perfectly, quite, thoroughly, totally, utterly, wholesale, wholly.

always *adv.* aye, consistently, constantly, continually, endlessly, eternally, ever, everlastingly, evermore, every time, forever, in perpetuum, invariably, perpetually, regularly, repeatedly, unceasingly, unfailingly, without exception.

amaze *v.* alarm, astonish, astound, bewilder, confound, daze, disconcert, dismay, dumbfound, electrify, flabbergast, floor, shock, stagger, startle, stun, stupefy, surprise, wow.

ambition *n.* aim, aspiration, avidity, craving, design, desire, dream, drive, eagerness, end, enterprise, goal, hankering, hope, hunger, ideal, intent, longing, object, objective, purpose, push, striving, target, wish, yearning, zeal.

ambush *n.* ambuscade, concealment, cover, hiding, hiding-place, retreat, shelter, snare, trap, waylaying. *v.* ambuscade, bushwhack, ensnare, entrap, surprise, trap, waylay.

amend *v.* adjust, alter, ameliorate, better, change, correct, emend, enhance, fix, improve, mend, modify, qualify, rectify, redress, reform, remedy, repair, revise.

amid *conj.* amidst, among, amongst, in the middle of, in the midst of, in the thick of, surrounded by.

among *prep.* amid, amidst, amongst, between, in the middle of, in the midst of, in the thick of, midst, mongst, surrounded by, together with, with.

amount *n.* addition, aggregate, bulk, entirety, expanse, extent, lot, magnitude, mass, measure, number, quantity, quantum, quota, sum, sum total, supply, total, volume, whole.

amuse *v.* absorb, beguile, charm, cheer, cheer up, delight, disport, divert, engross, enliven, entertain, enthrall, gladden, interest, occupy, please, recreate, regale, relax, slay, tickle.

amusing *adj.* charming, cheerful, cheering, comical, delightful, diverting, droll, enjoyable, entertaining, facetious, funny, gladdening, hilarious, humorous, interesting, jocular, jolly, killing, laughable, lively, ludicrous, merry, pleasant, pleasing, risible, sportive, witty.

analysis *n.* anatomy, assay, breakdown, dissection, dissolution, division, enquiry, estimation, evaluation, examination, explanation, exposition, interpretation, investigation, judgment, opinion, reasoning, reduction, resolution, review, scrutiny, separation, sifting, study, test.

analyze *v.* anatomize, assay, break down, consider, dissect, dissolve, divide, estimate, evaluate, examine, interpret, investigate, judge, reduce, resolve, review, scrutinize, separate, sift, study, test.

anesthetic *n.* analgesic, anodyne, narcotic, opiate, painkiller, palliative, sedative, soporific, stupefacient, stupefactive.

angel *n.* archangel, backer, benefactor, cherub, darling, divine messenger, fairy godmother, guardian spirit, ideal, paragon, principality, saint, seraph, supporter, treasure.

anger *n.* annoyance, antagonism, bad blood, bile, bitterness, choler, dander, displeasure, dudgeon, exasperation, fury, gall, indignation, ire, irritability, irritation, monkey, outrage, passion, pique, rage, rancor, resentment, spleen, temper, vexation, wrath.

angry *adj.* aggravated, annoyed, antagonized, bitter, burned up, choked, disgruntled, displeased, enraged, exasperated, furious, heated, hot, incensed, indignant, infuriated, irascible, irate, ireful, irked, irritable, irritated, mad, miffed, needled, nettled, outraged, passionate, provoked, raging, riled, tumultuous, uptight, wrathful, wroth.

anguish *n.* agony, angst, anxiety, desolation, distress, dole, dolor, grief, heartache, heartbreak, misery, pain, pang, rack, sorrow, suffering, torment, torture, tribulation, woe, wretchedness.

animate *v.* activate, arouse, embolden, encourage, energize, enliven, excite, fire, galvanize, goad, impel, incite, inspire, inspirit, instigate, invest, invigorate, irradiate, kindle, move, quicken, reactivate, revive, revivify, rouse, spark, spur, stimulate, stir, suffuse, urge, vitalize, vivify.

annex *v.* acquire, add, adjoin, affix, append, appropriate, arrogate, attach, connect, conquer, expropriate, fasten, incorporate, join, occupy, purloin, seize, subjoin, tack, take over, unite, usurp. *n.* addendum, additament, addition, adjunct, appendix, attachment, supplement.

announce *v.* advertise, blazon, broadcast, declare, disclose, divulge, intimate, leak, make known, notify, proclaim, promulgate, pro-pound, publicize, publish, report, reveal, state.

annoy *v.* aggravate, anger, badger, bore, bother, bug, chagrin, contrary, displease, disturb, exasperate, gall, get, harass, harm, harry, hip, irk, irritate, molest, needle, nettle, peeve, pester, pique, plague, provoke, rile, ruffle, tease, trouble, vex.

answer *n.* acknowledgment, defense, explanation, outcome, plea, rebuttal, reciprocation, rejoinder, reply, response, retort.

anxiety *n.* angst, anxiousness, apprehension, care, concern, craving, desire, disquiet, distress, dread, dysthymia, eagerness, foreboding, keenness, misgiving, nervousness, restlessness, solicitude, suspense, tension, torment, torture, uneasiness, watchfulness, worry.

anxious *adj.* afraid, apprehensive, avid, careful, concerned, desirous, distressed, disturbed, eager, expectant, fearful, fretful, impatient, keen, nervous, on tenterhooks, restless, solicitous, taut, tense, tormented, tortured, troubled, uneasy, unquiet, watchful, worried, yearning.

apartment *n.* accommodation, chambers, compartment, condominium, flat, living quarters, lodgings, maisonette, pad, penthouse, quarters, room, rooms, suite, tenement.

aperture *n.* breach, chink, cleft, crack, eye, eyelet, fissure, foramen, gap, hole, interstice, opening, orifice, passage, perforation, rent, rift, slit, slot, space, vent.

apology *n.* acknowledg-ment, apologia, confession, defense, excuse, explanation, extenuation, justification, palliation, plea, semblance, substitute, travesty, vindication.

appall *v.* alarm, astound, daunt, disconcert, disgust, dishearten, dismay, frighten, harrow, horrify, intimidate, outrage, petrify, scare, shock, terrify, unnerve.

apparent *adj.* clear, conspicuous, declared, discernible, distinct, evident, indubitable, manifest, marked, noticeable, obvious, on paper, open, ostensible, outward, overt, patent, perceptible, plain, seeming, specious, superficial, unmistakable, visible.

appeal¹ *n.* application, entreaty, imploration, invocation, petition, plea, prayer, request, solicitation, suit, supplication. *v.* address, adjure, apply, ask, beg, beseech, call, call upon, entreat, implore, invoke, petition, plead, pray, refer, request, resort to, solicit, sue.

appeal² *n.* allure, attraction, attractiveness, beauty, charisma, charm, enchantment, fascination, interest, magnetism, winsomeness. *v.* allure, attract, charm, draw, engage, entice, fascinate, interest, invite, lure, please, tempt.

appear *v.* act, arise, arrive, attend, be published, bob up, come into sight, come into view, come out, come to light, crop up, develop, emerge, enter, issue, leak out, look, loom, materialize, occur, perform, play, rise, seem, show, show up, surface, take part, transpire, turn out, turn up.

appearance *n.* advent, air, arrival, aspect, bearing, brow, cast, character, coming, demeanor, emergence, expression, face, favor, form, front, guise, illusion, image, impression, look, manner, mien, physiognomy, presence, pretense, seeming, semblance, show.

append *v.* add, adjoin, affix, annex, attach, conjoin, fasten, join, subjoin, tack on.

appetite *n.* appetency, craving, demand, desire, eagerness, hankering, hunger, inclination, keenness, liking, longing, orexis, passion, predilection, proclivity, propensity, relish, stomach, taste, willingness, yearning, zeal, zest.

appliance *n.* apparatus, contraption, contrivance, device, gadget, implement, instrument, machine, mechanism, tool.

apply¹ *v.* adhibit, administer, appose, assign, bring into play, bring to bear, direct, employ, engage, execute, exercise, implement, ply, practice, resort to, set, use, utilize, wield.

apply² *v.* appertain, be relevant, fit, have force, pertain, refer, relate, suit.

apply³ *v.* anoint, cover with, lay on, paint, place, put on, rub, smear, spread on, use.

apply[4] *v.* appeal, ask for, claim, indent for, inquire, petition, put in, request, requisition, solicit, sue.

apply[5] *v.* address, bend, buckle down, commit, devote, direct, give, persevere, settle down, study, throw.

appointment *n.* allotment, arrangement, assignation, assignment, choice, choosing, commissioning, consultation, date, delegation, election, engagement, installation, interview, job, meeting, naming, nomination, office, place, position, post, rendezvous, selection, session, situation, station, tryst.

appreciate *v.* acknowledge, admire, be sensible of, be sensitive to, cherish, comprehend, dig, do justice to, enjoy, esteem, estimate, know, like, perceive, prize, realize, recognize, regard, relish, respect, savor, sympathize with, take kindly to, treasure, understand, value.

apprehend[1] *v.* arrest, bust, capture, catch, collar, detain, get, grab, nab, nick, pinch, run in, seize, take.

apprehend[2] *v.* appreciate, believe, comprehend, conceive, consider, discern, grasp, imagine, know, perceive, realize, recognize, see, twig, understand.

apprehensive *adj.* afraid, alarmed, anxious, concerned, disquieted, distrustful, disturbed, doubtful, fearful, mistrustful, nervous, solicitous, suspicious, uneasy, worried.

approach *v.* advance, approximate, be like, come close, come near to, draw near, meet, near, resemble, sound out, undertake. *n.* access, advance, application, arrival, attitude, entrance, gesture, manner, modus operandi, overture, procedure, resemblance, technique, way.

approve *v.* accede to, accept, acclaim, admire, adopt, advocate, agree to, allow, applaud, appreciate, authorize, back, concur in, confirm, consent to, countenance, endorse, esteem, favor, like, mandate, OK, pass, permit, praise, ratify, recommend, regard, respect, sanction, second, support, take, kindly to, uphold, validate.

aptitude *n.* ability, aptness, bent, capability, capacity, cleverness, disposition, facility, faculty, flair, gift, inclination, intelligence, knack, leaning, penchant, predilection, proclivity, proficiency, proneness, propensity, quickness, talent, tendency.

area *n.* arena, bailiwick, ball-park, breadth, canvas, compass, department, district, domain, environs, expanse, extent, field, locality, neighborhood, part, patch, portion, province, range, realm, region, scope, section, sector, size, sphere, stretch, terrain, territory, tract, width, zone.

argue *v.* altercate, bicker, claim, contend, convince, debate, disagree, discuss, display, dispute, evidence, feud, fight, haggle, hold, imply, indicate, maintain, persuade, plead, prevail upon, prove, quarrel, question, reason, squabble, suggest, talk into, wrangle.

arid *adj.* baked, barren, boring, colorless, desert, desiccated, dreary, dry, dull, empty, flat, infertile, lifeless, monotonous, parched, spiritless, sterile, tedious, torrid, uninspired, uninteresting, unproductive, vapid, waste, waterless.

arise *v.* appear, ascend, begin, climb, come to light, commence, crop up, derive, emanate, emerge, ensue, flow, follow, get up, go up, grow, happen, issue, lift, mount, occur, originate, proceed, result, rise, set in, soar, spring, stand up, start, stem, tower, wake up.

arm[1] *n.* appendage, authority, bough, brachium, branch, channel, department, detachment, division, estuary, extension, firth, inlet, limb, offshoot, projection, section, sector, sound, strait, sway, tributary, upper limb.

arm[2] *v.* accouter, ammunition, array, brace, equip, forearm, fortify, furnish, gird, issue with, outfit, prepare, prime, protect, provide, reinforce, rig, steel, strengthen, supply.

arrange *v.* adjust, align, array, categorize, class, classify, collocate, concert, construct, contrive, coordinate, design, determine, devise, dispose, distribute, fettle, file, fix, form, group, lay out, marshal, methodize, order, organize, plan, position, prepare, project, range, rank, regulate, schedule, set out, settle, sift, sort, sort out, stage-manage, style, swing, systematize, tidy, trim.

arrangement[1] *n.* adjustment, agreement, alignment, array, battery, classification, compact, compromise, construction, deal, design, display, disposition, form, grouping, layout, line-up, marshaling, method, modus vivendi, order, ordering, organization, plan, planning, preparation, provision, ranging, rank, schedule, scheme, settlement, set-up, spacing, structure, system, tabulation, taxis, terms.

arrangement[2] *n.* adaptation, harmonization, instrumentation, interpretation, orchestration, score, setting, version.

arrest *v.* apprehend, bust, capture, catch, check, collar, delay, detain, engross, fascinate, halt, hinder, hold, impede, inhibit, nab, prevent, restrain, retard, seize, slow, stop, suppress.

arrival *n.* accession, advent, appearance, approach, caller, comer, coming, entrance, entrant, happening, landfall, newcomer, occurrence, visitant, visitor.

arrive *v.* alight, appear, attain, befall, come, enter, fetch, get to the top, happen, land, make it, materialize, occur, reach, show, show up, succeed, turn up.

art *n.* adroitness, aptitude, artifice, artistry, artwork, craft, craftiness, dexterity, draftsmanship, drawing, expertise, facility, finesse, knack, knowledge, mastery, meth-od, painting, sculpture, skill, trade, trick, trickery, virtu, virtuosity, visuals, wiliness.

article *n.* account, bit, clause, commodity, composition, constituent, count, detail, discourse, division, element, essay, feature, head, heading, item, matter, object, paper, paragraph, part, particular, piece, point, portion, report, review, section, story, thing, unit.

artificial *adj.* affected, assumed, bogus, contrived, counterfeit, ersatz, factitious, fake, false, feigned, forced, hyped up, imitation, insincere, made-up, manmade, mannered, manufactured, meretricious, mock, phony, plastic, pretended, pseudo, sham, simulated, specious, spurious, synthetic, unnatural.

artist *n.* colorist, craftsman, draftsman, expert, maestro, master, painter, portraitist, portrait-painter, sculptor, water-colorist.

ascend *v.* climb, float up, fly up, go up, lift off, move up, rise, scale, slope upwards, soar, take off, tower.

ashamed *adj.* abashed, apologetic, bashful, blushing, chagrined, confused, conscience-stricken, crestfallen, discomfited, discomposed, distressed, embarrassed, guilty, hesitant, humbled, humiliated, modest, mortified, prudish, red in the face, redfaced, reluctant, remorseful, self-conscious, shamefaced, sheepish, shy, sorry, unwilling.

ask *v.* appeal, apply, beg, beseech, bid, catechize, claim, clamor, crave, demand, enquire, entreat, implore, importune, indent, interrogate, invite, order, petition, plead, pray, press, query, question, quiz, request, require, seek, solicit, sue, summon, supplicate.

asleep *adj.* benumbed, comatose, dead to the world, dormant, dozing, fast asleep, inactive, inert, napping, numb, reposing, sleeping, slumbering, snoozing, sound asleep, unconscious.

aspect *n.* air, angle, appearance, attitude, bearing, condition, countenance, demeanor, direction, elevation, exposure, expression, face, facet, feature, look, manner, mien, outlook, physiognomy, point of view, position, prospect, scene, side, situation, standpoint, view, visage.

aspire *v.* aim, crave, desire, dream, hope, intend, long, purpose, pursue, seek, wish, yearn.

assail *v.* abuse, assault, attack, belabor, berate, beset, bombard, charge, criticize, encounter, fall upon, impugn, invade, lay into, malign, maltreat, pelt, revile, set about, set upon, strike, vilify.

assault *n.* aggression, attack, blitz, charge, incursion, invasion, offensive, onset, onslaught, raid, storm, storming, strike. *v.* assail, attack, beset, charge, fall on, hit, invade, lay violent hands on, set upon, storm, strike.

assemble *v.* accumulate, amass, build, collect, compose, congregate, construct, convene, convocate, convoke, erect, fabricate, flock, forgather, gather, group, join up, levy, make, manufacture, marshal, meet, mobilize, muster, muster (up), piece, rally, round up, set up, summon, together.

assembly *n.* agora, assemblage, caucus, collection, company, conclave, concourse, conference, congregation, congress, convention, crowd, fabrication, fitting, flock, gathering, group, manufacture, mass, meeting, multitude, rally, reception, setting up, soiree, synod, throng.

assert *v.* advance, affirm, allege, asseverate, attest, aver, avouch, avow, claim, contend, declare, defend, dogmatize, insist, lay down, maintain, predicate, press, profess, promote, pro-nounce, protest, state, stress, swear, testify to, thrust forward, uphold, vindicate.

assertion *n.* affirmance, affirmation, allegation, asseveration, attestation, averment, avowal, claim, contention, declaration, dictum, gratis, dictum, ipse dixit, predication, profession, pronouncement, statement, vindication, vouch, word.

assess *v.* appraise, compute, consider, demand, determine, estimate, evaluate, fix, gauge, impose, investigate, judge, rate, reckon, review, size up, tax, value, weigh.

assist *v.* abet, accommodate, aid, back, benefit, bestead, boost, collaborate, co-operate, enable, expedite, facilitate, further, help, rally round, reinforce, relieve, second, serve, succor, support, sustain.

associate *v.* accompany, affiliate, ally, combine, confederate, connect, consort, couple, fraternize, hang around, join, mingle, mix, pair, relate, socialize, unite, yoke. *n.* affiliate, ally, assistant, bedfellow, collaborator, colleague, companion, comrade, confederate, co-worker, fellow, follower, friend, leaguer, partner, peer, side-kick.

assume *v.* accept, acquire, adopt, affect, appropriate, believe, deduce, embrace, imagine, infer, opine, postulate, premise, presume, presuppose, pretend to, put on, seize, sham, suppose, surmise, suspect, take, undertake.

attach *v.* add, adhere, affix, annex, append, articulate, ascribe, assign, associate, attract, attribute, belong, bind, captivate, combine, connect, couple, fasten, fix, impute, join, link, place, put, relate to, secure, stick, tie, unite, weld.

attain *v.* accomplish, achieve, acquire, arrive at, bag, compass, complete, earn, effect, gain, get, grasp, net, obtain, procure, reach, realize, reap, secure, touch, win.

attitude *n.* affectation, air, approach, aspect, bearing, carriage, condition, demeanor, feeling, manner, mien, mood, opinion, outlook, perspective, point of view, pose, position, posture, stance, view.

authentic *adj.* accurate, actual, authoritative, bona fide, certain, dependable, actual, faithful, genuine, honest, kosher, legitimate, original, pure, real, reliable, simon-pure, true, true-to-life, trustworthy, valid, veracious, veritable.

author *n.* architect, begetter, composer, creator, designer, fabricator, fashioner, father, forger, founder, framer, initiator, inventor, maker, mover, originator, paper-stainer, parent, pen, penman, planner, prime mover, producer, volumist, writer.

authoritative *adj.* accurate, approved, authentic, authorized, commanding, decisive, definitive, dependable, factual, faithful, learned, legitimate, magisterial, masterly, official, reliable, sovereign, true, trustworthy, truthful, valid, veritable.

avarice *n.* acquisitiveness, covetousness, greed, greediness, miserliness, niggardliness, parsimoniousness, penny-pinching, penuriousness, stinginess, tight-fistedness.

average *n.* mean, mediocrity, medium, midpoint, norm, par, rule, run, standard.

aware *adj.* acquainted, alive to, appreciative, apprized, attentive, cognizant, conscious, conversant, enlightened, familiar,

heedful, informed, knowing, knowledgeable, mindful, observant, on the ball, sensible, sharp, shrewd.

awe *n.* admiration, amazement, apprehension, aston-ishment, dread, fear, respect, reverence, terror, veneration, wonder, wonderment.

awful *adj.* abysmal, alarming, atrocious, august, dire, dread, dreadful, fearful, fearsome, frightful, ghastly, gruesome, harrowing, horrendous, horrible, shocking, solemn, spine-chilling, terrible, tremendous, ugly, unpleasant.

B

baby *n.* babe, child, infant, suckling, tiny, toddler, youngling. *adj.* diminutive, dwarf, Lilliputian, little, midget, mini, miniature, minute, pygmy, small, tiny, toy, wee.

back[1] *v.* advocate, assist, boost, buttress, champion, countenance, countersign, encourage, endorse, favor, finance, sanction, second, side with, sponsor, subsidize, support, sustain, underwrite.

back[2] *n.* backside, end, hind part, hindquarters, posterior, rear, reverse, stern, tail, tail end, verso. *adj.* end, hind, hindmost, posterior, rear, reverse, tail.

back[3] *v.* backtrack, recede, recoil, regress, retire, retreat, reverse, withdraw.

back[4] *adj.* delayed, earlier, elapsed, former, outdated, overdue, past, previous, prior, superseded.

backing *n.* accompaniment, advocacy, aid, assistance, championing, championship, encouragement, endorsement, favor, funds, grant, helpers, moral support, patronage, sanction, seconding, sponsorship, subsidy, support.

bad *adj.* ailing, base, corrupt, dangerous, defective, deficient, disastrous, distressing, evil, fallacious, faulty, gloomy, grave, harmful, harsh, ill, imperfect, incorrect, inferior, naughty, offensive, putrid, rancid, rotten, sad, sick, sinful, spoilt, terrible, unsatisfactory, vile, wicked, wrong.

bag *v.* acquire, appropriate, capture, catch, commandeer, corner, gain, get, grab, kill, land, obtain, reserve, shoot, take, trap. *n.* carrier, container, grab-bag, grip, gripsack, handbag, haversack, holder, pack, poke, rucksack, sack, satchel, shoulder-bag, tote-bag, valise.

bail *n.* bond, guarantee, guaranty, pledge, security, surety, warranty.

bald *adj.* bald-headed, bare, barren, bleak, depilated, direct, downright, exposed, forthright, glabrous, hairless, naked, outright, peeled, plain, severe, simple, stark, straight, straightforward, treeless, unadorned, uncompromising, uncovered, undisguised, unvarnished.

balloon *v.* bag, belly, billow, blow up, bulge, dilate, distend, enlarge, expand, inflate, puff out, swell.

ballot *n.* election, plebiscite, poll, polling, referendum, vote, voting.

ban *v.* banish, bar, debar, disallow, exclude, forbid, interdict, ostracize, outlaw, prohibit, proscribe, restrict, suppress. *n.* boycott, censorship, condemnation, curse, denunciation, embargo, prohibition, proscription, restriction, stoppage, suppression, taboo.

band[1] *n.* bandage, binding, bond, chain, cord, fascia, manacle, ribbon, shackle, strap, strip, swath, tape, tie.

band[2] *n.* association, body, clique, club, combo, company, coterie, crew, ensemble, flock, gang, group, herd, horde, orchestra, party, range, society, troop, waits. *v.* affiliate, ally, amalgamate, collaborate, consolidate, federate, gather, group, join, merge, unite.

banish *v.* ban, bar, blacklist, debar, deport, discard, dislodge, dismiss, dispel, eject, eliminate, eradicate, evict, exclude, excommunicate, exile, expatriate, expel, get rid of, ostracize, oust, outlaw, remove, shut out, transport.

bar *n.* barricade, barrier, batten, check, cross-piece, deterrent, determent, hindrance, impediment, obstacle, obstruction, paling, pole, preventive, rail, railing, rod, shaft, stake, stanchion, stick, stop. *v.* ban, barricade, blackball, bolt, debar, exclude, fasten, forbid, hinder, latch, lock, obstruct, preclude, prevent, prohibit, restrain, secure.

bare *adj.* austere, bald, barren, basic, blank, defoliate, defoliated, denuded, empty, essential, explicit, exposed, hard, lacking, literal, mean, naked, napless, nude, open, peeled, plain, poor, scanty, scarce, severe, sheer, shorn, spare, stark, stripped, unclad, unclothed, uncovered, undressed, vacant, void, wanting.

barely[1] *adv.* almost, hardly, just, scarcely, sparingly, sparsely.

barely[2] *adv.* explicity, nakedly, openly, plainly.

bargain *n.* agreement, arrangement, compact, contract, discount, giveaway, negotiation, pact, pledge, promise, reduction, snip,

steal, stipulation, transaction, treaty, understanding. *v.* agree, barter, broke, buy, contract, covenant, deal, dicker, haggle, negotiate, promise, sell, stipulate, trade, traffic, transact.

barren *adj.* arid, boring, childless, desert, desolate, dry, dull, empty, flat, fruitless, infertile, jejune, lackluster, pointless, profitless, stale, sterile, unbearing, unfruitful, uninspiring, uninteresting, unproductive, unprolific, unrewarding, useless, vapid, waste.

barrier *n.* bail, bar, barricade, blockade, boom, boundary, bulkhead, check, difficulty, ditch, drawback, fence, fortification, handicap, hindrance, hurdle, impediment, limitation, obstacle, obstruction, railing, rampart, restriction, stop, stumbling-block, transverse, wall.

base[1] *n.* basis, bed, bottom, camp, center, core, essence, foundation, fundamental, headquarters, heart, home, key, pedestal, root, source, starting-point, substructure, underpinning.

base[2] *adj.* abject, contemptible, corrupt, counterfeit, depraved, disgraceful, disreputable, dog, evil, groveling, humble, ignoble, ignominious, immoral, infamous, low, lowly, low-minded, mean, menial, miserable, paltry, pitiful, poor, scandalous, servile, shameful, slavish, sordid, sorry, valueless, vile, villainous, vulgar, wicked, worthless, wretched.

base[3] *adj.* adulterated, alloyed, artificial, bastard, counterfeit, debased, fake, forged, fraudulent, impure, inferior, pinchbeck, spurious.

basic *adj.* central, elementary, essential, fundamental, important, indispensable, inherent, intrinsic, key, necessary, primary, radical, root, underlying, vital.

batter *v.* abuse, assault, bash, beat, belabor, bruise, buffet, crush, dash, deface, demolish, destroy, disfigure, distress, hurt, injure, lash, maltreat, mangle, manhandle, mar, maul, pelt, pound, pummel, ruin, shatter, smash, thrash, wallop.

battle *n.* action, affray, attack, campaign, clash, combat, conflict, contest, controversy, crusade, debate, disagreement, dispute, encounter, engagement, fight, fray, hostilities, row, skirmish, strife, struggle, war, warfare.

bearing *n.* air, application, aspect, attitude, behavior, carriage, comportment, connection, course, demeanor, deportment, direction, import, manner, mien, poise, posture, presence, reference, relation, relevance, significance.

bearings *n.* aim, course, direction, inclination, location, orientation, position, situation, track, way, whereabouts.

beat[1] *v.* bang, batter, bludgeon, bruise, buffet, cane, flog, hammer, hit, knock, lash, lay into, pelt, pound, punch, strike, thrash, whip. *n.* blow, hit, lash, punch, shake, slap, strike, swing, thump. *adj.* exhausted, fatigued, tired, wearied, worn out, zonked.

beat[2] *v.* best, conquer, defeat, excel, hammer, outdo, outrun, outstrip, overcome, overwhelm, slaughter, subdue, surpass, trounce, vanquish.

beat[3] *v.* flutter, palpitate, patter, pound, pulsate, pulse, quake, quiver, race, shake, throb, thump, tremble, vibrate. *n.* accent, cadence, flutter, measure, meter, palpitation, pulsation, pulse, rhyme, stress, throb, time.

beautiful *adj.* alluring, appealing, attractive, beau, beauteous, belle, charming, comely, delightful, exquisite, fair, fine, good-looking, gorgeous, graceful, handsome, lovely, pleasing, pulch-ritudinous, radiant, ravishing, stunning.

because *conj.* as, by reason of, for, forasmuch, in that, inasmuch as, on account of, owing to, since, thanks to.

becoming *adj.* appropriate, attractive, charming, comely, decent, flattering, graceful, pretty, proper, seemly, suitable, tasteful, worthy.

before *adv.* ahead, earlier, formerly, in advance, in front, previously, sooner.

beg *v.* beseech, crave, desire, entreat, implore, importune, petition, plead, pray, request, require, scrounge, solicit, sponge on, supplicate, touch.

begin *v.* activate, actuate, appear, arise, commence, crop up, dawn, emerge, happen, inaugurate, initiate, instigate, introduce, originate, prepare, set about, set in, spring, start.

beginning *n.* birth, commencement, embryo, establishment, germ, inception, introduction, onset, opening, origin, preface, prelude, seed, source, start, starting point.

behavior *n.* action, actions, bearing, carriage, comportment, conduct, dealings, demeanor, deportment, doings, functioning, habits, manner, manners, operation, performance, reaction, response, ways.

behind *prep.* after, backing, causing, following, for, initiating, instigating, later than,

responsible for, supporting. *adv.* after, afterwards, behindhand, following, in arrears, in debt, next, overdue, subsequently. *n.* ass, backside, bottom, butt, buttocks, derriere, fanny, posterior, prat, rear, rump, seat, sit-upon, tail, tush.

belief *n.* assurance, confidence, conviction, credence, credit, credo, creed, doctrine, dogma, expectation, faith, feeling, ideology, impression, intuition, ism, judgment, notion, opinion, persuasion, presumption, principle, principles, reliance, sureness, surety, tenet, theory, trust, view.

belligerent *adj.* aggressive, antagonistic, argumentative, bellicose, bullying, combative, contentious, forceful, militant, pugnacious, quarrelsome, violent, warlike, warring.

belonging *n.* acceptance, affinity, association, attachment, closeness, compatibility, fellow-feeling, fellowship, inclusion, kinship, link, linkage, loyalty, rapport, relationship.

below *adv.* beneath, down, infra, lower, lower down, under, underneath. *prep.* inferior to, lesser than, subject to, subordinate to, under, underneath, unworthy of.

belt[1] *n.* area, band, cincture, cingulum, cummerbund, district, girdle, girth, layer, region, sash, strait, stretch, strip, swathe, tract, waistband, zone, zonule. *v.* circle, encircle, girdle, ring, surround.

belt[2] *v.* bolt, career, charge, dash, hurry, race, rush, speed.

beneath *adv.* below, lower, lower down, under, underneath. *prep.* below, inferior to, infra dig(nitatem), lower than, 'neath, subject to, subordinate to, unbefitting, under, underneath, unworthy of.

benefit *n.* advantage, aid, asset, assistance, avail, blessing, boon, favor, gain, good, help, interest, profit, service, use, welfare.

beside *prep.* abreast of, abutting on, adjacent, bordering on, close to, near, neighboring, next door to, next to, overlooking, upsides with.

besides *adv.* additionally, also, as well, extra, further, furthermore, in addition, into the bargain, moreover, otherwise, to boot, too, withal. *prep.* apart from, in addition to, other than, over and above.

betray *v.* abandon, beguile, corrupt, deceive, delude, desert, disclose, discover, divulge, double cross, dupe, entrap, expose, give away, inform on, jilt, reveal, seduce, sell down the river, sell out, show, tell, testify against, turn state's evidence.

between *prep.* amidst, among, amongst, betwixt, inter-, mid.

beyond *prep.* above, across, apart from, away from, before, further than, out of range, out of reach of, over, past, remote from, superior to, yonder.

big *adj.* adult, altruistic, beefy, benevolent, boastful, bombastic, bulky, burly, buxom, colossal, considerable, corpulent, elder, eminent, enormous, extensive, gargantuan, generous, gigantic, gracious, great, grown, grown-up, heroic, huge, hulking, immense, important, influential, large, leading, lofty, magnanimous, mammoth, massive, mature, mighty, noble, ponderous, powerful, prime, principal, prodigious, prominent, serious, significant, sizable, spacious, stout, substantial, titanic, tolerant, unselfish, valuable, vast, voluminous, weighty.

bigot *n.* chauvinist, dogmatist, fanatic, racist, religionist, sectarian, sexist, zealot.

blade *n.* dagger, edge, knife, rapier, scalpel, sword.

blame *v.* accuse, admonish, censure, charge, chide, condemn, criticize, disapprove, find fault with, rebuke, reprimand, reproach, reprove, upbraid.

blank *adj.* apathetic, bare, deadpan, empty, expressionless, featureless, impassive, lifeless, plain, staring, uncomprehending, vacant, vacuous, vague, void, white.

bleak *adj.* bare, barren, cheerless, chilly, cold, colorless, depressing, desolate, dismal, dreary, empty, gloomy, joyless, somber, unsheltered, weather-beaten, windswept, windy.

blessed *adj.* adored, beatified, blissful, contented, divine, endowed, favored, fortunate, glad, hallowed, happy, holy, joyful, joyous, lucky, prosperous, revered, sacred, sanctified.

bluff[1] *n.* bank, brow, cliff, crag, escarp, escarpment, foreland, headland, height, knoll, peak, precipice, promontory, ridge, scarp, slope. *adj.* affable, blunt, candid, direct, downright, frank, genial, good-natured, hearty, open, outspoken, plain-spoken, straightforward.

bluff[2] *v.* bamboozle, blind, deceive, defraud, delude, fake, feign, grift, hoodwink, humbug, lie, mislead, pretend, sham. *n.* buster, boast, braggadocio, bravado, deceit, deception, fake, feint, fraud, grift, humbug,

idle boast, lie, pretence, sham, show, subterfuge, trick.

boast *v.* blow, bluster, bounce, brag, claim, crow, exaggerate, exhibit, show off, strut, swagger, talk big, trumpet, vaunt. *n.* avowal, brag, claim, joy, pride, swank, treasure, vaunt.

bold *adj.* adventurous, audacious, brash, brave, brazen, confident, courageous, daring, fearless, gallant, heroic, intrepid, jazzy, lively, loud, outgoing, prominent, shameless, showy, striking, valiant, valorous, venturesome, vivid.

boom[1] *v.* bang, blare, blast, crash, explode, resound, reverberate, roar, roll, rumble, sound, thunder. *n.* bang, blast, burst, clang, clap, crash, explosion, reverberation, roar, rumble, thunder.

boom[2] *v.* develop, escalate, expand, explode, flourish, gain, go from strength to strength, grow, increase, intensify, prosper, spurt, strengthen, succeed, swell, thrive. *n.* advance, boost, development, escalation, expansion, explosion, gain, growth, improvement, increase, jump, spurt, upsurge, upturn.

border *n.* borderline, bound, boundary, bounds, brim, brink, circumference, confine, confines, demarcation, edge, fringe, frontier, hem, limit, limits, lip, list, march, margin, perimeter, periphery, rand, rim, screed, skirt, surround, trimming, valance, verge. *adj.* boundary, dividing, frontier, marginal, perimeter, separating, side.

bore[1] *v.* burrow, countermine, drill, gouge, mine, penetrate, perforate, pierce, sap, sink, thrill, tunnel, undermine.

bore[2] *v.* annoy, bother, bug, fatigue, irk, irritate, jade, pester, tire, trouble, vex, weary, worry. *n.* annoyance, bind, bother, drag, dullard, headache, nuisance, pain, pain in the neck, pest, trial, vexation, vieux jeu, yawn.

bound[1] *adj.* bandaged, beholden, cased, certain, chained, committed, compelled, constrained, destined, doomed, duty-bound, fastened, fated, fixed, forced, held, liable, manacled, obligated, obliged, pinioned, pledged, required, restricted, secured, sure, tied, tied up.

bound[2] *v.* bob, bounce, caper, frisk, gambol, hurdle, jump, leap, lope, lunge, pounce, prance, skip, spring, vault. *n.* bob, bounce, caper, dance, frisk, gambol, jump, leap, lope, lunge, pounce, prance, scamper, skip, spring, vault.

bow[1] *v.* accept, acquiesce, bend, bob, capitulate, comply, concede, conquer, consent, crush, curtsey, defer, depress, droop, genuflect, give in, incline, kowtow, nod, overpower, stoop, subdue, subjugate, submit, surrender, vanquish, yield. *n.* acknowledgement, bending, bob, curtsey, genuflection, inclination, kowtow, nod, obeisance, salaam, salutation.

bow[2] *n.* beak, head, prow, rostrum, stem.

bowl[1] *n.* basin, container, cruse, dish, pan, porringer, receptacle, sink, tureen, vessel.

bowl[2] *n.* jack, wood. *v.* fling, hurl, pitch, revolve, roll, rotate, spin, throw, whirl.

bowl[3] *n.* amphitheater, arena, auditorium, coliseum, field, ground, hall, hippodrome, stadium.

box[1] *n.* bijou, carton, case, casket, chest, coffer, coffin, container, coop, fund, pack, package, portmanteau, present, receptacle, trunk. *v.* case, encase, pack, package, wrap.

box[2] *v.* buffet, butt, clout, cuff, fight, hit, punch, slap, sock, spar, strike, thwack, wallop, whack, wham. *n.* blow, buffet, clout, cuff, punch, slap, stroke, thump, wallop, wham.

brag *v.* bluster, boast, crow, swagger, talk big, trumpet.

brave *adj.* audacious, bold, courageous, daring, fearless, gallant, heroic, indomitable, intrepid, stalwart, stoic, unafraid, valiant, valorous.

brawl *n.* affray, altercation, argument, battle, clash, disorder, dispute, dog-fight, Donnybrook, fight, fracas, fray, free-for-all, melee, quarrel, row, ruckus, rumpus, scrap, squabble, tumult, uproar, wrangle.

brief *adj.* abrupt, blunt, brusque, compressed, concise, curt, fleeting, hasty, momentary, passing, quick, sharp, short-lived, succinct, swift, temporary, terse. *v.* advise, direct, explain, fill in, guide, inform, instruct, prepare, prime.

bright *adj.* ablaze, astute, blazing, brainy, brilliant, clever, dazzling, flashing, glaring, gleaming, glistening, illuminated, intelligent, joyful, lively, perceptive, quick, radiant, resplendent, sharp, shining, smart, sparkling, splendid, sunny, vivid.

brink *n.* bank, border, boundary, brim, edge, fringe, limit, lip, marge, margin, point, rim, skirt, threshold, verge, waterside.

brisk *adj.* active, agile, alert, allegro, bracing, bright, bustling, busy, crank, crisp, effervescing, energetic, exhilarating, expeditious, fresh, invigorating, keen, lively, nimble, nippy, no-nonsense, prompt, quick, refreshing, sharp, snappy, speedy, spirited, sprightly, spry, stimulating, vigorous.

broad *adj.* all-embracing, ample, blue, capacious, catholic, coarse, comprehensive, eclectic, encyclopedic, enlightened, expansive, extensive, far-reaching, general, generous, gross, improper, inclusive, indecent, indelicate, large, roomy, spacious, square, sweeping, tolerant, universal, unlimited, unrefined, vast, voluminous, vulgar, wide, wide-ranging, widespread.

broken *adj.* burst, crushed, defeated, demoralized, destroyed, faulty, fractured, fragmented, hesitating, incomplete, intermittent, out of order, ruptured, severed, shattered, subdued, tamed, vanquished.

brush[1] *n.* broom, sweeper. *v.* buff, burnish, caress, clean, contact, graze, paint, polish, rub, scrape, shine, stroke, sweep, touch, wash.

brush[2] *n.* brushwood, bushes, ground cover, scrub, shrubs, thicket, undergrowth.

brush[3] *n.* clash, conflict, confrontation, encounter, fight, fracas, incident, run-in, scrap, skirmish, tussle.

bud *n.* embryo, germ, shoot, sprig, sprout. *v.* burgeon, develop, grow, shoot, sprout.

bulky *adj.* big, colossal, cumbersome, enormous, heavy, hefty, huge, hulking, immense, large, mammoth, massive, massy, ponderous, substantial, voluminous, weighty.

burn *v.* blaze, brand, cauterize, char, combust, consume, flame, flare, flash, flicker, fume, glow, ignite, incinerate, kindle, light, scorch, simmer, singe, smoke, smolder, sting, tingle, toast.

busy *adj.* active, assiduous, brisk, diligent, employed, energetic, engaged, engrossed, exacting, full, fussy, hectic, industrious, inquisitive, interfering, lively, meddlesome, meddling, nosy, occupied, officious, persevering, prying, restless, slaving, stirring, strenuous, tireless, tiring, troublesome, versant, working. *v.* absorb, bother, concern, employ, engage, engross, immerse, interest, occupy.

buy *v.* acquire, bribe, corrupt, fix, get, obtain, procure, purchase, square, suborn. *n.* acquisition, bargain, deal, purchase.

by *prep.* along, beside, near, next to, over, past, through, via. *adv.* aside, at hand, away, beyond, close, handy, near, past.

bypass *v.* avoid, circumvent, ignore, neglect, outflank. *n.* detour, ring road.

C

cab *n.* hack, minicab, taxi, taxicab.

cabin *n.* berth, chalet, compartment, cot, cottage, crib, deck-house, hove, hut, lodge, quarters, room, shack, shanty, shed.

calamity *n.* adversity, affliction, cataclysm, catastrophe, desolation, disaster, distress, downfall, misadventure, mischance, misfortune, mishap, reverse, ruin, scourge, tragedy, trial, tribulation, woe, wretchedness.

calculate *v.* aim, cipher, compute, consider, count, determine, enumerate, estimate, figure, gauge, intend, judge, plan, rate, reckon, value, weigh, work out.

calculating *adj.* canny, cautious, contriving, crafty, cunning, designing, devious, manipulative, politic, scheming, sharp, shrewd, sly.

call *v.* announce, appoint, arouse, assemble, awaken, bid, christen, collect, consider, contact, convene, convoke, cry, declare, decree, denominate, designate, dub, elect, entitle, estimate, gather, hail, invite, judge, label, muster, name, ordain, order, phone, proclaim, rally, regard, rouse, shout, style, summon, telephone, term, think, waken, yell. *n.* announcement, appeal, cause, claim, command, cry, demand, excuse, grounds, hail, invitation, justification, need, notice, occasion, order, plea, reason, request, right, ring, scream, shout, signal, summons, supplication, urge, visit, whoop, yell.

calm *adj.* balmy, collected, composed, cool, dispassionate, equable, halcyon, impassive, imperturbable, laid back, mild, pacific, passionless, peaceful, placid, quiet, relaxed, restful, sedate, self-collected, self-possessed, serene, smooth, still, tranquil, unapprehensive, unclouded, undisturbed, unemotional, uneventful, unexcitable, unexcited, unflappable, unmoved, unperturbed, untroubled, windless.

candidate *n.* applicant, aspirant, competitor, contender, contestant, entrant, nominee, runner, solicitant, suitor.

capital[1] *adj.* cardinal, central, chief, controlling, essential, excellent, find, first, first-rate, foremost, great, important, leading, main, major, overruling, paramount, preeminent, primary, prime, principal, splendid, superb, upper-case.

capital[2] *n.* assets, cash, finance, finances, financing, fonds, funds, investment(s), means, money, principal, property, resources, stock, wealth, wherewithal.

care *n.* affliction, anxiety, attention, burden, carefulness, caution, charge, circumspection, concern, consideration, control, custody, direction, disquiet, forethought, guardianship, hardship, heed, interest, keeping, leading-strings, management, meticulousness, ministration, pains, perplexity, pressure, protection, prudence, regard, responsibility, solicitude, stress, supervision, tribulation, trouble, vexation, vigilance, ward, watchfulness, woe, worry.

careful *adj.* accurate, alert, attentive, cautious, chary, circumspect, concerned, conscientious, discreet, fastidious, heedful, judicious, meticulous, mindful, painstaking, particular, precise, protective, prudent, punctilious, scrupulous, softly-softly, solicitous, thoughtful, thrifty, vigilant, wary, watchful.

careless *adj.* absent-minded, casual, cursory, derelict, forgetful, heedless, hit-or-miss, inaccurate, incautious, inconsiderate, indiscreet, irresponsible, lackadaisical, messy, neglectful, negligent, nonchalant, offhand, perfunctory, regardless, remiss, slap-dash, slipshod, sloppy, thoughtless, uncaring, unconcerned, unguarded, unmindful, unstudied, unthinking.

caress *v.* cuddle, embrace, fondle, hug, kiss, pet, rub, stroke, touch. *n.* cuddle, embrace, fondle, hug, kiss, pat, stroke.

case[1] *n.* box, cabinet, canister, capsule, carton, chest, container, cover, covering, crate, envelope, holder, receptacle, suitcase, trunk. *v.* encase, enclose, skin.

case[2] *n.* argument, circumstances, condition, context, contingency, dilemma, event, example, illustration, instance, occasion, occurrence, plight, point, position, predicament, situation, specimen, state, thesis. *v.* investigate, reconnoiter.

case[3] *n.* action, argument, cause, dispute, lawsuit, proceedings, process, suit, trial.

cast[1] *v.* abandon, add, allot, appoint, assign, bestow, calculate, categorize, choose, chuck, compute, deposit, diffuse, distribute, drive, drop, emit, figure, fling, forecast, form, found, give, hurl, impel, launch, lob, model, mold, name, pick, pitch, project, radiate, reckon, reject, scatter, select, set, shape, shed, shy, sling, spread, throw, thrust, toss, total. *n.* air, appearance, complexion, demeanor, fling, form, lob, look, manner, mien, quality, semblance, shade, stamp, style, throw, thrust, tinge, tone, toss, turn.

cast² *n.* actors, artistes, characters, company, dramatis personae, entertainers, performers, players, troupe.

casual *adj.* accidental, apathetic, blasé, chance, contingent, cursory, fortuitous, incidental, indifferent, informal, insouciant, irregular, lackadaisical, negligent, nonchalant, occasional, offhand, perfunctory, random, relaxed, serendipitous, stray, unceremonious, uncertain, unconcerned, unexpected, unforeseen, unintentional, unpremeditated.

cease *v.* call a halt, call it a day, conclude, culminate, desist, die, discontinue, end, fail, finish, halt, pack in, poop out, refrain, stay, stop, terminate.

celebrate *v.* bless, commemorate, commend, emblazon, eulogize, exalt, extol, glorify, honor, keep, laud, live it up, observe, perform, praise, proclaim, publicize, rejoice, reverence, solemnize, toast, wassail, whoop it up.

center *n.* bull's-eye, core, crux, focus, heart, hub, mid, middle, mid-point, nucleus, pivot. *v.* cluster, concentrate, converge, focus, gravitate, hinge, pivot, revolve.

certain *adj.* ascertained, assured, bound, conclusive, confident, constant, convinced, convincing, decided, definite, dependable, destined, determinate, established, express, fated, fixed, incontrovertible, individual, indubitable, ineluctable, inescapable, inevitable, inexorable, irrefutable, known, one, particular, plain, positive, precise, regular, reliable, resolved, satisfied, settled, some, special, specific, stable, steady, sure, true, trustworthy, undeniable, undoubted, unequivocal, unfailing, unmistakable, unquestionable, valid.

certify *v.* ascertain, assure, attest, authentic, authorize, aver, avow, confirm, corroborate, declare, endorse, evidence, guarantee, notify, show, testify, validate, verify, vouch, witness.

character¹ *n.* attributes, bent, caliber, cast, complexion, constitution, disposition, feature, honor, individuality, integrity, kidney, make-up, nature, peculiarity, personality, physiognomy, position, quality, rank, rectitude, reputation, stamp, status, strength, temper, temperament, type, uprightness.

character² *n.* card, customer, eccentric, fellow, guy, individual, joker, oddball, oddity, original, part, person, persona, portrayal, role, sort, type.

character³ *n.* cipher, device, emblem, figure, hieroglyph, ideogram, ideograph, letter, logo, mark, rune, sign, symbol, type.

cheat *v.* baffle, bamboozle, check, chisel, deceive, defeat, defraud, deprive, double-cross, dupe, finagle, fleece, foil, fool, frustrate, fudge, hoax, hocus, hoodwink, mislead, prevent, queer, rip off, screw, short-change, skin, swindle, thwart, touch, trick, trim, victimize. *n.* artifice, bilker, cheater, chouse, deceit, deceiver, deception, dodger, double-crosser, extortioner, fraud, grifter, impostor, imposture, knave, rogue, shark, sharp, swindle, swindler, trickery, trickster, welsher.

check¹ *v.* compare, confirm, examine, give the onceover, inspect, investigate, monitor, note, probe, research, scrutinize, study, test, verify. *n.* audit, examination, inspection, investigation, research, scrutiny, tab, test.

check² *v.* arrest, bar, blame, bridle, chide, control, curb, damp, delay, halt, hinder, impede, inhibit, limit, obstruct, pause, rebuke, repress, reprimand, reprove, restrain, retard, scold, stop, thwart. *n.* blow, constraint, control, curb, damp, damper, disappointment, frustration, hindrance, impediment, inhibition, lim-itation, obstruction, rejection, restraint, reverse, setback, stoppage.

cheerful *adj.* animated, blithe, bright, bucked, buoyant, cheery, chipper, contented, enlivening, enthusiastic, eupeptic, gay, genial, glad, gladsome, happy, hearty, jaunty, jolly, jovial, joyful, joyous, light-hearted, lightsome, light-spirited, merry, optimistic, perky, pleasant, sparking, sprightly, sunny, upbeat, winsome.

chiefly *adv.* especially, essentially, for the most part, generally, mainly, mostly, predominantly, primarily, principally, usually.

choice *n.* alternative, choosing, decision, dilemma, discrimination, election, espousal, opting, option, pick, preference, say, selection, variety. *adj.* best, dainty, elect, élite, excellent, exclusive, exquisite, hand-picked, nice, plum, precious, prime, prize, rare, select, special, superior, uncommon, unusual, valuable.

chore *n.* burden, duty, errand, job, stint, task, trouble.

circle *n.* area, assembly, band, bounds, circumference, clique, disc, enclosure, field, group, orbit, perimeter, revolution, ring, round, set, society, sphere.

circumference *n.* border, boundary, bounds, circuit, edge, extremity, fringe, limits, margin, outline, perimeter, periphery, rim, verge.

civil *adj.* accommodating, affable, civic, civilized, complaisant, courteous, courtly, domestic, home, interior, internal, internecine, lay, municipal, obliging, polished, polite, political, refined, secular, temporal, urbane, well-bred, well-mannered.

claim *v.* affirm, allege, arrogate, ask, assert, challenge, collect, demand, exact, hold, insist, maintain, need, profess, request, require, state, take, uphold. *n.* affirmation, allegation, application, assertion, call, demand, insistence, petition, pretension, privilege, protestation, request, requirement, right, title.

clarify *v.* cleanse, define, elucidate, explain, gloss, illuminate, purify, refine, resolve, shed/throw light on, simplify.

classic *adj.* abiding, ageless, archetypal, best, characteristic, chaste, consummate, deathless, definitive, enduring, established, excellent, exemplary, finest, first-rate, ideal, immortal, lasting, master, masterly, model, quintessential, refined, regular, restrained, standard, time-honored, traditional, typical, undying, usual.

classify *v.* arrange, assort, catalog, categorize, codify, digest, dispose, distribute, file, grade, pigeon-hole, rank, sort, systematize, tabulate.

clear *adj.* apparent, bright, coherent, comprehensible, distinct, empty, evident, explicit, free, guiltless, innocent, lucid, manifest, obvious, positive, pronounced, pure, sharp, sunny, translucent, unambiguous, unquestionable. *v.* absolve, acquit, clarify, clean, emancipate, erase, excuse, exonerate, free, liberate, refine, unclog, vindicate.

climax *n.* acme, apogee, culmination, head, height, high point, highlight, orgasm, peak, summit, top, zenith.

clip^1 *v.* crop, curtail, cut, dock, pare, prune, shear, shorten, snip, trim.

clip^2 *v.* box, clout, cuff, hit, knock, punch, slap, smack, sock, thump, wallop, whack.

clip^3 *n.* gallop, lick, rate, speed.

clip^4 *v.* attach, fasten, fix, hold, pin, staple.

close^1 *v.* bar, block, cease, choke, clog, cloture, complete, conclude, confine, connect, cork, couple, culminate, discontinue, end, fill, finish, fuse, grapple, join, lock, mothball, obstruct, plug, seal, secure, shut, stop, terminate, unite, wind up.

close^2 *adj.* adjacent, adjoining, airless, confined, congested, crowded, earnest, hard by, impending, intimate, near, near-by, oppressive, packed, reserved, reticent, secret, stifling, suffocating, tight, tight-fisted, uncommunicative.

cloth *n.* dish-cloth, duster, fabric, face-cloth, material, rag, stuff, textiles, tissue, towel.

clumsy *adj.* awkward, blundering, bumbling, bungling, crude, ham-handed, inept, rough, uncoordinated, ungraceful, unwieldy.

collection *n.* accumulation, anthology, assortment, compilation, conglomeration, crowd, group, hoard, stockpile.

colorful *adj.* bright, brilliant, distinctive, graphic, intense, interesting, jazzy, kaleidoscopic, lively, motley, multicolored, parti-colored, picturesque, psychedelic, rich, stimulating, unusual, variegated, vibrant, vivid.

comely *adj.* attractive, beautiful, fair, good-looking, handsome, lovely, pleasing, pretty, wholesome, winsome.

comfort *v.* alleviate, assuage, cheer, console, ease, encourage, enliven, gladden, hearten, invigorate, reassure, refresh, relieve, solace, soothe, strengthen.

command *v.* bid, charge, compel, direct, dominate, enjoin, govern, head, lead, manage, order, reign over, require, rule, supervise, sway.

commence *v.* begin, embark on, inaugurate, initiate, open, originate, start.

commend *v.* acclaim, applaud, approve, commit, compliment, extol, praise, recommend.

common *adj.* commonplace, communal, conventional, familiar, hackneyed, ordinary, pedestrian, plain, prevailing, regular, routine, standard, trite, universal, usual, vulgar, widespread.

compete *v.* battle, challenge, contend, contest, duel, emulate, fight, oppose, rival, strive, struggle, tussle, vie.

competence *n.* ability, adequacy, appropriateness, aptitude, capability, capacity, expertise, facility, fitness, proficiency, skill, suitability, technique.

complete *v.* accomplish, achieve, cap, clinch, close, conclude, consummate, crown, discharge, do, effect, end, execute, finalize, finish, fulfil, perfect, perform, realize, settle, terminate, wind-up.

compromise *v.* adapt, adjust, agree, arbitrate, bargain, concede, make concessions, negotiate, retire, retreat, settle.

compute *v.* assess, calculate, count, enumerate, estimate, evaluate, figure, measure, rate, reckon, sum, tally, total.

computer *n.* adding machine, analog computer, data processor, digital computer, mainframe, processor, word processor.

conceal *v.* bury, camouflage, cloak, cover, disguise, dissemble, hide, keep, dark, mask, obscure, screen, secrete, shelter, sink, smother, submerge, suppress, veil.

concede *v.* accept, acknowledge, admit, allow, cede, confess, forfeit, grant, own, recognize, relinquish, sacrifice, surrender, yield.

conceive *v.* appreciate, apprehend, believe, comprehend, contrive, create, design, develop, devise, envisage, fancy, form, formulate, germinate, grasp, imagine, invent, originate, produce, project, purpose, realize, suppose, think, understand, visualize.

concern *n.* affair, anxiety, business, care, consideration, corporation, distress, enterprise, interest, involvement, job, organization, relevance, responsibility, stake, task, uneasiness, worry.

concerning *prep.* about, apropos of, as regards, germane to, in regard to, in the matter of, re, regarding, relating to, relevant to, respecting, touching, with reference to, with regard to.

conclude *v.* accomplish, assume, cease, clinch, close, complete, consummate, culminate, decide, deduce, determine, effect, end, establish, finish, fix, gather, infer, judge, opine, reckon, resolve, settle, suppose, surmise, terminate.

conduct *v.* accompany, acquit, act, administer, attend, bear, behave, carry, chair, comport, control, convoy, demean, deport, direct, escort, govern, guide, handle, lead, manage, orchestrate, organize, pilot, regulate, run, solicit, steer, supervise, transact, usher.

confidential *adj.* classified, close, closed, faithful, familiar, hush-hush, in camera, intimate, private, privy, secret, tête-à-tête, trusted, trustworthy, trusty.

confine *v.* bind, bound, cage, chamber, circumscribe, constrain, cramp, crib, enclose, immure, imprison, incarcerate, inhibit, intern, keep, keep prisoner, limit, mew, repress, restrain, restrict, shackle, shut up, thirl, trammel.

confirm *v.* approve, assure, attest, authenticate, back, buttress, clinch, corroborate, endorse, establish, evidence, fix, fortify, homologate, prove, ratify, reinforce, sanction, settle, strengthen, substantiate, support, validate, verify, witness to.

conflict *v.* battle, clash, collide, combat, contend, contest, contradict, differ, disagree, fight, interfere, oppose, strive, struggle, war, wrangle.

conform *v.* accommodate, accord, adapt, adjust, agree, assimilate, comply, correspond, follow, harmonize, match, obey, quadrate, square, suit, tally, yield.

confront *v.* accost, address, beard, brave, challenge, defy, encounter, face, front, oppose.

confuse *v.* baffle, befuddle, bewilder, confound, disconcert, disorientate, fluster, maze, mix up, mystify, nonplus, perplex, puzzle, upset.

congregate *v.* accumulate, assemble, bunch, clump, cluster, collect, concentrate, conglomerate, convene, converge, convoke, crowd, flock, foregather, gather, mass, meet, muster, rally, rendezvous, throng.

connect *v.* affix, ally, associate, cohere, combine, concatenate, couple, fasten, join, link, relate, unite.

consent *v.* accede, acquiesce, admit, agree, allow, comply, concede, concur, yield.

consequently *adv.* accordingly, consequentially, ergo, hence, inferentially, necessarily, subsequently, therefore, thus.

considerate *adj.* attentive, charitable, circumspect, concerned, discreet, forbearing, gracious, kind, kindly, mindful, obliging, patient, solicitous, tactful, thoughtful, unselfish.

consistent *adj.* agreeing, compatible, congruous, constant, dependable, harmonious, persistent, regular, steady, unchanging, uniform.

conspire *v.* cabal, collude, confederate, contrive, co-operate, devise, hatch, intrigue, maneuver, plot, scheme, treason.

contact *v.* approach, call, get hold of, notify, phone, reach, ring.

contaminate *v.* adulterate, befoul, corrupt, debase, defile, infect, pollute, sully, taint, tarnish.

contempt *n.* condescension, contemptuousness, contumely, derision, despite, disdain, disgrace, dishonor, disregard, disrespect, humiliation, loathing, mockery, neglect, scorn, shame, slight.

content *n.* burden, capacity, essence, gist, ideas, load, matter, meaning, measure, significance, size, subject, matter, substance, text, thoughts, volume.

contented *adj.* cheerful, comfortable, complacent, content, glad, gratified, happy, placid, pleased, relaxed, satisfied, serene, thankful.

contest *n.* affray, altercation, battle, combat, competition, conflict, controversy, debate, discord, dispute, encounter, fight, game, match, olympiad, set-to, shock, struggle, tournament, trial, *v.* argue, against, challenge, compete, contend, debate, deny, dispute, doubt, fight, litigate, oppose, question, refute, strive, vie.

contradict *v.* belie, challenge, contravene, controvert, counter, counteract, deny, disaffirm, dispute, gainsay, impugn, negate, oppose.

contrast *v.* compare, differ, differentiate, discriminate, distinguish, oppose, set off.

contribute *v.* add, afford, bestow, conduce, donate, furnish, give, help, kick in, lead, provide, subscribe, supply, tend.

controversy *n.* altercation, argument, contention, debate, disagreement, discussion, dispute, dissension, polemic, quarrel, squabble, strife, war of words, wrangle, wrangling.

conventional *adj.* accepted, arbitrary, bourgeois, common, commonplace, copybook, correct, customary, decorous, expected, formal, habitual, hackneyed, hidebound, nomic, normal, ordinary, orthodox, pedes-trian, prevailing, prevalent, proper, prosaic, regular, ritual, routine, run-of-the-mill, standard, stereotyped, straight, stylized, traditional, unoriginal, uptight, usual, wonted.

conversation *n.* chat, chitchat, colloquy, communication, communion, confab, confabulation, conference, converse, dialogue, discourse, discussion, exchange, gossip, intercourse, interlocution, powwow, tête-á-tête.

convict *v.* attaint, condemn, imprison, sentence. *n.* con, criminal, culprit, felon, jail-bird, lag, malefactor, prisoner.

cool *adj.* aloof, apathetic, calm, chilly, composed, deliberate, frigid, imperturbable, laidback, level-headed, lukewarm, placid, pleasant, relaxed, reserved, self-possessed, stand-offish, together, unexcited, urbane. *v.* abate, allay, assuage, calm, chill, dampen, freeze, lessen, moderate, quiet, refrigerate, temper.

cooperate *v.* abet, aid, assist, collaborate, conspire, help, play along, play ball.

copy *v.* ape, borrow, counterfeit, crib, duplicate, echo, emulate, facsimile, follow, imitate, mimic, mirror, parrot, photocopy, plagiarize, replicate, reproduce, simulate, transcribe.

correct *v.* adjust, admonish, amend, blue-pencil, chasten, chastise, chide, debug, discipline, rectify, reform, reprimand, reprove, right.

correspond *v.* accord, agree, answer, coincide, communicate, complement, concur, conform, correlate, dovetail, fit, harmonize, match, square, tally, write.

cost *n.* amount, charge, damage, deprivation, detriment, disbursement, expenditure, expense, figure, harm, hurt, injury, loss, outlay, payment, penalty, price, rate, sacrifice, worth.

council *n.* assembly, board, cabinet, committee, congress, panel, parliament, syndicate, synod.

counsel *v.* admonish, advise, advocate, caution, direct, exhort, guide, instruct, recommend, suggest, urge, warn.

courage *n.* boldness, bravery, daring, fearlessness, fortitude, grit, guts, heroism, mettle, nerve, spirit, spunk, valor.

courteous *adj.* affable, civil, courtly, debonair, elegant, gallant, gracious, polished, polite, refined, respectful, urbane, well-bred, well-mannered.

covert *adj.* clandestine, concealed, disguised, dissembled, hidden, private, secret, sneaky, stealthy, subreptitious, surreptitious, ulterior, under the table, underhand, unsuspected, veiled.

cower *v.* cringe, crouch, flinch, grovel, quail, shake, shiver, shrink, skulk, tremble.

creed *n.* articles, belief, canon, credo, doctrine, dogma, faith, persuasion, principles, tenets.

criminal *n.* con, convict, crook, culprit, delinquent, felon, jail-bird, law-breaker, malefactor, offender, sinner, transgressor. *adj.* bent, corrupt, crooked, culpable, felonious, illegal, immoral, indictable, lawless, malfeasant, nefarious, scandalous, senseless, unlawful, wrong.

critic *n.* analyst, animadverter, arbiter, attacker, authority, carper, caviler, censor, censurer, commentator, detractor, expert, expositor, fault-finder, judge, knocker, pundit, reviewer, reviler, vilifier.

crooked[1] *adj.* bent, corrupt, crafty, criminal, deceitful, discreditable, dishonest, dishonorable, dubious, fraudulent, illegal, knavish, nefarious, questionable, shady, shifty, treacherous, underhand, unethical, unlawful, unprincipled, unscrupulous.

crooked[2] *adj.* angled, askew, asymmetric, awry, bent, bowed, crank, cranky, crippled, curved, deformed, deviating, disfigured, distorted, irregular, lopsided, misshapen, off-center, slanted, slanting, tilted, tortuous, twisted, twisting, uneven, warped, zigzag.

cruel *adj.* barbarous, brutal, callous, cold-blooded, fierce, harsh, heartless, inhuman, merciless, murderous, ruthless, sadistic, savage, unfeeling, unmerciful, vicious.

cultivate *v.* aid, cherish, court, develop, elevate, encourage, enrich, farm, fertilize, forward, foster, further, harvest, help, improve, patronize, plant, plow, polish, prepare, promote, pursue, refine, school, support, tend, till, train, work.

cunning *adj.* adroit, arch, artful, astute, canny, crafty, deep, deft, devious, dexterous, foxy, guileful, imaginative, ingenious, knowing, leery, sharp, shifty, shrewd, skilful, sneaky, subtle, tricky, vulpine, wily.

curious *adj.* bizarre, exotic, extraordinary, inquisitive, interested, mysterious, nosy, novel, peculiar, puzzling, searching, unconventional, unorthodox, unusual, wonderful.

cursory *adj.* brief, careless, casual, desultory, fleeting, hasty, hurried, offhand, passing, perfunctory, quick, rapid, slap-dash, slight, summary, superficial.

curve *v.* arc, arch, bend, bow, coil, hook, inflect, spiral, swerve, turn, twist, wind. *n.* arc, bend, camber, curvature, half-moon, incurvation, loop, trajectory, turn.

cut *v.* abbreviate, abridge, carve, castrate, cleave, condense, contract, delete, dissect, divide, edit, engrave, excise, hack, harvest, hew, incise, nick, pare, part, prune, reduce, saw, scissor, sever, slash, slice, split, trim, truncate, whittle, wound.

cynical *adj.* contemptuous, derisive, distrustful, ironic, mephistophelian, mephistophilic, mocking, mordant, pessimistic,, sarcastic, sardonic, skeptical, scoffing, scornful, sharp-tongued, sneering.

D

dab *v.* blot, daub, pat, stipple, swab, tap, touch, wipe. *n.* bit, dollop, drop, fingerprint, fleck, flick, pat, peck, smear, smidgen, smudge, speck, spot, stroke, tap, touch, trace.

damage *n.* destruction, detriment, devastation, harm, hurt, impairment, injury, loss, mischief, mutilation, scathe, suffering. *v.* deface, harm, hurt, impair, incapacitate, injure, mar, mutilate, play hell with, ruin, spoil, tamper with, weaken, wreck.

damp *n.* clamminess, dampness, dankness, dew, drizzle, fog, humidity, mist, moisture, vapor, wet. *adj.* clammy, dank, dewy, dripping, drizzly, humid, misty, moist, muggy, sodden, soggy, wet. *v.* allay, check, chill, cool, curb, dampen, depress, diminish, discourage, dull, inhibit, moderate, restrain, stifle, wet.

dance *v.* frolic, gambol, hoof it, hop, jig, prance, rock, skip, spin, stomp, sway, swing, tread a measure, whirl. *n.* ball, hop, kick-up, knees-up, prom, shindig, social.

danger *n.* hazard, insecurity, jeopardy, liability, menace, peril, precariousness, risk, threat, trouble, venture, vulnerability.

dark *adj.* angry, black, bleak, cheerless, cloudy, concealed, cryptic, deep, dim, dingy, dismal, drab, dusky, ebony, forbidding, foul, gloomy, glowering, glum, grim, hidden, horrible, ignorant, indistinct, joyless, lightless, midnight, morbid, morose, murky, mysterious, mystic, obscure, ominous, overcast, pitch-black, scowling, secret, shadowy, shady, sinful, sinister, somber, sullen, sunless, swarthy, unenlightened, vile, wicked.

date[1] *n.* age, epoch, era, period, point in time, stage, time.

date[2] *n.* appointment, assignation, engagement, escort, friend, meeting, partner, rendezvous, steady, tryst.

dead[1] *adj.* apathetic, barren, boring, breathless, cold, deceased, defunct, departed, dull, exhausted, extinct, flat, frigid, glassy, glazed, gone, inactive, inanimate, indifferent, inert, inoperative, insipid, late, lifeless, lukewarm, numb, obsolete, paralyzed, perished, spent, spiritless, stagnant, stale, sterile, stiff, still, tasteless, tired, torpid, unemployed, uninteresting, unprofitable, unresponsive, useless, vapid, wooden, worn out.

dead[2] *adj.* absolute, complete, downright, entire, outright, perfect, thorough, total, unqualified, utter. *adv.* absolutely, completely, entirely, exactly, perfectly, quite, totally.

deal *v.* allot, apportion, assign, bargain, bestow, dispense, distribute, divide, dole out, give, mete out, negotiate, reward, sell, share, stock, trade, traffic, treat. *n.* agreement, amount, arrangement, bargain, buy, contract, degree, distribution, extent, hand, pact, portion, quantity, round, share, transaction, understanding.

dear *adj.* beloved, cherished, close, costly, darling, esteemed, expensive, familiar, favorite, high-priced, intimate, loved, overpriced, precious, pric(e)y, prized, respected, treasured, valued.

death *n.* annihilation, bane, bereavement, cessation, curtains, decease, demise, departure, destruction, dissolution, downfall, dying, end, eradication, exit, expiration, extermination, extinction, fatality, finish, grave, loss, obliteration, passing, quietus, release, ruin, ruination, undoing.

debate *v.* argue, cogitate, consider, contend, contest, controvert, deliberate, discuss, dispute, meditate on, mull over, ponder, question, reflect, revolve, ruminate, weigh, wrangle.

debt *n.* arrears, bill, claim, commitment, debit, due, duty, indebtedness, liability, obligation, score, sin.

deceit *n.* abuse, artifice, blind, cheat, cheating, chicanery, craftiness, cunning, deceitfulness, deception, duplicity, fake, feint, fraud, fraudulence, guile, hypocrisy, misrepresentation, pretense, ruse, sham, shift, slyness, stratagem, subterfuge, swindle, treachery, trick, trickery, underhandedness, wile.

deceive *v.* abuse, bamboozle, beguile, betray, camouflage, cheat, cog, con, delude, diddle, disappoint, dissemble, double-cross, dupe, entrap, fool, gag, hoax, impose upon, lead on, mislead, outwit, swindle.

decide *v.* adjudge, adjudicate, choose, conclude, decree, determine, dijudicate, elect, end, fix, judge, opt, purpose, reach a decision, resolve, settle.

decisive *adj.* absolute, conclusive, critical, crucial, crunch, decided, definite, definitive, determinate, determined, fateful, final, firm, forceful, forthright, incisive, influential, momentous, positive, resolute, significant, strong-minded, supreme, trenchant.

declare *v.* affirm, announce, assert, attest, aver, avouch, avow, certify, claim, confess, confirm, convey, disclose, maintain, manifest, nuncupate, proclaim, profess, pronounce, reveal, show, state, swear, testify, validate, witness.

decline[1] *v.* balk, decay, decrease, degenerate, deter-iorate, droop, dwindle, ebb, fade, fall, fall off, flag, forgo, languish, lessen, shrink, sink, turn down, wane, weaken, worsen.

decline[2] *v.* descend, dip, sink, slant, slope. *n.* brae, declination, declivity, descent, deviation, dip, divergence, hill, incline, obliqueness, obliquity, slope.

decorate[1] *v.* adorn, beautify, bedeck, color, deck, do up, embellish, enrich, furbish, grace, impearl, ornament, paint, paper, prettify, renovate, tart up, trick out, trim, wallpaper.

decorate[2] *v.* bemedal, cite, crown, garland, honor.

decoy *n.* attraction, bait, ensnarement, enticement, inducement, lure, pretence, roper (-in), trap. *v.* allure, attract, bait, beguile, deceive, draw, ensnare, entice, entrap, inveigle, lead, lure, seduce, tempt.

decrease *v.* abate, ablate, contract, curtail, cut down, decline, diminish, drop, dwindle, ease, fall off, lessen, lower, peter out, reduce, shrink, slacken, slim, subside, taper, wane.

dedicate *v.* address, assign, bless, commit, consecrate, devote, give over to, hallow, inscribe, offer, pledge, present, sacrifice, sanctify, set apart, surrender.

deep *adj.* abstruse, acute, astute, bass, booming, bottomless, broad, canny, cryptic, cunning, dark, designing, devious, esoteric, extreme, far, rave, great, hidden, immersed, insidious, intense, learned, lost, low, low-pitched, obscure, penetrating, preoccupied, profound, rapt, rich, sagacious, scheming, secret, shrewd, sonorous, strong, unfathomable, vivid, wide, wise, yawning.

defeat *v.* beat, best, conquer, crush, disappoint, down, foil, frustrate, overpower, overthrow, overwhelm, quell, repulse, rout, ruin, subdue, thwart, trounce, vanquish. *n.* beating, conquest, disappointment, discomfiture, failure, overthrow, rebuff, repulse, reverse, rout, setback, thwarting, trouncing, vanquishment, Waterloo.

defect *n.* absence, blemish, bug, default, deficiency, error, failing, fault, flaw, frailty, hamartia, imperfection, inadequacy, lack, mistake, shortcoming, spot, taint, want, weakness. *v.* apostatize, break faith, desert, rebel, revolt.

defend *n.* assert, bulwark, champion, contest, cover, endorse, espouse, fortify, guard, justify, maintain, plead, preserve, protect, safeguard, screen, secure, shelter, shield, speak up for, stand, by, stand up for, support, sustain, uphold, vindicate, watch over.

defer[1] *v.* adjourn, delay, hold over, postpone, procrastinate, prorogue, pro-tract, put off, put on ice, shelve, suspend, waive.

defer² *v.* accede, bow, capitulate, comply, give way, kowtow, respect, submit, yield.

define *v.* bound, characterize, circumscribe, delimit, delimitate, delineate, demarcate, describe, designate, detail, determine, explain, expound, interpret, limit, mark out, outline, specify, spell out.

definite *adj.* assured, certain, clear, clear-cut, decided, determined, exact, explicit, express, fixed, guaranteed, marked, obvious, particular, positive, precise, settled, specific, substantive, sure.

definition¹ *n.* clarification, delimitation, delineation, demarcation, description, determination, elucidation, explanation, exposition, interpretation, outlining, settling.

definition² *n.* clarity, clearness, contrast, distinctness, focus, precision, sharpness.

defunct *adj.* dead, deceased, departed, expired, extinct, gone, inoperative, invalid, kaput, non-existent, obsolete, passé.

defy *v.* baffle, beard, beat, brave, challenge, confront, contemn, dare, defeat, despise, disregard, elude, face, flout, foil, frustrate, provoke, repel, repulse, resist, scorn, slight, spurn, thwart, withstand.

delicate *adj.* choice, dainty, deft, detailed, diplomatic, discreet, discriminating, elegant, exquisite, faint, fine, flimsy, fragile, frail, graceful, hazardous, minute, pastel, precarious, precise, prudish, pure, refined, risky, savory, scrupulous, sensible, sensitive, sickly, skilled, slender, slight, soft, squeamish, sticky, subdued, subtle, tactful, tender, ticklish, touchy, weak.

delicious *adj.* agreeable, ambrosial, ambrosian, appetizing, charming, choice, dainty, delectable, delightful, enjoyable, entertaining, exquisite, flavorsome, luscious, mouthwatering, palatable, pleasant, pleasing, savory, scrumptious, tasty, toothsome, yummy.

delight *n.* bliss, ecstasy, enjoyment, felicity, gladness, gratification, happiness, heaven, joy, jubilation, pleasure, rapture, transport.

deliver *v.* acquit, administer, aim, announce, bear, bring, carry, cart, cede, commit, convey, deal, declare, direct, discharge, dispense, distribute, emancipate, feed, free, give, give forth, give up, grant, hand over, inflict, launch, liberate, loose, make over, pass, present, proclaim, pronounce, publish, ransom, read, redeem, release, relinquish, rescue, resign, save, strike, supply, surrender, throw, transfer, transport, turn over, utter, yield.

demand *v.* ask, call for, challenge, claim, exact, expect, inquire, insist on, interrogate, involve, necessitate, need, order, question, request, require, take, want.

demean *v.* abase, condescend, debase, degrade, deign, descend, humble, lower, stoop.

demeanor *n.* air, bearing, behavior, carriage, comportment, conduct, deportment, manner, mien, port.

demolish *v.* annihilate, bulldoze, consume, defeat, destroy, devour, dilapidate, dismantle, down, eat, flatten, gobble, gulp, guzzle, knock down, level, overthrow, overturn, pull down, pulverize, raze, ruin, tear down, undo, wreck.

demonstrate¹ *v.* describe, display, establish, evidence, evince, exhibit, explain, expound, illustrate, indicate, manifest, prove, show, substantiate, teach, testify to.

demonstrate² *v.* march, parade, picket, protest, rally, sit in.

den *n.* cave, cavern, cloister, cubby-hole, earth, haunt, hide-away, hide-out, hole, lair, retreat, sanctuary, sanctum, set(t), shelter, study.

deny *v.* abjure, begrudge, contradict, decline, disaffirm, disagree with, disallow, disavow, discard, disclaim, disown, disprove, forbid, gainsay, negative, oppose, rebuff, recant, refuse, refute, reject, renounce, repudiate, revoke, traverse, turn down, veto, withhold.

depart *v.* absent oneself, decamp, deviate, differ, digress, disappear, diverge, escape, exit, go, leave, levant, make off, migrate, quit, remove, retire, retreat, set forth, stray, swerve, take one's leave, toddle, vanish, vary, veer, withdraw.

dependable *adj.* certain, conscientious, faithful, gilt-edged, honest, reliable, responsible, steady, sure, trustworthy, trusty, unfailing.

depict *v.* caricature, characterize, delineate, describe, detail, draw, illustrate, limn, narrate, outline, paint, picture, portray, render, reproduce, sculpt, sketch, trace.

deposit¹ *v.* drop, dump, lay, locate, park, place, precipitate, put, settle, sit. *n.* accumulation, alluvium, deposition, dregs, hypostasis, lees, precipitate, sediment, silt.

deposit² *v.* amass, bank, consign, depone, entrust, file, hoard, lodge, reposit, save, store. *n.* bailment, down payment, installment, money, part payment, pledge, retainer, security, stake, warranty.

depress *v.* burden, cheapen, chill, damp, daunt, deject, depreciate, devaluate, devalue, devitalize, diminish, discourage, dishearten, enervate, exhaust, flatten, hip, impair, lessen, level, lower, oppress, overburden, press, reduce, sadden, sap, squash, tire, undermine, upset, weaken, weary.

depression[1] *n.* blues, de-cline, dejection, despair, despondency, doldrums, dolefulness, downheartedness, dullness, dumps, examination, gloominess, glumness, hard times, heart-heaviness, hopelessness, inactivity, low spirits, lowness, mal du siècle, megrims, melancholia, melancholy, recession, sadness, slump, stagnation, vapors.

depression[2] *n.* basin, bowl, cavity, concavity, dent, dimple, dint, dip, dish, excavation, fossa, fossula, fovea, foveola, hollow, hollowness, impression indentation, pit, sag, sink, umbilicus, valley.

deprive *v.* amerce, bereave, denude, deny, despoil, dispossess, divest, expropriate, mulct, rob, starve, strip.

descend *v.* alight, arrive, assail, assault, attack, condescend, degenerate, deign, derive, deteriorate, develop, dip, dismount, drop, fall, gravitate, incline, invade, issue, leap, originate, plummet, plunge, pounce, proceed, raid, sink, slant, slope, spring, stem, stoop, subside, swoop, tumble.

describe *v.* characterize, define, delineate, depict, detail, draw, enlarge on, explain, express, illustrate, mark out, narrate, outline, portray, present, recount, relate, report, sketch, specify, tell, trace.

desert[1] *n.* solitude, vacuum, vast, void, waste, wasteland, wilderness, wilds. *adj.* arid, bare, barren, desolate, dry, infertile, lonely, solitary, sterile, uncultivated, uninhabited, unproductive, untilled, waste, waterless, wild.

desert[2] *v.* abandon, abscond, apostatize, backslide, betray, decamp, deceive, defect, forsake, give up, jilt, leave, leave in the lurch, maroon, quit, rat on, relinquish, renounce, resign, strand, vacate.

desert[3] *n.* come-uppance, demerit, deserts, due, guerdon, meed, merit, payment, recompense, remuneration, requital, retribution, return, reward, right, virtue, worth.

design *n.* aim, arrangement, blueprint, composition, configuration, conformation, construction, contrivance, draft, figure, form, goal, guide, intent, meaning, model, objective, outline, pattern, plan, plot, project, prototype, scheme, shape, sketch, structure, style, target, undertaking. *v.* aim, conceive, construct, create, describe destine, develop, devise, draft, draw, draw up, fashion, form, intend, invent, make, mean, model, originate, outline, plan, project, propose, purpose, scheme, shape, sketch, structure, tailor, trace.

designate *v.* allot, appoint, assign, bill, call, characterize, choose, christen, deem, define, delegate, denominate, denote, depute, describe, docket, dub, earmark, entitle, indicate, label, name, nickname, nominate, select, show, specify, stipulate, style, term, ticket, title.

desire *v.* ask, aspire to, beg, covet, crave, desiderata, entreat, fancy, hanker after, hunger for, importune, lack, long for, need, request, solicit, want, wish for, yearn for, *n.* appeal, appetite, ardor, aspiration, covetousness, craving, cupidity, entreaty, greed, lasciviousness, lechery, libido, longing, lust, lustfulness, need, passion, petition, request, want, wish, yearning, yen.

desist *v.* abstain, break off, cease, come to a halt, discontinue, end, forbear, give over, give up, halt, leave off, pause, peter out, refrain, remit, stop, suspend.

despise *v.* abhor, condemn, deplore, deride, detest, disdain, dislike, disregard, ignore, loathe, revile, scorn, slight, spurn, undervalue, vilipend.

despondent *adj.* blue, broken-hearted, dejected, depressed, despairing, disconsolate, discouraged, disheartened, dispirited, doleful, down, downcast, downhearted, gloomy, glum, hopeless, inconsolable, low, low-spirited, melancholy, miserable, morose, mournful, overwhelmed, sad, sorrowful, wretched.

destitute *adj.* bankrupt, beggared, bereft, deficient, depleted, deprived, devoid of, distressed, down and out, impecunious, impoverished, indigent, innocent of, insolvent, lacking, necessitous, needy, penniless, penurious, poor, poverty-stricken, strapped, wanting.

destroy *v.* annihilate, break, canker, crush, demolish, destruct, devastate, dismantle, dispatch, eliminate, eradicate, extinguish, extirpate, gut, kill, level, nullify, overthrow, ravage, raze, ruin, sabotage, scuttle, shatter, slay, slight, smash, thwart, torpedo, undermine, undo, vaporize, waste, wreck, zap.

detail *n.* aspect, attribute, complexity, complication, component, count, elaborateness, elaboration, element, fact, factor, feature, ingredient, intricacy, item, meticulousness, nicety, particular, particularity, point, refinement, respect, specify, specificity, technicality, thoroughness, triviality. *v.* allocate, appoint, assign, catalog, charge, commission, delegate, delineate, depict, depute, describe, detach, enumerate, individualize, itemize, list, narrate, particularize, portray, recount, rehearse, relate, send, specify.

detect *v.* ascertain, catch, descry, discern, disclose, discover, distinguish, find, identify, note, notice, observe, perceive, recognize, reveal, scent, sight, spot, spy, track down, uncover, unmask.

determine *v.* affect, arbitrate, ascertain, certify, check, choose, conclude, control, decide, detect, dictate, direct, discover, elect, end, establish, finish, fix, govern, guide, identify, impel, impose, incline, induce, influence, intend, lead, learn, modify, ordain, point, purpose, regulate, resolve, rule, settle, shape, terminate, undertake, verify.

develop *v.* advance, amplify, augment, begin, bloom, blossom, branch out, breed, broaden, commence, contract, cultivate, diversify, elaborate, enlarge, ensue, establish, evolve, expand, flourish, follow, form, generate, grow, happen, invent, make headway, mature, move on, originate, progress, promote, prosper, result, ripen, sprout, start, unfold.

development *n.* advancement, blossoming, change, detail, elaboration, event, evolution, expansion, growth, happening, improvement, increase, issue, maturation, maturity, occurrence, outcome, progress, progression, promotion, refinement, result, ripening, situation, spread, unfolding, unraveling, upbuilding, upshot.

devilish *adj.* accursed, black-hearted, damnable, demoniac, demoniacal, diabolic, diabolical, execrable, fiendish, hellish, impious, infernal, iniquitous, mischievous, monstrous, nefarious, satanic, wicked.

devise *v.* arrange, compass, compose, conceive, concoct, construct, contrive, design, excogitate, forge, form, formulate, frame, imagine, invent, plan, plot, prepare, project, scheme, shape.

devote *v.* allocate, allot, apply, appropriate, assign, commit, consecrate, dedicate, enshrine, give oneself, pledge, reserve, sacrifice, set apart, set aside, surrender.

devour *v.* absorb, annihilate, bolt, consume, cram, destroy, dispatch, down, eat, engulf, feast on, feast one's eyes on, gobble, gorge, gormandize, gulp, guzzle, polish off, ravage, relish, revel in, spend, stuff, swallow, waste, wolf.

die *v.* breathe one's last, croak, decay, decease, decline, depart, desire, disappear, dwindle, ebb, end, expire, fade, finish, kick the bucket, languish, lapse, long for, pass, pass away, pass over, perish, peter out, sink, stop, subside, succumb, suffer, vanish, wane, wilt, wither, yearn.

difference *n.* argument, change, clash, conflict, contrast, controversy, debate, deviation, disagreement, discordance, discrepancy, disparateness, disparity, dispute, dissimilarity, distinctness, divergence, diversity, exception, idiosyncrasy, particularity, peculiarity, quarrel, remainder, rest, strife, tiff, unlikeness, variation, variety, wrangle.

different *adj.* altered, assorted, at odds, atypical, bizarre, contrasting, deviating, disparate, dissimilar, distinct, divers, diverse, inconsistent, manifold, many, miscellaneous, multifarious, numerous, peculiar, rare, several, singular, special, strange, sundry, uncommon, unconventional, unique, unlike, unusual, varied, various.

difficult *adj.* abstract, arduous, burdensome, complex, complicated, dark, delicate, formidable, hard, herculean, intricate, involved, knotty, laborious, onerous, painful, perplexing, perverse, problematic, rigid, sticky, stiff, straitened, strenuous, stubborn, thorny, ticklish, tiresome, toilsome, tough, troublesome, trying, unmanageable, uphill, wearisome.

difficulty *v.* arduousness, awkwardness, complication, dilemma, distress, hang-up, hardship, hurdle, impediment, laboriousness, mess, obstacle, opposition, pain, pitfall, plight, predicament, problem, protest, quandary, scruple, spot, strain, straits, strenuousness, stumbling-block, trial, tribulation, trouble, vexed, question.

dig[1] *v.* burrow, delve, drive, excavate, go into, gouge, graft, grub, hoe, investigate, jab, mine, penetrate, pierce, poke, probe, prod, punch, quarry, research, scoop, search, spit, thrust, till, tunnel. *n.* aspersion, barb, crack, cut, gibe, insinuation, insult, jab, jeer, poke, prod, punch, quip, sneer, taunt, thrust, wisecrack.

dig² *v.* adore, appreciate, be into, enjoy, fancy, follow, get a kick out of, get off on, go a bundle on, go for, go overboard about, groove, have the hots for, like, love, understand, warm to.

dignity *n.* courtliness, decorum, elevation, emi-nence, excellence, glory, grandeur, gravity, greatness, hauteur, honor, importance, loftiness, majesty, nobility, nobleness, pride, propriety, respectability, self-esteem, self-respect, solemnity, standing, stateliness, station, status.

diminish *v.* abate, bate, belittle, cheapen, contract, curtail, cut, deactivate, decline, decrease, demean, depreciate, devalue, dwindle, ebb, fade, lessen, lower, peter out, recede, reduce, retrench, shrink, shrivel, sink, slacken, subside, taper off, wane, weaken.

dip *v.* bathe, decline, descend, droop, drop, duck, dunk, fade, fall, immerse, plunge, rinse, sag, scoop, slope, slump, spoon, subside, tilt. *n.* basin, concoction, decline, depression, dilution, dive, fall, hole, hollow, immersion, incline, infusion, lowering, mixture, plunge, preparation, sag, slip, slope, slump, soaking, solution, suspension, swim.

direct¹ *v.* address, administer, advise, aim, bid, case, charge, command, conduct, control, dictate, dispose, enjoin, fix, focus, govern, guide, handle, indicate, instruct, intend, label, lead, level, mail, manage, mastermind, mean, order, oversee, point, regulate, route, rule, run, send, show, stage-manage, superintend, superscribe, supervise, train, turn.

direct² *adj.* absolute, blunt, candid, categorical, downright, explicit, express, face-to-face, first-hand, frank, head-on, honest, immediate, man-to-man, matter-of-fact, non-stop, open, outright, outspoken, personal, plain, plain-spoken, point-blank, shortest, sincere, straight, straightforward, through, unambig-uous, unbroken, undeviating, unequivocal, uninterrupted.

direction *n.* address, administration, aim, approach, bearing, bent, bias, charge, command, control, course, current, drift, end, government, guidance, label, leadership, line, management, mark, order, orientation, oversight, path, proclivity, purpose, road, route, superintendence, superscription, supervision, tack, tendency, tenor, track, trend, way.

dirty *adj.* angry, base, beggarly, begrimed, bitter, blue, clouded, contemptible, corrupt, cowardly, crooked, cruddy, dark, despicable, dishonest, dull, filthy, foul, grubby, ignomini-ous, illegal, indecent, low-down, maculate, mean, messy, miry, mucky, nasty, obscene, off-color, polluted, pornographic, salacious, scruffy, scurvy, shabby, sluttish, smutty, soiled, sordid, squalid, sullied, treacherous, unclean, unfair, unscrupulous, vile, vulgar.

disability *n.* affliction, ailment, complaint, defect, disablement, disorder, disqualification, handicap, impairment, impotency, inability, incapacitation, incapacity, incompetency, infirmity, malady, unfitness, weakness.

disable *v.* cripple, damage, debilitate, disenable, disqualify, enfeeble, hamstring, handicap, immobilize, impair, incapacitate, invalidate, lame, paralyze, prostrate, unfit, unman, weaken.

disagree *v.* altercate, argue, bicker, bother, clash, conflict, contend, contest, contradict, counter, depart, deviate, differ, discomfort, dissent, distress, diverge, hurt, object, oppose, quarrel, run counter to, sicken, spat, squabble, take issue with, tiff, trouble, upset, vary, wrangle.

disappear *v.* cease, dematerialize, depart, dissolve, ebb, end, escape, evanesce, evaporate, expire, fade, flee, fly, go, pass, perish, recede, retire, scarper, vamoose, vanish, wane, withdraw.

disappoint *v.* baffle, balk, chagrin, dash, deceive, defeat, delude, disconcert, disenchant, disgruntle, dishearten, disillusion, dismay, dissatisfy, fail, foil, frustrate, hamper, hinder, let down, miff, sadden, thwart, vex.

disaster *n.* accident, act of God, blow, calamity, cataclysm, catastrophe, curtains, debacle, misfortune, mishap, reverse, ruin, ruination, stroke, tragedy, trouble.

discard *v.* abandon, cashier, cast aside, dispense with, dispose of, ditch, drop, dump, jettison, leave off, reject, relinquish, remove, repudiate, scrap, shed.

discharge *v.* absolve, accomplish, acquit, carry out, detonate, disburden, discard, dismiss, dispense, drum out, eject, emit, empty, execute, expel, explode, exude, fire, free, fulfill, give off, gush, honor, leak, liberate, meet, oust, pardon, pay, perform, release, relieve, remove, sack, satisfy, set off, settle, shoot, unburden, unload, vent, void, volley.

disciple *n.* acolyte, adherent, apostle, believer, convert, devotee, follower, learner, partisan, proselyte, pupil, student, supporter, votary.

disconnect v. cut off, detach, disengage, divide, part, separate, sever, uncouple, unhitch, unhook, unlink, unplug, unyoke.

discontinue v. abandon, break off, cancel, cease, drop, end, finish, halt, interrupt, pause, quit, stop, suspend, terminate.

discourage v. abash, awe, check, chill, cow, curb, damp, dampen, dash, daunt, deject, demoralize, deprecate, depress, deter, discountenance, disfavor, dishearten, dismay, dispirit, dissuade, frighten, hinder, inhibit, intimidate, overawe, prevent, put off, restrain, scare, unman, unnerve.

discover v. ascertain, conceive, contrive, descry, design, detect, determine, devise, dig up, discern, disclose, espy, find, invent, learn, light on, locate, notice, originate, perceive, pioneer, realize, recognize, reveal, see, spot, suss out, uncover, unearth.

discreet adj. careful, cautious, circumspect, considerate, delicate, diplomatic, discerning, guarded, judicious, politic, prudent, reserved. sagacious, sensible, softly-softly, tactful, wary.

discretion n. acumen, care, carefulness, caution, choice, circumspection, consideration, diplomacy, discernment, heedfulness, inclination, judgment, judiciousness, liking, maturity, mind, option, pleasure, predilection, preference, prudence, responsibility, sagacity, tact, volition, wariness, will, wisdom, wish.

discriminating adj. acute, astute, critical, cultivated, discerning, discriminant, fastidious, particular, perceptive, selective, sensitive, tasteful.

discrimination n. bias, bigotry, favoritism, inequity, intolerance, Jim Crow, prejudice, unfairness.

discuss v. argue, confer, consider, consult, converse, debate deliberate, examine, lay heads together, rap.

disease n. affection, affliction, ailment, blight, cancer, canker, complaint, condition, contagion, contamination, disorder, distemper, epidemic, epizootic, idiopathy, ill-health, illness, indisposition, infection, infirmity, malady, malaise, murrain, pest, plague, sickness, upset.

disgrace n. aspersion, attaint, baseness, blemish, blot, contempt, defamation, degradation, discredit, disesteem, disfavor, dishonor, disrepute, dog-house, ignominy, infamy, obloquy, odium, opprobrium, reproach, scandal, shame, slur, stain, stigma.

disguise v. camouflage, cloak, conceal, cover, deceive, dissemble, dissimulate, dress up, explain away, fake, falsify, fudge, hide, mask, misrepresent, screen, secrete, shroud, veil.

disgust v. displease, nauseate, offend, outrage, put off, repel, revolt, scandalize, sicken.

dish n. bowl, fare, food, plate, platter, ramekin, recipe.

dishonor v. abase, blacken, corrupt, debase, debauch, defame, defile, deflower, degrade, demean, discredit, disgrace, disparage, pollute, rape, ravish, seduce, shame, sully.

dislike n. animosity, animus, antagonism, antipathy, aversion, detestation, disapprobation, disapproval, disgust, disinclination, displeasure, distaste, enmity, hatred, hostility, loathing, repugnance.

dismiss v. ax, banish, bounce, bowler-hat, cashier, chuck, disband, discharge, discount, dispel, disperse, disregard, dissolve, drop, fire, free, give (someone) the push, lay off, let go, oust, reject, release, relegate, remove, repudiate, sack, send packing, set aside, shelve, spurn.

disobedient adj. contrary, contumacious, defiant, disorderly, forward, insubordinate, intractable, mischievous, naughty, obstreperous, refactory, unruly, wayward, wilful.

disorder n. affliction, ailment, brawl, chaos, clamor, clutter, commotion, complaint, confusion, disarray, disease, disorganization, disturbance, fight, fracas, irregularity, jumble, malady, mess, muddle, quarrel, riot, rumpus, shambles, sickness, tumult, untidiness, uproar.

disorganized n. chaos, confusion, disordered, haphazard, jumbled, muddled, shuffled, topsy-turvy, unmethodical, unorganized, unregulated, unsifted, unsorted, unstructured, unsystematic, unsystematized.

disparage v. belittle, criticize, decry, defame, degrade, denigrate, deprecate, depreciate, deride, derogate, detract from, discredit, disdain, dishonor, dismiss, malign, minimize, ridicule, run down, scorn, slander, traduce, underestimate, underrate, undervalue, vilify, vilipend.

dispatch[1] v. accelerate, conclude, discharge, dismiss, dispose of, expedite, finish, hasten, hurry, perform, quicken, settle,

dispatch[2] v. consign, express, forward, remit, send, transmit. n. account, bulletin, communication, document, instruction, item, letter, message, missive, news, piece, report, story.

dispense *v.* administer, allocate, allot, apply, apportion, assign, deal out, direct, disburse, discharge, distribute, dole out, enforce, except, excuse, execute, exempt, exonerate, implement, let off, measure, mete out, mix, operate, prepare, release, relieve, reprieve, share, supply, undertake.

disperse *v.* broadcast, circulate, diffuse, disappear, disband, dismiss, dispel, disseminate, dissipate, dissolve, distribute, drive off, evanesce, melt away, rout, scatter, separate, spread, stew, vanish.

displeasure *n.* anger, annoyance, disapprobation, disapproval, discontent, disfavor, dudgeon, huff, indignation, irritation, offense, pique, resentment, vexation, wrath.

dispose *v.* actuate, adapt, adjust, align, arrange, array, bias, condition, determine, dispone, distribute, fix, group, incline, induce, influence, lay, lead, marshal, motivate, move, order, place, position, predispose, prompt, put, range, rank, regulate, set, settle, situate, stand, tempt.

disprove *v.* answer, confute, contradict, controvert, discredit, explode, expose, invalidate, negate, rebut, refute.

dispute *v.* altercate, argue, brawl, challenge, clash, contend, contest, contradict, controvert, debate, deny, discuss, doubt, gainsay, impugn, litigate, moot, oppugn, quarrel, question, spar, squabble, traverse, wrangle.

disqualify *v.* debar, disable, disentitle, incapacitate, invalidate, preclude, prohibit, rule out, unfit.

disregard *v.* brush aside, cold-shoulder, contemn, despise, discount, disdain, disobey, disparage, ignore, laugh off, make light of, neglect, overlook, pass over, pooh-pooh, slight, snub, turn a blind eye to.

disrespectful *adj.* bad-tempered, cheeky, contemptuous, discourteous, impertinent, impolite, impudent, insolent, insulting, irreverent, rude, uncivil, unmannerly.

dissect *v.* analyze, anatomize, break down, dismember, examine, explore, inspect, investigate, pore over, scrutinize, study.

dissolve *v.* break up, crumble, decompose, destroy, diffuse, disappear, discontinue, disintegrate, disorganize, disperse, dissipate, divorce, dwindle, end, evaporate fade, flux, fuse, liquefy, loose, melt, overthrow, perish, ruin,

separate sever, soften, suspend, thaw, vanish, wind up.

distant *adj.* abroad, afar, aloof, apart, ceremonious, cold, cool, disparate, dispersed, distinct, faint, far, faraway, far-flung, far-off, formal, haughty, indirect, indistinct, isolated, obscure, outlying, out-of-the-way, remote, removed, reserved, restrained, reticent, scattered, separate, slight, stand-offish, stiff, unapproachable, uncertain, unfriendly, withdrawn.

distinct *adj.* apparent, clear, clear-cut, decided, definite, detached, different, discrete, dissimilar, evident, individual, lucid, manifest, marked, noticeable, obvious, palpable, patent, plain, recognizable, separate, several, sharp, unambiguous, unconnected, unmistakable, well-defined.

distinction[1] *n.* characteristic, contradistinction, contrast, difference, differential, differentiation, discernment, discrimination, dissimilarity, distinctiveness, division, feature, individuality, mark, nuance, particularity, peculiarity, penetration, perception, quality, separation.

distinction[2] *n.* account, celebrity, consequence, credit, eminence, excellence, fame, glory, greatness, honor, importance, merit, name, note, prestige, prominence, quality, rank, renown, reputation, repute, significance, superiority, worth.

distinguish *v.* ascertain, categorize, celebrate, characterize, classify, decide, determine, differentiate, dignify, discern, discriminate, honor, immortalize, individualize, judge, know, make out, mark, perceive, pick out, recognize, see, separate, signalize, tell, tell apart.

distort *v.* bend, bias, buckle, color, contort, deform, disfigure, falsify, garble, misrepresent, misshape, pervert, skew, slant, torture, twist, warp, wrench, wrest, wring.

distract *v.* agitate, amuse, beguile, bewilder, confound, confuse, derange, discompose, disconcert, disturb, divert, engross, entertain, faze, harass, madden, occupy, perplex, puzzle, sidetrack, torment, trouble.

distress *n.* adversity, affliction, agony, anguish, anxiety, calamity, depravation, destitution, difficulties, discomfort, grief, hardship, heartache, indigence, katzen-jammer, misery, misfortune, need, pain, pauperism, poverty, privation, sadness, sorrow, strait(s), suffering, torment, torture, trial, trouble, woe, worry, wretchedness.

distribute v. administer, allocate, allot, apportion, arrange, assign, assort, bestow, carve up, categorize, circulate, class, classify, convey, deal, deliver, diffuse, dish out, dispense, disperse, dispose, disseminate, divide, dole, file, give, group, hand out, mete, scatter, share, spread, strew.

disturb v. affray, agitate, alarm, annoy, bother, concuss, confound, confuse, derange, disarrange, discompose, disorder, disorganize, disrupt, distract, distress, excite, fluster, harass, interrupt, muddle, perturb, pester, rouse, ruffle, shake, startle, trouble, unsettle, upset, worry.

diverse adj. assorted, different, differing, discrete, disparate, dissimilar, distinct, divergent, diversified, heterogeneous, manifold, many, miscellaneous, multifarious, multiform, numerous, separate, several, some, sundry, unlike, varied, various, varying.

divert v. amuse, avert, beguile, deflect, delight, detract, distract, entertain, gratify, hive off, recreate, redirect, regale, side-track, switch, tickle.

divide v. alienate, allocate, allot, apportion, arrange, bisect, , break up, categorize, classify, cleave, cut, deal out, detach, disconnect, dispense, distribute, disunite, divvy, estrange, grade, group, part, partition, portion, segment, segregate, separate, sever, share, shear, sort, split, subdivide, sunder.

divine adj. angelic, beatific, beautiful, blissful, celestial, consecrated, exalted, excellent, glorious, godlike, heavenly, holy, marvelous, mystical, perfect, rapturous, religious, sacred, sanctified, spiritual, splendid, superhuman, superlative, supernatural, supreme, transcendent, transcendental, wonderful.

divorce n. annulment, breach, break, break up, decree nisi, dissolution, rupture, separation, severance, split-up. v. annul, cancel, disconnect, dissever, dissociate, dissolve, disunite, divide, part, separate, sever, split up, sunder.

do v. accomplish, achieve, act, carry out, cause, complete, create, deceive, discharge, dupe, effect, end, execute, fix, fleece, hoax, implement, make, manage, organize, perform, prepare, present, proceed, produce, put on, render, resolve, satisfy, serve, solve, suffice, suit, swindle, travel, trick, undertake, visit, work, work out.

docile adj. amenable, biddable, complaisant, compliant, ductile, manageable, obedient, obliging, pliable, pliant, submissive, teachable, tractable, unprotesting, unquestioning.

dock¹ n. boat-yard, harbor, marina, pier, quay, water-front, wharf. v. anchor, berth, drop anchor, join up, land, link up, moor, put in, rendezvous, tie up, unite.

dock² v. clip, crop, curtail, cut, decrease, deduct, diminish, lessen, reduce, shorten, subtract, truncate, withhold.

doctor n. clinician, general practitioner, internist, medic, medical officer, medical practitioner, physician, pill(s).

doctrine n. belief, canon, concept, conviction, creed, dogma, ism, opinion, precept, principle, teaching, tenet.

document n. certificate, deed, form, instrument, paper, parchment, record, report. v. authenticate, back, certify, cite, corroborate, detail, enumerate, instance, list, particularize, prove, substantiate, support, validate, verify.

dodge v. avoid, dart, deceive, duck, elude, equivocate, evade, fend off, fudge, hedge, parry, shift, shirk, shuffle, side-step, swerve, swing the lead, trick. n. chicane, contrivance, device, feint, machination, maneuver, ploy, ruse, scheme, stratagem, subterfuge, trick, wheeze, wile.

dogma n. article, article of faith, belief, conviction, credo, creed, doctrine, opinion, precept, principle, , teaching, tenet.

domain n. area, authority, bailiwick, business, concern, demesne, department, discipline, dominion, empire, estate, field, jurisdiction, kingdom, lands, orbit, pidgin, policies, power, province, realm, region, scope, specialty, sphere, sway, territory.

dominate v. bestride, control, direct, domineer, dwarf, eclipse, govern, have-the-whip hand, keep under one's thumb, lead, master, monopolize, outshine, overbear, overlook, overrule, overshadow, predominate, prevail, rule, tyrannize.

domineering adj. arrogant, authoritarian, autocratic, bossy, coercive, despotic, dictatorial, harsh, high-handed, imperious, iron-handed, magisterial, masterful, oppressive, overbearing, severe, tyrannical.

donate v. bequeath, bestow, chip in, confer, contribute, cough up, fork out, give, impart, present, proffer, subscribe.

done adj. acceptable, accomplished, advised, agreed, completed, concluded, consummated, conventional, cooked, cooked to a turn, de rigueur, depleted, drained, ended, executed, exhausted, fatigued, finished, OK, over, perfected, proper, ready, realized, settled, spent, terminated, through, used up.

double *adj.* bifold, coupled, diploid, doubled, dual, duple, duplex, duplicate, paired, twice, twin, twofold. *v.* duplicate, enlarge, fold, geminate, grow, increase, magnify, multiply, repeat. *n.* clone, copy, counterpart, dead ringer, dead spit, duplicate, fellow, image, impersonator, lookalike, mate, replica, ringer, spitting image, twin.

doubt *v.* be dubious, be uncertain, demure, discredit, distrust, fear, fluctuate, hesitate, mistrust, query, question, scruple, suspect, vacillate, waver.

doubtless *adv.* apparently, assuredly, certainly, clearly, indisputably, most likely, of course, ostensibly, out of question, precisely, presumably, probably, seemingly, supposedly, surely, truly, undoubtedly, unquestionably, without doubt.

drab *adj.* cheerless, colorless, dingy, dismal, dreary, dull, flat, gloomy, gray, lackluster, mousy, shabby, somber, uninspired, vapid.

draft[1] *v.* compose, delineate, design, draw, draw up, formulate, outline, plan, sketch. *n.* abstract delineation, outline, plan, protocol, rough, sketch, version.

draft[2] *n.* bill, check, order, postal order.

draft[3] *n.* cup, current, dose, dragging, drawing, drench, drink, flow, haulage, influx, movement, portion, potation, puff, pulling, quantity, traction.

drag *v.* crawl, creep, dawdle, draw, hale, haul, inch, lag, linger, loiter, lug, pull, schlep, shamble, shuffle, straggle, sweep, tow, trail, tug, yank. *n.* annoyance, bore, bother, brake, drogue, nuisance, pain, pest, pill.

drain *v.* bleed, consume, deplete, discharge, dissipate, dry, effuse, empty, evacuate, exhaust, exude, leak, milk, ooze, quaff, remove, sap, seep, strain, swallow, tap, tax, trickle, use up, weary, withdraw

drama *n.* acting, crisis, dramatics, dramatization, dramaturgy, excitement, histrionics, kabuki, melodrama, play, scene, show, spectacle, stage-craft, theater, theatricals, Thespian art, turmoil.

draw[1] *v.* allure, attenuate, attract, borrow, breathe in, bring forth, choose, deduce, delineate, depict, derive, design, drag, drain, elicit, elongate, engage, entice, entrain, evoke, extend, extort, extract, get, haul, induce, infer, inhale, inspire, invite, lengthen, make, map out, mark out, outline, paint, pencil, persuade, pick, portray, puff, pull, respire,

select, sketch, stretch, suck, take, tow, trace, tug, unsheathe.

draw[2] *v.* be equal, be even, be neck and neck, dead-heat, tie. *n.* dead-heat, deadlock, impasse, stalemate, tie.

dread *v.* cringe at, fear, flinch, quail, shrink from, shudder, shy, tremble. *n.* alarm, apprehension, aversion, awe, dismay, disquiet, fear, fright, horror, misgiving, terror, trepidation, worry.

dream *n.* ambition, aspiration, beauty, daydream, delight, delusion, design, desire, fantasy, goal, hallucination, hope, illusion, imagination, joy, marvel, notion, phantasm, pipedream, pleasure, reverie, speculation, trance, treasure, vagary, vision, wish. *v.* conjure, daydream, envisage, fancy, fantasize, hallucinate, imagine, muse, think, visualize.

dress *n.* apparel, attire, clothing, costume, garb, garments, habit, outfit, robe, suit, togs, vestment. *v.* adjust, adorn, apparel, arrange, attire, clothe, deck, decorate, don, drape, embellish, fit, furbish, garb, groom, habit, ornament, prepare, put on, rig, robe, set, straighten, tend, treat, trim.

drill[1] *v.* coach, discipline, exercise, instruct, practice, rehearse, teach, train, tutor. *n.* coaching, discipline, exercise, instruction, practice, preparation, repetition, training, tuition.

drill[2] *v.* bore, penetrate, perforate, pierce, puncture. *n.* awl, bit, borer, gimlet.

drink *v.* absorb, booze, carouse, drain, gulp, guzzle, imbibe, indulge, partake of, quaff, revel, sip, swallow, swig, swill, tank up, tipple, water. *n.* alcohol, ambrosia, beverage, booze, dose, dram, draught, glass, liquor, potion, refreshment, slug, snifter, snort, spirits, swig, tipple, toss, tot.

drive *v.* actuate, bear, coerce, compel, constrain, dash, dig, direct, force, goad, guide, hammer, handle, harass, herd, hurl, impel, manage, motivate, motor, oblige, operate, overburden, overwork, plunge, press, prod, propel, push, ram, ride, rush, send, sink, spur, stab, steer, task, tax, thrust, travel, urge. *n.* action, advance, ambition, appeal, campaign, crusade, determination, effort, energy, enterprise, excursion, hurl, initiative, jaunt, journey, motivation, outing, pressure, push, ride, run, spin, surge, trip, turn, vigor, vim, zip.

drop *n.* abyss, bead, bubble, chasm, cut, dab, dash, decline, declivity, decrease, descent, deterioration, downturn, driblet, drip, droplet, fall, falling-off, glob, globule, lowering, mouthful, nip, pearl, pinch, plunge, precipice, reduction, shot, sip, slope, slump, spot, taste, tear, tot, trace, trickle. *v.* abandon, cease, chuck, decline, depress, descend, desert, diminish, discontinue, disown, dive, dribble, drip, droop, fall, forsake, give up, jilt, kick, leave, lower, plummet, plunge, quit, reject, relinquish, remit, renounce, repudiate, sink, stop, terminate, throw over, trickle, tumble.

drown *v.* deaden, deluge, drench, engulf, extinguish, flood, go under, immerse, inundate, muffle, obliterate, overcome, overpower, overwhelm, silence, sink, stifle, submerge, swallow up, swamp, wipe out.

drug *n.* depressant, dope, medicament, medication, medicine, Mickey, Mickey Finn, narcotic, opiate, physic, poison, potion, remedy, stimulant. *v.* anesthetize, deaden, dope, dose, knock out, load, medicate, numb, poison, stupefy, treat.

drunk *adj.* a sheet (three sheets) in the wind, blind, bottled, canned, cockeyed, corked, corny, drunken, inebriated, intoxicated, liquored, lit up, loaded, lushy, muddled, obfuscated, pickled, plastered, shickered, sloshed, soaked, sottish, soused, stewed, stoned, tanked up, tiddly, tight, tipsy, up the pole, well-oiled, wet.

dull *adj.* apathetic, blank, blunt, boring, dead, dense, depressed, dimwitted, dismal, drab, dreary, dry, edgeless, faded, featureless, flat, humdrum, insipid, lackluster, listless, monotonous, muted, opaque, overcast, passionless, plain, prosaic, stodgy, subdued, tedious, thick, tiresome, unexciting, uninteresting, vacuous, vapid.

duplicate *adj.* corresponding, geminate, identical, matched, matching, twin, twofold. *n.* carbon copy, copy, facsimile, match, photocopy, replica, repro-duction.

duplicity *n.* artifice, chicanery, deceit, deception, dishonesty, dissimulation, double-dealing, falsehood, fraud, guile, hypocrisy, mendacity, perfidy, treachery.

duty *n.* allegiance, assignment, business, calling, charge, chore, customs, debt, deference, devoir, due, engagement, excise, function, impost, job, levy, loyalty, mission, obedience, obligation, office, onus, province, respect, responsibility, reverence, role, service, tariff, task, tax, toll, work.

dying *adj.* at death's door, declining, disappearing, ebbing, expiring, fading, failing, final, going, in articulo mortis, in extremis, moribund, mortal, not long for this world,

obsolescent, passing, perishing, sinking, vanishing.

dynamic *adj.* active, driving, electric, energetic, forceful, go-ahead, go-getting, high-powered, lively, powerful, self-starting, spirited, vigorous, vital, zippy.

E

eager *adj.* agog, anxious, ardent, athirst, avid, desirous, earnest, enthusiastic, fervent, fervid, greedy, gung-ho, hot, hungry, impatient, intent, keen, longing, raring, unshrinking, vehement, yearning, zealous.

early *adj.* advanced, forward, matutinal, prehistoric, premature, primeval, primitive, primordial, undeveloped, untimely, young. *adv.* ahead of time, beforehand, betimes, in advance, in good time, prematurely, too soon.

earn *v.* acquire, attain, bring in, collect, deserve, draw, gain, get, gross, make, merit, net, obtain, procure, rate, realize, reap, receive, warrant, win.

ease *n.* affluence, aplomb, calmness, comfort, composure, content, contentment, deftness, dexterity, easiness, effortlessness, enjoyment, facileness, facility, flexibility, freedom, happiness, informality, insouciance, leisure, liberty, naturalness, nonchalance, peace, peace of mind, poise, quiet, quietude, readiness, realization, repose, rest, restfulness, serenity, simplicity, solace, tranquility, unaffectedness, unconstraint, unreservedness.

easy *adj.* a piece of cake, a pushover, accommodating, affable, calm, carefree, casual, child's play, clear, comfortable, contented, easy-going, effortless, facile, gentle, graceful, gracious, leisurely, lenient, liberal, light, manageable, mild, moderate, natural, open, peaceful, permissive, pleasant, quiet, relaxed, satisfied, simple, smooth, soft, straightforward, tolerant, tranquil, uncomplicated, yielding.

ebb *v.* abate, decay, decline, decrease, degenerate, deteriorate, diminish, drop, dwindle, fade away, fall away, fall back, flag, flow back, go out, lessen, peter out, recede, reflow, retire, retreat, retrocede, shrink, sink, slacken, subside, wane, weaken, withdraw.

effect *n.* action, aftermath, clout, conclusion, consequence, drift, effectiveness, efficacy, efficiency, enforcement, essence, event, execution, fact, force, fruit, impact, implementation, import, impression, influence, issue, meaning, operation, outcome, power, purport, purpose, reality, result, sense, significance, strength, tenor, upshot, use, validity, vigor, weight, work. *v.* accomplish, achieve, actuate, cause, complete, consummate, create, effectuate, execute, fulfill, initiate, make, perform, produce, wreak.

efficient *adj.* able, adept, businesslike, capable, competent, economic, effective, effectual, powerful, productive, proficient, ready, skilful, streamlined, well-ordered, well-regulated, workmanlike.

effort *n.* accomplishment, achievement, application, attempt, creation, deed, endeavor, energy, essay, exertion, feat, force, go, job, labor, molimen, nisus, pains, power, product, production, shot, stab, strain, stress, stretch, striving, struggle, toil, travail, trouble, try, work.

elated *adj.* animated, blissful, cheered, delighted, ecstatic, euphoric, excited, exhilarated, exultant, gleeful, joyful, joyous, jubilant, on the high ropes, over the moon, overjoyed, pleased, proud, roused.

elect *v.* adopt, appoint, choose, designate, determine, opt for, pick, prefer, select, vote. *adj.* choice, chosen, designate, designated, elite, hand-picked, picked, preferred, presumptive, prospective, select, selected, to be.

eliminate *v.* annihilate, bump off, cut out, delete, dispense with, dispose of, disregard, do away with, drop, eject, eradicate, exclude, expel, expunge, exterminate, extinguish, get rid of, ignore, kill, knock out, liquidate, murder, omit, reject, remove, rub out, slay, stamp out, take out, terminate, waste.

embrace *v.* accept, clasp, comprehend, comprise, contain, cover, cuddle, enclose, encompass, enfold, grab, grasp, hold, hug, include, incorporate, squeeze, take up, welcome.

emotion *n.* affect. agitation, ardor, excitement, feeling, fervor, passion, perturbation, reaction, sensation, sentiment, vehemence, warmth.

emotional *adj.* affecting, ardent, demonstrative, emotive, enthusiastic, excitable, exciting, feeling, fervent, fervid, fiery, heated, hot-blooded, impassioned, moved, moving, overcharged, passionate, pathetic, poignant, responsive, roused, sensitive, sentimental, stirred, stirring, susceptible, tear-jerking, temperamental, tempestuous, tender, thrilling, touching, volcanic, warm, zealous.

empty *adj.* absent, aimless, banal, bare, blank, bootless, cheap, clear, deserted, desolate, destitute, expressionless, famished,

frivolous, fruitless, futile, hollow, hungry, idle, inane, ineffective, insincere, insubstantial, meaningless, purposeless, ravenous, senseless, silly, starving, superficial, trivial, unfed, unfilled, uninhabited, unoccupied, unreal, unsatisfactory, vacant, vacuous, vain, valueless, void, waste, worthless.

encounter *v.* chance upon, clash with, combat, come upon, confront, contend, cross swords with, engage, experience, face, fight, happen on, meet, rencounter, run across, run into, strive, struggle.

encourage *v.* abet, advance, advocate, aid, animate, boost, buoy up, cheer, comfort, console, egg on, embolden, favor, forward, foster, further, hearten, help, incite, inspire, inspirit, promote, rally, reassure, rouse, second, spirit, spur, stimulate, strengthen, succor, support, urge.

end *n.* aim, annihilation, aspiration, attainment, bit, bound, boundary, butt, cessation, close, closure, completion, conclusion, consequence, consummation, culmination, curtain, death, demise, design, destruction, dissolution, doom, downfall, drift, edge, ending, expiration, expiry, extent, extermination, extinction, extreme, extremity, finale, fine, finis, finish, fragment, goal, intent, intention, issue, left-over, limit, object, objective, outcome, part, pay-off, piece, point, portion, purpose, reason, remainder, remnant, resolution, responsibility, result, ruin, ruination, scrap, share, side, stop, stub, termination, terminus, tip, upshot, wind-up.

endorse *v.* adopt, advocate, affirm, approve, authorize, back, champion, confirm, countenance, countersign, favor, indorse, ratify, recommend, sanction, sign, subscribe to, superscribe, support, sustain, undersign, vouch for, warrant.

endure *v.* abide, bear, brave, brook, cope with, experience, go through, hold, last, live, permit, persist, prevail, put up with, remain, stand, stay, stick, submit to, suffer, support, survive, sustain, swallow, tolerate, undergo, weather, withstand.

enemy *n.* adversary, antagonist, competitor, foe, foeman, opponent, Philistine, rival, the opposition.

engage *v.* absorb, activate, affiance, agree, allure, apply, appoint, arrest, assail, attach, attack, attract, bespeak, betroth, bind, book, busy, captivate, catch, charm, charter, combat, commission, commit, contract, covenant, draw, embark, employ, enamor, enchant, encounter, energize, engross, enlist, enrol, enter, fascinate, fit, fix, gain, grip, guarantee, hire, interact, interconnect, interlock, involve, join, lease, meet, mesh, obligate, oblige, occupy, operate, partake, participate, pledge, practice, prearrange, preoccupy, promise, rent, reserve, retain, secure, take on, tie up, undertake, vouch, vow, win.

enhance v. amplify, augment, boost, complement, elevate, embellish, escalate, exalt, heighten, improve, increase, intensify, lift, magnify, raise, reinforce, strengthen, swell.

enjoy v. appreciate, delight in, dig, experience, have, like, make a meal of, own, possess, rejoice in, relish, revel in, savor, take pleasure in, use.

enmity n. acrimony, ani-mosity, animus, antagonism, antipathy, aversion, bad blood, bitterness, feud, hate, hatred, hostility, ill-will, invidiousness, malevolence, malice, malignity, rancor, spite, venom.

enormous adj. abominable, astronomic(al), atrocious, Brobdingnagian, colossal, cyclopean, depraved, disgraceful, evil, excessive, gargantuan, gigantic, gross, heinous, herculean, huge, hulking, immense, jumbo, leviathan, mammoth, massive, monstrous, mountainous, nefarious, odious, outrageous, prodigious, titanic, tremendous, vast, vicious, vile, villainous, wicked.

enter v. arrive, begin, board, commence, embark upon, enlist, enrol, inscribe, insert, introduce, join, list, log, note, offer, participate, participate in, penetrate, pierce, present, proffer, record, register, set about, set down, sign up, start, submit, take down, take up, tender.

enterprise n. activity, adventure, adventurousness, alertness, audacity, boldness, business, company, concern, daring, dash, drive, eagerness, effort, endeavor, energy, enthusiasm, essay, establishment, firm, get-up-and-go, gumption, imagination, initiative, operation, plan, program, project, push, readiness, resource, resourcefulness, spirit, undertaking, venture, vigor, zeal.

entertain v. accommodate, amuse, charm, cheer, cherish, conceive, consider, contemplate, countenance, delight, divert, fête, foster, harbor, hold, imagine, lodge, maintain, occupy, please, ponder, put up, recreate, regale, support, treat.

entrance n. access, admission, admittance, appearance, arrival, atrium, avenue, beginning, commencement, debut, door, doorway, entrée, entry, gate, ingress, initiation, inlet, introduction, opening, outset, passage, portal, start.

entrance v. bewitch, captivate, charm, delight, enchant, enrapture, enthrall, fascinate, gladden, hypnotize, magnetize, mesmerize, ravish, spellbind, transport.

entreat v. appeal to, ask, beg, beseech, conjure, crave, enjoin, exhort, implore, importune, invoke, petition, plead with, pray, request, sue, supplicate.

environment n. ambience, atmosphere, background, conditions, context, domain, element, entourage, habitat, locale, medium, milieu, scene, setting, situation, surroundings, territory.

equal adj. able, adequate, alike, balanced, capable, commensurate, competent, corresponding, egalitarian, equable, equivalent, even, even-handed, evenly-balanced, evenly-matched, evenly-proportioned, fair, fifty-fifty, fit, identical, impartial, just, level-pegging, like, matched, proportionate, ready, regular, sufficient, suitable, symmetrical, tantamount, the same, unbiased, uniform, unvarying, up to.

equilibrium n. balance, calm, calmness, collectedness, composure, cool, coolness, counterpoise, equanimity, equipoise, evenness, poise, rest, self-possession, serenity, stability, steadiness, symmetry.

equity n. disinterestedness, equality, equitableness, even-handedness, fair play, fair-mindedness, fairness, honesty, impartiality, integrity, justice, justness, objectivity, reasonableness, rectitude, righteousness, uprightness.

era n. age, century, cycle, date, day, days, eon, epoch, generation, period, stage, time.

erase v. blot out, cancel, cleanse, delete, efface, eliminate, eradicate, expunge, get rid of, obliterate, remove, rub out.

erect adj. elevated, engorged, firm, hard, perpendicular, pricked, raised, rigid, standing, stiff, straight, taut, tense, tumescent, upright, upstanding, vertical.

err v. blunder, deviate, fail, go astray, lapse, misapprehend, misbehave, miscalculate, misjudge, mistake, misunderstand, offend, sin, slip up, stray, stumble, transgress, trespass, trip up, wander.

errand n. assignment, charge, commission, duty, job, message, mission, task.

error n. blunder, boner, delinquency, delusion, deviation, erratum, fallacy, fault, faux pas, flaw, inaccuracy, lapse, malapropism, miscalculation, misconception, mistake, offense, omission, oversight, slip-up, transgression, trespass, wrong, wrongdoing.

escort *n.* aide, attendant, beau, bodyguard, chaperon, companion, company, convoy, entourage, gigolo, guard, guardian, guide, partner, pilot, procession, protection, protector, retinue, safeguard, squire, suite, train. *v.* accompany, chaperon, chum, company, conduct, convoy, guard, guide, lead, partner, protect, shepherd, squire, usher.

establish *v.* affirm, attest to, authenticate, authorize, base, certify, confirm, constitute, corroborate, create, decree, demonstrate, enact, ensconce, entrench, fix, form, found, ground, implant, inaugurate, install, institute, introduce, invent, lodge, ordain, organize, plant, prove, radicate, ratify, root, sanction, seat, secure, set up, settle, show, start, station, substantiate, validate, verify.

eternal *adj.* abiding, ceaseless, changeless, constant, deathless, durable, endless, enduring, everlasting, illimitable, immortal, immutable, imperishable, incessant, indestructible, infinite, interminable, lasting, limitless, never-ending, perennial, permanent, perpetual, timeless, unceasing, unchanging, undying, unending, unextinguishable, unremitting.

ethical *adj.* commendable, conscientious, correct, decent, fair, fitting, good, honest, honorable, just, meet, moral, noble, principled, proper, right, righteous, seemly, upright, virtuous.

even *adj.* abreast, alongside, balanced, calm, coequal, commensurate, comparable, composed, constant, cool, disinterested, dispassionate, drawn, equable, equal, equalized, equitable, even-tempered, fair, fair and square, fifty-fifty, flat, fluent, flush, horizontal, identical, impartial, impassive, imperturbable, just, level, level-pegging, like, matching, metrical, monotonous, neck and neck, on a par, parallel, peaceful, placid, plane, proportionate, quits, regular, rhythmical, serene, side by side, similar, smooth, square, stable, steady, straight, symmetrical, tied, tranquil, true, unbiased, unbroken, undisturbed, unexcitable, unexcited, uniform, uninterrupted, unprejudiced, unruffled, unvarying, unwavering, well-balanced.

ever *adv.* always, at all, at all times, at any time, ceaselessly, constantly, continually, endlessly, eternally, everlastingly, evermore, for ever, in any case, in any circumstances, incessantly, on any account, perpetually, unceasingly, unendingly.

evidence *n.* affirmation, attestation, betray-al, confirmation, corroboration, data, declaration, demonstration, deposition, documentation, grounds, hint, indication, manifestation, mark, pledge, proof, sign, substantiation, suggestion, testimony, token, voucher, witness.

evil *adj.* adverse, bad, base, calamitous, corrupt, cruel, deadly, depraved, dire, disastrous, ghastly, grim, harmful, heinous, hurtful, immoral, malevolent, malic- ious, malignant, nefarious, noxious, offensive, painful, poisonous, putrid, reprobate, ruinous, sinful, sorrowful, ugly, unfortunate, unspeakable, vicious, vile, villainous, wicked, woeful, wrong.

exact *adj.* accurate, blow-by-blow, careful, close, correct, definite, detailed, explicit, express, factual, faithful, faultless, finicky, flawless, identical, letter-perfect, literal, methodical, metic-ulous, nice, orderly, painstaking, particular, perfectionist, precise, punc-tilious, right, rigorous, scrupulous, severe, specific, square, strict, true, unambiguous, unequivocal, unerring, veracious, very, word-perfect,

example *n.* admonition, archetype, case, case in point, caution, citation, exemplar, exemplification, ideal, illustration, instance, lesson, mirror, model, occurrence, paradigm, paragon, parallel, pattern, praxis, precedent, prototype, sample, specimen, standard, type, warning.

excel *v.* beat, better, cap, eclipse, exceed, outclass, outdo, outperform, outrank, outshine, outstrip, overshadow, pass, predominate, shine, stand out, surmount, surpass, top, transcend, trump.

except *prep.* apart from, bar, barring, besides, but, except for, excepting, excluding, exclusive of, leaving out, less, minus, not counting, omitting, other than, save, saving. *v.* ban, bar, debar, disallow, eliminate, exclude, leave out, omit, pass over, reject, rule out.

exclude *v.* anathematize, ban, bar, blackball, blacklist, bounce, boycott, debar, disallow, eject, eliminate, embargo, evict, except, excommunicate, expel, forbid, ignore, include out, interdict, keep out, leave out, omit, ostracize, oust, preclude, prohibit, proscribe, refuse, reject, remove, repudiate, rule out, shut out, veto.

exclusive *adj.* absolute, closed, complete, discriminative, entire, esoteric, fashionable, full, limited, monopolistic, private, restricted, restrictive, select, selective, sole, total, undivided, unique, unshared, whole.

excuse *v.* absolve, acquit, apologize for, condone, defend, discharge, exculpate, exempt, exonerate, explain, extenuate, forgive, free, ignore, indulge, justify, let off, liberate, mitigate, overlook, palliate, pardon, release, relieve, sanction, spare, tolerate, vindicate, warrant, wink at. *n.* alibi, apology, cop-out, defense, disguise, evasion, exculpation, exoneration, expedient, explanation, grounds, justification, make-shift, mitigation, mockery, palliation, parody, plea, pretense, pretext, put-off, reason, semblance, shift, substitute, subterfuge, vindication.

execute[1] *v.* behead, burn, crucify, decapitate, decollate, electrocute, guillotine, hang, kill, liquidate, put to death, shoot.

execute[2] *v.* accomplish, achieve, administer, complete, consummate, deliver, discharge, dispatch, do, effect, effectuate, enact, enforce, expedite, finish, fulfill, implement, perform, prosecute, realize, render, seal, serve, sign, validate.

exempt *v.* absolve, discharge, dismiss, except, excuse, exonerate, free, let off, liberate, make an exception of, release, relieve, spare.

exhibit *v.* air, demonstrate, disclose, display, evidence, evince, expose, express, flaunt, indicate, manifest, offer, parade, present, reveal, show, showcase, sport.

exonerate *v.* absolve, acquit, clear, discharge, dismiss, except, excuse, free, justify, liberate, pardon, release, relieve, vindicate.

expand *v.* amplify, augment, bloat, blow up, branch out, broaden, develop, diffuse, dilate, distend, diversify, elaborate, embellish, enlarge, expatiate, expound, extend, fatten, fill out, flesh out, grow, heighten, increase, inflate, lengthen, magnify, multiply, open, outspread, prolong, protract, snowball, spread, stretch, swell, thicken, unfold, unfurl, unravel, unroll, wax, widen.

expect *v.* anticipate, assume, await, bank on, bargain for, believe, calculate, conjecture, contemplate, count on, demand, envisage, forecast, foresee, hope for, imagine, insist on, look for, look forward to, predict, presume, project, reckon, rely on, require, suppose, surmise, think, trust, want, wish.

explore *v.* analyze, case, examine, inspect, investigate, probe, prospect, reconnoiter, research, scout, scrutinize, search, survey, tour, travel, traverse.

expose *v.* air, betray, bring to light, denounce, detect, disclose, display, divulge, endanger, exhibit, hazard, imperil, jeopardize, manifest, present, reveal, risk, show, uncover, unearth, unmask, unveil

express *v.* articulate, assert, asseverate, bespeak, communicate, conceive, convey, couch, declare, denote, depict, designate, disclose, divulge, embody, enunciate, evince, exhibit, extract, force out, formulate, indicate, intimate, manifest, phrase, pronounce, put, put across, represent, reveal, say, show, signify, speak, stand for, state, symbolize, tell, testify, utter, verbalize, voice, word. *adj.* accurate, certain, clear, clear-cut, definite, direct, distinct, especial, exact, explicit, fast, high-speed, manifest, non-stop, outright, particular, plain, pointed, precise, quick, rapid, singular, special, speedy, stated, swift, unambiguous, unqualified.

extend *v.* advance, amplify, attain, augment, bestow, broaden, confer, continue, develop, dilate, drag out, draw out, elongate, enhance, enlarge, expand, give, grant, hold out, impart, increase, last, lengthen, offer, present, proffer, prolong, protract, pull out, reach, spin out, spread, stretch, supplement, take, uncoil, unfold, unfurl, unroll, widen, yield.

exterminate *v.* abolish, annihilate, destroy, eliminate, eradicate, massacre, wipe out.

extinct *adj.* abolished, dead, defunct, doused, ended, exterminated, extinguished, gone, inactive, lost, obsolete, out, quenched, terminated, vanished, void.

extol *v.* acclaim, applaud, celebrate, commend, cry up, eulogize, exalt, glorify, laud, magnify, praise, puff.

extraordinary *adj.* amazing, bizarre, curious, exceptional, fantastic, marvelous, notable, noteworthy, odd, outstanding, particular, peculiar, phenomenal, rare, remarkable, significant, singular, special, strange, striking, surprising, uncommon, uncontemplated, unfamiliar, unheard-of, unimaginable, unique, unprecedented, unusual, unwonted, weird, wonderful.

extreme *adj.* acute, deep-dyed, dire, double-dyed, downright, drastic, egregious, exaggerated, exceptional, excessive, exquisite, extraordinary, extravagant, fanatical, faraway, far-off, farthest, final, great, greatest, harsh, high, highest, immoderate, inordinate, intemperate, intense, last, maximum, out-and-out, outermost, outrageous, radical, red-hot, remarkable, remotest, rigid, severe, sheer, stern, strict, supreme, terminal, ultimate, ultra, unbending, uncommon, uncompromising, unconventional, unreasonable, unusual, utmost, utter, uttermost, worst, zealous.

extricate *v.* clear, deliver, disembroil, disengage, disentangle, free, liberate, release, relieve, remove, rescue, withdraw.

eye *n.* appreciation, belief, discernment, discrimination, eyeball, judgment, mind, opinion, optic, orb, peeper, perception, recognition, taste, viewpoint. *v.* contemplate, examine, eye up, gaze at, glance at, inspect, leer at, look at, make eyes at, observe, ogle, peruse, regard, scan, scrutinize, stare at, study, survey, view, watch.

F

fable *n.* allegory, apologue, fabrication, fairy story, falsehood, fantasy, fib, fiction, figment, invention, legend, lie, myth, narrative, old wives' tale, parable, romance, saga, story, tale, tall story, untruth, yarn.

fabric *n.* cloth, constitution, construction, foundations, framework, infrastructure, make-up, material, organization, structure, stuff, textile, texture, web.

fabricate *v.* assemble, build, coin, concoct, construct, create, devise, erect, fake, falsify, fashion, feign, forge, form, frame, invent, make, manufacture, shape, trump up.

façade *n.* appearance, cloak, cover, disguise, exterior, face, front, frontage, guise, mask, pretense, semblance, show, veil, veneer.

face *n.* air, appearance, aspect, assurance, boldness, cheek, confidence, countenance, disguise, display, effrontery, exterior, facade, facet, features, front, grimace, image, impudence, kisser, look, mask, reputation, scowl, self-respect, semblance, side, smirk, surface, visage. *v.* clad, coat, confront, cover, deal with, encounter, experience, finish, front, give in to, meet, oppose, overlook, surface, tackle, veneer.

fact *n.* act, actuality, certainty, circumstance, datum, deed, detail, event, fait accompli, feature, gospel, happening, incident, item, occurrence, particular, point, reality, specific, truth.

factual *adj.* accurate, authentic, circumstantial, close, correct, credible, detailed, exact, faithful, genuine, literal, objective, precise, real, straight, sure, true, unadorned, unbiased, veritable.

fad *n.* affectation, craze, crotchet, fancy, fashion, mania, mode, rage, trend, vogue, whim.

fail *v.* abandon, cease, come to grief, conk out, crack up, crash, cut out, decline, desert, die, disappoint, droop, dwindle, fade, fall, flop, flub, flunk, fold, forget, forsake, founder, fudge, give out, give up, go bankrupt, go bust, go to the wall, go under, gutter, languish, lay an egg, let down, miscarry, misfire, miss, miss one's trip, neglect, omit, peter out, plow, sink, smash, underachieve, underperform, wane, weaken.

fair *adj.* adequate, all right, average, beauteous, beautiful, bonny, bright, clean, clement, cloudless, comely, decent, disinterested, dispassionate, dry, equal, equitable, evenhanded, favorable, fine, handsome, honest, honorable, impartial, just, lawful, legitimate, lovely, mediocre, middling, moderate, not bad, objective, OK, on the level, passable, pretty, proper, reasonable, respectable, satisfactory, so-so, square, sunny, sunshiny, tolerable, trustworthy, unbiased, unclouded, unprejudiced, upright, well-favored.

fair² *adj.* blond(e), fair-haired, fair-headed, flaxen, light, tow-headed.

fake *v.* affect, assume, copy, counterfeit, fabricate, feign, forge, phony, pretend, put on, sham, simulate. *n.* charlatan, copy, forgery, fraud, hoax, imitation, imposter, mountebank, phony, reproduction, sham, simulation. *adj.* affected, artificial, assumed, bastard, bogus, counterfeit, ersatz, false, forged, hyped up, imitation, mock, phony, pretended, pseudo, reproduction, sham, simulated, spurious.

fall *v.* abate, backslide, become, befall, capitulate, cascade, chance, collapse, come about, come to pass, crash, decline, decrease, depreciate, descend, die, diminish, dive, drop, drop down, dwindle, ebb, err, fall away, fall off, fall out, flag, give in, give up, give way, go astray, go down, happen, incline, keep over, lapse, lessen, measure one's length, meet one's end, perish, pitch, plummet, plunge, push, resign, settle, sin, sink, slope, slump, stumble, subside, succumb, surrender, take place, topple, transgress, trespass, trip, trip over, tumble, yield, yield to temptation.

false *adj.* artificial, bogus, concocted, counterfeit, deceitful, deceptive, dishonest, dishonorable, disloyal, duplicitous, erroneous, ersatz, fake, fallacious, faulty, feigned, fictitious, forged, fraudulent, hypocritical, imitation, improper, inaccurate, incorrect, inexact, lying, mendacious, misleading, mistaken, mock, perfidious, pseudo, sham, spurious, synthetic, treacherous, treasonable, trumped-up, two-faced, unfaithful, unfounded, unreal, unreliable, unsound, untrue, untrustworthy, untruthful, wrong.

fame *n.* celebrity, credit, eminence, esteem, glory, honor, illustriousness, kudos, name, prominence, renown, reputation, repute, stardom.

family *n.* ancestors, ancestry, birth, blood, brood, children, clan, class, classification, descendants, descent, dynasty, extraction, folk, forebears, forefathers, genealogy, genre, group, house, household, issue, kin, kind, kinsmen, kith and kin, line, lineage, network, offspring, parentage, pedigree, people, progeny, race, relations, relatives, sept, stirps, strain, subdivision, system, tribe.

famous *adj.* acclaimed, celebrated, conspicuous, distinguished, eminent, excellent, famed, glorious, great, honored, illustrious, legendary, lionized, notable, noted, prominent, remarkable, renowned, signal, well-known.

fan[1] *v.* aggravate, agitate, air-condition, aircool, arouse, blow, cool, enkindle, excite, impassion, increase, provoke, refresh, rouse, stimulate, stir up, ventilate, whip up, winnow, work up. *n.* air-conditioner, blower, extractor fan, flabellum, propeller, vane, ventilator.

fan[2] *n.* adherent, admirer, aficionado, buff, devotee, enthusiast, fiend, follower, freak, groupie, lover, rooter, supporter, zealot.

far *adv.* a good way, a long way, afar, considerably, decidedly, deep, extremely, greatly, incomparably, miles, much.

fare[1] *n.* charge, cost, fee, passage, passenger, pick-up, price, traveler.

fare[2] *n.* board, commons, diet, eatables, food, meals, menu, provisions, rations, sustenance, table, victuals.

fare[3] *v.* be, do, get along, get on, go, go on, happen, make out, manage, proceed, prosper, turn out.

fashion *n.* appearance, attitude, craze, custom, cut, demeanor, description, fad, figure, form, guise, haute couture, jet set, latest, line, look, make, manner, method, mode, model, mold, pattern, rage, shape, sort, style, trend, type, usage, vogue, way.

fast[1] *adj.* accelerated, brisk, fleet, flying, hasty, hurried, mercurial, nippy, quick, rapid, spanking, speedy, swift, winged.

fast[2] *adj.* close, constant, fastened, firm, fixed, fortified, immovable, impregnable, lasting, loyal, permanent, secure, sound, staunch, steadfast, tight, unflinching, unwavering.

fast[3] *adj.* dissipated, dissolute, extravagant, immoral, intemperate, licentious, loose, profligate, promiscuous, rakish, reckless, self-indulgent, wanton, whorish, wild.

fast[4] *v.* abstain, diet, go hungry, starve. *n.* abstinence, diet, fasting, starvation, xerophagy.

fat *adj.* abdominous, beefy, corpulent, fatty, fertile, fleshy, flourishing, greasy, gross, heavy, lucrative, obese, overweight, paunchy, plump, portly, pot-bellied, profitable, prosperous, pudgy, rotund, round, solid, stout, thriving, tubby.

fatal *adj.* baleful, baneful, calamitous, catastrophic, deadly, destructive, disastrous, final, incurable, killing, lethal, malignant, mortal, pernicious, ruinous, terminal, vital.

father *n.* ancestor, architect, author, begetter, confessor, creator, dad, daddy, elder, forebear, forefather, founder, genitor, governor, inventor, leader, maker, old boy, old man, originator, pa, padre, papa, pappy, parent, pastor, pater, paterfamilias, patriarch, patron, pop, poppa, pops, predecessor, priest, prime mover, procreator, progenitor, senator, sire. *v.* beget, conceive, create, dream up, engender, establish, found, get, institute, invent, originate, procreate, produce, sire.

favor *n.* acceptance, approbation, approval, backing, badge, benefit, bias, boon, championship, courtesy, decoration, esteem, favoritism, friendliness, gift, good turn, goodwill, grace, indulgence, keepsake, kindness, knot, love-token, memento, obligement, partiality, patronage, present, regard, rosette, service, smile, souvenir, support, token.

favorite *adj.* best-loved, choice, dearest, esteemed, favored, pet, preferred.

fear *n.* agitation, alarm, anxiety, apprehension, apprehensiveness, awe, bogey, bugbear, concern, consternation, cravenness, danger, dismay, disquietude, distress, doubt, dread, foreboding(s), fright, funk, heartquake, horror, likelihood, misgiving(s), nightmare, panic, phobia, phobism, qualms, reverence, risk, solicitude, specter, suspicion, terror, timidity, tremors, trepidation, unease, uneasiness, veneration, wonder, worry.

feast *n.* banquet, barbecue, beanfeast, beano, binge, blow-out, carousal, carouse, celebration, delight, dinner, enjoyment, entertainment, festival, fête, gala day, gaudy, gratification, holiday, holy day, pleasure, repast, revels, saint's day, spread, treat. *v.* delight, eat one's fill, entertain, gladden, gorge, gormandize, gratify, indulge, overindulge, regale, rejoice, stuff, stuff one's face, thrill, treat, wine and dine.

feature *n.* article, aspect, attraction, attribute, character, characteristic, column, comment, draw, facet, factor, hallmark, highlight, innovation, item, lineament, mark, peculiarity, piece, point, property, quality, report, special, specialty, story, trait. *v.* accentuate, emphasize, headline, highlight, play up, present, promote, push, recommend, show, spotlight, star.

feed *v.* augment, bolster, cater for, dine, eat, encourage, fare, foster, fuel, graze, grub, nourish, nurture, pasture, provide for, provision, strengthen, subsist, supply, sustain, victual. *n.* banquet, feast, fodder, food, forage, meal, nosh, pasturage, pasture, provender, repast, silage, spread, tuck-in, victuals.

feel *v.* appear, believe, caress, consider, deem, empathize, endure, enjoy, experience, explore, finger, fondle, fumble, go through, grope, handle, have, have a hunch, hold, intuit, judge, know, manipulate, maul, notice, observe, paw, perceive, reckon, resemble, seem, sense, sound, stroke, suffer, take to heart, test, think, touch, try, undergo.

feeling *n.* affection, air, ambience, appreciation, apprehension, ardor, atmosphere, aura, compassion, concern, consciousness, emotion, empathy, feel, fervor, fondness, heat, hunch, idea, impression, inclination, inkling, instinct, intensity, mood, notion, opinion, passion, perception, pity, point of view, presentiment, quality, sensation, sense, sensibility, sensitivity, sentiment, sentimentality, suspicion, sympathy, touch, understanding, vibes, vibrations, view, warmth.

fertile *adj.* abundant, fat, fecund, flowering, fruit-bearing, fruitful, generative, lush, luxuriant, plenteous, plentiful, potent, productive, prolific, rich, teeming, uberous, virile, yielding.

festive *adj.* carnival, celebratory, cheery, convivial, cordial, gala, gay, gleeful, happy, hearty, holiday, jolly, jovial, joyful, joyous, jubilant, merry, mirthful, rollicking, sportive, uproarious.

feud *n.* animosity, antagonism, argument, bad blood, bickering, bitterness, conflict, contention, disagreement, discord, dispute, dissension, enmity, estrangement, faction, feuding, grudge, hostility, ill will, quarrel, rivalry, row, strife, vendetta.

fight *v.* altercate, argue, assault, battle, bear arms against, brawl, clash, close, combat, conduct, conflict, contend, contest, dispute, do battle, engage, exchange blows, fence, feud, grapple, joust, lock horns, oppose, prosecute, quarrel, resist, scrap, scuffle, skirmish, spar, squabble, struggle, take the field, tilt, wage war, war, withstand, wrangle, wrestle. *n.* action, affray, altercation, argument, battle, belligerence, bout, brawl, brush, clash, combat, conflict, contest, courage, dispute, dissension, duel, encounter, engagement, free-for-all, hostilities, joust, quarrel, resistance, riot, row, rumble, scrap, scuffle, struggle, tenacity, tussle, war.

file[1] *v.* abrade, burnish, furbish, grate, hone, pare, plane, polish, rasp, refine, rub (down), sand, scour, scrape, shape, shave, smooth, trim, whet.

file[2] *n.* column, line, list, procession, queue, row, stream, string, trail, train. *v.* march, parade, stream, trail, troop.

fill *v.* assign, charge, clog, crowd, engage, glut, gorge, inflate, load, permeate, pervade, sate, satiate, satisfy, saturate, seal, soak, stuff, suffuse, supply, surfeit, swell, take up.

fine[1] *adj.* acceptable, admirable, agreeable, beautiful, clear, delicate, dry, elegant, excellent, exceptional, exquisite, first-class, fragile, honed, lovely, magnificent, pleasant, pure, satisfactory, slender, splendid, suitable, sunny, tasteful, virtuoso.

fine[2] *v.* amerce, mulct, penalize, punish, sting. *n.* amercement, damages, forfeit, forfeiture, mulct, penalty, punishment.

finish *v.* accomplish, achieve, annihilate, cease, complete, conclude, consummate, culminate, defeat, destroy, dispose of, empty, end, finalize, kill, overcome, polish, put an end to, rout, ruin, smooth, stop, terminate, texture, veneer, wind up.

firm[1] *adj.* abiding, braced, cast-iron, cemented, compressed, concentrated, definite, dense, dogged, enduring, fastened, fixed, grounded, hard, immovable, inflexible, motionless, obdurate, reliable, resolute, rigid, robust, secure, settled, solid, stable, steady, substantial, sure, taut, tight, unmoved, unshakable, unwavering, unyielding.

firm[2] *n.* association, business, company, concern, conglomerate, corporation, enterprise, establishment, house, institution, organization, outfit, partnership, set-up, syndicate.

fit[1] *adj.* able, able-bodied, appropriate, apt, becoming, blooming, capable, commensurate, competent, condign, convenient, correct, deserving, due, eligible, equipped, expedient, hale, hale and hearty, healthy, in the pink, prepared, proper, satisfactory, seemly, sound, strapping, sturdy, suitable, trained, trim, well, well-suited, worthy.

fit² *n.* access, attack, bout, burst, caprice, convulsion, eruption, explosion, fancy, humor, mood, outbreak, outburst, paroxysm, seizure, spasm, spell, storm, surge, whim.

fix¹ *v.* adjust, agree on, anchor, bind, cement, conclude, connect, correct, define, determine, direct, establish, fasten, install, limit, maneuver, mend, place, position, prearrange, repair, resolve, seat, secure, settle, stabilize, stick, tidy, tie.

fix² *n.* dose, hit, injection, jag, score, shot, slug.

flame *v.* beam, blaze, burn, flare, flash, glare, glow, radiate, shine. *n.* affection, ardor, beau, blaze, brightness, enthusiasm, fervency, fervor, fire, flake, heartthrob, intensity, keenness, light, lover, passion, radiance, sweetheart, warmth, zeal.

flat¹ *adj.* even, horizontal, lamellar, level, leveled, low, outstretched, planar, prone, prostrate, reclining, recumbent, smooth, spread-eagled, supine, uniform. *n.* lowland, marsh, morass, moss, mud flat, plain, shallow, shoal, strand, swamp.

flat² *adj.* bored, boring, burst, collapsed, dead, deflated, depressed, dull, empty, flavorless, insipid, jejune, lackluster, lifeless, monotonous, pointless, prosaic, punctured, spiritless, stale, tedious, uninteresting, unpalatable, vapid, watery, weak.

flattery *n.* adulation, backscratching, blandishment, blarney, bootlicking, butter, cajolement, cajolery, eulogy, fawning, flannel, fulsomeness, ingratiation, obsequiousness, servility, soap, soft soap, sugar, sweet talk, sycophancy, sycophantism, taffy, toadyism, unctuousness.

flavor *n.* aroma, aspect, character, essence, extract, feel, feeling, flavoring, hint, odor, piquancy, property, quality, relish, savor, savoriness, seasoning, smack, soupçon, stamp, style, suggestion, tang, taste, tastiness, touch, zest, zing. *v.* contaminate, ginger up, imbue, infuse, lace, leaven, season, spice, , taint.

flee *v.* abscond, avoid, beat a hasty retreat, bolt, bunk (off), cut and run, decamp, depart, escape, fly, get away, leave, make off, make oneself scarce, scarper, scram, shun, skedaddle, split, take flight, take it on the lam, take off, take to one's heels, vamoose, vanish, withdraw.

fleet¹ *n.* argosy, armada, flotilla, navy, squadron, task force.

fleet² *adj.* expeditious, fast, flying, light-footed, mercurial, nimble, quick, rapid, speedy, swift, velocipede, winged.

flexible *adj.* accommodating, adaptable, adjustable, agreeable, amenable, bendable, biddable, complaisant, compliant, discretionary, docile, double-jointed, ductile, elastic, gentle, limber, lissome, lithe, loose-limbed, manageable, mobile, open, plastic, pliable, pliant, responsive, springy, stretchy, supple, tensile, tractable, variable, willowy, yielding.

flourish¹ *v.* advance, bloom, blossom, boom, burgeon, develop, do well, flower, get on, grow, increase, mushroom, progress, prosper, succeed, thrive, wax.

flourish² *v.* brandish, display, flaunt, flutter, parade, shake, sweep, swing, swish, twirl, vaunt, wag, wave, wield. *n.* arabesque, brandishing, ceremony, decoration, display, embellishment, fanfare, ornament, ornamentation, parade, show.

flow *v.* arise, bubble, cascade, circulate, course, deluge, derive, emanate, emerge, flood, glide, originate, proceed, rush, spring, spurt, stream, teem, well, whirl.

fluent *adj.* articulate, easy, effortless, eloquent, facile, flowing, fluid, glib, mellifluous, natural, ready, smooth, smooth-talking, voluble, well-versed.

fly *v.* abscond, bolt, clear out, dart, dash, disappear, escape, flee, flutter, get away, hightail it, hurry, light out, pilot, race, retreat, run for it, rush, scamper, soar, speed, sprint, take off, vamoose, wing.

foe *n.* adversary, antagonist, enemy, foeman, ill-wisher, opponent, rival.

fold *v.* bend, clasp, close, collapse, crash, crumple, dog-ear, enclose, enfold, entwine, envelop, gather, hug, intertwine, pleat, ply, wrap, wrap up.

fond *adj.* absurd, adoring, affectionate, amorous, caring, credulous, deluded, devoted, doting, empty, foolish, indiscreet, indulgent, loving, naive, over-optimistic, sanguine, tender, uxorious, vain, warm.

food *n.* aliment, ambrosia, board, bread, cheer, chow, comestibles, commons, cooking, cuisine, diet, eatables, eats, edibles, fare, feed, fodder, foodstuffs, forage, grub, larder, meat, menu, nosh, nourishment, nutriment, nutrition, pabu-lum, pap, provend, provender, provisions, rations, refreshment, scoff, stores, subsistence, sustenance, table, tack, tucker, viands, victuals, vittles.

fool *v.* act up, bamboozle, bluff, deceive, delude, hoax, hoodwink, joke, kid, mislead, pretend, string along, swindle, take in, trifle.

foolish *adj.* absurd, brainless, crazy, daft, half-witted, idiotic, idle-headed, ill-advised, imbecilic, imprudent, incautious, indiscreet, inept, ludicrous, mad, moronic, nonsensical, ridiculous, senseless, simple-minded, stupid, unwise, witless.

forbid *v.* ban, block, contraindicate, debar, deny, disallow, exclude, hinder, inhibit, interdict, outlaw, preclude, prevent, prohibit, proscribe, refuse, rule out, veto.

force *v.* bulldoze, coerce, compel, constrain, drag, drive, exact, extort, impel, impose, lean on, make, necessitate, obligate, oblige, press, pressure, pressurize, prize, propel, push, strong-arm, thrust, urge, wrench, wring.

foreign *adj.* adventitious, alien, borrowed, distant, exotic, external, extraneous, extrinsic, imported, incongruous, irrelevant, outlandish, outside, overseas, remote, strange, uncharacteristic, unfamiliar, unknown, unrelated.

forever *adv.* always, ceaselessly, constantly, continually, endlessly, eternally, everlastingly, evermore, for all time, for good and all, for keeps, in perpetuity, in saecula saeculorum, incessantly, interminably, permanently, perpetually, persistently, till the cows come home, till the end of time, unremittingly

forget *v.* discount, dismiss, disregard, fail, ignore, lose sight of, neglect, omit, overlook, think no more of.

forgive *v.* absolve, acquit, condone, exculpate, excuse, exonerate, let off, overlook, pardon, remit, shrive.

formidable *adj.* alarming, appalling, arduous, awesome, challenging, colossal, dangerous, daunting, difficult, frightening, frightful, great, huge, impressive, intimidating, menacing, onerous, overwhelming, terrifying, threatening.

forte *n.* aptitude, bent, gift, long suit, skill, specialty, strength, strong point, talent.

fortunate *adj.* advantageous, auspicious, blessed, bright, convenient, encouraging, favorable, favored, felicitous, fortuitous, golden, happy, helpful, lucky, opportune, profitable, promising, propitious, prosperous, providential, rosy, serendipitous, successful, timely, well-off, well-timed.

foul *adj.* abhorrent, abominable, contaminated, crooked, despicable, detestable, dirty, disagreeable, disgusting, fetid, filthy, gross, impure, loathsome, low, malodorous, nasty, nauseating, nefarious, offensive, polluted, profane, putrid, rank, repulsive, revolting, rotten, smutty, squalid, stinking, tainted, unsportsmanlike, vile, vulgar, wet, wicked, wild.

fragile *adj.* breakable, brittle, dainty, delicate, feeble, fine, flimsy, frail, frangible, infirm, insubstantial, slight, weak.

fragrant *adj.* aromatic, balmy, odoriferous, odorous, perfumed, redolent, sweet, sweet-scented, sweet-smelling.

frail *adj.* breakable, brittle, decrepit, delicate, feeble, flimsy, fragile, insubstantial, puny, slight, tender, vulnerable, weak.

frank *adj.* artless, blunt, candid, direct, downright, forthright, four-square, free, honest, ingenuous, open, outright, outspoken, plain, plain-spoken, simple-hearted, sincere, straight, straightforward, transparent, truthful, unconcealed, undisguised, unreserved, unrestricted.

fraud[1] *n.* artifice, cheat, chicane, chicanery, craft, deceit, deception, double-dealing, duplicity, fake, forgery, guile, hoax, humbug, imposture, sham, sharp practice, spuriousness, swindling, swiz, swizzle, take-in, treachery, trickery.

fraud[2] *n.* bluffer, charlatan, cheat, counterfeit, double-dealer, hoaxer, impostor, malingerer, mountebank, phony, pretender, pseud, quack, swindler.

frequent[1] *adj.* common, commonplace, constant, continual, customary, everyday, familiar, habitual, incessant, numerous, persistent, recurrent, recurring, regular, reiterated, repeated, usual.

frequent[2] *v.* associate with, attend, crowd, hang about, hang out at, haunt, haunt about, patronize, resort, visit.

fresh *adj.* added, additional, alert, artless, auxiliary, blooming, bold, bouncing, bracing, brazen, bright, brisk, callow, cheeky, chipper, clean, clear, cool, crisp, crude, dewy, different, disrespectful, energetic, extra, fair, familiar, flip, florid, forward, further, glowing, green, hardy, healthy, impudent, inexperienced, innovative, insolent, inventive, latest, lively, modern, modernistic, more, natural, new, novel, original, raw, recent, refreshed, refreshing, re-newed, rested, restored, revived, rosy, spanking, sparkling, spick, sprightly, spry, stiff, supplementary, sweet, unspoiled, untrained, untried, up-to-date, vigorous, vital, vivid, warm, wholesome, young, youthful.

fright *n.* alarm, apprehension, consternation, dismay, dread, fear, horror, mess, monstrosity, panic, quaking, scare, scarecrow, shock, sight, spectacle, sweat, terror, the shivers, trepidation.

fruitful *adj.* abundant, advantageous, beneficial, copious, effective, fecund, feracious, fertile, flush, gainful, plenteous, plentiful, productive, profitable, pro-fuse, prolific, rewarding, rich, spawning, successful, teeming, uberous, useful, well-spent, worthwhile.

fulfill *v.* accomplish, achieve, answer, carry out, complete, conform to, execute, implement, perform, realize, satisfy.

full *adj.* abundant, ample, brimming, complete, comprehensive, copious, detailed, exhaustive, extensive, filled, jammed, loaded, orotund, packed, plentiful, replete, satiated, satisfied, saturated, sufficient, uncut, unedited, unexpurgated.

funny *adj.* a card, a caution, a scream, absurd, amusing, comic, comical, entertaining, farcical, hilarious, humorous, jocular, jolly, peculiar, perplexing, puzzling, queer, riotous, silly, slapstick, strange, suspicious, unusual, weird, witty.

fury *n.* anger, desperation, ferocity, fierceness, force, frenzy, impetuosity, intensity, ire, madness, passion, power, rage, savagery, severity, tempestuousness, turbulence, vehemence, violence, wax, wrath.

future *n.* expectation, futurity, hereafter, out-look, prospects.

G

gab *v.* babble, blabber, chatter, drivel, gossip, jaw, prattle, talk, yak.

gag[1] *v.* choke, choke up, curb, disgorge, gasp, heave, muffle, muzzle, puke, quiet, retch, silence, spew, stifle, still, stop up, suppress, throttle, throw up, vomit.

gag[2] *n.* funny, hoax, jest, joke, one-liner, pun, quip, wisecrack, witticism.

gaiety *n.* animation, blitheness, celebration, cheerfulness, effervescence, elation, exhilaration, festivity, high spirits, hilarity, joyousness, light-heartedness, liveliness, merriment, mirth, revelry, sparkle, sprightliness, vivacity.

gain *v.* achieve, acquire, advance, arrive at, attain, avail, bag, bring in, capture, clear, collect, come to, earn, enlist, gather, get, get to,

glean, harvest, improve, increase, make, net, obtain, pick up, procure, produce, profit, progress, reach, realize, reap, secure, win, win over, yield.

game[1] *n.* adventure, amusement, contest, diversion, entertainment, frolic, fun, lark, merriment, merry-making, pastime, recreation, romp, scheme, sport, strategy, tactic, tournament, trick, undertaking.

game[2] *n.* animals, bag, flesh, game-birds, meat, prey, quarry, spoils.

game[3] *adj.* bold, brave, courageous, dauntless, desirous, disposed, dogged, eager, fearless, gallant, gamy, heroic, inclined, interested, intrepid, persevering, persistent, plucky, prepared, ready, resolute, spirited, spunky, unflinching, valiant, valorous, willing.

game[4] *adj.* bad, crippled, deformed, disabled, gouty, hobbling, incapacitated, injured, lame, maimed.

gang *n.* band, circle, clique, club, company, core, coterie, crew, crowd, group, herd, horde, lot, mob, pack, party, ring, set, shift, squad, team, troupe.

gap *n.* blank, breach, break, chink, cleft, crack, cranny, crevice, diastema, difference, disagreement, discontinuity, disparateness, disparity, divergence, divide, hiatus, hole, inconsistency, interlude, intermission, interruption, interspace, interstice, interval, lacuna, lull, opening, pause, recess, rent, rift, space, vacuity, void.

gather *v.* accumulate, amass, assemble, collect, congregate, convene, deduce, enfold, garner, glean, harvest, hoard, hold, hug, increase, infer, pile up, reap, round up, stockpile, surmise, understand.

generous *adj.* abundant, ample, beneficent, benevolent, big-hearted, bounteous, bountiful, charitable, copious, disinterested, free, full, good, high-minded, lavish, liberal, lofty, magnanimous, munificent, noble, open-handed, over-flowing, plentiful, princely, rich, soft-boiled, soft-hearted, ungrudging, unresentful, unselfish, unsparing, unstinted, unstinting.

give *v.* accord, administer, admit, allow, announce, award, bend, bestow, break, cause, cede, collapse, commit, communicate, concede, confer, consign, contribute, deliver, demonstrate, devote, display, do, emit, engender, entrust, evidence, fall, furnish, grant, hand, hand over, impart, indicate, issue, lead, lend, make, make over, manifest, notify, occasion, offer, pay, perform, permit, present, produce, proffer, pronounce, provide, publish, recede, render, retire, set forth, show, sink, state, supply, surrender, vouchsafe, yield.

glad *adj.* animated, blithe, cheerful, cheering, cheery, delighted, delightful, gleeful, happy, jovial, joyful, joyous, merry, overjoyed, pleasant, pleased.

glance *v.* browse, dip, flip, gaze, glimpse, leaf, look, peek, peep, riffle, scan, skim, thumb, touch on, view. *n.* allusion, coup d'oiel, gander, glimpse, look, mention, once over, peek, peep, reference, squint, view.

glance *v.* bounce, brush, cannon, carom, coruscate, flash, gleam, glimmer, glint, glisten, glitter, graze, rebound, reflect, ricochet, shimmer, shine, skim, twinkle.

gleam *n.* beam, brightness, brilliance, coruscation, flash, flicker, glimmer, glint, gloss, glow, hint, inkling, luster, ray, sheen, shimmer, sparkle, splendor, suggestion, trace. *v.* coruscate, flare, flash, glance, glimmer, glint, glisten, glitter, glow, scintillate, shimmer, shine, sparkle.

glee *n.* cheerfulness, delight, elation, exhilaration, exuberance, exultation, fun, gaiety, gladness, gratification, hilarity, jocularity, jollity, joviality, joy, joyfulness, joyousness, liveliness, merriment, mirth, pleasure, sprightliness, triumph, verve.

glint *v.* flash, gleam, glimmer, glitter, reflect, shine, sparkle, twinkle. *n.* flash, gleem, glimmer, glimmering, glitter, shine, sparkle, twinkle, twinkling.

globe *n.* ball, earth, orb, planet, round, sphere, world.

gloom *n.* blackness, blues, cloud, cloudiness, damp, dark, darkness, dejection, depression, desolation, despair, despondency, dimness, downheartedness, dullness, dusk, gloominess, glumness, low spirits, melancholy, misery, murk murkiness, obscurity, sadness, shade, shadow, sorrow, twilight, unhappiness, woe.

goal *n.* aim, ambition, aspiration, design, destination, destiny, end, grail, intention, limit, mark, object, objective, purpose, target.

good *adj.* able, accomplished, adept, adroit, agreeable, ample, approved, approving, beneficent, beneficial, benevolent, calm, capable, choice, clear, clever, competent, complete, congenial, considerate, decorous, dependable, efficient, enjoyable, ethical, excellent, exemplary, fair, favorable, first-rate, gracious, gratifying, great, helpful, honest, honorable, humane, kind, kindly, large, legitimate, long, loyal, mannerly, merciful, meritorious, mild, moral, nice, noble, nourishing, nutritious, obedient, pleasing, pleasurable, polite, positive, praiseworthy, precious, presentable, professional proficient, profitable, proper, propitious, rattling, real, reliable, right, righteous, safe, salubrious, salutary, satisfactory, satisfying, seemly, serviceable, sizeable, skilful, skilled, solid, sound, special, splendid, substantial, sufficient, suitable, sunny, super, superior, sustaining, talented, tested, thorough, tranquil, true, trustworthy, useful, valid, valuable, virtuous, wholesome, worthwhile, worthy.

govern *v.* administer, allay, bridle, check, command, conduct, contain, control, curb, decide, determine, direct, discipline, guide, influence, inhibit, lead, manage, master, order, oversee, pilot, preside, quell, regulate, reign, restrain, rule, steer, subdue, superintend, supervise, sway, tame, underlie.

gracious *adj.* accommodating, affable, amenable, amiable, beneficent, benevolent, chivalrous, considerate, courteous, hospitable, indulgent, kind, obliging, polite, refined.

grand *adj.* A1, admirable, chief, dignified, elevated, eminent, exalted, excellent, fine, first-class, glorious, grandiose, great, highest, illustrious, imposing, impressive, large, leading, lofty, magnificent, main, monumental, opulent, palatial, regal, splendid, sumptuous, super, superb, supreme, wonderful.

grant *v.* accede to, accord, acknowledge, admit, agree to, allocate, allot, allow, apportion, assign, award, bestow, cede, concede, confer, consent to, convey, deign, dispense, donate, give, impart, permit, present, provide, transfer, transmit, vouchsafe, yield.

grateful *adj.* appreciative, aware, beholden, indebted, mindful, obligated, obliged, sensible, thankful.

gratitude *n.* acknowledgment, appreciation, awareness, gratefulness, indebtedness, mindfulness, obligation, recognition, thankfulness, thanks.

greed *n.* acquisitiveness, anxiety, avidity, covetousness, craving, cupidity, desire, eagerness, edacity, gluttony, gormandizing, gourmandism, gormandize, greediness, hunger, insatiability, insatiableness, itchy palm, land-hunger, longing. plutolatry, rapacity, ravenousness, selfishness, voraciousness, voracity.

grief *n.* ache, affliction, agony, anguish, bereavement, glow, burden, dejection, distress, dole, grievance, heartache, heart-break, misery, mournfulness, pain, regret, remorse, sadness, sorrow, suffering, tragedy, trial, woe.

grim *adj.* adamant, cruel, dour, fierce, forbidding, formidable, gruesome, harsh, horrible, morose, repellent, resolute, ruthless, severe, sinister, stern, sullen, surly, terrible, unpleasant.

gross[1] *adj.* apparent, arrant, bawdy, bestial, big, blatant, blue, boorish, broad, brutish, bulky, callous, coarse, crass, crude, egregious, fat, foul, heavy, heinous, huge, impure, indecent, large, lewd, obscene, offensive, rank, shocking, tasteless, uncouth, vulgar.

gross[2] *adj.* aggregate, all-inclusive, complete, entire, inclusive, total, whole. *v.* accumulate, aggregate, bring, earn, make, rake in, take, total.

grounds[1] *n.* acres, area, country, district, domain, estate, fields, gardens, habitat, holding, land, park, property, realm, surroundings, terrain, territory, tract.

grounds[2] *n.* account, argument, base, basis, call, cause, excuse, factor, foundation, inducement, justification, motive, occasion, premise, pretext, principle, rationale, reason, score, vindication.

grounds[3] *n.* deposit, dregs, grouts, lees, precipitate, sediment, settlings.

grow *v.* advance, arise, augment, become, branch out, breed, broaden, burgeon, cultivate, develop, diversify, enlarge, evolve, expand, extend, farm, flourish, flower, germinate, get, heighten, improve, increase, issue, mature, multiply, nurture, originate, produce, progress, proliferate, propagate, prosper, raise, ripen, rise, shoot, spread, spring, sprout, stem, stretch, succeed, swell, thicken, thrive, turn, vegetate, wax, widen.

guarantee *n.* assurance, attestation, bond, certainty, collateral, covenant, earnest, endorsement, guaranty, insurance, oath, pledge, promise, security, surety, testimonial, undertaking, voucher, warranty, word, word of honor. *v.* answer for, assure, avouch, certify, ensure, insure, maintain, make certain, make sure of, pledge, promise, protect, secure, swear, underwrite, vouch for, warrant.

guard *v.* beware, conserve, cover, defend, escort, keep, look out, mind, oversee, patrol, police, preserve, protect, safeguard, save, screen, secure, sentinel, shelter, shield, supervise, tend, ward, watch. *n.* attention, backstop, barrier, buffer, bulwark, bumper, care, caution, convoy, custodian, defense, defender, escort, guarantee, heed, lookout, minder, pad, patrol, picket, precaution, protection, protector, rampart, safeguard, screen, security, sentinel, sentry, shield, vigilance, wall, warder, wariness, watch, watchfulness, watchman.

guess *v.* assume, believe, conjecture, estimate, fancy, fathom, feel, guesstimate, hazard, hypothesize, imagine, intuit, judge, opine, penetrate, predict, reckon, solve, speculate, suppose, surmise, suspect, think, work out. *n.* assumption, belief, conjecture, fancy, feeling, guesstimate, hypothesis, intuition, judgment, notion, opinion, prediction, reckoning, shot (in the dark), speculation, supposition, surmise, suspicion, theory.

gutter *n.* channel, conduit, ditch, drain, duct, pipe, sluice, trench, trough, tube.

H

habit[1] *n.* accustomedness, addiction, assuetude, bent, constitution, convention, custom, dependence, disposition, fixation, frame of mind, habitude, inclination, makeup, manner, mannerism, mode, mores, nature, obsession, practice, proclivity, propensity, quirk, routine, rule, second nature, tendency, usage, vice, way, weakness, wont.

habit[2] *n.* apparel, attire, clothes, clothing, dress, garb, garment, habiliment.

hack[1] *v.* bark, chop, cough, cut, gash, haggle, hew, kick, lacerate, mangle, mutilate, notch, rasp, slash. *n.* bark, chop, cough, cut, gash, notch, rasp, slash.

hack[2] *adj.* banal, hackneyed, mediocre, pedestrian, poor, stereotyped, tired, undistinguished, uninspired, unoriginal.

hand *n.* ability, agency, aid, applause, art, artistry, assistance, calligraphy, clap, daddle, direction, fist, flipper, handwriting, help, influence, mitt, ovation, palm, part, participation, paw, penmanship, script, share, skill, support. *v.* aid, assist, conduct, convey, deliver, give, guide, help, lead, offer, pass, present, provide, transmit, yield.

harass *v.* annoy, badger, bait, beleaguer, bother, distress, disturb, exasperate, exhaust, fatigue, harry, hassle, hound, perplex, persecute, pester, plague, tease, tire, torment, trash, trouble, vex, wear out, weary, worry.

hard *adj.* acrimonious, actual, arduous, backbreaking, bitter, burdensome, cold, compact, complex, complicated, cruel, definite, disagreeable, disastrous, distressing, exhausting, fa- tiguing, forceful, grievous, grim, hostile, impenetrable, implacable, intolerable, laborious, obdurate, plain, powerful, puzzling, resentful, rigid, severe, solid, stern, stiff, stony, strong, stubborn, tough, undeniable, unjust, unkind, unpleasant, uphill, violent, wearying.

harm *n.* abuse, damage, detriment, disservice, evil, hurt, ill, immorality, impairment, iniquity, injury, loss, mischief, misfortune, scathe, sin, sinfulness, vice, wickedness, wrong.

harmful *adj.* baleful, baneful, damaging, deleterious, destructive, detrimental, disadvantageous, evil, hurtful, injurious, noxious, pernicious, pestiferous, pestilent, scatheful.

harmless *adj.* gentle, innocent, innocuous, innoxious, inoffensive, non-toxic, safe, scatheless, unharmed, uninjured, unobjectionable, unscathed.

hate *v.* abhor, abominate, despise, detest, dislike, execrate, loathe, spite.

head *n.* apex, boss, brain, captain, chief, chieftain, commander, crown, director, forefront, front, intellect, intelligence, leader, manager, master, mastermind, principal, promontory, rise, skull, source, start, summit, top, vanguard, vertex.

heal *v.* alleviate, ameliorate, balsam, compose, conciliate, cure, harmonize, mend, patch up, physic, reconcile, regenerate, remedy, restore, salve, settle, soothe, treat.

healthy *adj.* active, beneficial, blooming, bracing, fine, fit, flourishing, good, hale (and hearty), hardy, healthful, hearty, hygienic, in fine feather, in fine fettle, in fine form, in good condition, in good shape, in the pink, invigorating, nourishing, nutritious, physically fit, robust, salubrious, salutary, sound, strong, sturdy, vigorous, well, wholesome.

hearty *adj.* active, affable, ample, ardent, cordial, eager, earnest, ebullient, effusive, energetic, enthusiastic, exuberant, genial, genuine, hale, hardy, jovial, nourishing, robust, sound, stalwart, strong, substantial, true, vigorous, whole-hearted.

heat *n.* ardor, excitement, fervor, fever, fury, hotness, intensity, passion, sizzle, sultriness, swelter, vehemence, violence, warmness, warmth, zeal.

height *n.* acme, altitude, apex, apogee, ceiling, climax, crest, crown, culmination, degree, dignity, elevation, eminence, exaltation, extremity, grandeur, highness, hill, limit, loftiness, maximum, mountain, ne plus ultra, peak, pinnacle, prominence, stature, summit, tallness, top, ultimate, utmost, uttermost, vertex, zenith.

help *v.* abet, abstain, aid, alleviate, ameliorate, assist, avoid, back, befriend, bestead, control, cooperate, cure, ease, eschew, facilitate, forbear, heal, hinder, improve, keep from, lend a hand, mitigate, prevent, promote, rally round, refrain from, relieve, remedy, resist, restore, save, second, serve, shun, stand by, succor, support, withstand.

helpful *adj.* accommodating, adjuvant, advantageous, beneficent, beneficial, benevolent, caring, considerate, constructive, cooperative, favorable, fortunate, friendly, kind, neighborly, practical, productive, profitable, serviceable, supportive, sympathetic, timely, useful.

helpless *adj.* abandoned, debilitated, defenseless, dependent, destitute, disabled, exposed, feeble, forlorn, friendless, impotent, incapable, incompetent, infirm, paralyzed, powerless, unfit, unprotected, vulnerable, weak.

herd *n.* assemblage, canaille, collection, cowherd, crowd, crush, drove, flock, herd-boy, herdsman, horde, mass, mob, multitude, populace, press, rabble, riff-raff, shepherd, swarm, the hoi polloi, the masses, the plebs, throng, vulgus.

heritage *n.* bequest, birthright, deserts, due, endowment, estate, history, inheritance, legacy, lot, past, patrimony, record, share, tradition.

hide *v.* abscond, bury, cache, camouflage, cloak, conceal, cover, disguise, earth, eclipse, ensconce, go to ground, go underground, hole up, keep dark, lie low, mask, obscure, occult, screen, secret, shadow, shelter, shroud, stash, suppress, take cover, veil, withhold.

hint *v.* allude, imply, indicate, inkle, innuendo, insinuate, intimate, mention, prompt, suggest, tip off.

hire *v.* appoint, book, charter, commission, employ, engage, lease, let, rent, reserve, retain, sign up, take on.

history *n.* account, annals, antecedents, antiquity, auto-biography, biography, chronicle, chronology, days of old, days of yore, genealogy, memoirs, narration, narrative, olden days, recapitulation, recital, record, relation, saga, story, tale, the past.

hobby *n.* avocation, diversion, pastime, pursuit, recreation, relaxation, sideline.

holocaust *n.* annihilation, carnage, conflagration, destruction, devastation, extermination, extinction, flames, genocide, immolation, inferno, mass murder, massacre, pogrom, sacrifice, slaughter.

holy *adj.* blessed, consecrated, dedicated, devout, divine, evangelical, evangelistic, faithful, god-fearing, godly, good, hallowed, perfect, pious, pure, religious, righteous, sacred, sacrosanct, saintly, sanctified, sanctimonious, spiritual, sublime, unctuous, venerable, venerated, virtuous.

honest *adj.* above-board, authentic, bona fide, decent, direct, fair, forthright, genuine, impartial, legitimate, on the level, real, reputable, scrupulous, sincere, straight, true, trustworthy, trusty, truthful, upright, veracious, virtuous.

hope *n.* ambition, anticipation, aspiration, assumption, assurance, belief, confidence, conviction, desire, dream, expectancy, expectation, faith, longing, optimism, promise, prospect, wish.

hospitable *adj.* accessible, amenable, amicable, approachable, bountiful, congenial, convivial, cordial, friendly, gemutlich, generous, genial, gracious, kind, liberal, liv(e)able, receptive, responsive, sociable, tolerant, welcoming.

hostile *adj.* adverse, alien, antagonistic, anti, antipathetic, bellicose, belligerent, contrary, ill-disposed, inhospitable, inim- ical, malevolent, opposed, opposite, rancorous, unfriendly, unkind, unpropitious, unsympathetic, unwelcoming, warlike.

hue *n.* aspect, cast, character, color, complexion, dye, light, nuance, shade, tincture, tinge, tint, tone.

hug *v.* cherish, clasp, cling to, cuddle, embrace, enclose, enfold, follow, grip, hold, lock, nurse, retain, skirt, squeeze. *n.* clasp, clinch, cuddle, embrace, squeeze.

humane *adj.* beneficent, benevolent, benign, charitable, civilizing, clement, compassionate, forbearing, forgiving, gentle, good, good-natured, human, humanizing, kind, kind-hearted, kindly, lenient, loving, magnanimous, merciful, mild, sympathetic, tender, understanding.

humiliate *v.* abase, abash, bring low, chagrin, chasten, confound, crush, debase, deflate, degrade, discomfit, discredit, disgrace, embarrass, humble, mortify, shame, subdue, undignify.

humor *n.* amusement, ban-ter, caprice, comedy, conceit, disposition, farce, fun, funniness, gags, jesting, jocularity, jokes, joking, quirk, temperament, vein, whim, wisecracks, wit, witticisms, wittiness.

hunger *n.* appetence, appetite, craving, desire, emptiness, famine, greediness, hungriness, itch, lust, rapacity, ravenousness, starvation, voracity, yearning, yen.

hurry *v.* accelerate, belt, bustle, dash, dispatch, expedite, fly, get a move on, goad, hasten, hightail it, hump, hustle, jump to it, look lively, move, pike, quicken, rush, scoot, scurry, scuttle, shake a leg, shift, speed up, step on it, step on the gas, urge.

hurt *v.* abuse, ache, afflict, annoy, bruise, burn, damage, disable, distress, grieve, harm, impair, injure, maim, pain, sadden, smart, spoil, sting, throb, tingle, torture, upset, wound.

hypothesis *n.* assumption, conjecture, guess, postulate, premise, premiss, presumption, proposition, starting-point, supposition, theory, thesis.

I

idea *n.* abstraction, belief, clue, concept, design, doctrine, end, essence, estimate, guess, hypothesis, impression, interpretation, judgement, notion, opinion, perception, scheme, suggestion, surmise, suspicion, teaching, theory, thought, viewpoint, vision.

ideal *n.* archetype, epitome, example, image, model, paradigm, paragon, perfection, prototype, standard, type.

identify *v.* catalog, classify, detect, diagnose, distinguish, finger, know, label, make out, name, pick out, pinpoint, place, recognize, single out, specify, spot, tag.

identity *n.* accord, coincidence, correspondence, empathy, existence, individuality, oneness, particularity, personality, rapport, sameness, self, selfhood, singularity, unanimity, uniqueness, unity.

idiom *n.* colloquialism, expression, idiolect, idiotism, jargon, language, locution, parlance, phrase, regionalism, set phrase, style, talk, turn of phrase, usage, vernacular.

idle *adj.* abortive, dormant, frivolous, fruitless, futile, good-for-nothing, inactive, indolent, lackadaisical, lazy, purposeless, shiftless, slothful, unemployed, useless, vain, worthless.

idol *n.* beloved, darling, deity, favorite, fetish, god, graven image, hero, icon, image, joss, ju-ju, mumbo-jumbo, pet, pin-up, superstar.

idolize v. admire, adore, apotheosize, deify, dote on, exalt, glorify, hero-worship, iconize, lionize, love, revere, reverence, venerate, worship.

ignorant adj. clueless, dense, green, gross, half-baked, idealess, ill-informed, illiterate, ill-versed, inexperienced, innocent, innumerate, insensitive, know-nothing, naive, nascent, oblivious, pig-ignorant, stupid, thick, unacquainted, unaware, unconscious, uncultivated, uneducated, unenlightened, uninformed, uninitiated, uninstructed, unknowing, unlearned, unlettered, unread, unscholarly, unschooled, untaught, untrained, untutored, unwitting.

ignore v. blink, cold-shoulder, cut, disregard, neglect, omit, overlook, pass over, pay no attention to, pigeon-hole, reject, set aside, shut one's eyes to, slight, take no notice of, turn a blind eye to, turn a deaf ear to, turn one's back on.

ill adj. ailing, diseased, frail, indisposed, infirm, laid up, out of sorts, queasy, sick, under the weather, unhealthy.

illegal adj. actionable, banned, black-market, contraband, criminal, felonious, forbidden, illicit, outlawed, pirate, prohibited, proscribed, unauthorized, unconstitutional, under-the-counter, unlawful, unlicensed, wrongful, wrongous.

illustrate v. adorn, clarify, decorate, demonstrate, depict, draw, elucidate, emphasize, exemplify, exhibit, explain, illuminate, instance, interpret, ornament, picture, show, sketch.

image n. appearance, conceit, concept, conception, counterpart, dead ringer, Doppelgänger, double, effigies, effigy, eidolon, facsimile, figure, icon, idea, idol, impression, likeness, perception, picture, portrait, reflection, replica, representation, semblance, similitude, simulacrum, spit, spitting image, statue, trope.

imagine v. apprehend, assume, believe, conceive, conceptualize, conjecture, conjure up, create, deduce, deem, devise, dream up, envisage, envision, fancy, fantasize, frame, gather, guess, ideate, infer, invent, judge, picture, plan, project, realize, scheme, suppose, surmise, suspect, take it, think, think of, think up, visualize.

imitate v. affect, ape, burlesque, caricature, clone, copy, copycat, counterfeit, do, duplicate, echo, emulate, follow, follow suit, forge, impersonate, mimic, mirror, mock, monkey, parody, parrot, personate, repeat,

reproduce, send up, simulate, spoof, take off, travesty.

immature adj. adolescent, babyish, callow, childish, crude, green, immatured, imperfect, inexperienced, infantile, jejune, juvenile, premature, puerile, raw, under-age, undeveloped, unfinished, unfledged, unformed, unripe, unseasonable, untimely, young.

immediate adj. actual, adjacent, close, contiguous, current, direct, existing, extant, instant, instantaneous, near, nearest, neighboring, next, on hand, present, pressing, primary, prompt, proximate, recent, unhesitating, up-to-date, urgent.

immense adj. colossal, elephantine, enormous, giant, herculean, huge, jumbo, large, mammoth, massive, titanic, tremendous, vast.

immoral adj. abandoned, bad, corrupt, debauched, degenerate, depraved, dishonest, dissolute, evil, foul, impure, indecent, lecherous, lewd, licentious, nefarious, obscene, pornographic, profligate, reprobate, sinful, unchaste, unethical, unprincipled, unrighteous, unscrupulous, vicious, vile, wanton, wicked, wrong.

immortal adj. abiding, ambrosial, constant, deathless, endless, enduring, eternal, everlasting, imperishable, incorruptible, inde-structible, lasting, perennial, perpetual, timeless, undying, unfading, unforgettable.

impartial adj. detached, disinterested, dispassionate, equal, equitable, even-handed, fair, just, neutral, nondiscriminating, nonpartisan, objective, open-minded, unbiased, uncommitted, unprejudiced.

impasse n. blind alley, cul-de-sac, dead end, deadlock, halt, nonplus, stalemate, stand-off, standstill.

impending adj. approaching, brewing, coming, forthcoming, imminent, looming, menacing, near, threatening.

imperfection n. blemish, blot, blotch, crack, defect, deficiency, dent, failing, fallibility, fault, flaw, foible, frailty, glitch, inadequacy, incompleteness, insufficiency, peccadillo, shortcoming, stain, taint, weakness.

impersonate v. act, ape, caricature, do, imitate, masquerade as, mimic, mock, parody, personate, pose as, take off.

implore v. ask, beg, beseech, crave, entreat, importune, plead, pray, solicit, supplicate, wheedle.

imply v. betoken, connote, denote, entail, evidence, hint, import, indicate, insinuate, intimate, involve, mean, point to, presuppose, require, signify, suggest.

important *adj.* basic, eminent, essential, far-reaching, foremost, grave, heavy, high-level, high-ranking, influential, key, keynote, large, leading, material, meaningful, momentous, notable, noteworthy, on the map, outstanding, powerful, pre-eminent, primary, prominent, relevant, salient, seminal, serious, signal, significant, substantial, urgent, valuable, valued, weighty.

impossible *adj.* absurd, hopeless, impracticable, inadmissible, inconceivable, insoluble, intolerable, ludicrous, outrageous, preposterous, unacceptable, unachievable, unattainable, ungovernable, unobtainable, unreasonable, untenable, unthinkable, unworkable.

impress *v.* affect, emboss, emphasize, engrave, excite, fix, grab, imprint, inculcate, indent, influence, inspire, instill, make one's mark, mark, move, namedrop, print, slay, stamp, stand out, stir, strike, sway, touch, wow.

improve *v.* advance, ameliorate, amend, augment, better, correct, culture, develop, embourgeoise, enhance, gentrify, help, increase, look up, perk up, pick up, polish, progress, rally, recover, rectify, recuperate, reform, rise, touch up, turn over a new leaf, turn the corner, up, upgrade.

impulsive *adj.* hasty, headlong, impetuous, instinctive, intuitive, passionate, precipitant, precipitate, quick, rash, reckless, spontaneous, unconsidered, unpredictable, unpremeditated.

in effect actually, effectively, essentially, for practical purposes, in actuality, in fact, in reality, in the end, in truth, really, to all intents and purposes, virtually, when all is said and done.

in spite of despite, notwithstanding.

inaccurate *adj.* careless, defective, discrepant, erroneous, faulty, imprecise, in error, incorrect, inexact, loose, mistaken, out, unfaithful, unreliable, unrepresentative, unsound, wide of the mark, wild, wrong.

inadequate *adj.* defective, deficient, faulty, imperfect, inapt, incapable, incommensurate, incompetent, incomplete, ineffective, ineffectual, inefficacious, inefficient, insubstantial, insufficient, leaving a little/a lot/much to be desired, meager, niggardly, scanty, short, sketchy, skimpy, sparse, unequal, unfitted, unqualified, wanting.

inaugurate *v.* begin, christen, commence, commission, consecrate, dedicate, enthrone, han(d)sel, induct, initiate, install, instate, institute, introduce, invest, kick off, launch, open, ordain, originate, set up, start, start off, usher in.

incessant *adj.* ceaseless, constant, continual, continuous, endless, eternal, everlasting, interminable, never-ending, nonstop, perpetual, persistent, relentless, unbroken, unceasing, unending, unrelenting, unremitting, weariless.

incident *n.* adventure, affair(e), brush, circumstance, clash, commotion, confrontation, contretemps, disturbance, episode, event, fight, happening, mishap, occasion, occurrence, scene, skirmish.

incinerate *v.* burn, char, cremate, reduce to ashes.

incite *v.* abet, animate, drive, egg on, encourage, excite, foment, goad, impel, inflame, instigate, prompt, provoke, put up to, rouse, set on, solicit, spur, stimulate, stir up, urge, whip up.

inconsiderate *adj.* careless, imprudent, indelicate, insensitive, intolerant, rash, rude, self-centered, selfish, tactless, thoughtless, unconcerned, ungracious, unkind, unthinking.

inconsistent *adj.* at odds, at variance, capricious, changeable, conflicting, contradictory, contrary, discordant, discrepant, erratic, fickle, incoherent, incompatible, incongruous, inconstant, irreconcilable, irregular, unpredictable, unstable, unsteady, variable, varying.

incorrect *adj.* erroneous, false, faulty, flawed, inaccurate, inappropriate, inexact, mistaken, out, specious, untrue, wrong.

increase *v.* add to, advance, amplify, augment, build up, develop, enhance, escalate, expand, extend, heighten, inflate, intensify, magnify, multiply, proliferate, snowball, swell.

incredible *adj.* absurd, amazing, astonishing, astounding, extraordinary, fabulous, far-fetched, great, implausible, impossible, improbable, inconceivable, inspired, marvelous, preposterous, prodigious, superb, superhuman, unbelievable, unimaginable, unthinkable, wonderful.

indefinite *adj.* ambiguous, confused, doubtful, equivocal, evasive, general, ill-defined, imprecise, indeterminate, indistinct, inexact, loose, obscure, uncertain, unclear, undecided, undefined, undetermined, unfixed, unfocus(s)ed, unformed, unformulated, unknown, unlimited, unresolved, unsettled, vague.

independent *adj.* absolute, autarchical, autocephalous, autogenous, autonomous, bold, crossbench, free, individualistic, liberated, nonaligned, one's own man, self-contained, self-determining, self-governing, self-reliant, self-sufficient, self-supporting, separate, separated, sovereign, unaided, unbiased, unconnected, unconstrained, uncontrolled, unconventional, unrelated, upon one's legs.

indignant *adj.* angry, annoyed, disgruntled, exasperated, fuming, furibund, furious, heated, huffy, in a paddy, in a wax, incensed, irate, livid, mad, marked, miffed, peeved, provoked, resentful, riled, scornful, sore, waxy, wrathful, wroth.

indirect *adj.* ancillary, backhanded, circuitous, circumlocutory, collateral, contingent, crooked, devious, incidental, meandering, mediate, oblique, rambling, roundabout, secondary, slanted, subsidiary, tortuous, unintended, wandering, winding, zigzag.

indulge *v.* baby, coddle, give in to, gratify, humor, pamper, pander to, spoil, yield to.

inept *adj.* absurd, awkward, bungling, back-handed, clumsy, fatuous, futile, gauche, improper, inappropriate, inapt, incompetent, inexpert, infelicitous, irrelevant, maladroit, malapropos, meaningless, ridiculous, unfit, unhandy, unskillful, unworkmanlike.

inexperienced *adj.* amateur, callow, fresh, green, immature, inexpert, innocent, nascent, new, raw, unaccustomed, unacquainted, unbearded, unfamiliar, unpractical, unpracticed, unschooled, unseasoned, unskilled, unsophisticated, untrained, untraveled, untried, unused, unversed, verdant.

infect *v.* affect, blight, canker, contaminate, corrupt, defile, enthuse, influence, inject, inspire, pervert, poison, pollute, taint, touch, vitiate.

infer *v.* assume, conclude, conjecture, construe, deduce, derive, extract, extrapolate, gather, presume, surmise, understand.

infinite *adj.* absolute, bottomless, boundless, countless, enormous, eternal, everlasting, fathomless, illimitable, immeasurable, immense, incomputable, inestimable, inexhaustible, interminable, limitless, measureless, never-ending, numberless, perpetual, stupendous, total, unbounded, uncountable, uncounted, unfathomable, untold, vast, wide.

inform[1] *v.* acquaint, advise, apprise, brief, clue up, communicate, enlighten, fill in, illuminate, impart, instruct, intimate, leak, notify, teach, tell, tip off, wise up.

inform[2] *v.* animate, characterize, endue, fill, illuminate, imbue, inspire, invest, irradiate, light up, permeate, suffuse, typify.

information *n.* advises, blurb, briefing, bulletin, clues, communique, data, databank, database, dope, dossier, enlightenment, facts, gen, illumination, info, input, instruction, intelligence, knowledge, low-down, message, news, notice, report, tidings, word.

ingenuous *adj.* artless, candid, childlike, frank, guileless, honest, innocent, open, plain, simple, sincere, trustful, trusting, unreserved, unsophisticated.

ingredient *n.* component, constituent, element, factor, part.

inhabit *v.* abide, bide, dwell, habit, live, lodge, make one's home, occupy, people, populate, possess, reside, settle, settle in, stay, take up one's abode, tenant.

inherent *adj.* basic, characteristic, congenital, connate, essential, fundamental, hereditary, immanent, inborn, inbred, inbuilt, ingrained, inherited, innate, instinctive, intrinsic, native, natural.

inheritance *n.* accession, bequest, birthright, descent, heredity, heritage, legacy, patrimony, succession.

initial *adj.* beginning, early, embryonic, first, formative, inaugural, inauguratory, inceptive, incipient, infant, introductory, opening, original, primary.

injure *v.* abuse, aggrieve, blemish, blight, break, cripple, damage, deface, disable, disfigure, disserve, harm, hurt, ill-treat, impair, maim, maltreat, mar, ruin, scathe, spoil, tarnish, undermine, vandalize, vitiate, weaken, wound, wrong.

injury *n.* abase, annoyance, damage, damnification, detriment, disservice, evil, grievance, harm, hurt, ill, impairment, injustice, insult, lesion, loss, mischief, prejudice, ruin, scathe, trauma, vexation, wound, wrong.

innocent *adj.* artless, benign, blameless, faultless, guileless, guiltless, harmless, honest, immaculate, naive, natural, pure, spotless, stainless, unblemished, virginal, well-intentioned, well-meaning.

inquire *v.* ask, catechize, delve, enquire, examine, explore, inspect, interrogate, investigate, look into, probe, query, quest, question, reconnoiter, scout, scrutinize, search.

insane *adj.* barmy, batty, bizarre, bonkers, brainsick, cracked, crackers, crazed, cuckoo, daft, delirious, demented, deranged, distracted, disturbed, fatuous, foolish, idiotic, impractical, irrational, irresponsible, loony, loopy, lunatic, mad, manic, mental, mentally ill, non compos mentis, nuts, nutty, preposterous, psychotic, queer, schizoid, schizophrenic, screwy, senseless, stupid, touched, unbalanced, unhinged.

insecure *adj.* afraid, anxious, apprehensive, dangerous, defenseless, diffident, exposed, expugnable, flimsy, frail, hazardous, insubstantial, jerry-built, loose, nervous, perilous, precarious, pregnable, rickety, rocky, shaky, uncertain, unconfident, uneasy, unguarded, unprotected, unsafe, unsound, unstable, unsteady, unsure, vulnerable, weak, wobbly, worried.

insight *n.* acumen, acuteness, apprehension, awareness, comprehension, discernment, grasp, ingenuity, intelligence, intuition, intuitiveness, judgment, knowledge, observation, penetration, perception, percipience, perspicacity, sensitivity, shrewdness, understanding, vision, wisdom.

insincere *adj.* artificial, canting, deceitful, deceptive, devious, dishonest, disingenuous, dissembling, dissimulating, double-dealing, duplicitous, evasive, faithless, false, hollow, hypocritical, lip-deep, lying, mendacious, perfidious, phony, pretended, synthetic, two-faced, unfaithful, ungenuine, untrue, untruthful.

insinuate *v.* allude, get at, hint, imply, indicate, innuendo, intimate, suggest.

insist *v.* assert, asseverate, aver, claim, contend, demand, dwell on, emphasize, harp on, hold, maintain, persist, reiterate, repeat, request, require, stand firm, stress, swear, urge, vow.

inspect *v.* audit, check, examine, give the once-over, investigate, look over, oversee, peruse, reconnoiter, scan, scrutinize, search, study, superintend, supervise, survey, vet, visit.

instal(l) *v.* consecrate, ensconce, establish, fix, inaugurate, induct, instate, institute, introduce, invest, lay, locate, lodge, ordain, place, plant, position, put, set, set up, settle, site, situate, station.

instance *n.* advice, application, behest, demand, entreaty, exhortation, importunity, impulse, incitement, initiative, insistence,

instigation, pressure, prompting, request, solicitation, urging.

instant *n.* flash, jiffy, juncture, minute, mo, moment, occasion, point, second, shake, split second, tick, time, trice, twinkling, two shakes. *adj.* convenience, direct, fast, immediate, instantaneous, on-the-spot, prompt, quick, rapid, ready-mixed, split-second, unhesitating, urgent.

instinct *n.* ability, aptitude, faculty, feel, feeling, flair, gift, gut feeling, gut reaction, id, impulse, intuition, knack, nose, predisposition, proclivity, sixth sense, talent, tendency, urge.

institute[1] *v.* appoint, begin, commence, constitute, create, enact, establish, fix, found, inaugurate, induct, initiate, install, introduce, launch, open, ordain, organize, originate, pioneer, set up, settle, start.

institute[2] *n.* custom, decree, doctrine, dogma, edict, law, maxim, precedent, precept, principle, regulation, rescript, rule, tenet, ukase.

institute[3] *n.* academy, association, college, conservatory, foundation, guild, institution, organization, poly, polytechnic, school, seminary, society.

instruct *v.* acquaint, advise, apprise, bid, brief, catechize, charge, coach, command, counsel, direct, discipline, drill, educate, enjoin, enlighten, ground, guide, inform, mandate, notify, order, school, teach, tell, train, tutor.

insult *v.* abuse, affront, call names, fling/throw mud at, give offense to, injure, libel, miscall, offend, outrage, revile, slag, slander, slight, snub, vilify, vilipend.

insure *v.* assure, cover, guarantee, indemnify, protect, underwrite, warrant.

intelligent *adj.* acute, alert, apt, brainy, bright, clever, deep-browed, discerning, enlightened, instructed, knowing, penetrating, perspicacious, quick, quick-witted, rational, razor-sharp, sharp, smart, thinking, well-informed.

intend *v.* aim, consign, contemplate, design, destine, determine, earmark, have a mind, mark out, mean, meditate, plan, project, propose, purpose, scheme, set apart.

intent *adj.* absorbed, alert, attentive, bent, committed, concentrated, concentrating, determined, eager, earnest, engrossed, fixed, hell-bent, industrious, intense, mindful, occupied, piercing, preoccupied, rapt, resolute, resolved, set, steadfast, steady, watchful, wrapped up.

intercourse[1] *n.* association, commerce, communication, communion, congress, connection, contact, conversation, converse, correspondence, dealings, intercommunication, traffic, truck.

intercourse[2] *n.* carnal knowledge, coition, coitus, copulation, embraces, intimacy, love-making, sex, sexual relations, venery.

interest *n.* activity, advantage, affair, affection, attention, attentiveness, attraction, authority, bag, benefit, business, care, claim, commitment, concern, consequence, curiosity, diversion, finger, gain, good, hobby, importance, influence, investment, involvement, line of country, matter, moment, note, notice, participation, pastime, portion, preoccupation, profit, pursuit, regard, relaxation, relevance, right, share, significance, stake, study, suspicion, sympathy, weight.

interfere *v.* block, butt in, clash, collide, conflict, hamper, handicap, hinder, impede, intervene, intrude, meddle, obstruct, tamper.

intimate[1] *v.* allude, announce, communicate, declare, hint, impart, imply, indicate, insinuate, state, suggest, tell.

intimate[2] *adj.* as thick as thieves, bosom, cherished, close, confidential, cozy, dear, deep, deep-seated, detailed, exhaustive, friendly, gremial, informal, innermost, internal, near, penetrating, personal, private, privy, profound, secret, warm.

intrigue[1] *v.* attract, charm, fascinate, interest, puzzle, rivet, tantalize, tickle one's fancy, titillate.

intrigue[2] *n.* affair, amour, cabal, chicanery, collusion, conspiracy, double-dealing, intimacy, knavery, liaison, machination, machination(s), maneuver, manipulation, plot, romance, ruse, scheme, sharp practice, stratagem, string-pulling, trickery, wheeler-dealing, wile, wire-pulling. *v.* connive, conspire, machinate, maneuver, plot, scheme.

introduce *v.* acquaint, add, advance, air, announce, begin, bring in, bring up, broach, commence, conduct, establish, familiarize, found, inaugurate, initiate, inject, insert, institute, interpolate, interpose, launch, lead in, lead into, moot, offer, open, organize, pioneer, preface, present, propose, put forward, put in, recommend, set forth, start, submit, suggest, throw in, ventilate.

intrude *v.* aggress, butt in, encroach, infringe, interfere, interrupt, meddle, obtrude, trespass, violate.

invade *v.* assail, assault, attack, burst in, come upon, descend upon, encroach, enter, fall upon, infest, infringe, irrupt, occupy, overrun, overspread, penetrate, pervade, raid, rush into, seize, swarm over, violate

invalid[1] *adj.* ailing, bedridden, disabled, feeble, frail, ill, infirm, invalidish, poorly, sick, sickly, valetudinarian, valetudinary, weak.

invalid[2] *adj.* baseless, fallacious, false, ill-founded, illogical, incorrect, inoperative, irrational, nugatory, null, null and void, unfounded, unscientific, unsound, untrue, void, worthless.

invent *v.* coin, conceive, concoct, contrive, cook up, create, design, devise, discover, dream up, fabricate, formulate, frame, imagine, improvise, make up, originate, think up, trump up.

inventory *n.* account, catalog, equipment, file, list, listing, record, register, roll, roster, schedule, stock.

investigate *v.* consider, enquire into, examine, explore, go into, inspect, look into, probe, scrutinize, search, see how the land lies, sift, study.

invisible *adj.* concealed, disguised, hidden, imperceptible, inappreciable, inconspicuous, indiscernible, infinitesimal, microscopic, out of sight, unperceivable, unseeable, unseen.

invite *v.* allure, ask, ask for, attract, beckon, beg, bid, bring on, call, court, draw, encourage, entice, lead, provoke, request, seek, solicit, summon, tempt, welcome.

involve *v.* absorb, affect, associate, bind, commit, comprehend, comprise, compromise, concern, connect, contain, cover, draw in, engage, engross, entail, grip, hold, implicate, imply, include, incorporate, incriminate, mean, mix up, necessitate, number among, preoccupy, presuppose, require, rivet, take in, touch.

irate *adj.* angered, angry, annoyed, enraged, exasperated, fuming, furibund, furious, gusty, in a paddy, incensed, indignant, infuriated, ireful, irritated, livid, mad, piqued, provoked, riled, up in arms, waxy, worked up, wrathful, wroth.

ire *n.* anger, annoyance, choler, displeasure, exasperation, fury, indignation, passion, rage, wax, wrath.

irk *v.* aggravate, annoy, bug, disgust, distress, gall, get, get to, irritate, miff, nettle, peeve, provoke, put out, rile, rub up the wrong way, ruffle, vex, weary.

irrational *adj.* aberrant, absurd, alogical, brainless, crazy, demented, foolish, illogical, injudicious, insane, mindless, muddle-headed, nonsensical, preposterous, raving, senseless, silly, unreasonable, unreasoning, unsound, unstable, unthinking, unwise, wild.

irregular *adj.* abnormal, anomalistic(al), anomalous, asymmetrical, broken, bumpy, capricious, craggy, crooked, disconnected, disorderly, eccentric, erratic, exceptional, extraordinary, extravagant, fitful, fluctuating, fragmentary, haphazard, holey, immoderate, improper, inappropriate, inordinate, intermittent, jagged, lopsided, lumpy, occasional, odd, patchy, peculiar, pitted, queer, quirky, ragged, random, rough, serrated, shifting, spasmodic, sporadic, uncertain, unconventional, unequal, uneven, unofficial, unorthodox, unprocedural, unpunctual, unsteady, unsuitable, unsymmetrical, unsystematic, unusual, variable, wavering.

irrelevant *adj.* alien, extraneous, foreign, immaterial, impertinent, inapplicable, inapposite, inappropriate, inapt, inconsequent, peripheral, tangential, unapt, unconnected, unnecessary, unrelated.

irresponsible *adj.* carefree, careless, feather-brained, feckless, flighty, footloose, giddy, hare-brained, harum-scarum, heedless, ill-considered, immature, lighthearted, madcap, negligent, rash, reckless, scatterbrained, shiftless, thoughtless, undependable, unreliable, untrustworthy, wild.

irritate *v.* acerbate, aggravate, anger, annoy, bedevil, bother, bug, chafe, embroil, enrage, exacerbate, exasperate, faze, fret, get on one's nerves, get to, give the pip, gravel, harass, incense, inflame, infuriate, intensify, irk, needle, nettle, offend, pain, peeve, pester, pique, provoke, put out, rankle, rile, rouse, rub, ruffle, vex.

isolate *v.* abstract, cut off, detach, disconnect, divorce, exclude, identify, insulate, keep apart, ostracize, pinpoint, quarantine, remove, seclude, segregate, separate, sequester, set apart.

issue¹ *n.* affair, argument, concern, controversy, crux, debate, matter, point, problem, question, subject, topic.

issue² *n.* announcement, broadcast, circulation, copy, delivery, dispersal, dissemination, distribution, edition, emanation, flow, granting, handout, impression, installment, issuance, issuing, number, printing, promulgation, propagation, publication, release, supply, supplying, vent. *v.* announce, broadcast, circulate, deal out, deliver, distribute,

emit, give out, mint, produce, promulgate, publicize, publish, put out, release, supply.

issue³ *n.* conclusion, consequence, culmination, denouement, effect, end, finale, outcome, pay-off, product, result, termination, upshot. *v.* arise, burst forth, debouch, emanate, emerge, flow, leak, originate, proceed, rise, spring, stem.

issue⁴ *n.* brood, children, descendants, heirs, offspring, progeny, scions, seed, young.

itemize *v.* count, detail, document, enumerate, instance, inventory, list, mention, number, overname, particularize, record, specify, tabulate.

itinerant *adj.* ambulatory, drifting, journeying, migratory, nomadic, peripatetic, rambling, roaming, rootless, roving, traveling, vagabond, vagrant, wandering, wayfaring.

itinerary *n.* circuit, course, journey, line, plan, program, route, schedule, tour.

J

jab *v.* dig, elbow, jag, lunge, nudge, poke, prod, punch, push, shove, stab, tap, thrust.

jacket *n.* case, casing, coat, cover covering, envelope, folder, jerkin, mackinaw, sheath, shell, skin, wrap, wrapper, wrapping.

jackpot *n.* award, big time, bonanza, kitty, pool, pot, prize, reward, stakes, winnings.

jail *n.* borstal, bridewell, brig, calaboose, can, cells, clink, cooler, coop, custody, guardhouse, hoos(e)gow, house of correction, inside, jailhouse, jankers, jug, lock-up, nick, pen, penitentiary, pokey, prison, quod, reformatory, slammer, stir, tollbooth. *v.* confine, detail, immure, impound, imprison, incarcerate, intern, lock up, quod, send down.

janitor *n.* caretaker, concierge, custodian, door-keeper, doorman, janitress, porter.

jar *v.* agitate, annoy, clash, convulse, disagree, discompose, disturb, grate, grind, interfere, irk, irritate, jangle, jolt, nettle, offend, quarrel, rasp, rattle, rock, shake, upset, vibrate. *n.* clash, disagreement, discord, dissonance, grating, irritation, jangle, jolt, quarrel, rasping, wrangling.

jealous *adj.* anxious, apprehensive, attentive, careful, covetous, desirous, emulous, envious, green, green-eyed, grudging, guarded, heedful, invidious, mistrustful, possessive, proprietorial, protective, resentful, rival, solicitous, suspicious, vigilant, wary, watchful, zealous.

jerk[1] *n.* bounce, jog, jolt, lurch, pluck, pull, shrug, throw, thrust, tug, tweak, twitch, wrench, yank. *v.* bounce, flirt, jigger, job, jolt, jounce, lurch, peck, pluck, pull, shrug, throw, thrust, tug, tweak, twitch, wrench, yank.

jerk[2] *n.* bum, clod, clown, creep, dimwit, dolt, dope, fool, halfwit, idiot, klutz, ninny, prick, schlep, schmo, schmuck, twit.

job *n.* activity, affair, assignment, calling, career, craft, duty, employment, enterprise, livelihood, lot, message, occupation, position, post, profession, pursuit, role, share, trade, undertaking, venture, vocation, work.

jog *v.* activate, arouse, bounce, jar, jerk, joggle, jolt, jostle, jounce, nudge, poke, prod, prompt, push, remind, rock, shake, shove, stimulate, stir. *n.* jerk, jiggle, jolt, nudge, poke, prod, push, reminder, shake, shove.

jog[2] *v., n.* bump, canter, dogtrot, jogtrot, lope, lumber, pad, run, trot.

join *v.* abut, accompany, accrete, add, adhere, adjoin, affiliate, amalgamate, annex, append, associate, attach, border, border on, butt, cement, coincide, combine, conglutinate, conjoin, conjugate, connect, couple, dock, enlist, enrol, enter, fasten, knit, link, march with, marry, meet, merge, reach, sign up, splice, team, tie, touch, unite, verge on, yoke.

joke *n.* buffoon, butt, clown, conceit, frolic, fun, funny, gag, guy, hoot, jape, jest, lark, laughing-stock, play, pun, quip, quirk, sally, simpleton, sport, target, whimsy, wisecrack, witticism, yarn, yell. *v.* banter, chaff, clown, deride, fool, frolic, gambol, jest, kid, laugh, mock, quip, ridicule, spoof, taunt, tease, wisecrack.

journey *n.* career, course, excursion, expedition, eyre, itinerary, jaunt, odyssey, outing, passage, peregrination, pilgrimage, progress, ramble, route, tour, travel, trek, trip, voyage, wanderings.

joy *n.* blessedness, bliss, charm, delight, ecstacy, elation, exaltation, exultation, felicity, festivity, gaiety, gem, gladness, gladsomeness, glee, gratification, happiness, hilarity, jewel, joyance, joyfulness, joyousness, pleasure, pride, prize, rapture, ravishment, satisfaction, transport, treasure, treat, triumph, wonder.

judge *n.* adjudicator, alcalde, arbiter, arbiter, arbitrator, assessor, authority, beak, connoisseur, critic, Daniel, deemster, doomster, elegantiarum, evaluator, expert, hakim, justice, justiciar, justiciary, Law Lord, magistrate, mediator, moderator, pundit, referee, umpire, virtuoso, wig. *v.* adjudge, adjudicate, appraise, appreciate, arbitrate, ascertain, assess, conclude, condemn, consider, criticize, decide, decree, determine, dijudicate, discern, distinguish, doom, esteem, estimate, evaluate, examine, find, gauge, mediate, opine, rate, reckon, referee, review, rule, sentence, sit, try, umpire, value.

judgment *n.* acumen, appraisal, arbitration, assessment, assize, award, belief, common sense, conclusion, conviction, damnation, decision, decree, decreet, deduction, determination, diagnosis, discernment, discretion, discrimination, doom, enlightenment, estimate, expertise, fate, finding, intelligence, mediation, misfortune, opinion, order, penetration, perceptiveness, percipience, perspicacity, prudence, punishment, result, retribution, ruling, sagacity, sense, sentence, shrewdness, taste, understanding, valuation, verdict, view, virtuosity, wisdom.

jump[1] *v.* bounce, bound, caper, clear, dance, frisk, frolic, gambol, hop, hurdle, jig, leap, pounce, prance, skip, spring, vault. *n.* bounce, bound, capriole, curvet, dance, frisk, frolic, ho, leap, pounce, prance, saltation, skip, spring, vault.

jump[2] *v.* avoid, bypass, digress, disregard, evade, ignore, leave out, miss, omit, overshoot, pass over, skip, switch. *n.* breach, break, gap, hiatus, interruption, interval, lacuna, lapse, omission, saltation, switch.

jump[3] *v.* advance, appreciate, ascend, boost, escalate, gain, hike, increase, mount, rise, spiral, surge. *n.* advance, ascent, augmentation, boost, escalation, increase, increment, mounting, rise, upsurge, upturn.

jump[4] *v.* flinch, jerk, jump out of one's skin, leap in the air, quail, recoil, resile, shrink, start, wince. *n.* jar, jerk, jolt, lurch, quiver, shiver, shock, spasm, start, swerve, twitch, wrench.

jump[5] *n.* barricade, barrier, fence, gate, hedge, hurdle, impediment, obstacle, pons asinorum, rail.

jumpy *adj.* agitated, anxious, apprehensive, discomposed, edgy, fidgety, jittery, nervous, nervy, restive, restless, shaky, tense, tremulous, uneasy.

just *adj.* accurate, apposite, appropriate, apt, blameless, condign, conscientious, correct, decent, deserved, disinterested, due, equitable, even-handed, exact, fair, fairminded, faithful, fitting, four-square, good, honest, honorable, impartial, impeccable, irreproachable, justified, lawful, legitimate, merited, normal, precise, proper, pure, reasonable, regular, right, righteous, rightful, sound, suitable, true, unbiased, unimpeachable, unprejudiced, upright, virtuous, well-deserved.

justice *n.* amends, appositeness, appropriateness, compensation, correction, dharma, equitableness, equity, fairness, honesty, impartiality, integrity, justifiableness, justness, law, legality, legitimacy, nemesis, penalty, propriety, reasonableness, recompense, rectitude, redress, reparation, requital, right, rightfulness, rightness, satisfaction.

justify *v.* absolve, acquit, condone, confirm, defend, establish, exculpate, excuse, exonerate, explain, forgive, legalize, legitimize, maintain, pardon, substantiate, support, sustain, uphold, validate, vindicate, warrant.

juvenile *n.* adolescent, boy, child, girl, halfling, infant, kid, minor, young person, youngster, youth.

K

keen *adj.* acid, acute, anxious, ardent, assiduous, astute, avid, biting, brilliant, canny, caustic, clever, cutting, devoted, diligent, discerning, discriminating, eager, earnest, ebullient, edged, enthusiastic, fervid, fierce, fond, forthright, impassioned, incisive, industrious, intense, intent, mordant, penetrating, perceptive, perfervid, perspicacious, piercing, pointed, pungent, quick, razorlike, sagacious, sapient, sardonic, satirical, scathing, sedulous, sensitive, sharp, shrewd, shrill, tart, trenchant, wise, zealous.

keep[1] *v.* accumulate, amass, carry, collect, conserve, control, deal in, deposit, furnish, garner, hang on to, heap, hold, hold on to, maintain, pile, place, possess, preserve, retain, stack, stock, store.

keep[2] *v.* be responsible for, board, care for, defend, feed, foster, guard, have charge of, have custody of, look after, maintain, manage, mind, nourish, nurture, operate, protect, provide for, provision, safeguard, shelter, shield, subsidize, support, sustain, tend, victual, watch, watch over. *n.* board, food, livelihood, living, maintenance, means, nourishment, nurture, subsistence, support, upkeep.

keep[3] *v.* arrest, block, check, constrain, control, curb, delay, detain, deter, hamper, hamstring, hinder, hold, hold back, hold up, impede, inhibit, interfere with, keep back, limit, obstruct, prevent, restrain, retard, shackle, stall, trammel, withhold.

keg *n.* barrel, butt, cask, drum, firkin, hogshead, puncheon, round, tun, vat.

key *n.* answer, clue, code, crib, cue, digital, explanation, glossary, guide, index, indicator, interpretation, lead, means, pointer, secret, sign, solution, table, translation. *adj.* basic, cardinal, central, chief, core, crucial, decisive, essential, fundamental, hinge, important, leading, main, major, pivotal, principal, salient.

kill *v.* abolish, annihilate, assassinate, beguile, bump off, butcher, cancel, cease, deaden, defeat, destroy, dispatch, do away with, do in, do to death, eliminate, eradicate, execute, exterminate, extinguish, extirpate, fill, finish off, halt, kibosh, knock off, knock on the head, liquidate, mar, martyr, massacre, murder, neutralize, nip in the bud, nullify, obliterate, occupy, pass, pip, put to death, quash, quell, rub out, ruin, scotch, slaughter, slay, smite, smother, spoil, stifle, still, stop, suppress, top, veto, vitiate, while away, zap. *n.* climax, conclusion, coup de grâce, death, deathblow, denouement, dispatch, end, finish, mop-up, shoot-out.

killing[1] *n.* big hit, bonanza, coup, fortune, gain, hit, lucky break, profit, smash, success, windfall, winner.

killing[2] *adj.* absurd, amusing, comical, funny, hilarious, ludicrous, side-splitting, uproarious.

kind[1] *n.* brand, breed, category, character, class, description, essence, family, genus, habit, ilk, kidney, manner, mold, nature, persuasion, race, set, sort, species, stamp, style, temperament, type, variety.

kind[2] *adj.* accommodating, affectionate, altruistic, amiable, amicable, avuncular, beneficent, benevolent, benign, benignant, bonhomous, boon, bounteous, bountiful, brotherly, charitable, clement, compassionate, congenial, considerate, cordial, courteous, diplomatic, fatherly, friendly, generous, gentle, giving, good, gracious, hospitable, humane, indulgent, kind-hearted, kindly, lenient, loving, mild, motherly, neighborly, obliging, philanthropic, propitious, sisterly, soft-boiled, soft-hearted, sweet, sympathetic, tactful, tender-hearted, thoughtful, understanding.

kink *n.* bend, coil, complication, corkscrew, crick, crimp, defect, dent, difficulty, entanglement, flaw, hitch, imperfection, indentation, knot, loop, tangle, twist, wrinkle. *v.* bend, coil, crimp, curl, tangle, twist, wrinkle.

kiss *v.* buss, neck, peck, salute, smooch.

knife *n.* blade, carver, cutter, dagger, flick-knife, jackknife, machete, pen-knife, pocket-knife, skene, switchblade, whittle. *v.* cut, impale, lacerate, pierce, rip, slash, stab, wound.

knock[1] *v.* buffet, clap, cuff, ding, hit, knobble, (k)nubble, punch, rap, slap, smack, smite, strike, thump, thwack. *n.* blow, box, chap, clip, clout, con, cuff, hammering, rap, slap, slam, vilify, vilipend. *n.* blame, censure, condemnation, criticism, defeat, failure, rebuff, rejection, reversal, setback, stricture.

knock[2] *v.* abuse, belittle, carp, cavil, censure, condemn, criticize, deprecate, disparage, find fault, lambaste, run down, slam, vilify, vilipend. *n.* blame, censure, condemnation, criticism, defeat, failure, rebuff, rejection, reversal, setback, stricture.

knot *v.* bind, entangle, entwine, knit loop, secure, tangle, tether, tie, weave.

know *v.* apprehend, comprehend, discern, distinguish, experience, fathom, identify, intuit, ken, learn, make out, notice, perceive, realize, recognize, see, tell, undergo, understand, wist.

knowledge *n.* ability, acquaintance, acquaintanceship, apprehension, book learning, booklore, cognition, cognizance, comprehension, consciousness, discernment, education, enlightenment, erudition, familiarity, grasp, information, instruction, intelligence, intimacy, judgment, learning, notice, recognition, scholarship, schooling, science, wisdom.

knowledgeable *adj.* acquainted, au courant, aware, bright, cognizant, conscious, conversant, educated, erudite, intelligent, learned, lettered, scholarly, well-informed.

kudos *n.* acclaim, applause, distinction, esteem, fame, glory, honor, laudation, laurels, plaudits, praise, prestige, regard, renown, repute.

L

label *n.* badge, brand, categorization, characterization, classification, company, description, docket, epithet, mark, marker, sticker, tag, tally, ticket, trademark. *v.* brand, call, categorize, characterize, class, classify, define, describe, designate, docket, dub, identify, mark, name, stamp, tag.

labor[1] *n.* chore, drudgery, effort, employees, exertion, grind, job, labor, laborers, pains, painstaking, sweat, task, toil, undertaking, work, workers, workmen.

labor[2] *n.* birth, childbirth, contractions, delivery, labor pains, pains, parturition, throes, travail. *v.* dwell on, elaborate, overdo, overemphasize, overstress, strain.

lace[1] *n.* crochet, filigree, mesh-work, netting, open-work, tatting.

lace[2] *n.* bootlace, cord, lanyard, shoelace, string, thong, tie. *v.* attach, bind, close, do up, fasten, intertwine, interweave, interwork, string, thread, tie.

lace[3] *v.* add to, fortify, intermix, mix in, spike.

laceration *n.* cut, gash, injury, maim, mutilation, rent, rip, slash, tear, wound.

lack *n.* absence, dearth, deficiency, deprivation, destitution, emptiness, insufficiency, need, privation, scantiness, scarcity, shortage, shortcoming, shortness, vacancy, void, want.

lad *n.* boy, chap, fellow, guy, juvenile, kid, schoolboy, stripling, youngster, youth.

lady *n.* dame, damsel, gentlewoman, madam(e), matron, noblewoman, woman.

lag *v.* dawdle, delay, hang back, idle, linger, loiter, mosey, saunter, shuffle, straggle, tarry, trail.

land *n.* country, countryside, dirt, district, earth, estate, farmland, fatherland, ground, grounds, loam, motherland, nation, property, real estate, realty, region, soil, terra firma, territory, tract. *v.* alight, arrive, berth, bring, cause, come to rest, debark, deposit, dock, drop, end up, plant, touch down, turn up, wind up.

language *n.* argot, cant, conversation, dialect, diction, discourse, expression, idiolect, idiom, interchange, jargon, lingo, lingua franca, parlance, parole, patois, phraseology, phrasing, speech, style, talk, terminology, tongue, utterance, vernacular, vocabulary, wording.

large *adj.* abundant, ample, big, broad, bulky, capacious, colossal, comprehensive, considerable, copious, colossal, enormous, extensive, full, generous, giant, gigantic, goodly, grand, grandiose, great, huge, immense, jumbo, king-sized, liberal, man-sized, massive, monumental, plentiful, roomy, sizeable, spacious, spanking, substantial, sweeping, swinging, tidy, vast, wide.

last[1] *adj.* aftermost, closing, concluding, conclusive, definitive, extreme, final, furthest, hindmost, latest, rearmost, remotest, terminal, ultimate, utmost.

last² *v.* abide, carry on, continue, endure, hold on, hold out, keep (on), perdure, persist, remain, stand up, stay, survive, wear.

late¹ *adj.* behind, behind-hand, belated, delayed, dilatory, last-minute, overdue, slow, tardy, unpunctual.

late² *adj.* dead, deceased, defunct, departed, ex-, former, old, past, preceding, previous.

lately *adv.* formerly, heretofore, latterly, recently.

latitude *n.* breadth, clearance, compass, elbowroom, extent, field, freedom, indulgence, laxity, leeway, liberty, license, play, range, reach, room, scope, space, span, spread, sweep, width.

laugh *v.* cachinnate, chortle, chuckle, crease up, fall about, giggle, guffaw, snicker, snigger, te(e)hee, titter.

launch *n.* begin, cast, commence, discharge, dispatch, embark on, establish, fire, float, found, inaugurate, initiate, instigate, introduce, open, project, propel, send off, set in motion, start, throw.

lay *v.* advance, allay, alleviate, allocate, allot, appease, apply, arrange, ascribe, assess, assign, assuage, attribute, bet, burden, calm, charge, concoct, contrive, deposit, design, devise, dispose, encumber, establish, gamble, hatch, hazard, impose, impute, leave, locate, lodge, offer, organize, place, plan, plant, plot, posit, position, prepare, present, put, quiet, relieve, risk, saddle, set, set down, set out, settle, soothe, spread, stake, still, submit, suppress, tax, wager, work out.

lazy *adj.* dormant, drowsy, idle, inactive, indolent, inert, languid, languorous, lethargic, shiftless, slack, sleepy, slobby, slothful, slow, slow-moving, sluggish, somnolent, torpid, work-shy.

leach *v.* drain, extract, filter, filtrate, osmose, percolate, seep, strain.

lead *v.* antecede, cause, command, conduct, direct, dispose, draw, escort, exceed, excel, experience, govern, guide, have, head, incline, induce, influence, live, manage, outdo, outstrip, pass, persuade, pilot, precede, preside over, prevail, prompt, spend, steer, supervise, surpass, transcend, undergo, usher.

leak *n.* aperture, chink, crack, crevice, disclosure, divulgence, drip, fissure, hole, leakage, leaking, oozing, opening, percolation, perforation, puncture, seepage. *v.* discharge, disclose, divulge, drip, escape, exude, give away, let slip, let the cat out of the bag, make known, make public, make water, ooze, pass,
pass on, percolate, reveal, seep, spill, spill the beans, tell, trickle, weep.

lean¹ *v.* bend, confide, count on, depend, favor, incline, list, prefer, prop, recline, rely, repose, rest, slant, slope, tend, tilt, tip, trust.

lean² *adj.* angular, bare, barren, bony, emaciated, gaunt, inadequate, infertile, lank, meager, pitiful, poor, rangy, scanty, scraggy, scrawny, skinny, slender, slim, slink(y), spare, sparse, thin, unfruitful, unproductive, wiry.

learn *v.* acquire, ascertain, assimilate, attain, cognize, con, detect, determine, discern, discover, find out, gather, get off pat, grasp, hear, imbibe, learn by heart, master, memorize, pick up, see, understand.

least *adj.* fewest, last, lowest, meanest, merest, minimum, minutest, poorest, slightest, smallest, tiniest.

leave¹ *v.* abandon, allot, assign, bequeath, cause, cease, cede, commit, consign, decamp, depart, deposit, desert, desist, disappear, do a bunk, drop, entrust, exit, flit, forget, forsake, generate, give over, give up, go, go away, hand down, leave behind, levant, move, produce, pull out, quit, refer, refrain, relinquish, renounce, retire, set out, stop, surrender, take off, transmit, will, withdraw.

leave² *n.* allowance, author-ization, concession, consent, dispensation, exeat, freedom, furlough, holiday, indulgence, liberty, permission, sabbatical, sanction, time off, vacation.

legal *adj.* aboveboard, allowable, allowed, authorized, constitutional, forensic, judicial, juridical, lawful, legalized, legitimate, licit, permissible, proper, rightful, sanctioned, valid, warrantable.

legend *n.* caption, celebrity, cipher, code, device, fable, fiction, folk tale, household name, inscription, key, luminary, marvel, motto, myth, narrative, phenomenon, prodigy, saga, spectacle, story, tale, tradition, wonder.

legible *adj.* clear, deciph-erable, discernible, distinct, intelligible, neat, readable.

legislation *n.* act, authorization, bill, charter, codification, constitutionalization, enactment, law, law making, measure, prescription, regulation, ruling, statute.

leisure *n.* breather, ease, freedom, holiday, letup, liberty, opportunity, pause, quiet, recreation, relaxation, respite, rest, retirement, spare time, time off, vacation.

lend v. add, advance, afford, bestow, confer, contribute, furnish, give, grant, impart, lease, loan, present, provide, supply.

length n. distance, duration, elongation, extensiveness, extent, lengthiness, longitude, measure, period, piece, portion, prolixity, reach, section, segment, space, span, stretch, tediousness, term.

lessen v. abate, abridge, bate, contract, curtail, deaden, decrease, deescalate, de-grade, die down, diminish, dwindle, ease, erode, fail, flag, impair, lighten, lower, minimize, moderate, narrow, reduce, shrink, slack, slow down, weaken

lesson n. admonition, assignment, censure, chiding, class, coaching, deterrent, drill, example, exemplar, exercise, homework, instruction, lecture, message, model, moral, period, practice, precept, punishment, reading, rebuke, recitation, reprimand, reproof, schooling, scolding, task, teaching, tutorial, tutoring, warning.

let[1] v. agree to, allow, authorize, cause, charter, consent to, empower, enable, entitle, give leave, give permission, give the go-ahead, give the green light, grant, hire, lease, make, permit, rent, sanction, tolerate.

let[2] n. check, constraint, hindrance, impediment, interference, obstacle, obstruction, prohibition, restraint, restriction.

level[1] adj. aligned, balanced, calm, champaign, commensurate, comparable, consistent, equable, equal, equiv-alent, even, even-tempered, flat, flush, horizontal, neck and neck, on a par, plain, proportionate, smooth, stable, steady, uniform.

level[2] v. admit, avow, come clean, confess, divulge, open up, tell.

leverage n. advantage, ascendancy, authority, clout, force, influence, pull, purchase, rank, strength, weight.

libel n. aspersion, calumny, defamation, denigration, obloquy, slander, slur, smear, vilification, vituperation.

liberal adj. abundant, advanced, altruistic, ample, beneficent, bounteous, bountiful, broad, broad-minded, catholic, charitable, copious, enlightened, flexible, free, free-handed, general, generous, handsome, high-minded, humanistic, humanitarian, indulgent, inexact, kind, large-hearted, latitudinarian, lavish, lenient, libertarian, loose, magnanimous, munificent, open-hearted, permissive, plentiful, profuse, progressive, radical, reformist, rich, tolerant, unbiased, unbigoted, unprejudiced, unstinting.

liberty n. authorization, autonomy, carte blanche, dispensation, emancipation, exemption, franchise, free rein, freedom, immunity, independence, latitude, leave, liberation, license, permission, prerogative, privilege, release, right, sanction, self-determination, sovereignty.

license[1] n. authorization, authority, carte blanche, certificate, charter, dispensation, entitlement, exemption, freedom, immunity, imprimatur, independence, latitude, leave, liberty, permission, permit, privilege, right, warrant.

license[2] n. abandon, amorality, anarchy, debauchery, disorder, dissipation, dissoluteness, excess, immoderation, impropriety, indulgence, intemperance, irresponsibility, lawlessness, laxity, profligacy, unruliness.

lick[1] v. brush, dart, flick, lap, play over, smear, taste, tongue, touch, wash. n. bit, brush, dab, hint, little, sample, smidgeon, speck, spot, stroke, taste, touch.

lick[2] v. beat, best, defeat, excel, flog, outdo, outstrip, overcome, rout, slap, smack, spank, strike, surpass, thrash, top, trounce, vanquish, wallop.

lie[1] v. dissimulate, equivocate, fabricate, falsify, fib, forswear oneself, invent, misrepresent, perjure, prevaricate. n. bounce, caulker, cram, crammer, deceit, fabrication, falsehood, falsification, falsity, fib, fiction, flam, invention, plumper, prevarication, stretcher, tar(r)adiddle, untruth, whacker, white lie, whopper.

lie[2] v. be, belong, couch, dwell, exist, extend, inhere, laze, loll, lounge, recline, remain, repose, rest, slump, stretch out.

life n. activity, animation, autobiography, behavior, being, biography, breath, brio, career, conduct, confessions, continuance, course, creatures, duration, élan vital, energy, entity, essence, existence, fauna, flora and fauna, go, growth, heart, high spirits, history, memoirs, soul, span, sparkle, spirit, story, the world, this mortal coil, time, verve, viability, vigor, vita, vital flame, vital spark, vitality, vivacity, way of life, wildlife, zest.

lift v. advance, ameliorate, annul, appropriate, arrest, ascend, boost, buoy up, cancel, climb, collar, copy, countermand, crib, dignify, disappear, disperse, dissipate, draw up, elevate, end, enhance, exalt, half-inch, heft, hoist, improve, mount, nab, nick, pick up, pilfer, pinch, pirate, plagiarize, pocket, promote, purloin, raise, rear, relax, remove, rescind, revoke, rise, steal, stop, take, terminate, thieve, up, upgrade, uplift, upraise, vanish.

light¹ *n.* beacon, blaze, brightness, brilliance, bulb, candle, cockcrow, dawn, day, daybreak, daylight, daytime, effulgence, flame, flare, flash, glare, gleam, glim, glint, glow, illumination, incandescence, lambency, lamp, lantern, lighter, lighthouse, luminescence, luminosity, luster, match, morn, morning, phosphorescence, radiance, ray, refulgence, scintillation, shine, sparkle, star, sunrise, sunshine, taper, torch, window, Yang.

light² *n.* angle, approach, aspect, attitude, awareness, clue, comprehension, context, elucidation, enlightenment, example, exemplar, explanation, hint, illustration, information, insight, interpretation, knowledge, model, paragon, point of view, slant, understanding, viewpoint.

light³ *adj.* agile, airy, amusing, animated, blithe, buoyant, carefree, cheerful, cheery, crumbly, delicate, delirious, digestible, diverting, dizzy, easy, effortless, entertaining, facile, faint, fickle, flimsy, friable, frivolous, frugal, funny, gay, gentle, giddy, graceful, humorous, idle, imponderous, inconsequential, inconsiderable, indistinct, insignificant, insubstantial, light-footed, light-headed, light-hearted, lightweight, lithe, lively, loose, manageable, merry, mild, minute, moderate, modest, nimble, pleasing, portable, reeling, restricted, sandy, scanty, simple, slight, small, soft, spongy, sprightly, sunny, thin, tiny, trifling, trivial, unchaste, undemanding, underweight, unheeding, unsteady, unsubstantial, untaxing, volatile, wanton, weak, witty, worthless.

lighten¹ *v.* beacon, brighten, illume, illuminate, illumine, light up, shine.

lighten² *v.* alleviate, amel-iorate, assuage, brighten buoy up, cheer, disburden, disencumber, ease, elate, encourage, facilitate, gladden, hearten, inspire, inspirit, lessen, lift, mitigate, perk up, reduce, relieve, revive, unload, uplift.

like¹ *adj.* akin, alike, allied, analogous, approximating, cognate, corresponding, equivalent, identical, parallel, related, relating, resembling, same, similar.

like² *v.* admire, adore, appreciate, approve, care to, cherish, choose, choose to, delight in, desire, dig, enjoy, esteem, fancy, feel inclined, go for, hold dear, love, prefer, prize, relish, revel in, select, take a shine to, take kindly to, want, wish.

limb *n.* appendage, arm, bough, branch, extension, extremity, leg, member, offshoot, part, projection, ramus, spur, wing.

limit *n.* bitter end, border, bound, boundary, brink, ceiling, check, compass, confines, curb, cut-off point, deadline, edge, end, extent, frontier, limitation, maximum, mete, obstruction, perimeter, periphery, precinct, restraint, restriction, rim, saturation point, termination, terminus, terminus a quo, terminus ad quem, threshold, ultimate, utmost, verge. *v.* bound, check, circumscribe, condition, confine, constrain, curb, delimit, delimitate, demarcate, fix, hem in, hinder, ration, restrain, restrict, specify.

limp¹ *v.* dot, falter, halt, hitch, hobble, hop, shamble, shuffle. *n.* claudication, hitch, hobble, lameness.

limp² *adj.* debilitated, drooping, enervated, exhausted, flabby, flaccid, flexible, flexile, floppy, hypotonic, lax, lethargic, limber, loose, pliable, pooped, relaxed, slack, soft, spent, tired, toneless, weak, worn out.

line¹ *n.* band, bar, border, borderline, boundary, cable, chain, channel, column, configuration, contour, cord, crease, crocodile, crow's foot, dash, demarcation, disposition, edge, features, figure, filament, file, firing line, formation, front, front line, frontier, furrow, groove, limit, mark, outline, position, procession, profile, queue, rank, rope, row, rule, score, scratch, sequence, series, silhouette, stipe, strand, streak, string, stroke, tail, thread, trail, trenches, underline, wire, wrinkle. *v.* border, bound, crease, cut, draw, edge, fringe, furrow, hatch, inscribe, mark, rank, rim, rule, score, skirt, verge.

line² *n.* activity, approach, area, avenue, axis, belief, business, calling, course, course of action, department, direction, employment, field, forte, ideology, interest, job, line of country, method, occupation, path, policy, position, practice, procedure, profession, province, pursuit, route, scheme, specialism, specialization, specialty, system, track, trade, trajectory, vocation.

line³ *n.* ancestry, breed, family, lineage, pedigree, race, stock, strain, succession.

link *n.* association, attachment, bond, communication, component, connection, constituent, division, element, joint, knot, liaison, member, part, piece, relationship, tie, tie-up, union. *v.* associate, attach, bind, bracket, catenate, concatenate, connect, couple, fasten, identify, join, relate, tie, unite, yoke.

liquid *n.* drink, fluid, juice, liquor, lotion, potation, sap, solution. *adj.* aqueous, clear, convertible, dulcet, flowing, fluid, limpid, liquefied, mellifluent, mellifluous, melted, molten, running, runny, serous, shining, smooth, soft, sweet, thawed, translucent, transparent, watery, wet.

liquidate *v.* abolish, annihilate, annul, assassinate, bump off, cancel, cash, clear, destroy, discharge, dispatch, dissolve, do away with, do in, eliminate, exterminate, finish off, honor, kill, massacre, murder, pay, pay off, realize, remove, rub out, sell off, sell up, settle, silence, square, terminate, wipe out.

list[1] *n.* catalog, directory, enumeration, file, index, inventory, invoice, listing, litany, record, register, roll, schedule, series, syllabus, table, tabulation, tally. *v.* alphabetize, bill, book, catalog, enroll, enter, enumerate, file, index, itemize, note, record, register, schedule, set down, tabulate, write down.

list[2] *v.* cant, careen, heel, heel over, incline, lean, slope, tilt, tip. *n.* cant, leaning, slant, slope, tilt.

listen *v.* attend, get a load of, give ear, give heed to, hang on (someone's) words, hang on (someone's) lips, hark, hear, hearken, heed, keep one's ears open, lend an ear, mind, obey, observe, pay attention, pin back one's ears, take notice.

literal *adj.* accurate, actual, boring, close, colorless, down-to-earth, dull, exact, factual, faithful, genuine, matter-of-fact, plain, prosaic, prosy, real, simple, strict, true, unimaginative, uninspired, unvarnished, verbatim, word-for-word.

literary *adj.* bookish, cultivated, cultured, erudite, formal, learned, lettered, literate, refined, scholarly, well-read.

litter[1] *n.* clutter, confusion, debris, detritus, disarray, disorder, fragments, jumble, mess, muck, refuse, rubbish, scatter, scoria, shreds, untidiness, wastage. *v.* bestrew, clutter, derange, disarrange, disorder, mess up, scatter, strew.

litter[2] *n.* brood, family, offspring, progeny, quiverfull, young.

little *adj.* babyish, base, brief, cheap, diminutive, dwarf, elfin, fleeting, hasty, immature, inconsiderable, infant, infinitesimal, insignificant, insufficient, junior, Lilliputian, meager, mean, microscopic, miniature, minor, minute, negligible, paltry, passing, petite, petty, pickaninny, pint-size(d), pygmy, scant, short, short-lived, skimpy, slender, small, sparse, tiny, transient, trifling, trivial, undeveloped, unimportant, wee, young.

live[1] *v.* abide, breathe, continue, draw breath, dwell, earn a living, endure, exist, fare, feed, get along, inhabit, last, led, lodge, pass, persist, prevail, remain, reside, settle, stay, subsist, survive.

live[2] *adj.* active, alert, alive, animate, blazing, breathing, brisk, burning, connected, controversial, current, dynamic, earnest, energetic, existent, glowing, hot, ignited, lively, living, pressing, prevalent, relevant, sentient, smoldering, topical, vigorous, vital, vivid, wide-awake.

livelihood *n.* employment, income, job, living, maintenance, means, occupation, subsistence, support, sustenance, work.

lively *adj.* active, agile, alert, animated, astir, blithe, blithesome, breezy, bright, brisk, buckish, bustling, busy, buxom, buzzing, cheerful, chipper, chirpy, colorful, crowded, energetic, eventful, exciting, forceful, frisky, frolicsome, gay, invigorating, keen, lifesome, lightsome, merry, moving, nimble, perky, quick, racy, refreshing, sparkling, spirited, sprightly, spry, stimulating, stirring, swinging, vigorous, vivacious, vivid, zippy.

livid[1] *adj.* angry, beside oneself, boiling, enraged, exasperated, fuming, furibund, furious, incensed, indignant, infuriated, irate, ireful, mad, outraged, waxy.

livid[2] *adj.* angry, ashen, black-and-blue, blanched, bloodless, bruised, contused, discolored, doughy, grayish, leaden, pale, pallid, pasty, purple, wan, waxen, waxy.

living *adj.* active, alive, animated, breathing, existing, live, lively, strong, vigorous, vital.

load *n.* affliction, albatross, bale, burden, cargo, consignment, encumbrance, freight, goods, lading, millstone, onus, oppression, pressure, shipment, trouble, weight, worry. *v.* adulterate, burden, charge, cram, doctor, drug, encumber, fill, fortify, freight, hamper, heap, lade, oppress, overburden, pack, pile, prime, saddle with, stack, stuff, trouble, weigh down, weight, worry.

loan *n.* accommodation, advance, allowance, credit, lend-lease, loan translation, loan-word, mortgage, touch. *v.* accommodate, advance, allow, credit, lend, let out, oblige.

loathe *v.* abhor, abominate, despise, detest, dislike, execrate, hate.

locate *v.* detect, discover, establish, find, fix, identify, lay one's hands on, pin-point, place, put, run to earth, seat, set, settle, situate, track down, unearth.

location *n.* bearings, locale, locus, place, point, position, site, situation, spot, venue, whereabouts.

lock[1] *n.* bolt, clasp, fastening, padlock. *v.* bolt, clasp, clench, close, clutch, disengage, embrace, encircle, enclose, engage, entangle, entwine, fasten, grapple, grasp, hug, join, latch, link, mesh, press, seal, secure, shut, unite, unlock.

lock[2] *n.* curl, plait, ringlet, strand, tress, tuft.

log[1] *n.* billet, bole, chunk, stump, timber, trunk.

log[2] *n.* account, chart, daybook, diary, journal, listing, logbook, record, tally. *v.* book, chart, note, record, register, report, tally, write down, write in, write up.

logic *n.* argumentation, deduction, dialectic(s), rationale, rationality, reason, reasoning, sense.

lone *adj.* deserted, isolated, lonesome, one, only, separate, separated, single, sole, solitary, unaccompanied, unattached, unattended.

loneliness *n.* aloneness, desolation, forlornness, friendlessness, isolation, lonesomeness, seclusion, solitariness, solitude.

lonely *adj.* abandoned, alone, apart, companionless, destitute, estranged, forlorn, forsaken, friendless, isolated, lonely-heart, lone-some, outcast, out-of-the-way, remote, secluded, sequestered, solitary, unfrequented, uninhabited, untrodden.

long *adj.* dragging, elongated, expanded, expansive, extended, extensive, far-reaching, interminable, late, lengthy, lingering, long-drawn-out, marathon, prolonged, protracted, slow, spread out, stretched, sustained, tardy.

look *v.* appear, behold, consider, contemplate, display, evidence, examine, exhibit, eye, gape, gawk, gaze, get a load of, glance, goggle, inspect, observe, ogle, peep, regard, rubberneck, scan, scrutinize, see, seem, show, stare, study, survey, view, watch. *n.* air, appearance, aspect, bearing, cast, complexion, countenance, effect, examination, eyeful, eye-glance, face, fashion, gaze, glance, glimpse, guise, inspection, look-see, manner, mien, observation, once-over, peek, review, semblance, sight, squint, survey, view.

loose[1] *adj.* baggy, crank, diffuse, disconnected, disordered, easy, floating, free, hanging, ill-defined, imprecise, inaccurate, indefinite, indistinct, inexact, insecure, loosened, movable, rambling, random, relaxed, released, shaky, slack, slackened, sloppy, solute, unattached, unbound, unconfined, unfastened, unfettered, unrestricted, unsecured, untied, vague, wobbly.

loose[2] *adj.* abandoned, careless, debauched, disreputable, dissipated, dissolute, fast, heedless, immoral, imprudent, lax, lewd, libertine, licentious, negligent, profligate, promiscuous, rash, unchaste, unmindful, wanton.

lose *v.* capitulate, come a cropper, come to grief, consume, default, deplete, displace, dissipate, dodge, drain, drop, duck, elude, escape, evade, exhaust, expend, fail, fall short, forfeit, forget, get the worst of, give (someone) the slip, lap, lavish, leave behind, lose out on, misfile, mislay, misplace, miss, misspend, outdistance, outrun, outstrip, overtake, pass, pass up, shake off, slip away, squander, stray from, suffer defeat, take a licking, throw off, use up, wander from, waste, yield.

loss *n.* bereavement, cost, damage, debit, debt, defeat, deficiency, deficit, depletion, deprivation, destruction, detriment, disadvantage, disappearance, failure, forfeiture, harm, hurt, impairment, injury, losing, misfortune, privation, ruin, shrinkage, squandering, waste, write-off.

lost *adj.* abandoned, abolished, absent, absorbed, abstracted, adrift, annihilated, astray, baffled, bewildered, confused, consumed, corrupt, damned, demolished, depraved, destroyed, devastated, disappeared, disoriented, dissipated, dissolute, distracted, dreamy, engrossed, entranced, eradicated, exterminated, fallen, forfeited, frittered away, irreclaimable, licentious, misapplied, misdirected, mislaid, misplaced, missed, missing, misspent, misused, mystified, obliterated, off-course, off-track, perished, perplexed, preoccupied, profligate, puzzled, rapt, ruined, spell-bound, squandered, strayed, unrecallable, unrecapturable, unrecoverable, untraceable, vanished, wanton, wasted, wayward, wiped out, wrecked.

loud *adj.* blaring, blatant, boisterous, booming, brash, brassy, brazen, clamorous, coarse, crass, crude, deafening, ear-piercing, ear-splitting, flamboyant, flashy, garish, gaudy, glaring, high-sounding, loud-mouthed, lurid, noisy, offensive, ostentatious, piercing, raucous, rowdy, showy, sonorous, stentorian, strident, strong, tasteless, tawdry, thundering, tumultuous, turbulent, vehement, vocal, vociferous, vulgar.

love *v.* adore, adulate, appreciate, cherish, delight in, desire, dote on, enjoy, fancy, hold dear, idolize, like, prize, relish, savor, take pleasure in, think the world of, treasure, want, worship.

lovely *adj.* admirable, adorable, agreeable, amiable, attractive, beautiful, captivating, charming, comely, delightful, enchanting, engaging, enjoyable, exquisite, graceful, gratifying, handsome, idyllic, nice, pleasant, pleasing, pretty, sweet, taking, winning.

lover *n.* admirer, beau, beloved, boyfriend, Casanova, flame, gigolo, girlfriend, mistress, paramour, philanderer, suitor, swain, sweetheart.

loving *adj.* affectionate, amative, amatorial, amatorian, amatorious, amorous, ardent, cordial, dear, demonstrative, devoted, doting, fond, friendly, kind, passionate, solicitous, tender, warm, warm-hearted.

low *adj.* abject, base, base-born, blue, browned off, cheap, coarse, common, contemptible, crude, dastardly, debilitated, deep, deficient, degraded, dejected, depleted, depraved, depressed, despicable, despondent, disgraceful, disheartened, dishonorable, disreputable, down, down in the dumps, downcast, dying, economical, exhausted, fed up, feeble, forlorn, frail, gloomy, glum, gross, humble, hushed, ignoble, ill, ill-bred, inadequate, inexpensive, inferior, insignificant, little, low-born, low-grade, lowly, low-lying, meager, mean, mediocre, meek, menial miserable, moderate, modest, morose, muffled, muted, nasty, obscene, obscure, paltry, plain, plebeian, poor, prostrate, puny, quiet, reasonable, reduced, rough, rude, sad, scant, scurvy, second-rate, servile, shallow, shoddy, short, simple, sinking, small, soft, sordid, sparse, squat, stricken, stunted, subdued, substandard, sunken, trifling, unbecoming, undignified, unhappy, unpretentious, unrefined, unworthy, vile, vulgar, weak, whispered, worthless.

lower *adj.* inferior, insignificant, junior, lesser, low-level, lowly, minor, secondary, second-class, smaller, subordinate, subservient, under, unimportant. *v.* abase, abate, belittle, condescend, couch, curtail, cut, debase, decrease, degrade, deign, demean, demolish, depress, devalue, diminish, discredit, disgrace, downgrade, drop, fall, humble, humiliate, lessen, let down, minimize, moderate, prune, raze, reduce, sink, slash, soften stoop, submerge, take down, tone down.

loyal *adj.* attached, constant, dependable, devoted, dutiful, faithful, honest, patriotic, sincere, staunch, steadfast, true, true-blue, true-hearted, trustworthy, trusty, unswerving, unwavering.

luck *n.* accident, blessing, break, chance, destiny, fate, fluke, fortuity, fortune, godsend, good fortune, hap, happenstance, hazard, jam, joss, prosperity, serendipity, stroke, success, windfall.

lucrative *adj.* advantageous, fecund, fertile, fruitful, gainful, paying, productive, profitable, remunerative, well-paid.

ludicrous *adj.* absurd, amusing, burlesque, comic, comical, crazy, droll, farcical, funny, incongruous, laughable, nonsensical, odd, outlandish, preposterous, ridiculous, risible, silly, zany.

lull *v.* abate, allay, calm, cease, compose, decrease, diminish, dwindle, ease off, hush, let up, lullaby, moderate, pacify, quell, quiet, down, sedate, slacken, soothe, still, subdue, subside, tranquilize, wane.

luminous *adj.* bright, brilliant, glowing, illuminated, lighted, lit, lucent, luminescent, luminiferous, lustrous, radiant, resplendent, shining, vivid.

lump *n.* ball, bulge, bump, bunch, cake, chuck, chump, chunk, clod, cluster, cyst, dab, gob, gobbet, group, growth, hunch, hunk, (k)nub, (k)nubble, lob, mass, nugget, piece, protrusion, protuberance, spot, swelling, tuber, tumescence, tumor, wedge, wen. *v.* coalesce, collect, combine, consolidate, group, mass, unite.

lunge *v.* bound, charge, cut, dash, dive, fall upon, grab (at), hit(at), jab, leap, pitch into, plunge, poke, pounce, set upon, stab, strike (at), thrust, *n.* charge, cut, jab, pass, pounce, spring, stab, swing, swipe, thrust.

lure *v.* allure, attract, beckon, decoy, draw, ensnare, entice, inveigle, invite, lead on, seduce, tempt, trepan. *n.* allurement, attraction, bait, carrot, come-on, decoy, enticement, inducement, magnet, siren, song, temptation, train.

lurk *v.* crouch, hide, hide out, lie in wait, lie low, prowl, skulk, slink, sneak, snoop.

lush *adj.* abundant, dense, elaborate, extravagant, flourishing, grand, green, juicy, lavish, luxuriant, luxurious, opulent, ornate, overgrown, palatial, plush, prolific, rank, ripe, ritzy, succulent, sumptuous, superabundant, teeming, tender, verdant.

lust *n.* appetence, appetency, appetite, avidity, carnality, concupiscence, covetousness, craving, cupidity, desire, greed, lasciviousness, lechery, lewdness, libido, licentiousness, longing, passion, prurience, randiness, salaciousness, sensuality, thirst, wantonness.

luxury *n.* affluence, bliss, comfort, delight, dolce vita, enjoyment, extra, extravagance, flesh-pots, flesh-pottery, frill, gratification, hedonism, indulgence, milk and honey, non-essential, opulence, pleasure, richness, satisfaction, splendor, sumptuousness, treat, voluptuousness, well-being.

lying *adj.* accumbent, deceitful, dishonest, dissembling, duplicitous, false, guileful, mendacious, perfidious, untruthful.

M

macabre *adj.* cadaverous, deathlike, deathly, dreadful, eerie, frightening, frightful, ghastly, ghostly, ghoulish, grim, grisly, gruesome, hideous, horrible, horrid, morbid, sick, weird.

Machiavellian *adj.* amoral, artful, astute, calculating, crafty, cunning, cynical, deceitful, designing, double-dealing, foxy, guileful, intriguing, opportunist, perfidious, scheming, shrewd, sly, underhand, unscrupulous, wily.

machine *n.* agency, agent, apparatus, appliance, automaton, contraption, contrivance, device, engine, gadget, gizmo, instrument, machinery, mechanism, organization, party, puppet, robot, setup, structure, system, tool, zombie.

mad *adj.* abandoned, aberrant, absurd, agitated, angry, ardent, avid, bananas, bats, batty, berserk, boisterous, bonkers, crackers, crazed, crazy, cuckoo, daft, delirious, demented, deranged, devoted, distracted, dotty, ebullient, enamored, energetic, enraged, enthusiastic, exasperated, excited, fanatical, fond, foolhardy, foolish, frantic, frenetic, frenzied, fuming, furious, gay, have bats in the belfry, hooked, impassioned, imprudent, in a paddy, incensed, infatuated, infuriated, insane, irate, irrational, irritated, keen, livid, loony, loopy, ludicrous, lunatic, madcap, mental, moon-stricken, moon-struck, non compos mentis, nonsensical, nuts, nutty, off one's chump, off one's head, off one's nut, off one's rocker, off one's trolley, out of one's mind, possessed, preposterous, psychotic, rabid, raging, raving, resentful, riotous, round the bend, screwball, screwy, senseless, uncontrolled, unhinged, unreasonable, unrestrained, unsafe, unsound, unstable, up the pole, waxy, wild, wrathful, zealous.

magic *n.* allurement, black art, charm, conjuring, enchantment, fascination, illusion, legerdemain, magnetism, medicine, necromancy, occultism, prestidigitation, sleight of hand, sorcery, spell, trickery, voodoo, witchcraft, wizardry.

magnanimous *adj.* altruistic, beneficent, big, big-hearted, bountiful, charitable, free, generous, great-hearted, handsome, high-minded, kind, kindly, large-hearted, large-minded, liberal, munificent, noble, open-handed, philanthropic, selfless, ungrudging, unselfish, unstinting.

magnet *n.* appeal, attraction, bait, draw, enticement, lodestone, lure, solenoid.

magnify *v.* aggrandize, aggravate, amplify, augment, blow up, boost, build up, deepen, dilate, dramatize, enhance, enlarge, exaggerate, expand, greaten, heighten, increase, inflate, intensify, lionize, overdo, overemphasize, overestimate, overplay, overrate, overstate, praise.

main[1] *adj.* absolute, brute, capital, cardinal, central, chief, critical, crucial, direct, downright, entire, essential, extensive, first, foremost, general, great, head, leading, mere, necessary, outstanding, paramount, particular, predominant, preeminent, premier, primary, prime, principal, pure, sheer, special, staple, supreme, undisguised, utmost, utter, vital.

main[2] *n.* cable, channel, conduit, duct, line, pipe.

maintain *v.* advocate, affirm, allege, argue, assert, asseverate, aver, avouch, avow, back, care for, carry on, champion, claim, conserve, contend, continue, declare, defend, fight for, finance, hold, insist, justify, keep, keep up, look after, make good, nurture, observe, perpetuate, plead for, practice, preserve, profess, prolong, provide, retain, stand by, state, supply, support, sustain, take care of, uphold, vindicate.

majestic *adj.* august, awesome, dignified, distinguished, elevated, exalted, grand, grandiose, imperial, imperious, imposing, impressive, kingly, lofty, magisterial, magnificent, monumental, noble, pompous, princely, queenly, regal, royal, splendid, stately, sublime, superb.

make *v.* accomplish, acquire, act, add up to, amount to, appoint, arrive at, assemble, assign, attain, beget, bring about, build, calculate, carry out, catch, cause, clear, coerce, compel, compose, conclude, constitute, constrain, construct, contract, contribute, convert, create, designate, do, dragoon, draw up, drive, earn, effect elect, embody, enact, engage in, engender, establish, estimate, execute, fabricate, fashion, fix, flow, force, forge, form, frame, gain, gar, generate, get, give rise to, impel, induce, install, invest, judge, lead to, manufacture, meet, mold, net, oblige, obtain, occasion, ordain, originate, pass, perform, practice, press, pressurize, prevail upon, proceed, produce, prosecute, put together, reach, reckon, render, require, secure, shape, smith(y), suppose, synthesize, take in, tend, think, turn, win.

makeup[1] *n.* cosmetics, greasepaint, paint, powder, war paint, white-face.

makeup[2] *n.* arrangement, assembly, build, cast, character, complexion, composition, configuration, constitution, construction, disposition, figure, form, format, formation, make, nature, organization, stamp, structure, style, temper, temperament.

malicious *adj.* baleful, bitchy, bitter, catty, despiteful, evil-minded, hateful, ill-natured, injurious, malevolent, malignant, mischievous, pernicious, rancorous, resentful, sham, spiteful, vengeful, venomous, vicious.

malignant *adj.* baleful, bitter, cancerous, cankered, dangerous, deadly, destructive, devilish, evil, fatal, harmful, hostile, hurtful, inimical, injurious, irremediable, malevolent, malicious, malign, pernicious, spiteful, uncontrollable, venomous, vicious, viperous, virulent.

malleable *adj.* adaptable, compliant, impressionable, manageable, plastic, pliable, tractable.

man[1] adult, attendant, beau, bloke, body, boyfriend, cat, chap, employee, fellow, follower, gentleman, guy, hand, hireling, hombre, human, human being, husband, individual, lover, male, partner, person, retainer, servant, soldier, spouse, subject, subordinate, valet, vassal, worker, workman. *v.* crew, fill, garrison, occupy, operate, people, staff, take charge of.

man[2] *n.* Homo sapiens, human race, humanity, humankind, humans, mankind, mortals, people.

manage *v.* accomplish, administer, arrange, bring about, bring off, carry on, command, concert, conduct, contrive, control, cope, cope with, deal with, direct, dominate, effect, engineer, fare, get along, get by, get on, govern, guide, handle, influence, make do, make out, manipulate, muddle through, operate, oversee, pilot, ply, preside over, rule, run, shift, solicit, stage-manage, steer, succeed, superintend, supervise, survive, train, use, wield.

manageable *adj.* amenable, biddable, compliant, controllable, convenient, docile, easy, governable, handy, submissive, tamable, tractable, wieldy.

mandatory *adj.* binding, compulsory, imperative, necessary, obligatory, required, requisite.

maneuver *n.* action, artifice, device, dodge, exercise, gambit, intrigue, move, movement, operation, plan, plot, ploy, ruse, scheme, stratagem, subterfuge, tactic, trick. *v.* contrive, deploy, devise, direct, drive, engineer, guide, handle, intrigue, jockey, machinate, manage, manipulate, move, navigate, negotiate, pilot, plan, plot, pull strings, scheme, steer, wangle.

manipulate *v.* conduct, control, cook, direct, employ, engineer, gerrymander, guide, handle, influence, juggle with, maneuver, negotiate, operate, ply, shuffle, steer, use, wield, work.

manner *n.* address, air, appearance, approach, aspect, bearing, behavior, brand, breed, category, character, comportment, conduct, custom, demeanor, deportment, description, fashion, form, genre, habit, kind, line, look, means, method, mien, mode, nature, practice, procedure, process, routine, sort, style, tack, tenor, tone, type, usage, variety, way, wise, wont.

mannerism *n.* characteristic, feature, foible, habit, idiosyncrasy, peculiarity, quirk, trick.

manufacture *v.* assemble, build, churn out compose, concoct, construct, cook up, create, devise, fabricate, forge, form, hatch, invent, make, make up, mass-produce, mold, process, produce, shape, think up, turn out. *n.* assembly, construction, creation, fabrication, formation, making, mass production, production.

many *adj.* abundant, copious, countless, divers, frequent, innumerable, manifold, multifarious, multifold, multitudinous, myriad, numerous, profuse, sundry, umpteen, varied, various, zillion.

march *v.* countermarch, file, flounce, goose-step, pace, parade, slog, stalk, stride, strut, stump, tramp, tread, walk. *n.* advance, career, demonstration, development, evolution, footslog, gait, hike, pace, parade, passage, procession, progress, progression, step, stride, tramp, trek, walk.

margin *n.* allowance, border, bound, boundary, brim, brink, compass, confine, edge, extra, latitude, leeway, limit, marge, perimeter, play, rand, rim, room, scope, side, skirt, space, surplus, verge.

marine *adj.* maritime, nautical, naval, ocean-going, oceanic, saltwater, sea, seafaring, seagoing.

mark *n.* aim, badge, blaze, blemish, blot, blotch, brand, bruise, character, characteristic, consequence, criterion, dent, device, dignity, distinction, earmark, emblem, eminence, end, evidence, fame, feature, fingermark, footmark, footprint, goal, hallmark, importance, impression, incision, index, indication, influence, label, level, line, lineament, marque, measure, nick, norm, notability, note, noteworthiness, notice, object, objective, pock, prestige, print, proof, purpose, quality, regard, scar, scratch, seal, sign, smudge, splotch, spot, stain, stamp, standard, standing, streak, symbol, symptom, target, token, trace, track, trail, vestige, yardstick. *v.* appraise, assess, attend, betoken, blemish, blot, blotch, brand, bruise, characterize, correct, denote, dent, distinguish, evaluate, evince, exemplify, grade, hearken, heed, identify, illustrate, impress, imprint, label, list, listen, mind, nick, note, notice, observe, print, regard, remark, scar, scratch, show, smudge, splotch, stain, stamp, streak, take to heart, traumatize, watch.

marriage *n.* alliance, amalgamation, association, confederation, coupling, espousal, link, match, matrimony, merger, nuptials, union, wedding, wedlock.

marry *v.* ally, bond, espouse, get hitched, get spliced, join, jump the broomstick, knit, link, match, merge, spice, tie, tie the knot, unify, unite, wed, wive, yoke.

marvelous *adj.* amazing, astonishing, astounding, beyond belief, breathtaking, excellent, extraordinary, fabulous, fantastic, glorious, great, implausible, improbable, incredible, magnificent, miraculous, phenomenal, prodigious, remarkable, sensational, singular, smashing, spectacular, splendid, stupendous, super, superb, surprising, terrific, unbelievable, unlikely, wonderful, wondrous.

masculine *adj.* bold, brave, butch, gallant, hardy, macho, male, manlike, manly, mannish, muscular, powerful, red-blooded, robust, stout-hearted, strapping, strong, tomboyish, vigorous, virile.

mass[1] *n.* accumulation, aggregate, aggregation, assemblage, band, batch, block, body, bulk, bunch, chunk, collection, combination, concretion, congeries, conglomeration, crowd, dimension, entirety, group, heap, horde, host, hunk, lion's share, load, lot, lump, magnitude, majority, mob, number, piece, pile, preponderance, quantity, size, stack, sum, sum total, throng, totality, troop, welter, whole. *adj.* across-the-board, blanket, comprehensive, extensive, general, indiscriminate, large-scale, pandemic, popular, sweeping, wholesale, widespread.

mass[2] *n.* communion, eucharist, holy communion, Lord's Supper, Lord's Table.

massacre *v.* annihilate, butcher, decimate, exterminate, kill, mow down, murder, slaughter, slay, wipe out.

master *n.* ace, adept, baas, boss, bwana, captain, chief, commander, controller, dab hand, deacon, director, doyen, employer, expert, genius, governor, guide, guru, head, Herr, instructor, lord, maestro, manager, overlord, overseer, owner, past master, pedagogue, preceptor, principal, pro, ruler, schoolmaster, skipper, superintendent, swami, teacher, tutor, virtuoso, wizard.

masterpiece *n.* chef d'oeuvre, classic, jewel, magnum opus, masterwork, museum piece, pièce de résistance, tour de force.

match[1] *n.* bout, competition, contest, game, main, test, trial, venue. *v.* compete, contend, oppose, pit against, rival, vie.

match[2] *n.* affiliation, alliance, combination, companion, complement, copy, counterpart, couple, dead ringer, double, duet, duplicate, equal, equivalent, fellow, like, look-alike, marriage, mate, pair, pairing, parallel, partnership, peer, replica, ringer, rival, spit, spitting image, tally, twin, union. *v.* accompany, accord, adapt, agree, ally, blend, combine, compare, coordinate, correspond, couple, emulate, equal, fit, gee, go together, go with, harmonize, join, link, marry, mate, measure up to, pair, relate, rival, suit, tally, team, tone with, unite, yoke.

match[3] *n.* fuse, fusee, light, lucifer, lucifer match, safety match, spill, taper, vesta, vesuvian.

material *n.* body, cloth, constituents, data, element, evidence, fabric, facts, information, literature, matter, notes, stuff, substance, textile, work.

materialize *v.* appear, arise, happen, occur, take shape, turn up.

maternal *adj.* loving, motherly, protective.

matter[1] *n.* affair, amount, argument, body, business, complication, concern, consequence, context, difficulty, distress, episode, event, import, importance, incident, issue, material, moment, note, occurrence, problem, proceeding, purport, quantity, question, sense, significance, situation, stuff, subject, substance, sum, text, thesis, thing, topic, transaction, trouble, upset, weight, worry.

matter² *n.* discharge, purulence, pus, secretion, suppuration. *v.* discharge, secrete.

mature *adj.* adult, complete, due, fit, full-blown, full-grown, fully fledged, grown, grown-up, matured, mellow, nubile, perfect, perfected, reaped, ready, ripe, ripened, seasoned, well-thought-out.

maybe *adv.* haply, happen, perchance, perhaps, possibly.

meal¹ *n.* banquet, barbecue, blow-out, breakfast, brunch, collation, déjeuner, déjeuner à la fourchette, dinner, feast, lunch, luncheon, nosh, nosh-up, petit déjeuner, picnic, repast, scoff, snack, supper, tea, tuck-in.

meal² *n.* farina, flour, grits, powder.

mean¹ *adj.* abject, base, callous, common, contemptible, despicable, disgraceful, hard-hearted, hostile, humble, inconsiderable, inferior, lowly, malicious, miserable, miserly, nasty, near, niggardly, obscure, parsimonious, penurious, petty, pusillanimous, rude, run-down, scrub, scurvy, selfish, servile, shabby, small-minded, squalid, stingy, tight, tight-fisted, vicious, vile, vulgar, wretched.

mean² *v.* adumbrate, aim, aspire, augur, betoken, cause, connote, contemplate, convey, denote, design, desire, destine, drive at, engender, entail, express, fate, fit, foreshadow, foretell, get at, give rise to, herald, hint, imply, indicate, insinuate, intend, involve, lead to, make, match, necessitate, omen, plan, portend, predestine, preordain, presage, produce, promise, propose, purport, purpose, represent, result in, say, set out, signify, spell, stand for, suggest, suit, symbolize, want, wish.

mean³ *adj.* average, half-way, intermediate, medial, median, medium, middle, middling, normal, standard.

meaning *n.* aim, connotation, construction, denotation, design, drift, end, explanation, force, gist, goal, idea, implication, import, intention, interpretation, matter, message, object, plan, point, purport, purpose, sense, significance, signification, substance, thrust, trend, upshot, validity, value, worth.

measure *n.* act, action, allotment, allowance, amount, amplitude, beat, bill, bounds, cadence, capacity, control, course, criterion, deed, degree, démarche, enactment, example, expedient, extent, foot, gauge, jigger, law, limit, limitation, magnitude, maneuver, means, method, meter, model, moderation, norm, portion, procedure, proceeding, proportion, quantity, quota, range, ration, reach, resolution, restraint, rhythm, rule, scale, scope, share, size, standard, statute, step, system, test, touchstone, verse, yardstick. *v.* admeasure, appraise, assess, calculate, calibrate, choose, compute, determine, estimate, evaluate, fathom, gauge, judge, mark out, measure off, measure out, plumb, quantify, rate, size, sound, step, survey, value, weigh.

meat¹ *n.* chow, comestibles, eats, fare, food, grub, nourishment, nutriment, provisions, rations, sustenance, viands, victuals.

meat² *n.* core, crux, essence, fundamentals, gist, heart, kernel, marrow, nub, nucleus, pith, point, substance.

mechanic *n.* artificer, engineer, machinist, operative, operator, repairman, technician.

medal *n.* award, decoration, gong, honor, medallion, prize, reward, trophy.

meddle *v.* interfere, interlope, interpose, intervene, intrude, mell, pry, put one's oar in, tamper,

mediate *v.* arbitrate, conciliate, incubate, intercede, interpose, intervene, moderate, negotiate, reconcile, referee, resolve, settle, step in, umpire.

medium¹ *adj.* average, fair, intermediate, mean, medial, median, medi-ocre, middle, middling, midway, standard. *n.* average, center, compromise, golden mean, mean, middle, middle ground, midpoint, via media, way.

medium² *n.* agency, avenue, base, channel, excipient, form, instrument, instrumentality, means, mode, organ, vehicle, way.

medium³ *n.* clairvoyant, psychic, spiritualist.

medium⁴ *n.* ambience, atmosphere, circumstances, conditions, element, environment, habitat, influences, milieu, setting, surroundings.

meet *v.* abut, adjoin, answer, assemble, bear, bump into, chance on, collect, come across, come together, comply, confront, congregate, connect, contact, convene, converge, cross, discharge, encounter, endure, equal, experience, face, find, forgather, fulfill, gather, go through, gratify, handle, happen on, intersect, join, link up, match, measure up to, muster, perform, rally, rencounter, run across, run into, satisfy, suffer, touch, undergo, unite.

melancholy *adj.* blue, dejected, depressed, despondent, disconsolate, dismal, dispirited, doleful, down, down in the dumps, down in the mouth, downcast, downhearted, gloomy, glum, heavy-hearted, hipped, joyless, low, low-spirited, lugubrious, melancholic, miserable, moody, mournful, pensive, sad, somber, sorrowful, splenific, unhappy, woebegone, woeful.

member *n.* appendage, arm, associate, component, constituent, element, extremity, fellow, initiate, leg, limb, organ, part, portion, representative.

memento *n.* keepsake, memorial, record, relic, remembrance, reminder, souvenir, token, trophy.

memory *n.* celebrity, commemoration, fame, glory, honor, memorial, name, recall, recollection, remembrance, reminiscence, renown, reputation, repute, retention.

menial *adj.* abject, attending, base, boring, degrading, demeaning, dull, fawning, groveling, helping, humble, humdrum, ignoble, ignominious, low, lowly, mean, obsequious, routine, servile, slavish, sorry, subservient, sycophantic, unskilled, vile.

mental[1] *adj.* abstract, cerebral, cognitive, conceptual, ideational, intellectual, noetic, rational, theoretical.

mental[2] *adj.* crazy, deranged, disturbed, insane, loony, lunatic, mad, psychiatric, psychotic, unbalanced, unstable.

merchandise *n.* cargo, commodities, freight, goods, produce, products, shipment, staples, stock, stock in trade, truck, vendibles, wares. *v.* carry, deal in, distribute, market, peddle, retail, sell, supply, trade, traffic in, vend.

mercy *n.* benevolence, blessing, boon, charity, clemency, compassion, favor, forbearance, forgiveness, godsend, grace, humanitarianism, kindness, lenience, pity, quarter, relief.

merit *n.* advantage, asset, claim, credit, desert, due, excellence, good, goodness, integrity, justification, quality, right, strong point, talent, value, virtue, worth, worthiness.

merry *adj.* amusing, blithe, blithesome, boon, carefree, cheerful, chirpy, comic, comical, convivial, crank, elevated, facetious, festive, frolicsome, fun-loving, funny, gay, glad, gleeful, happy, heartsome, hilarious, humorous, jocular, jocund, jolly, joyful, joyous, light-hearted, mellow, mirthful, rol-

licking, saturnalian, sportful, sportive, squiffy, tiddly, tipsy, vivacious.

messenger *n.* agent, ambassador, bearer, carrier, courier, delivery boy, emissary, envoy, errand boy, go-between, harbinger, herald, in-between, internuncio, mercury, nuncio, runner, send, vaunt-courier.

messy *adj.* chaotic, cluttered, confused, dirty, disheveled, disordered, disorganized, grubby, littered, muddled, sloppy, slovenly, unkempt, untidy, yucky.

method *n.* approach, arrangement, course, design, fashion, form, manner, mode, modus operandi, order, orderliness, organization, pattern, plan, planning, practice, procedure, process, program, purpose, regularity, routine, rule, scheme, structure, style, system, technique, way.

middle *adj.* central, halfway, inner, inside, intermediate, intervening, mean, medial, median, mediate, medium, mid, middle-bracket.

might *n.* ability, capability, capacity, clout, efficacy, efficiency, energy, force, heftiness, muscularity, potency, power, powerfulness, prowess, puissance, strength, sway, valor, vigor.

migrate *v.* drift, emigrate, journey, move, roam, rove, shift, travel, trek, voyage, wander.

migratory *adj.* gipsy, itinerant, migrant, nomadic, peripatetic, roving, shifting, transient, transitory, traveling, vagrant, wandering.

mild *adj.* amiable, balmy, bland, clam, clement, compassionate, docile, easy, easygong, equable, forgiving, gentle, indulgent, kind, lenient, meek, mellow, merciful, moderate, pacific, passive, peaceable, placid, pleasant, serene, smooth, soft, temperate, tender, tranquil, warm.

militant *adj.* active, aggressive, assertive, belligerent, combating, combative, contending, embattled, fighting, hawkish, pugnacious, vigorous, warring. *n.* activist, aggressor, belligerent, combatant, fighter, partisan, struggler, warrior.

mind[1] *n.* attention, attitude, believe, bent, brains, concentration, desire, disposition, fancy, feeling, genius, gray matter, head, imagination, inclination, inner, intellect, intellectual, intelligence, intention, judgment, leaning, marbles, memory, mentality, notion, opinion, outlook, point of view, psyche, purpose, rationality, reason, recollection, remembrance, sanity, sense, senses, sensorium, sensory, sentiment, spirit, tendency, thinker, thinking, thoughts, understanding, urge, view, will, wish, wits.

mind² v. care, demur, disapprove, dislike, object, resent, take offense.

mind³ v. adhere to, attend, attend to, be careful, be on one's guard, comply with, ensure, follow, guard, have charge of, heed, keep an eye on, listen to, look after, make certain, mark, note, notice, obey, observe, pay attention, pay heed to, regard, respect, take care, take care of, take heed, tend, watch.

mine¹ n. abundance, deposit, excavation, fund, hoard, lode, pit, source, stock, store, supply, treasury, tunnel, vein, wealth. v. delve, dig up, excavate, extract, quarry, remove, tunnel, unearth, weaken.

mine² n. bomb, depth charge, egg, explosive, land mine.

minimum n. bottom, least, lowest point, nadir, slightest.

minister n. administrator, agent, aide, ambassador, assistant, churchman, clergyman, cleric, delegate, diplomat, divine, ecclesiastic, envoy, executive, officeholder, official, parson, pastor, plenipotentiary, preacher, priest, servant, subordinate, vicar, vizier. v. accommodate, administer, attend, cater to, nurse, pander to, serve, take care of, tend.

minor adj. inconsequential, inconsiderable, inferior, insignificant, junior, lesser, light, negligible, paltry, petty, piddling, secondary, slight, small, smaller, subordinate, trifling, trivial, unclassified, unimportant, younger.

minute¹ n. flash, instant, jiff, jiffy, mo, moment, sec, second, shake, tick, trice.

minute² adj. close, critical, detailed, diminutive, exact, exhaustive, fine, inconsiderable, infinitesimal, itsy-bitsy, Lilliputian, little, meticulous, microscopic, miniature, minimum, minuscule, negligible, painstaking, paltry, petty, piddling, precise, punctilious, puny, slender, slight, small, tiny, trifling, trivial, unimportant.

misbehave v. act up, carry on, get up to mischief, kick over the traces, mess about, muck about, offend, transgress, trespass.

miscalculate v. blunder, boob, err, get wrong, misjudge, overestimate, overrate, overvalue, slip up, underestimate, underrate, undervalue.

miscellaneous adj. assorted, confused, diverse, diversified, indiscriminate, jumbled, manifold, many, mingled, mixed, mot-

ley, multifarious, multiform, promiscuous, sundry, varied, various.

mischief¹ n. bane, damage, detriment, devilment, deviltry, disruption, evil, harm, hurt, impishness, injury, misbehavior, misfortune, monkey business, naughtiness, pranks, roguery, roguishness, shenanigans, trouble, waggery, waywardness.

mischief² n. devil, imp, monkey, nuisance, pest, rapscallion, rascal, rapscallion, rogue, scallywag, scamp, tyke, villain.

miserable adj. abject, anguished, contemptible, dejected, deplorable, depressed, despondent, destitute, detestable, dismal, distressed, dolorous, down, downcast, dreary, forlorn, gloomy, glum, heartbroken, ignominious, low, luckless, lugubrious, meager, mean, melancholic, melancholy, mournful, needy, niggardly, paltry, pathetic, penniless, piteous, pitiable, pitiful, poor, sad, scanty, scurvy, shabby, shameful, sordid, sorrowful, sorrowing, sorry, squalid, starcrossed, stricken, tearful, unhappy, vile, woebegone, worthless, wretched.

misery¹ n. abjectness, adversity, affliction, agony, anguish, bale, bane, bitter pill, blow, burden, calamity, catastrophe, cross, curse, depression, desolation, despair, destitution, disaster, discomfort, distress, dole, dolor, extremity, gloom, grief, hardship, heartache, heartbreak, humiliation, indigence, living death, load, melancholia, melancholy, misfortune, need, oppression, ordeal, penury, poverty, privation, prostration, sadness, sordidness, sorrow, squalor, suffering, torment, torture, trial, tribulation, trouble, unhappiness, want, woe, wretchedness.

misery² n. grouch, Jeremiah, Job's comforter, killjoy, moaner, pessimist, prophet of doom, ray of sunshine, sourpuss, spoil-sport, Weary Willie, wet blanket, whiner.

misfortune n. accident, adversity, affliction, bad luck, blow, buffet, calamity, catastrophe, disaster, failure, grief, hardship, harm, ill-luck, infelicity, loss, misadventure, mischance, misery, mishap, reverse, setback, sorrow, tragedy, trial, tribulation, trouble, woe.

misjudge v. miscalculate, mistake, overestimate, overrate, underestimate, undervalue.

mislead v. beguile, bluff, deceive, delude, fool, give a bum steer, hoodwink, misadvise, misdirect, misguide, misinform, pull the wool over someone's eyes, snow, take for a ride, take in.

miss[1] *v.* avoid, bypass, circumvent, err, escape, evade, fail, forego, jump, lack, leave out, let go, let slip, lose, miscarry, mistake, obviate, omit, overlook, pass over, pass up, sidestep, skip, slip, trip. *n.* blunder, error, failure, fault, fiasco, flop, lack, lacuna, loss, mistake, need, omission, oversight, want.

miss[2] *v.* grieve for, lack, lament, long for, mourn, need, pine for, regret, sorrow for, want, wish, yearn for.

miss[3] *n.* child, damsel, demoiselle, flapper, Fraulein, girl, junior miss, kid, lass, lassie, mademoiselle, maid, maiden, missy, Ms., schoolgirl, spinster, teenager, young thing.

missing *adj.* absent, astray, disappeared, gone, lacking, lost, minus, mislaid, misplaced, strayed, unaccounted-for, wanting.

mistake *n.* aberration, blunder, boner, boob, boo-boo, clinker, corrigendum, erratum, error, fallacy, false move, fault, faux pas, floater, folly, gaffe, gaucherie, goof, howler, inaccuracy, indiscretion, inexactitude, lapse, lapsus, lapsus calami, lapsus linguae, lapsus memoriae, literal, malapropism, misapprehension, miscalculation, misconception, misjudgment, misprint, misprision, mispronunciation, misreading, misspelling, misunderstanding, oversight, scape, slip, slip-up, solecism, tactlessness, trespass. *v.* blunder, confound, confuse, err, get the wrong end of the stick, goof, misapprehend, miscalculate, misconceive, misconstrue, misinterpret, misjudge, misread, misreckon, misunderstand, slip up.

misunderstand *v.* get the wrong end of the stick, get wrong, misapprehend, miscomprehend, misconceive, misconstrue, mishear, misinterpret, misjudge, misread, miss the point, mistake, take up wrong(ly).

mix *v.* allay, alloy, amalgamate, associate, blend, coalesce, combine, commingle, compound, consort, cross, dash, fold in, fraternize, fuse, hobnob, homogenize, incorporate, intermingle, intermix, interweave, join, jumble, mell, merge, mingle, shuffle, socialize, synthesize, unite.

mixture *n.* admixture, alloy, amalgam, amalgamation, association, assortment, blend, brew, coalescence, combination, combine, composite, compost, compound, concoction, conglomeration, cross, fusion, gallimaufry, half-breed, hotch-potch, hybrid, miscegenation, miscellany, mix, mixed bag, mongrel, olio, olla-podrida, pastiche, potpourri, salad, salmagundi, synthesis, union, variety.

mock *v.* ape, baffle, befool, burlesque, caricature, chaff, cheat, counterfeit, debunk, deceive, defeat, defy, delude, deride, disappoint, disparage, dupe, elude, explode, fleer, flout, foil, fool, frustrate, guy, imitate, insult, jeer, lampoon, laugh at, laugh in (someone's) face, laugh to scorn, make fun of, make sport of, mimic, parody, parrot, poke fun at, queer, quiz, ridicule, satirize, scoff, scorn, send up, sneer, take the mickey, taunt, tease, thwart, travesty, twit.

moderate *adj.* abstemious, average, calm, centrist, continent, controlled, cool, deliberate, disciplined, equable, fair, fairish, frugal, gentle, indifferent, judicious, limited, mediocre, medium, middle-of-the-road, middling, mild, modest, nonextreme, ordinary, passable, peaceable, quiet, rational, reasonable, restrained, sensible, sober, softshell(ed), so-so, steady, temperate, unexceptional, well-regulated. *v.* abate, allay, alleviate, appease, assuage, blunt, calm, chasten, check, control, curb, cushion, decrease, diminish, dwindle, ease, lessen, mitigate, modify, modulate, pacify, palliate, play down, quiet, regulate, repress, restrain, slake, soften, soft-pedal, subdue, subside, tame, temper, tone down.

modern *adj.* advanced, avant-garde, contemporary, current, emancipated, fashionable, fresh, go-ahead, innovative, inventive, jazzy, late, latest, mod, modernistic, modish, new, newfangled, novel, present, present-day, progressive, recent, stylish, trendy, twentieth-century, up-to-date, up-to-the-minute, with-it.

modest *adj.* bashful, blushing, chaste, chastened, coy, demure, diffident, discreet, fair, humble, limited, maidenly, meek, middling, moderate, ordinary, proper, quiet, reserved, reticent, retiring, seemly, self-conscious, self-effacing, shame-faced, shy, simple, small, timid, unassuming, unexceptional, unpresuming, unpresumptuous, unpretending, unpretentious, verecund.

modify *v.* abate, adapt, adjust, allay, alter, temper, change, convert, improve, lessen, limit, lower, moderate, modulate, qualify, recast, redesign, redo, reduce, refashion, reform, remodel, reorganize, re-shape, restrain, restrict, revise, rework, soften, temper, tone down, transform, vary.

moist *adj.* clammy, damp, dampish, dampy, dank, dewy, dripping, drizzly, humid, marshy, muggy, rainy, soggy, swampy, tearful, vaporous, watery, wet, wettish.

mold[1] *n.* arrangement, brand, build, caliber, cast, character, configuration, construction, cut, design, die, fashion, form, format, frame, framework, ilk, kidney, kind, line, make, matrix, model, nature, pattern, quality, shape, sort, stamp, structure, style, template, type. *v.* affect, carve, cast, construct, control, create, design, direct, fashion, fit, forge, form, hew, influence, make, model, sculpt, sculpture, shape, stamp, work.

mold[2] *n.* black, black spot, blight, fungus, mildew, moldiness, must, mustiness, rust.

mold[3] *n.* clods, dirt, dust, earth, ground, humus, loam, soil.

moment[1] *n.* breathing-while, flash, hour, instant, jiff, jiffy, juncture, less than no time, minute, second, shake, split second, stage, tick, time, trice, twink, twinkling.

moment[2] *n.* concern, consequence, gravity, import, importance, note interest, seriousness, significance, substance, value, weight, weightiness, worth.

money *n.* baksheesh, banco, banknotes, bankroll, boodle, brass, bread, capital, cash, chips, coin, currency, dough, dumps, fat, filthy lucre, fonds, funds, gelt, gold, gravy, greens, hard cash, hard money, legal tender, mazuma, mint-sauce, money of account, moolah, pelf, readies, ready, money, riches, scrip, shekels, silver, specie, sugar, the needful, the ready, the wherewithal, tin, wealth.

monkey[1] *n.* ape, primate, simian.

monkey[2] *n.* dupe, fool, imp, jackanapes, laughing-stock, mug, rapscallion, rascal, rogue, scallywag, scamp. *v.* fiddle, fidget, fool, interfere, meddle, mess, play, potter, tamper, tinker, trifle.

monster *n.* abortion, barbarian, basilisk, beast, behemoth, bogeyman, brute, centaur, chimera, cockatrice, colossus, Cyclops, demon, devil, fiend, freak, giant, Gorgon, harpy, hellhound, hippocampus, leviathan, mammoth, monstrosity, mutant, ogre, ogress, prodigy, savage, villain.

monument *n.* ancient monument, antiquity, barrow, commemoration, cross, dolmen, evidence, gravestone, headstone, marker, mausoleum, memento, memorial, obelisk, pillar, record, relic, remembrance, reminder, shaft, shrine, statute, testament, token, tombstone.

mood *n.* blues, caprice, depression, disposition, doldrums, dumps, fit, frame of mind, grumps, humor, melancholy, pique, spirit, state of mind, sulk, temper, tenor, the sulks, vein, whim.

moral *adj.* blameless, chaste, clean-living, decent, equitable, ethical, good, high-minded, honest, honorable, incorruptible, innocent, just, meritorious, moralistic, noble, principled, proper, pure, responsible, right, righteous, square, straight, temperate, upright, upstanding, virtuous.

morale *n.* confidence, espirit de corps, heart, mettle, mood, resolve, self-esteem, spirit, spirits, state of mind, temper.

morality *n.* chastity, conduct, decency, deontology, equity, ethicality, ethicalness, ethics, ethos, goodness, habits, honesty, ideals, integrity, justice, manners, morals, mores, philosophy, principle, principles, probity, propriety, rationale, rectitude, righteousness, standards, tightness, uprightness, virtue.

morbid *adj.* ailing, brooding, corrupt, deadly, diseased, dreadful, ghastly, ghoulish, gloomy, grim, grisly, gruesome, hideous, horrid, hypochondriacal, infected, lugubrious, macabre, malignant, melancholy, neurotic, peccant, pessimistic, putrid, sick, sickly, somber, unhealthy, unsound, unwholesome, vicious.

more *adj.* added, additional, alternative, extra, fresh, further, increased, new, other, renewed, repeated, spare, supplementary. *adv.* again, better, further, longer.

morsel *n.* atom, bit, bite, crumb, fraction, fragment, grain, modicum, mouthful, nibble, part, piece, scrap, segment, slice, soupçon, taste, tidbit.

mortal *adj.* agonizing, awful, bodily, corporeal, deadly, deathful, dire, earthly, enormous, ephemeral, extreme, fatal, fleshly, grave, great, human, impermanent, implacable, intense, irreconcilable, lethal lethiferious, mortiferous, passing, perishable, relentless, remorseless, severe, sublunary, sworn, temporal, terrible, transient, unrelenting, worldly.

mortified *adj.* abashed, affronted, annoyed, ashamed, chagrined, chastened, confounded, crushed, dead, decayed, deflated, discomfited, displeased, embarrassed, gangrenous, humbled, humiliated, necrotic, put out, put to shame, putrefied, putrid, rotted, rotten, shamed, vexed.

motion *n.* action, change, dynamics, flow, flux, gesticulation, gesture, inclination, kinesics, kinetics, locomotion, mechanics, mobility, motility, move, movement, nod, passage, passing, progress, proposal, proposition, recommendation, sign, signal, submission, suggestion, transit, travel, wave. v. beckon, direct, gesticulate, gesture, nod, sign, signal, usher, wave.

motivate v. actuate, arouse, bring, cause, draw, drive, encourage, impel, incite, induce, inspire, inspirit, instigate, kindle, lead, move, persuade, prompt, propel, provoke, push, spur, stimulate, stir, trigger, urge.

motive n. cause, consideration, design, desire, encouragement, ground(s), impulse, incentive, incitement, inducement, influence, inspiration, intention, mainspring, motivation, object, occasion, purpose, rationale, reason, spur, stimulus, thinking, urge.

mourn v. bemoan, bewail, beweep, deplore, grieve, keen, lament, miss, regret, rue, sorrow, wail, weep.

move v. activate, actuate, adjust, advance, advise, advocate, affect, agitate, budge, carry, cause, change, cover the ground, decamp, depart, disturb, drift, drive, ease, edge, excite, flit, get, give rise to, go, go away, gravitate, impel, impress, incite, induce, influence, inspire, instigate, jiggle, lead, leave, locomote, make strides, march, migrate, motivate, move house, operate, persuade, proceed, progress, prompt, propel, propose, pull, push, put forward, quit, recommend, relocate, remove, rouse, run, set going, shift, shove, start, stimulate, stir, submit, suggest, switch, take, touch, transfer, transport, transpose, turn, urge, walk. n. act, action, deed, démarche, dodge, drift, flit, flitting, go, maneuver, measure, migration, motion, movement, ploy, relocation, removal, ruse, shift, step, stratagem, stroke, tack, tactic, transfer, turn.

movement n. act, action, activity, advance, agitation, beat, cadence, campaign, change, crusade, current, development, displacement, division, drift, drive, evolution, exercise, faction, flow, front, gesture, ground swell, group, grouping, innards, machinery, maneuver, measure, mechanism, meter, motion, move, moving, operation, organization, pace, part, party, passage, progress, progression, rhythm, section, shift, steps, stir, stirring, swing, tempo, tendency, transfer, trend, workings, works.

moving adj. affecting, ambulant, ambulatory, arousing, dynamic, emotional, emotive, exciting, impelling, impressive, inspirational, inspiring, locomobile, mobile, motile, motivating, movable, pathetic, persuasive, poignant, portable, propelling, running, stimulating, stimulative, stirring, touching, unfixed.

much adv. considerably, copiously, decidedly, exceedingly, frequently, greatly, often. adj. a lot of, abundant, ample, considerable, copious, great, plenteous, plenty of, sizable, substantial. n. heaps, lashings, loads, lots, oodles, plenty, scads.

muddle v. befuddle, bewilder, confound, confuse, daze, disarrange, disorder, disorganize, disorient(ate), fuddle, jumble, make a mess of, mess, mix up, mull, perplex, scramble, spoil, stupefy, tangle. n. balls up, chaos, clutter, cock-up, confusion, daze, disarray, disorder, disorganization, jumble, mess, mix-up, mull, perplexity, pie, plight, predicament, puddle, snarl-up, tangle.

mug[1] n. breaker, cup, flagon, jug, pot, tankard, jug.

mug[2] n. chump, fool, gull, innocent, mark, sap, saphead, simpleton, soft touch, sucker.

mug[3] n. clock, countenance, dial, face, features, mush, puss, visage.

mug[4] v. attack, bash, batter, beat up, garrote, jump (on), mill, rob, roll, set upon, steal from, waylay.

multiply v. accumulate, augment, boost, breed, build up, expand, extend, increase, intensify, proliferate, propagate, reproduce, spread.

multitude n. army, assemblage, assembly, collection, commonalty, concourse, congregation, crowd, herd, hive, hoi polloi, horde, host, legion, lot, lots, mass, mob, myriad, populace, proletariat, public, rabble, sea, swarm, throng.

mundane adj. banal, commonplace, day-to-day, earthly, everyday, fleshly, human, humdrum, material, mortal, ordinary, prosaic, routine, secular, temporal, terrestrial, workaday, worldly.

murder n. agony, assassination, bloodshed, butchery, carnage, danger, difficulty, fratricide, hell, homicide, infanticide, killing, manslaughter, massacre, misery, ordeal, parricide, patricide, slaying, trial, trouble. v. abuse, assassinate, bump off, butcher, destroy, dispatch, do in, drub, eliminate, hammer, hit, kill, mangle, mar, massacre, misuse, rub out, ruin, slaughter, slay, spoil, thrash, waste.

murderer n. assassin, butcher, cut-throat, hitman, homicide, killer, matricide, parricide, patricide, slaughterer, slayer.

muscle n. brawn, clout, depressor, force, forcefulness, levator, might, potency, power, sinew, stamina, strength, sturdiness, tendon, weight.

musical *adj.* dulcet, euphonious, harmonious, lifting, lyrical, melodic, melodious, sweet-sounding, tuneful.

mutter *v.* complain, grouch, grouse, grumble, mumble, murmur, rumble.

mutual *adj.* common, communal, complementary, exchanged, interchangeable, interchanged, joint, reciprocal, reciprocated, requited, returned, shared.

myriad *adj.* boundless, countless, immeasurable, incalculable, innumerable, limitless, multitudinous, untold. *n.* army, flood, horde, host, millions, mountain, multitude, scores, sea, swarm, thousands, throng.

mystery *n.* arcanum, conundrum, enigma, problem, puzzle, question, riddle, secrecy, secret.

myth *n.* allegory, delusion, fable, fairy tale, fancy, fantasy, fiction, figment, illusion, legend, old wives' tale, parable, saga, story, superstition, tradition.

N

nag *v.* annoy, badger, berate, chivvy, goad, harass, harry, henpeck, irritate, kvetch, pain, pester, plague, scold, torment, upbraid, vex.

naked *adj.* bare, blatant, defenseless, denuded, disrobed, divested, evident, exposed, helpless, in puris in the altogether, in the buff, insecure, manifest, mother-naked, nude, open, overt, patent, plain, simple, skyclad, stark, starkers, stark naked, stripped, unadorned, unarmed, unclothed, unconcealed, uncovered, undisguised, undraped, undressed, unexaggerated, unguarded, unmistakable, unprotected, unqualified, unvarnished, vulnerable.

name *n.* acronym, agnomen, appellation, character, cognomen, compilation, credit, denomination, designation, distinction, eminence, epithet, esteem, fame, handle, honor, moni(c)ker, nickname, note, praise, renown, reputation, repute, sobriquet, stage name, term, title, to-name. *v.* appoint, baptize, bename, betitle, call, choose, christen, cite, classify, cognominate, commission, designate, dub, entitle, identify, label, mention, nominate, select, specify, style, term, title.

nap[1] *v.* catnap, doze, drop off, drowse, kip, nod, nod off, rest, sleep, snooze. *n.* catnap, forty winks, kip, rest, shuteye, siesta, sleep.

nap[2] *n.* down, downiness, fuzz, grain, pile, shag, weave.

narcotic *n.* anesthetic, analgesic, drug, opiate, pain-killer, sedative, tranquilizer.

narrate *v.* chronicle, describe, detail, recite, recount, rehearse, relate, repeat, report, set forth, state, tell, unfold.

narrow *adj.* attenuated, avaricious, biased, bigoted, circumscribed, close, confined, constricted, contracted, cramped, dogmatic, exclusive, fine, illiberal, incapacious, intolerant, limited, meager, mean, mercenary, narrow-minded, near, niggardly, partial, pinched, prejudiced, reactionary, restricted, scanty, select, simplistic, slender, slim, small-minded, spare, straitened, tapering, thin, tight, ungenerous.

nasty *adj.* abusive, annoying, bad, bad-tempered, base, critical, dangerous, despicable, dirty, disagreeable, disgusting, distasteful, filthy, foul, gross, horrible, impure, indecent, lascivious, lewd, licentious, loathsome, low-down, malicious, malodorous, mean, mephitic, nauseating, noisome, objectionable, obnoxious, obscene, odious, offensive, painful, polluted, pornographic, repellent, repugnant, ribald, serious, severe, sickening, smutty, spiteful, unappetizing, unpleasant, unsavory, vicious, vile, waspish.

native *adj.* aboriginal, autochthonous, built-in, congenital, domestic, endemic, genuine, hereditary, home, home-born, home-bred, home-grown, home-made, inborn, inbred, indigenous, ingrained, inherent, inherited, innate, instinctive, intrinsic, inveterate, local, mother, natal, natural, original, real, vernacular. *n.* aborigine, citizen, country-man, dweller, indigent, inhabitant, national, resident.

natural *adj.* artless, candid, characteristic, common, congenital, constitutional, essential, everyday, frank, genuine, inborn, indigenous, ingenuous, inherent, innate, instinctive, intuitive, legitimate, logical natal, native, normal, open, ordinary, organic, plain, pure, real, regular, simple, spontaneous, typical, unaffected, unbleached, unforced, unlabored, unlearned, unmixed, unpolished, unpretentious, unrefined, unsophisticated, unstudied, untaught, usual, whole.

naturally *adv.* absolutely, artlessly, as a matter of course, candidly, certainly, customarily, frankly, genuinely, informally, normally, of course, plainly, simply, spontaneously, typically, unaffectedly, unpretentiously.

nature[1] *n.* attributes, category, character, complexion, constitution, cosmos, creation, description, disposition, earth, environment, essence, features, humor, inbeing, kind, mood, outlook quality, sort, species, style, temper, temperament, traits, type, universe, variety, world.

nature² *n.* country, countryside, landscape, natural history, scenery.

naval *adj.* marine, maritime, nautical, sea.

near *adj.* accessible, adjacent, adjoining, akin, allied, alongside, approaching, at close quarters, attached, beside, bordering, close, connected, contiguous, dear, familiar, forthcoming, handy, imminent, impending, in the offing, intimate, looming, near at hand, nearby, neighboring, next, nigh, on the cards, proximal, related, touching.

nearly *adv.* about, all but, almost, approaching, approximately, as good as, closely, not quite, practically, pretty much, pretty well, roughly, virtually.

necessary *adj.* certain, compulsory, de rigueur, essential, fated, imperative, indispensable, ineluctable, inescapable, inevitable, inexorable, mandatory, needed, needful, obligatory, required, requisite, unavoidable, vital.

need *v.* call for, crave, demand, lack, miss, necessitate, require, want. *n.* demand, deprivation, desideratum, destitution, distress, emergency, essential, exigency, extremity, impecuniousness, inadequacy, indigence, insufficiency, lack, longing, necessity, neediness, obligation, paucity, penury, poverty, privation, requirement, requisite, shortage, urgency, want, wish.

needed *adj.* called for, compulsory, desired, essential, lacking, necessary, obligatory, required, requisite, wanted.

needless *adj.* causeless, dispensable, excessive, expendable, gratuitous, groundless, inessential, nonessential, pointless, purposeless, redundant, superfluous, uncalled-for, unessential, unnecessary, unwanted, useless.

needy *adj.* deprived destitute, disadvantaged, impecunious, impoverished, indigent, penniless, penurious, poor, poverty-stricken, underprivileged.

neglect *v.* contemn, disdain, disprovide, disregard, forget, ignore, leave alone, let slide, omit, overlook, pass by, rebuff, scorn, shirk, skimp, slight, spurn.

negligent *adj.* careless, cursory, disregardful, forgetful, inattentive, indifferent, lax, neglectful, nonchalant, off-hand, remiss, slack, thoughtless, uncaring, unmindful, unthinking.

negotiate *v.* adjudicate, arbitrate, arrange, bargain, broker, clear, conciliate, confer, consult, contract, cross, deal, debate, discuss, get past, handle, manage, mediate, parley, pass, settle, surmount, transact, transverse, treat, work out.

neighborhood *n.* community, confines, district, environs, locale, locality, precincts, proximity, purlieus, quarter, region, surroundings, vicinage, vicinity.

nerve *n.* audacity, boldness, bottle, brass, bravery, brazenness, cheek, chutzpah, coolness, courage, daring, determination, effrontery, endurance, energy, fearlessness, firmness, force, fortitude, gall, gameness, grit, guts, hardihood, impertinence, impudence, insolence, intrepidity, mettle, might, pluck, resolution, sauce, spirit, spunk, steadfastness, temerity, vigor, will.

nervous *adj.* agitated, anxious, apprehensive, edgy, excitable, fearful, fidgety, flustered, hesitant, highly strung, high-strung, hysterical, jittery, jumpy, nervy, neurotic, on edge, shaky, tense, timid, timorous, twitchy, uneasy, uptight, weak, windy, worried.

net¹ *n.* drag, dragnet, drift, driftnet, dropnet, lattice, mesh, netting, network, openwork, reticulum, tracery, web. *v.* apprehend, bag, benet, capture, catch, enmesh, ensnare, entangle, nab, trap.

net² *adj.* after tax, clear, final, lowest. *v.* accumulate, bring in, clear, earn, gain, make, obtain, reap, receive, secure.

neurotic *adj.* abnormal, anxious, compulsive, deviant, disordered, distraught, disturbed, maladjusted, manic, morbid, nervous, obsessive, overwrought, unhealthy, unstable, wearisome.

neutral *adj.* colorless, disinterested, dispassionate, dull, evenhanded, expressionless, impartial, indeterminate, indifferent, indistinct, indistinguishable, intermediate, nonaligned, noncommittal, nondescript, nonpartisan, unbia(s)sed, uncommitted, undecided, undefined, uninvolved, unprejudiced.

new *adj.* added, advanced, altered, changed, contemporary, current, different, extra, fresh, improved, latest, modern, modernistic, modernized, modish, more, newborn, newfangled, novel, original, recent, redesigned, renewed, restored, supplementary, topical, trendy, ultramodern, unfamiliar, unknowns, unused, unusual, up-to-date, up-to-the-minute, virgin.

news *n.* account, advice, bulletin, communique, disclosure, dispatch, exposé, gen, gossip, hearsay, information, intelligence, latest, leak, release, report, revelation, rumor, scandal, statement, story, tidings, update, word.

next *adj.* adjacent, adjoining, closest, consequent, ensuing, following, later, nearest, neighboring, sequent, sequential, subsequent, succeeding.

nice *adj.* accurate, agreeable, amiable, attractive, careful, charming, commendable, courteous, critical, cultured, dainty, delicate, delightful, discriminating, exact, exacting, fastidious, fine, finical, friendly, genteel, good, kind, likable, meticulous, neat, particular, pleasant, pleasurable, polite, precise, prepossessing, purist, refined, respectable, rigorous, scrupulous, strict, subtle, tidy, trim, virtuous, well-bred, well-mannered.

niche[1] *n.* alcove, corner, cubby, cubbyhole, hollow, nook, opening, recess.

niche[2] *n.* calling, métier, pigeon-hole, place, position, slot, vocation.

nick[1] *n.* chip, cut, damage, dent, indent, indentation, mark, notch, scar, score, scratch, snick. *v.* chip, cut, damage, dent, indent, mark, notch, scar, score, scratch, snick.

nick[2] *v.* finger, knap, knock off, lag, pilfer, pinch, snitch, steal.

nil *n.* duck, goose-egg, love, naught, nihil, none, nothing, zero.

nip[1] *v.* bite, catch, check, clip, compress, grip, nibble, pinch, snag, snap, snip, squeeze, tweak, twitch.

nip[2] *n.* dram, draught, drop, finger, mouthful, peg, portion, shot, sip, slug, snifter, soupçon, sup, swallow, taste.

noise *n.* babble, ballyhoo, blare, clamor, clash, clatter, coil, commotion, cry, din, fracas, hubbub, outcry, pandemonium, racket, row, sound, talk, tumult, uproar.

noisome *adj.* bad, baneful, deleterious, disgusting, fetid, foul, fulsome, harmful, hurtful, injurious, malodorous, mephitic, mischievous, noxious, offensive, pernicious, pestiferous, pestilential, poisonous, putrid, reeking, smelly, stinking, unhealthy, unwholesome.

noisy *adj.* boisterous, cacophonous, chattering, clamorous, deafening, ear-piercing, ear-splitting, loud, obstreperous, piercing, plangent, rackety, riotous, strident, tumultuous, turbulent, uproarious, vocal, vociferous.

nonessential *adj.* dispensable, excessive, expendable, extraneous, extrinsic(al), inessential, peripheral, superfluous, unimportant, unnecessary.

nonexistent *adj.* chimerical, fancied, fictional, hallucinatory, hypothetical, illusory, imaginary, imagined, immaterial, incorporeal, insubstantial, legendary, missing, mythical, null, unreal.

nonplus *v.* astonish, astound, baffle, bewilder, confound, confuse, discomfit, disconcert, discountenance, dismay, dumbfound, embarrass, flabbergast, flummox, mystify, perplex, puzzle, stump, stun, take aback.

nonsense *n.* absurdity, balderdash, balls, baloney, bilge, blah, blather, bombast, bosh, bull, bunk, bunkum, claptrap, cobblers, crap, double-Dutch, drivel, faddle, fandangle, fatuity, fiddle-de-dee, fiddle-faddle, folly, foolishness, fudge, gaff, gas and gaiters, gibberish, gobbledygook, hogwash, hooey, inanity, jest, ludicrousness, moonshine, nomeaning, piffle, pulp, ridiculousness, rot, rubbish, senselessness, silliness, squish, stuff, stupidity, tommy-rot, trash, twaddle, twattle.

normal *adj.* accustomed, acknowledged, average, common, common-or-garden, conventional, habitual, mainstream, natural, ordinary, par for the course, popular, rational, reasonable, regular, routine, sane, standard, straight, typical, usual, well-adjusted.

note *n.* annotation, apostill(e), billet, celebrity, character, comment, communication, consequence, distinction, eminence, epistle, epistolet, fame, gloss, heed, indication, jotting, letter, line, mark, memo, memorandum, message, minute, notice, observation, prestige, record, regard, remark, reminder, renown, reputation, signal, symbol, token. *v.* denote, designate, detect, enter, indicate, mark, mention, notice, observe, perceive, record, register, remark, see, witness.

noted *adj.* acclaimed, celebrated, conspicuous, distinguished, eminent, famous, great, illustrious, notable, notorious, prominent, recognized, renowned, respected, well-known.

notice *v.* descry, detect, discern, distinguish, espy, heed, mark, mind, note, observe, perceive, remark, see, spot.

nourish *v.* attend, cherish, comfort, cultivate, encourage, feed, foster, furnish, harbor, maintain, nurse, nurture, promote, supply, support, sustain, tend.

novel *adj.* different, fresh, imaginative, innovative, new, original, rare, singular, strange, surprising, uncommon, unconventional, unfamiliar, unusual.

novice *n.* amateur, apprentice, beginner, learner, neophyte, newcomer, novitiate, probationer, proselyte, pupil.

now *adv.* at once, at present, directly, immediately, instanter, instantly, next, nowadays, presently, promptly, straightaway, these days.

nude *adj.* au natural, bare, disrobed, exposed, in one's birthday suit, in puris naturalibus, in the altogether, in the buff, naked, starkers, stark naked, stripped, unattired, unclad, unclothed, uncovered, undraped, undressed, without a stitch.

nuisance *n.* annoyance, bore, bother, drawback, inconvenience, infliction, irritation, offense, pain, pest, plague, problem, trouble, vexation.

number[1] *n.* aggregate, amount, character, collection, company, count, crowd, digit, figure, folio, horde, index, integer, many, multitude, numeral, quantity, several, sum, throng, total, unit.

number[2] *n.* copy, edition, impression, imprint, issue, printing, volume.

numeral *n.* character, cipher, digit, figure, folio, integer, number.

numerous *adj.* abundant, copious, divers, many, multitudinous, myriad, plentiful, profuse, several, sundry.

nutrition *n.* eutrophy, food, nourishment, nutriment, sustenance.

O

oasis *n.* enclave, haven, island, refuge, resting place, retreat, sanctuary, sanctum, watering hole.

oath *n.* affirmation, assurance, avowal, blasphemy, bond, curse, cuss, expletive, imprecation, malediction, pledge, plight, profanity, promise, swearword, vow, word, word of honor.

obedient *adj.* acquiescent, amenable, biddable, compliant, deferential, docile, duteous, dutiful, law-abiding, observant, passive, regardful, respectful, submissive, subservient, tractable, unquestioning, unresisting, well-trained, yielding.

obey *v.* abide by, act upon, adhere to, be ruled by, bow to, carry out, comply, conform, defer (to), discharge, embrace, execute, follow, fulfill, give in, give way, heed, implement, keep, knuckle under, mind, observe, perform, respond, serve, submit, surrender, take orders from, toe the line, yield.

object[1] *n.* aim, article, body, butt, design, end, entity, fact, focus, goal, idea, intent, intention, item, motive, objective, phenomenon, point, purpose, raison d'être, reality, reason, recipient, target, thing, victim, visible.

object[2] *v.* argue, complain, demur, dissent, expostulate, oppose, protest, rebut, refuse, repudiate, take exception.

objective *adj.* calm, detached, disinterested, dispassionate, equitable, evenhanded, fair, impartial, impersonal, judicial, just, open-minded, sensible, sober, unbiased, uncolored, unemotional, unimpassioned, uninvolved, unprejudiced.

oblige *v.* accommodate, assist, benefit, bind, coerce, compel, constrain, do a favor, favor, force, gratify, help, impel, indulge, make, necessitate, obligate, please, require, serve.

obsequious *adj.* abject, cringing, deferential, doughfaced, fawning, flattering, groveling, ingratiating, kneecrooking, menial, oily, servile, slavish, slimy, smarmy, submissive, subservient, sycophantic, toadying, unctuous.

observe *v.* abide by, adhere to, celebrate, commemorate, comment, comply, conform to, contemplate, declare, detect, discern, discover, espy, follow, fulfill, heed, honor, keep, keep an eye on, keep tabs on, mention, mind, monitor, note, notice, obey, opine, perceive, perform, regard, remark, remember, respect, say, scrutinize, see, solemnize, spot, state, study, surveille, survey, view, watch, witness.

obstruct *v.* arrest, bar, barricade, block, check, choke, clog, crab, cumber, curb, cut off, frustrate, hamper, hide, hinder, hold, up, impede, inhibit, interfere with, interrupt, mask, obscure, occlude, prevent, restrict, retard, shield, shut off, slow down, stall, stonewall, stop, stuff, thwart.

obtain[1] *v.* achieve, acquire, attain, come by, compass, earn, gain, get, procure, secure.

obtain[2] *v.* be in force, be prevalent, be-the-case, exist, hold, prevail, reign, rule, stand.

obvious *adj.* apparent, clear, conspicuous, discernible, distinct, evident, glaring, indisputable, manifest, noticeable, open, open-and-shut, overt, palpable, patent, perceptible, plain, prominent, pronounced, recognizable, self-evident, self-explanatory, straight-forward, transparent, unconcealed, undeniable, undisguised, unmistakable, unsubtle, visible.

occasion *n.* affair, call, case, cause, celebration, chance, convenience, event, excuse, experience, ground(s), incident, inducement, influence, instance, justification, moment, motive, occurrence, opening, opportunity, prompting, provocation, reason, time. *v.* bring about, bring on, cause, create, effect, elicit, engender, evoke, generate, give rise to, induce, influence, inspire, lead to, make, originate, persuade, produce, prompt, provoke.

occupy *v.* absorb, amuse, beguile, busy, capture, conquer, cover, divert, dwell in, employ, engage, engross, ensconce oneself in, entertain, establish oneself in, fill, garrison, hold, immerse, inhabit, interest, invade, involve, keep, keep busy, live in, monopolize, own, permeate, pervade, possess, preoccupy, reside in, seize, stay in, take over, take possession of, take up, tenant, tie up, use, utilize.

occur *v.* appear, arise, be found, be met with, be present, befall, betide, chance, come about, come off, come to pass, crop up, develop, eventuate, exist, happen, intervene, manifest itself, materialize, obtain, result, show itself, take place, transpire, turn up.

ocean *n.* briny, main, profound, sea, the deep, the drink.

odd¹ *adj.* abnormal, atypical, bizarre, curious, deviant, different, eccentric, exceptional, extraordinary, fantastic, freak, freakish, freaky, funky, funny, irregular, kinky, outlandish, peculiar, quaint, queer, rare, remarkable, singular, strange, uncanny, uncommon, unconventional, unexplained, unusual, weird, whimsical.

odd² *adj.* auxiliary, casual, fragmentary, ill-matched, incidental, irregular, left-over, lone, miscellaneous, occasional, periodic, random, remaining, single, solitary, spare, sundry, surplus, uneven, unmatched, unpaired, varied, various.

odor *n.* air, aroma, atmosphere, aura, bouquet, breath, emanation, essence, flavor, fragrance, perfume, quality, redolence, scent, smell, spirit, stench, stink.

off *adj.* abnormal, absent, bad, below par, canceled, decomposed, disappointing, disheartening, displeasing, finished, gone, high, inoperative, moldy, poor, postponed, quiet, rancid, rotten, slack, sour, substandard, turned, unavailable, unsatisfactory, wrong.

adv. apart, aside, at a distance, away, elsewhere, out.

offend *v.* affront, annoy, disgruntle, disgust, displease, fret, gall, hip, hurt, insult, irritate, miff, nauseate, outrage, pain, pique, provoke, repel, repulse, rile, sicken, slight, snub, transgress, turn off, upset, vex, violate, wound, wrong.

offense *n.* affront, anger, annoyance, crime, delict, delinquency, displeasure, fault, hard feelings, harm, huff, hurt, indignation, indignity, infraction, infringement, injury, injustice, insult, ire, lapse, misdeed, misdemeanor, needle, outrage, peccadillo, pique, put-down, resentment, sin, slight, snub, transgression, trespass, umbrage, violation, wrath, wrong.

offer *v.* advance, afford, bid, extend, furnish, give, hold out, make available, move, present, proffer, propose, propound, provide, put forth, put forward, show, submit, suggest, tender, volunteer. *n.* approach, attempt, bid, endeavor, essay, overture, presentation, proposal, proposition, submission, suggestion, tender.

often *adv.* again and again, frequently, generally, habitually, many a time, much, oft, over and over, regularly, repeatedly, time after time, time and again.

ogle *v.* eye, eye up, leer, look, make eyes at, stare.

old *adj.* aboriginal, aged, age-old, ancient, antediluvian, antiquated, antique, archaic, bygone, cast-off, crumbling, dated, decayed, decrepit, done, earlier, early, elderly, erstwhile, ex-, experienced, familiar, former, gray, gray-haired, grizzled, hackneyed, hardened, hoary, immemorial, long-established, long-standing, mature, obsolete, of old, of yore, olden, old-fashioned, one-time, original, out-of-date, outdated, outmoded, over the hill, passé, patriarchal, practiced, prehistoric, previous, primitive, pristine, remote, senescent, senile, skilled, stale, superannuated, time-worn, traditional, unfashionable, unoriginal, venerable, versed, veteran, vintage, worn-out.

omen *n.* augury, auspice, boding, foreboding, foretoken, indication, portent, premonition, presage, prognostic, prognostication, sign, straw in the wind, warning, writing on the wall.

omit *v.* disregard, drop, edit out, eliminate, exclude, fail, forget, give something a miss, leave out, leave undone, let slide, miss out, neglect, overlook, pass over, pretermit, skip.

omnipotent *adj.* all-powerful, almighty, plenipotent, supreme.

omniscient *adj.* all-knowing, all-seeing, pansophic.

once *adv.* at one time, formerly, heretofore, in the old days, in the past, in times gone by, in times past, long ago, once upon a time, previously.

only *adv.* at most, barely, exclusively, just, merely, purely, simply, solely. *adj.* exclusive, individual, lone, single, sole, solitary, unique.

open *adj.* above-board, accessible, ajar, apparent, available, bare, blatant, conspicuous, evident, expanded, exposed, flagrant, frank, free, gaping, honest, innocent, liberal, natural, navigable, noticeable, obvious, overt, public, receptive, sincere, unconcealed, unconditional, unobstructed, unoccupied, unsealed, vacant, visible, wide, wide-open, yawning.

opening *n.* adit, aperture, beginning, birth, breach, break, chance, chasm, chink, cleft, commencement, crack, dawn, fissure, fistula, foramen, gap, hole, inauguration, inception, initiation, interstice, kick-off, launch, launching, occasion, onset, opportunity, orifice, outset, perforation, place, rent, rupture, slot, space, split, start, vacancy, vent, vista.

operate *v.* act, function, go, handle, manage, maneuver, perform, run, serve, use, utilize, work.

opponent *n.* adversary, antagonist, challenger, competitor, contestant, disputant, dissentient, dissident, enemy, foe, objector, opposer, opposition, rival.

opportunity *n.* break, chance, convenience, hour, moment, occasion, opening, scope, shot, time, turn.

oppose *v.* bar, beard, breast, check, combat, compare, confront, contradict, contrary, contrast, contravene, controvert, counter, counter-attack, counterbalance, defy, face, fight, fly in the face of, gainsay, hinder, obstruct, pit against, play off, prevent, resist, stand up to, take a stand against, take issue with, thwart, withstand.

opposite *adj.* adverse, antagonistic, antipodal, antipodean, antithetical, conflicting, contradictory, contrary, contrasted, corresponding, different, differing, diverse, facing, fronting, hostile, inconsistent, inimical, irreconcilable, opposed, reverse, unlike.

opposition *n.* antagonism, antagonist, clash, competition, contraposition, contrariety, counteraction, counterstand, countertime, counterview, disapproval, foe, hostility, obstruction, opponent, other side, prevention, resistance, rival.

optimistic *adj.* assured, bright, bullish, buoyant, cheerful, idealistic, Panglossian, positive, sanguine, upbeat, Utopian.

option *n.* alternative, choice, election, possibility, preference, selection.

orate *v.* declaim, discourse, harangue, hold forth, pontificate, sermonize, speak, speechify, talk.

ordeal *n.* affliction, agony, anguish, nightmare, pain, persecution, suffering, test, torture, trial, tribulation(s), trouble(s).

order[1] *n.* application, arrangement, array, behest, booking, calm, categorization, chit, classification, codification, command, commission, control, cosmos, decree, dictate, direction, directive, discipline, disposal, disposition, grouping, harmony, injunction, instruction, law, line, line-up, mandate, method, neatness, ordering, orderliness, ordinance, organization, pattern, peace, placement, plan, precept, progression, propriety, quiet, regularity, regulation, request, requisition, reservation, rule, sequence, series, structure, succession, symmetry, system, tidiness, tranquility.

order[2] *n.* association, breed, brotherhood, cast, caste, class, community, company, degree, family, fraternity, genre, genus, grade, guild, hierarchy, ilk, kind, league, lodge, organization, pecking order, phylum, position, rank, sect, sisterhood, society, sort, species, status, subclass, tribe, type, union.

ordinary *adj.* average, common, common-or-garden, commonplace, established, everyday, familiar, habitual, humdrum, inferior, mediocre, modest, normal, pedestrian, plain, prosaic, routine, standard, stock, typical, unremarkable, usual, wonted, workaday.

organ *n.* agency, channel, device, element, forum, harmonium, hurdy-gurdy, implement, instrument, means, medium, member, mouthpiece, newspaper, paper, part, process, publication, structure, tool, unit, vehicle, viscus, voice.

organization *n.* arrangement, assembling, assembly, association, body, business, chemistry, combine, company, composition, concern, confederation, configuration, conformation, consortium, constitution, construction, coordination, corporation, design,

organize *v.* arrange, catalog, classify, codify, constitute, construct, coordinate, dispose, establish, form, frame, group, marshal, regiment, run, see to, set up, shape, structure, systematize, tabulate.

disposal, federation, firm, format, formation, formulation, frame-work, group, grouping, institution, league, makeup, management, method, methodology, organism, outfit, pattern, plan, planning, regulation, running, standardization, structure, structuring, syndicate, system, unity, whole.

origin *n.* ancestry, base, basis, beginning, beginnings, birth, cause, commencement, creation, dawning, derivation, descent, emergence, etymology, foundation, fountain, genesis, heritage, inauguration, inception, launch, lineage, occasion, origination, outset, parentage, paternity, pedigree, provenance, root, roots, source, spring, start, stirps, stock, well-spring.

original *adj.* aboriginal, archetypal, authentic, autochthonous, commencing, creative, earliest, early, embryonic, fertile, first, first-hand, fresh, genuine, imaginative, ingenious, initial, innovative, new, novel, opening, primal, primary, primitive, primordial, prototypical, resourceful, rudimentary, seminal, starting.

originate *v.* arise, be born, begin, come, commence, conceive, create, derive, develop, discover, emanate, emerge, establish, evolve, flow, form, formulate generate, give birth to, inaugurate, initiate, institute, introduce, invent, issue, launch, pioneer, proceed, produce, result, rise, set up, spring, start, stem.

ornament *n.* accessory, adornment, bauble, decoration, embellishment, flower, frill, garnish, gaud, honor, jewel, treasure, trimming, trinket.

other *adj.* added, additional, alternative, auxiliary, contrasting, different, differing, dissimilar, distinct, diverse, extra, fresh, further, more, new, remaining, separate, spare, supplementary, unrelated.

out¹ *adj.* abroad, absent, away, disclosed, elsewhere, evident, exposed, gone, manifest, outside, public, revealed.

out² *adj.* antiquated, banned, blacked, dated dead, disallowed, ended, excluded, exhausted, expired, extinguished, impossible, not on, old hat, old-fashioned, out of date, passé, square, taboo, unacceptable, unfashionable, used up.

outcome *n.* aftereffect, aftermath, conclusion, consequence, effect, end, end result, issue, payoff, result, sequel, upshot.

outfit¹ *n.* clothes, costume, ensemble, equipment, garb, gear, kit, rig, suit, togs, trappings,

outfit² *n.* business, clan, clique, company, corps, coterie, crew, firm, gang, group, organization, set, setout, set-up, squad, team, unit.

outlaw *n.* bandit, brigand, desperado, fugitive, highwayman, marauder, robber. *v.* ban, banish, bar, condemn, debar, exclude, excommunicate, forbid, illegalize, prohibit, proscribe, waive.

outline *n.* bare facts, configuration, contour, draft, form, frame, framework, plan, profile, résumé, rough, scenario, schema, shape, silhouette, sketch, summary, synopsis, thumbnail sketch, tracing.

outlook *n.* angle, aspect, attitude, forecast, frame of mind, future, panorama, perspective, point of view, prognosis, prospect, slant, vantage point, view, vista.

outside¹ *adj.* exterior, external, extramural, extraneous, extreme, outdoor, outer, outermost, outward, superficial, surface.

outside² *adj.* distant, faint, infinitesimal, marginal, minute, negligible, remote, slight, slim, small, unlikely.

outsmart *v.* beat, best, deceive, dupe, get the better of, outfox, outmaneuver, outperform, outthink, outwit, trick.

outstanding¹ *adj.* ace, arresting, celebrated, distinguished, eminent, excellent, exceptional, extraordinary, great, important, impressive, notable, noteworthy, prominent, remarkable, salient, signal, singular, special, striking, superior, superlative.

outstanding² *adj.* due, left, ongoing, open, over, owing, payable, pending, remaining, uncollected, undone, unpaid, unresolved, unsettled.

outwit *v.* beat, best, better, cheat, circumvent, deceive, defraud, dupe, get the better of, gull, outfox, outmaneuver, outsmart, outthink, swindle, trick.

ovation *n.* acclaim, acclamation, applause, bravos, cheering, cheers, clapping, éclat, laudation, plaudits, praises, tribute.

over¹ *adj.* accomplished, bygone, closed, completed, concluded, done with, ended, finished, forgotten, gone, in the past, past, settled up.

over² *prep.* above, exceeding, in charge of, in command of, in excess of, more than, on, on top of, superior to, upon.

overcome v. beat, best, better, conquer, crush, defeat, lick, master, overpower, overthrow, overwhelm, prevail, subjugate, surmount, triumph over, vanquish, weather, worst.

overflow v. brim over, bubble over, cover, deluge, discharge, drown, flood, inundate, pour over, shower, soak, spill, spray, submerge, surge, swamp, well over. n. flood, inundation, overabundance, spill, superfluity, surplus.

overlook v. condone, disregard, excuse, forget, forgive, ignore, neglect, omit, pardon, pass, pass over, skip, slight, wink at.

overpower v. beat, best, conquer, crush, defeat, floor, immobilize, master, overcome, overthrow, overwhelm, quell, subdue, subjugate, vanquish.

overrun v. choke, infest, inundate, invade, occupy, overflow, overwhelm, permeate, ravage, swamp, swarm over.

overseer n. boss, chief, foreman, manager, master, super, superintendent, superior, supervisor, surveyor, work-master.

overthrow v. abolish, beat, bring down, conquer, crush, defeat, destroy, dethrone, displace, level, master, oust, overcome, overpower, overturn, subjugate, subvert, topple, unseat, upset, vanquish.

own[1] adj. idiosyncratic, individual, inimitable, particular, personal, private.

own[2] v. acknowledge, admit, agree, allow, avow, concede, confess, disclose, enjoy, grant, have, hold, keep, possess, recognize, retain.

P

pace n. celerity, clip, gait, lick, measure, momentum, motion, movement, progress, quickness, rapidity, rate, speed, step, stride, tempo, time, tread, velocity, walk.

pack n. assemblage, backpack, band, bunch, bundle, collection, company, crew, crowd, gang, group, haversack, herd, knapsack, load, lot, mob, outfit, package, parcel, rucksack, set, troop, truss. v. batch, bundle, burden, charge, compact, compress, cram, crowd, fill, jam, load, package, store, stow, stuff, wedge.

package n. agreement, amalgamation, arrangement, bale, box, carton, combination, consignment, container, deal, entity, kit, pack, packet, parcel, proposal, proposition, unit, whole. v. batch, box, pack, pack up, packet, parcel, parcel up, wrap, wrap up.

pact n. agreement, alliance, arrangement, bargain, bond, cartel, compact, concord, concordat, contract, convention, covenant, deal, entente, league, protocol, treaty, understanding.

pain n. ache, affliction, aggravation, agony, anguish, annoyance, bitterness, burden, cramp, discomfort, distress, dole, dolor, drag, grief, gyp, headache, heartache, heartbreak, hurt, irritation, misery, nuisance, pang, pest, smart, soreness, spasm, suffering, tenderness, throb, throe, torment, torture, tribulation, trouble, twinge, vexation, woe, wretchedness. v. afflict, aggrieve, agonize, annoy, chagrin, cut to the quick, disappoint, disquiet, distress, exasperate, gall, grieve, harass, hurt, irritate, nettle, rile, sadden, torment, torture, vex, worry, wound, wring.

pair n. brace, combination, couple, doublet, doubleton, duo, dyad, match, span, twins, two of a kind, twosome, yoke. v. bracket, couple, join, link, marry, match, match up, mate, pair off, put together, splice, team, twin, wed, yoke.

pal n. amigo, buddy, chum, companion, comrade, confidant(e), crony, friend, gossip, mate, partner, sidekick, soul mate.

pale adj. anemic, ashen, bleached, bloodless, chalky, colorless, dim, faded, faint, pallid, pasty, poor, wan, washed-out, white.

pamper v. baby, cocker, coddle, cosset, fondle, gratify, humor, indulge, mollycoddle, mother, overindulge, pet, spoil.

panic n. agitation, alarm, consternation, dismay, fear, fright, hassle, horror, hysteria, scare, terror, tizzy, to-do.

pardon v. absolve, acquit, amnesty, condone, emancipate, exculpate, excuse, exonerate, forgive, free, let off, liberate, overlook, release, remit, reprieve, respite, vindicate. n. absolution, acquittal, allowance, amnesty, compassion, condonation, discharge, excuse, forgiveness, grace, humanity, indulgence, mercy, release, remission, reprieval, reprieve.

pare v. clip, crop, cut, cut back, decrease, diminish, dock, float, lop, peel, prune, reduce, retrench, shave, shear, skin, trim.

part n. area, behalf, bit, branch, business, capacity, cause, character, charge, clause, complement, component, concern, constituent, department, district, division, duty, element, faction, factor, fraction, fragment, function, heft, ingredient, interest, involvement, limb, lines, lot, member, module, neck of the woods, neighborhood, office, organ, particle, partwork, party, piece, place, portion, quarter, region, responsibility, role, scrap, section, sector, segment, share, side, slice, task, territory, tip of the iceberg, unit, vicinity, work. *v.* break, break up, cleave, come apart, depart, detach, disband, disconnect, disjoin, dismantle, disperse, disunite, divide, go, go away, leave, part company, quit, rend, scatter, separate, sever, split, split up, sunder, take leave, tear, withdraw.

partial[1] *adj.* fragmentary, imperfect, incomplete, inexhaustive, limited, part, uncompleted, unfinished.

partial[2] *adj.* affected, biased, colored, discriminatory, ex parte, influenced, interested, one-sided, partisan, predisposed, prejudiced, tendentious, unfair, unjust.

participant *n.* associate, contributor, co-operator, helper, member, partaker, participator, party, shareholder, worker.

partisan *n.* adherent, backer, champion, devotee, disciple, factionist, follower, guerrilla, irregular, party man, stalwart, supporter, upholder, votary. *adj.* biased, discriminatory, factional, guerrilla, interested, irregular, one-sided, partial, predisposed, prejudiced, resistant, sectarian, tendentious, underground.

passion *n.* adoration, affection, anger, animation, ardor, attachment, avidity, bug, chafe, craving, craze, desire, eagerness, emotion, enthusiasm, excitement, fancy, fascination, feeling, fervor, fire, fit, flare-up, fondness, frenzy, fury, heat, idol, indignation, infatuation, intensity, ire, itch, joy, keenness, love, lust, mania, monomania, obsession, outburst, paroxysm, rage, rapture, resentment, spirit, storm, transport, vehemence, verve, vivacity, warmth, wax, wrath, zeal, zest.

passive *adj.* acquiescent, compliant, docile, enduring, impassive, inactive, indifferent, indolent, inert, lifeless, long-suffering, non-participating, nonviolent, patient, quiescent, receptive, resigned, submissive, supine, unaffected, unassertive, uninvolved, unresisting.

patrol *n.* defense, garrison, guard, guarding, policing, protecting, sentinel, surveillance, watch, watching, watchman. *v.* cruise, go the rounds, guard, inspect, perambulate, police, range, tour.

pause *v.* break, cease, cut, delay, desist, discontinue, halt, hesitate, interrupt, rest, take a break, take a breather, take five, wait, waver. *n.* abatement, break, breather, caesura, ces-sation, delay, discontinuance, gap, halt, hesitation, interlude, intermission, interruption, interval, letup, lull, respite, rest, slackening, stay, stoppage, suspension, wait.

pay *v.* ante, benefit, bestow, bring in, clear, compensate, cough up, disburse, discharge, extend, foot, get even with, give, grant, honor, indemnify, liquidate, meet, offer, pay out, present, produce, proffer, profit, punish, reciprocate, reimburse, remit, remunerate, render, repay, requite, return, reward, serve, settle, square, square up, yield. *n.* allowance, compensation, consideration, earnings, fee, hire, honorarium, income, payment, recompense, reimbursement, remuneration, reward, salary, stipend, takings, wages.

peak *n.* acme, apex, apogee, brow, climax, crest, crown, culmination, cuspid, high point, maximum, ne plus ultra, pinnacle, point, summit, tip, top, visor, zenith.

peculiar[1] *adj.* abnormal, bizarre, curious, eccentric, exceptional, extraordinary, far-out, freakish, funky, funny, odd, offbeat, outlandish, out-of-the-way, quaint, queer, singular, strange, uncommon, unconventional, unusual, way-out, weird.

peculiar[2] *adj.* appropriate, characteristic, discriminative, distinct, distinctive, distinguishing, endemic, idiosyncratic, individual, local, particular, personal, private, quintessential, restricted, special, specific, unique.

peek *v.* glance, look, peep, peer, spy. *n.* blink, gander, glance, glimpse, look, looksee, peep.

pen *n.* cage, coop, crib, enclosure, fold, hutch, stall, sty. *v.* cage, confine, coop, corral, crib, enclose, fence, hedge, hem in, hurdle, mew (up), shut up.

perceive *v.* appreciate, apprehend, be aware of, behold, catch, comprehend, conclude, deduce, descry, discern, discover, distinguish, espy, feel, gather, get, grasp, intuit, know, learn, make out, note, observe, realize, recognize, remark, see, sense, spot, understand.

perfect *adj.* absolute, accomplished, accurate, adept, complete, completed, consummate, copybook, correct, entire, exact, excellent, expert, faithful, faultless, finished, flawless, full, ideal, immaculate, impeccable, irreproachable, masterly, model, polished, practiced, precise, pure, right, sheer, skilled, skillful, spotless, spot-on, strict, sublime, superb, superlative, unadulterated, unalloyed, unblemished, unmarred, unmitigated, untarnished, utter, whole.

perfection *n.* accomplishment, achievement, acme, completeness, completion, consummation, crown, evolution, exactness, excellence, exquisiteness, flawlessness, fulfillment, ideal, integrity, maturity, nonpareil, paragon, perfectness, pinnacle, precision, purity, realization, sublimity, superiority, wholeness.

perform *v.* accomplish, achieve, act, appear as, bring about, bring off, carry out, complete, depict, discharge, do, effect, enact, execute, fulfill, function, functionate, manage, observe, play, present, produce, pull off, put on, render, represent, satisfy, stage, transact, work.

perhaps *adv.* conceivably, feasibly, happen, maybe, mayhap, peradventure, perchance, possibly, you never know.

peril *n.* danger, exposure, hazard, imperilment, insecurity, jeopardy, menace, pitfall, risk, threat, uncertainty, vulnerability.

period *n.* age, course, cycle, date, days, end, eon, epoch, era, generation, interval, season, space, span, spell, stage, stint, stop, stretch, term, time, turn, while, years.

perish *v.* collapse, croak, crumble, decay, decline, decompose, decrease, die, disappear, disintegrate, end, expire, fall, molder, pass away, rot, vanish, waste, wither.

permit *v.* admit, agree, allow, authorize, consent, empower, enable, endorse, endure, give leave, grant, let, warrant.

perpetrate *v.* carry out, commit, do, effect, enact, execute, inflict, perform, practice, wreak.

perpetual *adj.* abiding, ceaseless, constant, continual, continuous, endless, enduring, eternal, everlasting, immortal, incessant, infinite, interminable, lasting, never-ending, never-failing, perennial, permanent, persistent, recurrent, repeated, unceasing, unchanging, undying, unending, unfailing, unflagging, uninterrupted, unremitting, unvarying.

perplex *v.* baffle, befuddle, beset, bewilder, complicate, confound, confuse, dumbfound, encumber, entangle, gravel, hobble, involve, jumble, mix up, muddle, mystify, nonplus, pother, pudder, puzzle, stump, tangle, thicken, throw.

persist *v.* abide, carry on, continue, endure, insist, keep at it, last, linger, perdure, persevere, remain, stand fast, stand firm.

person *n.* being, body, character, customer, human, human being, individual, living soul, party, soul, specimen.

persuade *v.* actuate, advise, allure, bring round, cajole, coax, convert, convince, counsel, entice, impel, incite, induce, influence, inveigle, lead on, lean on, prevail upon, prompt, satisfy, sway, sweet-talk, talk into, urge, win over.

pertain *v.* appertain, apply, be appropriate, be part of, be relevant, bear on, befit, belong, come under, concern, refer, regard, relate.

pervade *v.* affect, charge, diffuse, extend, fill, imbue, infuse, osmose, overspread, penetrate, percolate, permeate, saturate, suffuse.

perverse *adj.* abnormal, balky, cantankerous, churlish, contradictory, contrary, contumacious, crabbed, cross, cross-grained, cussed, delinquent, depraved, deviant, disobedient, dogged, fractious, forward, headstrong, ill-natured, ill-tempered, improper, incorrect, intractable, intransigent, miscreant, mulish, obdurate, obstinate, peevish, petulant, pigheaded, rebellious, recalcitrant, refractory, spiteful, stubborn, surly, thwart, troublesome, unhealthy, unmanageable, unreasonable, unyielding, uppity, wayward, wilful, wrong-headed, wry.

pest *n.* annoyance, bane, blight, bore, bother, bug, canker, curse, irritation, nuisance, pain (in the neck), scourge, thorn in one's flesh, trial, vexation.

phantom *n.* apparition, chimera, eidolon, figment (of the imagination), ghost, hallucination, illusion, manes, phantasm(a), shade, simulacrum, specter, spirit, spook, vision, wraith.

phony *adj.* affected, assumed, bogus, counterfeit, fake, false, forged, imitation, pseudo, put-on, quack, quack-salving, sham, spurious, trick.

pick *v.* break into, break open, choose, collect, crack, cull, cut, decide on, elect, embrace, espouse, fix upon, foment, gather, harvest, incite, instigate, opt for, pluck, prize, provoke, pull, screen, select, settle on, sift out, single out, start.

pile[1] *n.* accumulation, assemblage, assortment, bomb, building, cock, collection, edifice, erection, fortune, heap, hoard, mass, mint, money, mound, mountain, mow, packet, pot, stack, stockpile, structure, wealth. *v.* accumulate, amass, assemble, build up, charge, climb, collect, crowd, crush, flock, flood, gather, heap, hoard, jam, load up, mass, pack, rush, stack, store, stream.

pile² *n.* bar, beam, column, foundation, pier, piling, pill, post, rib, stanchion, support, upright.

pile³ *n.* down, fur, fuzz, fuzziness, hair, nap, plush, shag.

plain *adj.* apparent, artless, austere, bare, basic, blunt, candid, clear, clinical, common, commonplace, comprehensible, direct, discreet, distinct, downright, even, everyday, evident, flat, forthright, frank, frugal, guileless, homebred, homely, homespun, honest, ill-favored, level, lowly, lucid, manifest, modest, muted, obvious, open, ordinary, outspoken, patent, penny-plain, plane, pure, restrained, self-colored, severe, simple, sincere, smooth, spartan, stark, straightforward, transparent, ugly, unadorned, unaffected, unambiguous, unattractive, unbeautiful, understandable, undistinguished, unelaborate, unembellished, unfigured, unhandsome, unlovely, unmistakable, unobstructed, unornamented, unpatterned, unprepossessing, unpretentious, untrimmed, unvarnished, visible, whole-colored, workaday.

plan *n.* blueprint, design, diagram, illustration, plot, proposal, scenario, scheme, sketch, strategy, suggestion, system. *v.* arrange, conspire, contrive, draft, formulate, frame, invent, outline, plot, represent, scheme.

play *v.* act, bet, caper, challenge, chance, compete, contend, execute, fiddle, fidget, flirt, fool around, frisk, frolic, gamble, gambol, hazard, impersonate, interfere, lilt, participate, perform, personate, portray, punt, represent, revel, risk, rival, romp, speculate, sport, string along, take, take on, take part, take the part of, trifle, vie with, wager.

plead *v.* adduce, allege, appeal, argue, ask, assert, beg, beseech, crave, entreat, implore, importune, maintain, moot, petition, put forward, request, solicit, supplicate.

pleasant *adj.* acceptable, affable, agreeable, amiable, amusing, charming, cheerful, cheery, congenial, cool, delectable, delightful, delightsome, engaging, enjoyable, fine, friendly, genial, good-humored, gratifying, likable, lovely, nice, pleasing, pleasurable, refreshing, satisfying, sunshiny, toothsome, welcome, winsome.

please *v.* amuse, captivate, charm, cheer, choose, content, delight, desire, enchant, entertain, gladden, go for, gratify, humor, indulge, like, opt, prefer, rejoice, satisfy, see fit, suit, think fit, tickle, tickle pink, want, will, wish.

plot *n.* action, cabal, conspiracy, covin, design, intrigue, machination(s), narrative, outline, plan, scenario, scheme, story, story line, stratagem, subject, theme, thread. *v.* brew, cabal, calculate, chart, collude, compass, compute, conceive, concoct, conspire, contrive, cook up, design, devise, draft, draw, frame, hatch, imagine, intrigue, lay, locate, machinate, maneuver, map, mark, outline, plan, project, scheme.

plump *adj.* beefy, burly, buxom, chopping, chubby, corpulent, dumpy, embonpoint, endomorphic, fat, fleshy, full, matronly, obese, podgy, portly, roly-poly, rotund, round, stout, tubby, well-upholstered.

plunder *v.* depredate, despoil, devastate, loot, pillage, raid, ransack, ravage, rifle, rob, sack, spoil, steal, strip. *n.* booty, despoilment, ill-gotten gains, loot, pickings, pillage, prey, prize, rapine, spoils, swag.

point *n.* aim, aspect, attribute, burden, characteristic, circumstance, condition, core, crux, degree, design, detail, dot, drift, end, essence, extent, fact, feature, full stop, gist, goal, import, instance, instant, intent, intention, item, juncture, location, mark, marrow, matter, meaning, moment, motive, nicety, nub, object, objective, particular, peculiarity, period, pith, place, position, property, proposition, purpose, quality, question, reason, respect, score, side, site, speck, spot, stage, station, stop, subject, tally, text, theme, thrust, time, trait, unit, use, usefulness, utility. *v.* aim, denote, designate, direct, draw attention to, hint, indicate, level, show, signal, signify, suggest, train.

pointless *adj.* absurd, aimless, bootless, fruitless, futile, inane, ineffectual, irrelevant, meaningless, nonsensical, profitless, senseless, silly, stupid, unavailing, unbeneficial, unproductive, unprofitable, useless, vague, vain, worthless.

poise *n.* aplomb, assurance, calmness, collectedness, composure, cool, coolness, dignity, elegance, equanimity, equilibrium, grace, presence, presence of mind, sangfroid, savoir faire, self-possession, serenity. *v.* balance, float, hang, hold, hover, position, support, suspend.

polish *v.* brighten, brush up, buff, burnish, clean, correct, cultivate, emend, emery, enhance, file, finish, furbish, improve, luster, perfect, refine, rub, rub up, shine, shine up, slick, slicken, smooth, touch up, wax.

pollute *v.* adulterate, befoul, besmirch, canker, contaminate, corrupt, debase, debauch, defile, deprave, desecrate, dirty, dishonor, foul, infect, mar, poison, profane, soil, spoil, stain, sully, taint, violate, vitiate.

ponder *v.* analyze, brood, cerebrate, cogitate, contemplate, consider, deliberate, examine, excogitate, give thought to, incubate, meditate, mull over, muse, puzzle over, ratiocinate, reason, reflect, ruminate over, study, think, weigh.

pool¹ *n.* dub, lake, lasher, leisure pool, mere, pond, puddle, splash, stank, swimming bath, swimming pool, tarn, water hole, watering hole.

pool² *n.* accumulation, bank, cartel, collective, combine, consortium, funds, group, jackpot, kitty, pot, purse, reserve, ring, stakes, syndicate, team, trust. *v.* amalgamate, chip in, combine, contribute, merge, muck, put together, share.

poor¹ *adj.* badly off, bankrupt, beggared, beggarly, broke, deficient, destitute, distressed, embarrassed, exiguous, hard up, impecunious, impoverished, in reduced circumstances, inadequate, indigent, lacking, meager, miserable, moneyless, necessitous, needy, niggardly, on one's beam-ends, on one's uppers, on the rocks, pauperized, penniless, penurious, pinched, pitiable, poverty-stricken, reduced, scanty, skimpy, skint, slight, sparse, stony-broke, straitened, without means, without the wherewithal.

poor² *adj.* bad, bare, barren, below par, depleted, exhausted, faulty, feeble, fruitless, grotty, humble, imperfect, impoverished, inferior, infertile, insignificant, je-june, low-grade, lowly, mean, mediocre, modest, paltry, pathetic, pitiful, plain, ropy, rotten, rubbishy, second-rate, shabby, shoddy, sorry, spiritless, sterile, substandard, third-rate, trivial, unfruitful, unimpressive, unproductive, unsatisfactory, valueless, weak, worthless.

poor³ *adj.* accursed, cursed, forlorn, hapless, ill-fated, luckless, miserable, pathetic, pitiable, star-crossed, unfortunate, unhappy, unlucky, wretched.

popular *adj.* accepted, approved, celebrated, common, conventional, current, democratic, famous, fashionable, favored, favorite, fêted, general, household, idolized, in, in demand, in favor, liked, lionized, modish, overpopular, overused, prevailing, prevalent, public, sought-after, standard, stock, trite, ubiquitous, universal, vernacular, voguish, vulgar, well-liked, widespread.

portable *adj.* carriageable, compact, convenient, handy, light, lightweight, manageable, movable, transportable.

portray *v.* act, capture, characterize, delineate, depict, describe, draw, emblazon, encapsulate, evoke, figure, illustrate, impersonate, limn, paint, personate, personify, picture, play, present, render, represent, sketch, suggest.

position *n.* angle, area, arrangement, attitude, bearings, belief, berth, billet, capacity, character, circumstances, condition, deployment, disposition, duty, employment, function, grade, importance, job, level, locale, locality, location, niche, occupation, office, opinion, outlook, pass, perspective, pinch, place, placement, placing, plight, point, point of view, pose, positioning, post, posture, predicament, prestige, rank, reference, reputation, role, set, setting, site, situation, slant, slot, spot, stance, stand, standing, standpoint, state, station, stature, status, view, viewpoint, whereabouts. *v.* arrange, array, deploy, dispose, fix, lay out, locate, place, pose, put, range, set, settle, stand, stick.

positive *adj.* absolute, actual, affirmative, arrant, assertive, assured, authoritative, beneficial, categorical, certain, clear, clear-cut, cocksure, complete, conclusive, concrete, confident, constructive, consummate, convinced, decided, decisive, definite, direct, dogmatic, downright, effective, efficacious, emphatic, explicit, express, firm, forceful, forward-looking, helpful, hopeful, incontestable, incontrovertible, indisputable, irrefragable, irrefutable, open-and-shut, opinionated, optimistic, out-and-out, peremptory, perfect, practical, productive, progressive, promising, rank, real, realistic, resolute, secure, self-evident, sheer, stubborn, sure, thorough, thoroughgoing, uncompromising, undeniable, unequivocal, unmistakable, useful, utter.

possess *v.* acquire, be endowed with, control, dominate, enjoy, have, hold, obtain, occupy, own, possess oneself of, seize, take, take over, take possession of.

postpone *v.* adjourn, defer, delay, freeze, hold over, pigeonhole, prorogue, put back, put off, put on ice, shelve, suspend, table, waive.

potency *n.* authority, capacity, cogency, control, effectiveness, efficaciousness, efficacy, energy, force, headiness, influence, kick, might, muscle, persuasiveness, potential, power, puissance, punch, strength, sway, vigor.

pound[1] v. bang, bash, baste, batter, beat, belabor, bray, bruise, clobber, clomp, clump, comminute, crush, drum, hammer, march, palpitate, pelt, powder, pulsate, pulse, pulverize, pummel, smash, stomp, strike, strum, thrash, throb, thrum, thud, thump, thunder, tramp, triturate.

pound[2] n. compound, corral, enclosure, fold, pen, yard.

power n. ability, ascendancy, authority, authorization, brawn, capability, capacity, clout, clutches, command, competence, competency, control, dominance, domination, dominion, efficience, energy, faculty, force, forcefulness, heavy metal, hegemony, imperium, influence, intensity, juice, license, mastery, might, muscle, omnipotence, plenipotence, potency, potential, prerogative, privilege, right, rule, sovereignty, strength, supremacy, sway, teeth, vigor, virtue, vis, voltage, warrant, weight.

practical adj. accomplished, active, applicative, applied, businesslike, common sense, commonsensical, down-to-earth, efficient, empirical, everyday, expedient, experienced, experimental, factual, feasible, functional, hardheaded, hard-nosed, material, matter-of-fact, mundane, nuts-and-bolts, ordinary, practicable, pragmatic, proficient, qualified, realistic, seasoned, sensible, serviceable, skilled, sound, trained, unsentimental, useful, utilitarian, workable, workaday, working.

practice[1] n. action, application, business, career, clientele, convention, custom, discipline, frill, dry run, dummy run, effect, exercise, experience, habit, ism, method, mode, modus operandi, operation, patronage, performance, policy, practic, practicalities, practicum, praxis, preparation, procedure, profession, rehearsal, repetition, routine, rule, run-through, study, system, tradition, training, usage, use, vocation, way, wont, work, workout.

practice[2] v. apply, carry out, discipline, do, drill, enact, engage in, execute, exercise, follow, implement, live up to, observe, perfect, perform, ply, prepare, pursue, put into practice, rehearse, repeat, run through, study, train, undertake, warm up.

pragmatic adj. businesslike, efficient, factual, hard-headed, opportunistic, practi-

cal, realistic, sensible, unidealistic, unsentimental, utilitarian.

praise n. acclaim, acclamation, accolade, acknowledgment, adoration, adulation, applause, approbation, approval, bouquet, cheering, comment, commendation, compliment, compliments, congratulation, devotion, encomium, eulogy, extolment, flattery, glory, homage, honor, kudos, laud, laudation, ovation, panegyric, plaudit, puff, rave, recognition, salvos, testimonial, thanks, thanksgiving, tribute, worship.

precise adj. absolute, accurate, actual, authentic, blow-by-blow, buckram, careful, ceremonious, clear-cut, correct, definite, delimitative, determinate, distinct, exact, explicit, express, expressis verbis, factual, faithful, fastidious, finical, finicky, fixed, formal, identical, literal, meticulous, minute, nice, particular, prim, punctilious, puritanical, rigid, scrupulous, specific, strict, succinct, unequivocal verbatim, word for word.

predilection n. affection, affinity, bent, bias, enthusiasm, fancy, fondness, inclination, leaning, liking, love, partiality, penchant, predisposition, preference, proclivity, proneness, propensity, soft spot, taste, tendency, weakness.

preeminent adj. chief, consummate, distinguished, excellent, exceptional, facile princeps, foremost, incomparable, inimitable, leading, matchless, nonpareil, outstanding, paramount, passing, peerless, predominant, prominent, renowned, superior, superlative, supreme, surpassing, transcendent, unequaled, unmatched, unrivaled, unsurpassed.

prefer[1] v. adopt, advocate, back, be partial to, choose, desire, elect, endorse, fancy, favor, go for, incline toward, like better, opt for, pick, plump for, recommend, select, single out, support, want, wish, would rather, would sooner.

prefer[2] v. bring, file, lodge, place, present, press.

prefer[3] v. advance, aggrandize, dignify, elevate, exalt, promote, raise, upgrade.

prejudice[1] n. bias, bigotry, chauvinism, discrimination, injustice, intolerance, narrow-mindedness, partiality, partisanship, preconception, prejudgment, racism, sexism, unfairness, viewiness, warp.

prejudice[2] n. damage, detriment, disadvantage, harm, hurt, impairment, injury, loss, mischief, ruin, vitiation, wreck.

premature adj. abortive, early, embryonic, forward, green, half-formed, hasty, ill-considered, ill-timed, immature, imperfect, impulsive, incomplete, inopportune, over-hasty, precipitate, precocious, preterm, previous, rash, raw, undeveloped, unfledged, unripe, unseasonable, untimely.

prepare v. accouter, adapt, adjust, anticipate, arrange, assemble, brace, brief, coach, compose, concoct, construct, contrive, develop, devise, dispose, do one's homework, draft, draw up, dress, equip, fashion, fettle, fit, fit out, fix up, forearm, form, fortify, furnish, get up, gird, groom, instruct, limber up, make, make ready, outfit, plan, practice, predispose, prime, produce, provide, psych up, ready, rehearse, rig out, steel, strengthen, supply, train, trim, warm up.

prescribe v. appoint, assign, command, decree, define, dictate, direct, enjoin, fix, impose, lay down, limit, ordain, require, rule, set, set bounds to, specify, stipulate.

present[1] adj. at hand, attending, available, contemporary, current, existent, extant, here, immediate, instant, near, ready, there, to hand.

present[2] v. acquaint with, adduce, advance, award, bestow, confer, declare, demonstrate, display, donate, entrust, exhibit, expound, extend, furnish, give, grant, hand over, hold out, introduce, mount, offer, pose, produce, proffer, put on, raise, recount, relate, show, stage, state, submit, suggest, tender.

presume v. assume, bank on, believe, conjecture, count on, dare, depend on, go so far, have the audacity, hypothesize, infer, make bold, make so bold, posit, postulate, presuppose, rely on, suppose, surmise, take for granted, take it, take the liberty, think, trust, undertake, venture.

pretend v. act, affect, allege, aspire, assume, claim, counterfeit, dissemble, dissimulate, fake, falsify, feign, go through the motions, imagine, impersonate, make believe, pass oneself off, profess, purport, put on, sham, simulate, suppose.

prey n. booty, dupe, fall guy, game, kill, mark, mug, plunder, quarry, target, victim.

primary adj. aboriginal, basic, beginning, best, capital, cardinal, chief, dominant, earliest, elemental, elementary, essential, first, first-formed, first-made, fundamental, greatest, highest, initial, introductory, leading, main, original, paramount, primal, prime, primeval, primitive, primordial, principal, pristine, radical, rudimentary, simple, top, ultimate, underlying.

principal[1] adj. capital, cardinal, chief, controlling, dominant, essential, first, foremost, highest, key, leading, main, paramount, pre-eminent, primary, prime, strongest, truncal.

principal[2] n. assets, capital, capital funds, money.

principle n. assumption, attitude, axiom, belief, canon, code, conscience, credo, criterion, dictum, doctrine, dogma, duty, element, ethic, formula, fundamental, golden rule, honor, institute, integrity, law, maxim, moral, morality, morals, opinion, precept, principium, probity, proposition, rectitude, rule, scruples, standard, tenet, truth, uprightness, verity.

private adj. clandestine, closet, concealed, confidential, exclusive, home-felt, hush-hush, in camera, independent, individual, inside, intimate, intraparietal, inward, isolated, off the record, own, particular, personal, privy, reserved, retired, secluded, secret, separate, sequestrated, solitary, special, unofficial, withdrawn.

prize[1] n. accolade, aim, ambition, award, conquest, desire, gain, goal, haul, honor, hope, jackpot, premium, purse, reward, stake(s), trophy, windfall, winnings. adj. award-winning, best, champion, excellent, first-rate, outstanding, top, top-notch, winning.

prize[2] n. booty, capture, loot, pickings, pillage, plunder, spoils, trophy.

problem n. brainteaser, complication, conundrum, difficulty, dilemma, disagreement, dispute, doubt, enigma, no laughing matter, poster, predicament, puzzle, quandary, question, riddle, trouble, vexata quaestio, vexed question. adj. delinquent, difficult, intractable, perverse, refractory, uncontrollable, unmanageable, unruly.

procedure n. action, conduct, course, custom, form, formula, method, modus operandi, move, operation, performance, plan of action, policy, practice, process, routing, scheme, step, strategy, system, transaction.

proceed v. advance, arise, carry on, come, continue, derive, emanate, ensue, flow, follow, go ahead, issue, originate, progress, result, set in motion, spring, start, stem.

procrastinate v. adjourn, dally, defer, delay, dillydally, drag one's feet, gain time, play for time, postpone, prolong, protract, put off, retard, stall, temporize.

procreate v. beget, breed, conceive, engender, father, generate, mother, produce, propagate, reproduce, sire, spawn.

procure v. acquire, appropriate, bag, buy, come by, earn, effect, find, gain, get, induce, lay hands on, obtain, pander, pick up, pimp, purchase, secure, win.

prod v. dig, drive, egg on, elbow, goad, impel, incite, jab, motivate, move, nudge, poke, prick, prompt, propel, push, rouse, shove, sup, stimulate, urge. n. boost, cue, dig, elbow, jab, nudge, poke, prompt, push, reminder, shove, signal, stimulus.

product n. artefact, commodity, concoction, consequence, creation, effect, fruit, goods, invention, issue, legacy, merchandise, offshoot, offspring, outcome, output, produce, production, result, returns, spin-off, upshot, work, yield.

profess v. acknowledge, admit, affirm, allege, announce, assert, asseverate, aver, avow, certify, claim, confess, confirm, declare, enunciate, fake, feign, maintain, make out, own, pretend, proclaim, propose, propound, purport, sham, state, vouch.

profit n. a fast buck, advancement, advantage, avail, benefit, boot, bottom line, earnings, emoluments, fruit, gain, gelt, good, graft, gravy, grist, interest, melon, percentage, proceeds, receipts, return, revenue, surplus, takings, use, value, velvet, winnings, yield.

progress n. advance, advancement, amelioration, betterment, breakthrough, circuit, continuation, course, development, gain, growth, headway, improvement, increase, journey, movement, passage, procession, progression, promotion, step forward, way.

prohibit v. ban, bar, constrain, debar, disallow, forbid, hamper, hinder, impede, interdict, obstruct, outlaw, preclude, prevent, proscribe, restrict, rule out, stop, veto.

project n. activity, assignment, conception, design, enterprise, idea, job, occupation, plan, program, proposal, purpose, scheme, task, undertaking, venture, work. v. beetle, bulge, calculate, cast, contemplate, contrive, design, devise, discharge, draft, estimate, exert, extend, extrapolate, extrude, fling, forecast, frame, gauge, hurl, jut, launch, map out, outline, overhand, plan, predetermine, predict, propel, prophesy, propose, protrude, purpose, reckon, scheme, shoot, stand out, stick out, throw, transmit.

prolific adj. abounding, abundant, bountiful, copious, fecund, fertile, fertilizing, fruitful, generative, luxuriant, productive, profuse, rank, reproductive, rich, teeming, voluminous.

promise v. assure, augur, bespeak, betoken, bid fair, contract, denote, engage, guarantee, hint at, indicate, look like, pledge, plight, predict, presage, prophesy, stipulate, suggest, swear, take an oath, undertake, vouch, vow, warrant. n. ability, aptitude, assurance, bond, capability, capacity, commitment, compact, covenant, engagement, flair, guarantee, oath, pledge, pollicitation, potential, talent, undertaking, vow, word, word of honor.

promote v. advance, advertise, advocate, aggrandize, aid, assist, back, blazon, boost, champion, contribute to, develop, dignify, elevate, encourage, endorse, espouse, exalt, forward, foster, further, help, honor, hype, kick upstairs, nurture, plug, popularize, prefer, publicize, puff, push, raise, recommend, sell, sponsor, stimulate, support, trumpet, upgrade, urge.

prompt[1] adj. alert, brisk, eager, early, efficient, expeditious, immediate, instant, instantaneous, on time, punctual, quick, rapid, ready, responsive, smart, speedy, swift, timely, timeous, unhesitating, willing.

prompt[2] v. advise, assist, call forth, cause, cue, elicit, evoke, give rise to, impel, incite, induce, inspire, instigate, motivate, move, occasion, prod, produce, provoke, remind, result in, spur, stimulate, urge.

prone[1] adj. apt, bent, disposed, given, inclined, liable, likely, predisposed, subject, susceptible, tending, vulnerable.

prone[2] adj. facedown, flat, full-length, horizontal, procumbent, prostrate, recumbent, stretched.

pronounce v. accent, affirm, announce, articulate, assert, breathe, declaim, declare, decree, deliver, enunciate, judge, proclaim, say, sound, speak, stress, utter, vocalize, voice.

proper adj. accepted, accurate, appropriate, apt, becoming, befitting, characteristic, conventional, correct, decent, decorous, established, exact, fit, fitting, formal, genteel, gentlemanly, individual, kosher, ladylike, legitimate, mannerly, meet, orthodox, own, particular, peculiar, polite, precise, prim, prissy, refined, respectable, respective, right, sedate, seemly, special, specific, suitable, suited, well-becoming, well-beseeming.

property[1] n. acres, assets, belongings, building(s), capital, chattels, effects, estate, freehold, goods, holding, holdings, house(s), land, means, meum et tuum, possessions, real estate, realty, resources, riches, title, wealth.

property² *n.* ability, affection, attribute, characteristic, feature, hallmark, idiosyncrasy, peculiarity, quality, trait, virtue.

prophecy *n.* augury, divination, forecast, foretelling, prediction, prognosis, prognostication, revelation, second sight, soothsaying, vaticination.

prophesy *v.* augur, divine, forecast, foresee, foretell, forewarn, predict, presage, prognosticate, soothsay, vaticinate.

proposal *n.* bid, design, draft, manifesto, motion, offer, outline, overture, plan, platform, presentation, proffer, program, project, proposition, recommendation, scheme, sketch, suggestion, suit, tender, terms.

propose *v.* advance, aim, bring up, design, enunciate, have in mind, intend, introduce, invite, lay before, mean, move, name, nominate, pay suit, plan, pop the question, present, proffer, propound, purpose, put forward, put up, recommend, scheme, submit, suggest, table, tender.

prospect *n.* calculation, chance, contemplation, expectation, future, hope, landscape, likelihood, odds, opening, outlook, panorama, perspective, plan, possibility, presumption, probability, promise, proposition, scene, sight, spectacle, thought, view, vision, vista.

prosper *v.* advance, bloom, boom, burgeon, fare well, flourish, flower, get on, grow rich, make good, progress, succeed, thrive, turn out well.

protest *n.* complaint, declaration, demur, demurral, disapproval, dissent, formal complaint, objection, obtestation, outcry, protestation, remonstrance.

proud *adj.* appreciative, arrogant, august, boastful, conceited, content, contented, disdainful, distinguished, egotistical, eminent, exalted, glad, glorious, grand, gratified, gratifying, great, haughty, high and mighty, honored, illustrious, imperious, imposing, lofty, lordly, magnificent, majestic, memorable, noble, overbearing, pleased, pleasing, presumptuous, prideful, red-letter, rewarding, satisfied, satisfying, self-important, self-respecting, snobbish, snobby, snooty, splendid, stately, stuck-up, supercilious, toffee-nosed, vain.

prove *v.* analyze, ascertain, assay, attest, authenticate, bear out, check, confirm, corroborate, demonstrate, determine, document, establish, evidence, evince, examine, experience, experiment, justify, show, substantiate, suffer, test, try, turn out, verify.

provide *v.* accommodate, add, afford, anticipate, arrange for, bring, cater, contribute, determine, equip, forearm, furnish, give, impart, lay down, lend, outfit, plan for, prepare, present, produce, provision, render, require, serve, specify, state, stock up, suit, supply, take measures, take precautions, yield.

prowl *v.* creep, cruise, hunt, lurk, nose, patrol, range, roam, rove, scavenge, search, skulk, slink, sneak, stalk, steal.

prudent *adj.* canny, careful, cautious, circumspect, discerning, discreet, economical, farsighted, frugal, judicious, politic, provident, sagacious, sage, sensible, shrewd, sparing, thrift, vigilant, wary, well-advised, wise, wise-hearted.

pry *v.* delve, dig, ferret, interfere, intrude, meddle, nose, peep, peer, poke, poke one's nose in, snoop.

psyche *n.* anima, awareness, consciousness, individuality, intellect, intelligence, mind, personality, pneuma, self, soul, spirit, subconscious, understanding.

public *adj.* accessible, acknowledged, circulating, civic, civil, common, communal, community, exposed, general, important, known, national, notorious, obvious, open, overt, patent, plain, popular, prominent, published, recognized, respected, social, state, universal, unrestricted, well-known, widespread.

pull *v.* attract, cull, dislocate, drag, draw, draw out, entice, extract, gather, haul, jerk, lure, magnetize, pick, pluck, remove, rend, rip, schlep, sprain, strain, stretch, take out, tear, tow, track, trail, tug, tweak, uproot, weed, whang, wrench, yank.

punish *v.* abuse, amerce, batter, beat, castigate, chasten, chastise, correct, crucify, discipline, flog, give a lesson to, give someone harm, hurt, injure, keelhaul, kneecap, lash, maltreat, manhandle, masthead, misuse, oppress, penalize, rough up, scour, scourge, sort, strafe, trounce.

pure *adj.* absolute, abstract, academic, antiseptic, authentic, blameless, chaste, clean, clear, disinfected, flawless, genuine, germ-free, guileless, high-minded, honest, hygienic, immaculate, innocent, maidenly, modest, natural, neat, pasteurized, perfect, philosophical, real, refined, sanitary, Saturnian, sheer, simple, sincere, snow-white, speculative, spirituous, spotless, stainless, sterile, sterilized, straight, taintless, theoretical, thorough, true, unadulterate, unadulterated, unalloyed, unblemished, uncontaminated, uncorrupted, unmixed, unpolluted, unqualified, unsoiled, unspoiled, unspotted, unstained, unsullied, untainted, untarnished, upright, utter, virgin, virginal, virtuous, wholesome.

purpose *n.* advantage, aim, ambition, aspiration, assiduity, avail, benefit, constancy, contemplation, decision, dedication, design, determination, devotion, drive, effect, end, firmness, function, gain, goal, good, hope, idea, ideal, intention, motive, object, objective, outcome, persistence, pertinacity, plan, point, principle, rationale, reason, resolution, resolve, result, return, scheme, service, single-mindedness, steadfastness, target, tenacity, use, usefulness, utility, view, vision, will, wish, zeal. *v.* aim, aspire, contemplate, decide, design, desire, determine, intend, mean, meditate, plan, propose, resolve.

pursue *v.* accompany, adhere to, aim at, aim for, aspire to, attend, bedevil, beset, besiege, carry on, chase, check out, conduct, continue, course, court, cultivate, desire, dog, engage, in, follow, follow up, go for, gun for, harass, harry, haunt, hold to, hound, hunt, inquire into, investigate, keep on, maintain, perform, persecute, persevere in, plague, ply, practice, proceed, prosecute, purpose, seek, set one's cap at, shadow, stalk, strive for, tackle, tail, track, trail, try for, wage, woo.

push *v.* advance, bully, coerce, drive, egg on, encourage, force, incite, inveigle, maneuver, persuade, prod, shove, urge.

puzzle¹ *v.* baffle, bamboozle, beat, bewilder, confound, confuse, fickle, floor, flummox, mystify, nonplus, perplex, pother, stump, worry. *n.* acrostic, anagram, brainteaser, confusion, conundrum, cross-word, difficulty, dilemma, enigma, knot, koan, maze, mind-bender, mystery, paradox, poser, problem, quandary, question, rebus, riddle, Sphinx, tickler.

puzzle² *v.* brood, cogitate, consider, deliberate, figure, meditate, mull over, muse, ponder, rack one's brains, ratiocinate, reason, rum-inate, study, think, wonder, worry.

Q

quack *n.* charlatan, cowboy, empiric, fake, fraud, humbug, impostor, masquerader, mountebank, phony, pretender, pseud, quacksalver, sham, spieler, swindler, trickster, witch doctor. *adj.* bogus, counterfeit, fake, false, fraudulent, phony, pretended, sham, so-called, spurious, supposed, unqualified.

quagmire *n.* bog, everglade, fen, marsh, mire, morass, moss, mudflat, quag, quicksand, slough, swamp.

quake *v.* convulse, heave, jolt, move, pulsate, quail, quiver, rock, shake, shiver, shudder, sway, throb, totter, tremble, vibrate, waver, wobble.

quantity *n.* aggregate, allotment, amount, breadth, bulk, capacity, content, dosage, expanse, extent, greatness, length, lot, magnitude, mass, measure, number, part, portion, proportion, quantum, quota, share, size, spread, strength, sum, total, volume, weight.

quarrel *n.* affray, altercation, argument, beef, bicker, clash, conflict, controversy, debate, discord, dispute, dissension, feud, fight, fray, row, scrap, spat, squabble, tiff, wrangle.

quarry *n.* game, goal, kill, object, objective, prey, prize, target, victim.

quarter¹ *n.* area, direction, district, division, locality, location, neighborhood, part, place, point, position, province, quartier, region, section, sector, side, spot, station, territory, vicinity, zone.

quarter² *n.* clemency, compassion, favor, forgiveness, grace, indulgence, leniency, mercy, pardon, pity.

quarter³ *n.* fourth, quartern, term. *v.* decussate, divide in four, quadrisect.

quarter⁴ *v.* accommodate, bed, billet, board, house, install, lodge, place, post, put up, shelter, station.

queer *adj.* aberrant, abnormal, absurd, anomalous, atypical, bizarre, cranky, crazy, curious, daft, demented, deranged, deviant, disquieting, dizzy, doubtful, droll, dubious, eccentric, eerie, erratic, exceptional, extraordinary, faint, fanciful, fantastic, fey, fishy, freakish, funny, giddy, grotesque, homosexual, idiosyncratic, ill, irrational, irregular, light-headed, mad, mysterious, odd, offbeat, outlandish, outré, peculiar, preternatural, puzzling, quaint, queasy, questionable, reeling, remarkable, rum, screwy, shady, shifty, singular, strange, suspect, suspicious, touched, unaccountable, unbalanced, uncanny, uncommon, unconventional, uneasy, unhinged, unnatural, unorthodox, unusual, unwell, unwonted, weird.

quench *v.* allay, appease, check, cool, crush, damp down, destroy, douse, end, extinguish, overcome, put out, quash, quell, sate, satisfy, silence, slake, smother, snuff out, stifle, suppress.

query *v.* ask, be skeptical of, call in question, challenge, disbelieve, dispute, distrust, doubt, enquire, misdoubt, mistrust, quarrel with, question, suspect.

question *v.* ask, be skeptical of, catechize, challenge, controvert, cross-examine, debrief, dispute, distrust, doubt, enquire, examine, grill, impugn, interpellate, interrogate, interview, investigate, misdoubt, mistrust, oppose, probe, pump, quarrel with, query, quiz, suspect. *n.* argument, confusion, contention, controversy, debate, dispute, doubt, dubiety, examination, inquiry, interrogation, investigation, misgiving, motion, point, problem, proposal, proposition, quaere, query, quibble, skepsis, subject, theme, topic, uncertainty.

quick *adj.* able, active, acute, adept, adroit, agile, alert, animated, apt, astute, awake, brief, bright, brisk, clever, cursory, deft, dexterous, discerning, energetic, expeditious, express, fast, fleet, flying, hasty, hurried, immediate, instant, instantaneous, intelligent, keen, lively, nifty, nimble, penetrating, perceptive, perfunctory, prompt, quick-witted, rapid, ready, receptive, responsive, sharp, shrewd, skillful, smart, snappy, speedy, spirited, sprightly, spry, sudden, summary, swift, unhesitating, vivacious, wide-awake, winged.

quiet *adj.* calm, composed, conservative, contemplative, contented, docile, dumb, even-tempered, gentle, hushed, inaudible, isolated, lonely, low, low-pitched, meek, mild, modest, motionless, noiseless, pacific, passive, peaceable, peaceful, placid, plain, private, removed, reserved, restful, restrained, retired, retiring, secluded, secret, sedate, self-contained, sequestered, serene, shy, silent, simple, smooth, sober, soft, soundless, still, subdued, taciturn, thoughtful, tranquil, uncommunicative, undisturbed, uneventful, unexcitable, unexciting, unin- terrupted, unobtrusive, untroubled.

quit *v.* abandon, abdicate, apostatize, cease, conclude, decamp, depart, desert, disappear, discontinue, drop, end, exit, forsake, give up, go, halt, leave, relinquish, renege, renounce, repudiate, resign, retire, stop, surrender, suspend, vamoose, vanish, withdraw.

quite *adv.* absolutely, comparatively, completely, entirely, exactly, fairly, fully, moderately, perfectly, precisely, rather, relatively, somewhat, totally, utterly, wholly.

quota *n.* allocation, allowance, assignment, cut, part, percentage, portion, proportion, quotum, ration, share, slice, whack.

quotation[1] *n.* citation, crib, cutting, excerpt, extract, gobbet, locus classicus, passage, piece, quote, reference, remnant.

quote *v.* adduce, attest, cite, detail, echo, instance, name, parrot, recall, recite, recollect, refer to, repeat, reproduce, retell.

R

race[1] *n.* chase, competition, contention, contest, dash, derby, footrace, marathon, pursuit, quest, rat race, regatta, rivalry, scramble, sprint. *v.* career, compete, contest, dart, dash, fly, gallop, hare, hasten, hurry, run, rush, speed, sprint, tear, zoom.

race[2] *n.* ancestry, blood, breed, clan, descent, family, folk, house, issue, kin, kindred, line, lineage, nation, offspring, people, progeny, seed, stirps, stock, strain, tribe, type.

rage *n.* agitation, anger, bate, chafe, conniption, craze, enthusiasm, fad, fashion, frenzy, fury, ire, madness, mania, obsession, paddy, passion, style, vehemence, violence, vogue, wrath. *v.* chafe, explode, fret, fulminate, fume, inveigh, ramp, rampage, rant, rave, seethe, storm, surge, thunder.

raid *n.* attack, break-in, bust, descent, foray, incursion, inroad, invasion, irruption, onset, onslaught, sally, seizure, sortie, strike, swoop. *v.* attack, bust, descend on, do, forage, foray, invade, loot, maraud, pillage, plunder, ransack, rifle, rush, sack.

rail *v.* abuse, arraign, attack, castigate, censure, criticize, decry, denounce, fulminate, inveigh, jeer, mock, revile, ridicule, scoff, upbraid, vituperate, vociferate.

rain *n.* cloudburst, deluge, downpour, drizzle, fall, flood, hail, mizzle, precipitation, raindrops, rainfall, rains, shower, spate, squall, stream, torrent, volley. *v.* bestow, bucket, deluge, deposit, drizzle, drop, expend, fall, heap, lavish, mizzle, pour, shower, spit, sprinkle, teem.

raise *v.* abandon, activate, advance, aggrandize, aggravate, amplify, arouse, assemble, augment, awaken, boost, breed, broach, build, cause, collect, construct, create, cultivate, develop, discontinue, elate, elevate, emboss, embourgeoise, end, engender, enhance, enlarge, erect, escalate, evoke, exaggerate, exalt, excite, foment, form, foster, father, gentrify, get, grow, heave, heighten, hoist, incite, increase, inflate, instigate, intensify, introduce, kindle, levy, lift, loft, magnify, mass, mobilize, moot, motivate, muster, nurture, obtain, occasion, originate, pose, prefer, produce, promote, propagate, provoke, rally, rear, recruit, reinforce, relinquish, remove, sky, start, strengthen, sublime, suggest, terminate, up, upgrade, uplift.

rampage *v.* rage, rant, rave, run amok, run riot, run wild, rush, storm, tear. *n.* destruction, frenzy, furor, fury, rage, storm, tempest, tumult, uproar, violence.

rancid *adj.* bad, fetid, foul, fusty, musty, off, putrid, rank, rotten, sour, stale, strong-smelling, tainted.

rancor *n.* acrimony, animosity, animus, antipathy, bitterness, enmity, grudge, hate, hatred, hostility, ill-feeling, ill-will, malevolence, malice, malignity, resentfulness, resentment, spite, spleen, venom, vindictiveness.

random *adj.* accidental, adventitious, aimless, arbitrary, casual, chance, desultory, fortuitous, haphazard, incidental, indiscriminate, purposeless, scattershot, spot, stray, unfocused, unplanned, unpremeditated.

rant *v.* bellow, bluster, cry, declaim, mouth it, rave, roar, shout, slang-whang, spout, vociferate, yell. *n.* bluster, bombast, declamation, diatribe, fanfaronade, harangue, philippic, rhetoric, storm, tirade, vociferation.

rapid *adj.* brisk, expeditious, express, fast, fleet, flying, hasty, headlong, hurried, precipitate, prompt, quick, speedy, swift.

rare *adj.* admirable, choice, curious, excellent, exceptional, exquisite, extreme, few, fine, great, incomparable, infrequent, invaluable, peerless, precious, priceless, recherche, rich, scarce, singular, sparse, sporadic, strange, superb, superlative, uncommon, unusual.

rash[1] *adj.* adventurous, audacious, brash, careless, foolhardy, harebrained, harumscarum, hasty, headlong, headstrong, heedless, helter-skelter, hotheaded, ill-advised, ill-considered, impetuous, imprudent, impulsive, incautious, indiscreet, injudicious, incipient, madcap, precipitant, precipitate, premature, reckless, slapdash, thoughtless, unguarded, unthinking, unwary, venturesome.

rash[2] *n.* epidemic, eruption, exanthem(a), flood, hives, nettlerash, outbreak, plague, pompholyx, series, spate, succession, wave.

ration *n.* allocation, allotment, allowance, amount, dole, helping, measure, part, provision, quota, share. *v.* allocate, allot, apportion, budget, conserve, control, deal, dispense, distribute, dole, issue, limit, mete, restrict, save, supply.

rational *adj.* balanced, cerebral, cognitive, compos mentis, enlightened, intelligent, judicious, logical, lucid, normal, ratiocinative, realistic, reasonable, reasoning, sagacious, sane, sensible, sound, thinking, well-founded, well-grounded, wise.

ravishing *adj.* alluring, beautiful, bewitching, charming, dazzling, delightful, enchanting, entrancing, gorgeous, lovely, radiant, seductive, stunning.

raw *adj.* abraded, bare, basic, biting, bitter, bleak, bloody, blunt, brutal, callow, candid, chafed, chill, chilly, coarse, cold, crude, damp, frank, freezing, fresh, grazed, green, harsh, ignorant, immature, inexperienced, naked, natural, new, open, organic, piercing, plain, realistic, rough, scraped, scratched, sensitive, skinned, sore, tender, unadorned, uncooked, undisciplined, undisguised, undressed, unfinished, unpleasant, unpracticed, unprepared, unprocessed, unrefined, unripe, unseasoned, unskilled, untrained, untreated, untried, unvarnished, verdant, wet.

raze *v.* bulldoze, delete, demolish, destroy, dismantle, efface, erase, expunge, extinguish, extirpate, flatten, level, obliterate, remove, ruin.

react *v.* acknowledge, act, answer, behave, emote, function, operate, proceed, reply, respond, work.

real *adj.* absolute, actual, authentic, bona fide, certain, dinkum, dinky-di(e), essential, existent, factual, genuine, heartfelt, honest, intrinsic, legitimate, positive, right, rightful, simon-pure, sincere, substantial, substantive, sure-enough, tangible, true, unaffected, unfeigned, valid, veritable.

rear[1] *n.* back, backside, bottom, buttocks, croup, end, hindquarters, posterior, rearguard, rump, stern, tail.

rear[2] *v.* breed, build, construct, cultivate, educate, elevate, erect, fabricate, foster, grow, hoist, lift, loom, nurse, nurture, parent, raise, rise, soar, tower, train.

reasonable *adj.* acceptable, advisable, arguable, average, believable, credible, equitable, fair, fit, honest, inexpensive, intelligent, judicious, just, justifiable, logical, moderate, modest, OK, passable, plausible, possible, practical, proper, rational, reasoned, right, sane, satisfactory, sensible, sober, sound, tenable, tolerable, viable, well-advised, well thought-out, wise.

rebel *v.* defy, disobey, dissent, flinch, kick, over the traces, mutiny, recoil, resist, revolt, rise up, run riot, shrink. *n.* apostate, dissenter, heretic, insurgent, insurrectionary, Jacobin, malcontent, mutineer, nonconformist, revolutionary, revolutionist, schismatic, secessionist. *adj.* insubordinate, insurgent, insurrectionary, malcontent(ed), mutinous, rebellious, revolutionary.

recede *v.* abate, decline, decrease, diminish, dwindle, ebb, fade, lessen, regress, retire, retreat, retrogress, return, shrink, sink, slacken, subside, wane, withdraw.

receive *v.* accept, accommodate, acquire, admit, apprehend, bear, collect, derive, encounter, entertain, experience, gather, get, greet, hear, meet, obtain, perceive, pick up, react to, respond to, suffer, sustain, take, undergo, welcome.

recession *n.* decline, depression, downturn, slump, stagflation.

recite *v.* articulate, declaim, deliver, describe, detail, enumerate, itemize, narrate, orate, perform, recapitulate, recount, rehearse, relate, repeat, speak, tell.

reckless *adj.* careless, daredevil, devil-may-care, foolhardy, harebrained, hasty, headlong, heedless, ill-advised, imprudent, inattentive, incautious, indiscreet, irresponsible, madcap, mindless, negligent, precipitate, rash, regardless, tearaway, thoughtless, wild.

recognize *v.* accept, acknowledge, admit, allow, appreciate, approve, avow, concede, confess, grant, greet, honor, identify, know, notice, own, perceive, place, realize, recall, recollect, remember, respect, salute, see, spot, understand.

recover *v.* convalesce, heal, improve, mend, pick up, pull through, rally, recapture, reclaim, recoup, recuperate, redeem, regain, repair, replevy, repossess, restore, retake, retrieve, revive.

recreation *n.* amusement, distraction, diversion, enjoyment, entertainment, exercise, fun, games, hobby, leisure activity, pastime, play, pleasure, refreshment, relaxation, relief, sport.

recur *v.* persist, reappear, repeat, return.

reduce *v.* abate, abridge, bankrupt, break, cheapen, conquer, contract, curtail, cut, debase, decimate, decrease, degrade, demote, deoxidate, deoxidize, depress, diet, dilute, diminish, discount, downgrade, drive, force, humble, humiliate, impair, impoverish, lessen, lower, master, moderate, overpower, pauperize, rebate, ruin, scant, shorten, slake, slash, slenderize, slim, subdue, trim, truncate, vanquish, weaken.

reek *v.* exhale, fume, hum, pong, smell, smoke, stink.

refine *v.* chasten, civilize, clarify, cultivate, distill, elevate, exalt, filter, hone, improve, perfect, polish, process, purify, rarefy, spiritualize, sublimate, subtilize, temper.

refrain[1] *v.* abstain, avoid, cease, desist, eschew, forbear, leave off, quit, renounce, stop, swear off.

refrain[2] *n.* burden, chorus, epistrophe, melody, song, tune, undersong, wheel.

refresh *v.* brace, cheer, cool, energize, enliven, freshen, inspirit, jog, prod, prompt, reanimate, reinvigorate, rejuvenate, renew, renovate, repair, replenish, restore, revitalize, revive, revivify, stimulate.

regard *v.* account, adjudge, attend, behold, believe, concern, consider, deem, esteem, estimate, eye, heed, hold, imagine, interest, judge, mark, mind, note, notice, observe, pertain to, rate, relate to, remark, respect, scrutinize, see, suppose, think, treat, value, view, watch.

regret *v.* bemoan, bewail, deplore, grieve, lament, miss, mourn, repent, rue, sorrow. *n.* bitterness, compunction, contrition, disappointment, grief, lamentation, penitence, remorse, repentance, ruefulness, self-reproach, shame, sorrow.

regulate *v.* adjust, administer, arrange, balance, conduct, control, direct, fit, govern, guide, handle, manage, moderate, modulate, monitor, order, organize, oversee, regiment, rule, run, settle, square, superintend, supervise, systematize, tune.

reimburse *v.* compensate, indemnify, recompense, refund, remunerate, repay, requite, restore, return, square up.

reject *v.* condemn, decline, deny, despise, disallow, discard, eliminate, exclude, explode, jettison, jilt, pip, rebuff, refuse, renounce, repel, reprobate, repudiate, repulse, scrap, spike, spurn, veto.

rejoice *v.* celebrate, delight, exult, glory, joy, jubilate, revel, triumph.

relative *adj.* allied, applicable, apposite, appropriate, appurtenant, apropos, associated, comparative, connected, contingent, correlative, corresponding, dependent, germane, interrelated, pertinent, proportionate, reciprocal, related, relevant, respective. *n.* cognate, connection, german, kinsman, kinswoman, relation, sib.

relatively *adv.* comparatively, fairly, quite, rather, somewhat.

relax *v.* abate, diminish, disinhibit, ease, ebb, lessen, loosen, lower, mitigate, moderate, reduce, relieve, remit, rest, slacken, soften, tranquilize, unbend, unclench, unwind, weaken.

relent *v.* acquiesce, capitulate, drop, ease, fall, forbear, give in, melt, relax, slacken, slow, soften, unbend, weaken, yield.

reluctant *adj.* averse, backward, disinclined, grudging, hesitant, indisposed, loath, loathful, loth, recalcitrant, slow, squeamish, unenthusiastic, unwilling.

rely *v.* bank, bet, count, depend, lean, reckon, swear by, trust.

remain *v.* abide, bide, cling, continue, delay, dwell, endure, last, linger, persist, prevail, rest, sojourn, stand, stay, survive, tarry, wait.

remark *v.* animadvert, comment, declare, espy, heed, mark, mention, note, notice, observe, perceive, reflect, regard, say, see, state. *n.* acknowledgment, assertion, attention, comment, consideration, declaration, heed, mention, notice, observation, opinion, recognition, reflection, regard, say, statement, thought, utterance, word.

remarkable *adj.* amazing, conspicuous, distinguished, exceptional, extraordinary, famous, impressive, miraculous, notable, noteworthy, odd, outstanding, phenomenal, preeminent, prominent, rare, signal, singular, strange, striking, surprising, unco, uncommon, unusual, wonderful.

remember *v.* commemorate, place, recall, recognize, recollect, reminisce, retain, summon up, think back.

remit *v.* abate, alleviate, cancel, decrease, defer, delay, desist, desist from, diminish, dispatch, dwindle, forbear, forward, halt, mail, mitigate, moderate, post, postpone, put back, reduce, relax, repeal, rescind, send, send back, shelve, sink, slacken, stop, suspend, transfer, transmit, wane, weaken. *n.* authorization, brief, guidelines, instructions, orders, responsibility, scope, terms of reference.

renew *v.* continue, extend, mend, modernize, overhaul, prolong, reaffirm, recommence, recreate, reestablish, refashion, refit, refresh, refurbish, regenerate, rejuvenate, remodel, renovate, reopen, repair, repeat, replace, replenish, restate, restock, restore, resume, revitalize, transform.

renounce *v.* abandon, abdicate, abjure, abnegate, decline, deny, discard, disclaim, disown, yank, eschew, forgo, forsake, forswear,

put away, quit, recant, reject, relinquish, repudiate, resign, spurn.

repeal *v.* abolish, annul, cancel, invalidate, nullify, rescind, revoke, set aside, void, withdraw.

repeat *v.* duplicate, echo, iterate, quote, rebroadcast, recapitulate, recite, redo, rehearse, reiterate, relate, renew, replay, reproduce, rerun, reshow, restate, retell. *n.* duplicate, echo, rebroadcast, recapitulation, reiteration, repetition, replay, reproduction, rerun, reshowing.

repel *v.* check, confront, decline, disadvantage, disgust, fight, hold off, nauseate, offend, oppose, parry, rebuff, refuse, reject, repulse, resist, revolt, sicken, ward off.

repent *n.* atone, bewail, deplore, lament, regret, relent, rue, sorrow.

reply *v.* acknowledge, answer, reciprocate, respond, retort, return, riposte.

report *n.* account, announcement, article, bang, blast, boom, bruit, character, communication, communique, crack, crash, declaration, description, detail, detonation, discharge, dispatch, esteem, explosion, fame, gossip, information, message, narrative, news, noise, note, paper, piece, record, regard, relation, reputation, repute, reverberation, rumor, sound, statement, story, summary, tale, talk, version, word, write-up. *v.* air, announce, appear, arrive, broadcast, bruit, circulate, come, communicate, cover, declare, describe, detail, document, mention, narrate, note, notify, proclaim, publish, recite, record, recount, relate, relay, state, tell.

represent *v.* act, appear as, be, betoken, delineate, denote, depict, describe, designate, embody, enact, epitomize, equal, evoke, exemplify, exhibit, express, illustrate, mean, outline, perform, personify, picture, portray, produce, render, reproduce, show, sketch, stage, symbolize, typify.

reprimand *n.* admonition, blame, castigation, censure, dressing-down, lecture, rebuke, reprehension, reproach, reprove, scold, slate, tongue-lash, upbraid.

request *v.* ask, ask for, beg, beseech, demand, desire, entreat, importune, petition, pray, requisition, seek, solicit, supplicate. *n.* appeal, application, asking, begging, call, demand, desire, entreaty, impetration, petition, prayer, representation, requisition, solicitation, suit, supplication.

require *v.* ask, beg, beseech, bid, command, compel, constrain, crave, demand, desire, direct, enjoin, exact, force, instruct, involve, lack, make, miss, necessitate, need, oblige, order, request, take, want, wish.

requirement n. demand, desideratum, essential, lack, must, necessity, need, precondition, prerequisite, provision, proviso, qualification, requisite, sine qua non, specification, stipulation, term, want.

rescue v. deliver, extricate, free, liberate, ransom, recover, redeem, release, salvage, save.

reside v. abide, consist, dwell, exist, inhabit, inhere, lie, live, lodge, remain, settle, sit, sojourn, stay.

resign v. abandon, abdicate, cede, forgo, forsake, leave, quit, relinquish, renounce, sacrifice, stand down, surrender, vacate, waive, yield.

resilience n. adaptability, bounce, buoyancy, elasticity, flexibility, give, hardiness, plasticity, pliability, recoil, spring, springiness, strength, suppleness, toughness, unshockability.

resist v. avoid, battle, check, combat, confront, counteract, curb, defy, dispute, fight back, forbear, forgo, hinder, oppose, refuse, repel, thwart, weather, withstand.

respect n. admiration, appreciation, approbation, aspect, bearing, characteristic, connection, consideration, deference, detail, esteem, estimation, facet, feature, homage, honor, matter, particular, point, recognition, reference, regard, relation, reverence, sense, veneration, way.

response n. acknowledgment, answer, comeback, counterblast, feedback, reaction, rejoinder, reply, respond, retort, return, riposte.

rest[1] n. base, break, breather, breathing space, breathing time, breathing while, calm, cessation, cradle, doze, halt, haven, holiday, idleness, inactivity, interlude, intermission, interval, leisure, lie-down, lie-in, lodging, lull, motionlessness, nap, pause, prop, refreshment, refuge, relaxation, relieve, repose, retreat, shelf, shelter, shut-eye, siesta, sleep, slumber, snooze, somnolence, spell, stand, standstill, stillness, stop, support, tranquillity, trestle, vacation.

rest[2] n. balance, core, excess, leftovers, majority, others, remainder, remains, remnants, residue, residuum, rump, surplus.

restrict v. bound, circumscribe, confine, constrain, contain, impede, inhibit, limit, regulate, restrain, restringe.

retard v. arrest, brake, check, clog, decelerate, defer, delay, detain, encumber, handi-cap, hinder, impede, keep back, obstruct, slow, stall.

retreat v. depart, ebb, leave, quit, recede, recoil, retire, shrink, turn tail, withdraw.

retrieve v. fetch, make good, recall, recapture, recoup, recover, redeem, regain, repair, repossess, rescue, restore, return, salvage, save.

return v. answer, choose, communicate, convey, deliver, earn, elect, make, net, pick, reappear, rebound, reciprocate, recoil, recompense, recur, redound, reestablish, refund, reimburse, reinstate, rejoin, remit, render, repair, repay, replace, reply, report, requite, respond, restore, retort, retreat, revert, send, submit, transmit, volley, yield.

reveal v. announce, bare, betray, broadcast, communicate, disbosom, disclose, dismask, display, divulge, exhibit, expose, impart, leak, lift the lid off, manifest, open, proclaim, publish, show, tell, unbare, uncover, unearth, unfold, unmask, unshadow, unveil.

revenge n. a dose/taste of one's own medicine, reprisal, requital, retaliation, retribution, revengement, satisfaction, vengeance, vindictiveness. v. avenge, even the score, get one's own back, get satisfaction, repay, requite, retaliate, vindicate.

revere v. adore, defer to, exalt, honor, pay homage to, respect, reverence, venerate, worship.

reverse v. alter, annul, back, backtrack, cancel, change, countermand, hark back, invalidate, invert, negate, overrule, overset, overthrow, overturn, quash, repeal, rescind, retract, retreat, revert, revoke, transpose, undo, upend, upset.

revert v. backslide, lapse, recur, regress, relapse, resume, retrogress, return, reverse.

revise v. alter, amend, change, correct, edit, emend, memorize, modify, recast, reconsider, reconstruct, redo, reexamine, reread, revamp, review, rewrite, study, update.

revive v. animate, awaken, cheer, comfort, invigorate, quicken, rally, reactivate, reanimate, recover, refresh, rekindle, renew, renovate, restore, resuscitate, revitalize, revivify, rouse.

revolt[1] n. breakaway, defection, insurgency, insurrection, jacquerie, mutiny, putsch, rebellion, revolution, rising, secession, sedition, uprising. v. defect, mutiny, rebel, resist, riot, rise.

revolt[2] v. disgust, nauseate, offend, outrage, repel, repulse, scandalize, shock, sicken.

revolution *n.* cataclysm, change, circle, circuit, coup, coup d'état, cycle, gyration, innovation, insurgency, jacquerie, lap, metamorphosis, mutiny, orbit, putsch, rebellion, reformation, revolt, rising, rotation, round, shift, spin, transformation, turn, upheaval, uprising, volution, wheel, whirl.

revulsion *n.* abhorrence, abomination, aversion, detestation, disgust, dislike, distaste, hatred, loathing, recoil, repugnance, repulsion.

reward *n.* benefit, bonus, bounty, come-up(p)ance, compensation, desert, gain, guerdon, honor, meed, merit, payment, payoff, premium, prize, profit, punishment, recompense, remuneration, repayment, requital, retribution, return, wages.

rich *adj.* abounding, abundant, affluent, ample, bright, copious, costly, creamy, deep, delicious, dulcet, elaborate, elegant, expensive, exquisite, exuberant, fatty, fecund, fertile, fine, flavorsome, flush, fruitful, full, full-bodied, full-flavored, full-toned, gay, gorgeous, heavy, highly flavored, humorous, in the money, intense, juicy, laughable, lavish, loaded, ludicrous, luscious, lush, luxurious, mellifluous, mellow, moneyed, opulent, palatial, pecunious, plenteous, plentiful, plutocratic, precious, priceless, productive, prolific, propertied, property, prosperous, resonant, rrisible, rolling, savory, sidesplitting, spicy, splendid, strong, succulent, sumptuous, superb, sweet, tasty, uberous, valuable, vibrant, vivid, warm, wealthy, well-heeled, well-off, well-provided, well-stocked, well-supplied, well-to-do.

ridiculous *adj.* absurd, comical, contemptible, damfool, derisory, farcical, foolish, funny, hilarious, incredible, laughable, laughworthy, ludicrous, nonsensical, outrageous, preposterous, risible, silly, stupid, unbelievable.

right *adj.* absolute, accurate, admissible, advantageous, appropriate, authentic, balanced, becoming, characteristic, comme il faut, complete, compos mentis, conservative, correct, deserved, desirable, dexter, dextral, direct, done, due, equitable, ethical, exact, factual, fair, favorable, fine, fit, fitting, genuine, good, healthy, honest, honorable, ideal, just, lawful, lucid, moral, normal, opportune, out-and-out, perpendicular, precise, proper, propitious, rational, reactionary, real, reasonable, righteous, rightful, rightist, rightward, right-wing, sane, satisfactory, seemly, sound, spot-on, straight, suitable, thorough, thoroughgoing, Tory, true, unerring, unimpaired, upright, utter, valid, veracious, veritable, virtuous, well.

rile *v.* anger, annoy, bug, exasperate, gall, get, irk, irritate, miff, nettle, peeve, pique, provoke, put out, upset, vex.

ring[1] *n.* association, band, cartel, cell, circle, circuit, circus, clique, collar, collet, combine, coterie, crew, enclosure, gang, group, gyre, halo, hoop, knot, loop, mob, organization, rink, round, syndicate. *v.* circumscribe, encircle, enclose, encompass, gash, gird, girdle, mark, score, surround.

ring[2] *v.* bell, buzz, call, chime, clang, clink, peal, phone, resonate, resound, reverberate, sound, tang, telephone, ting, tinkle, tintinnabulate, toll. *n.* buzz, call, chime, clang, clink, knell, peal, phone call, tang, ting, tinkle, tintinnabulation.

rinse *v.* bathe, clean, cleanse, dip, sluice, splash, swill, wash, wet. *n.* bath, dip, dye, splash, tint, wash, wetting.

rise *v.* advance, appear, arise, ascend, buoy, climb, crop up, emanate, emerge, enlarge, eventuate, flow, get up, grow, happen, improve, increase, intensify, issue, levitate, lift, mount, mutiny, occur, originate, progress, prosper, rebel, resist, revolt, slope, slope up, soar, spring, spring up, stand up, surface, swell, tower, volume, wax.

risk *n.* adventure, chance, danger, gamble, hazard, jeopardy, peril, possibility, speculation, uncertainty, venture.

rite *n.* act, ceremonial, ceremony, custom, form, formality, liturgy, mystery, observance, office, ordinance, practice, procedure, ritual, sacrament, service, solemnity, usage, worship.

rival *n.* adversary, antagonist, challenger, collateral, compeer, competitor, contender, contestant, emulator, equal, equivalent, fellow, match, opponent, peer, rivaless.

roam *v.* drift, meander, prowl, ramble, range, rove, squander, stray, stroll, travel, walk, wander.

roar *v.* bawl, bay, bell, bellow, blare, clamor, crash, cry, guffaw, hoot, howl, rumble, shout, thunder, vociferate, yell.

rob *v.* bereave, bunko, cheat, con, defraud, deprive, despoil, dispossess, do, flake, gyp, heist, hold up, loot, mill, pillage, plunder, raid, ramp, ransack, rifle, rip off, roll, sack, sting, strip, swindle.

rock[1] *n.* anchor, boulder, bulwark, cornerstone, danger, foundation, hazard, logan, log(g)an-stone, mainstay, obstacle, pebble, problem, protection, stone, support.

rock² *v.* astonish, astound, daze, dumbfound, jar, lurch, pitch, reel, roll, shake, shock, stagger, stun, surprise, way, swing, tilt, tip, toss, wobble.

rocky *adj.* craggy, flinty, hard, pebbly, rocklike, rough, rugged, stony.

romance *n.* absurdity, adventure, affair(e), amour, attachment, charm, color, exaggeration, excitement, fabrication, fairy tale, falsehood, fantasy, fascination, fiction, gest(e), glamour, idyll, intrigue, invention, legend, liaison, lie, love affair, love story, melodrama, mystery, novel, passion, relationship, sentiment, story, tale, tear-jerker. *v.* exaggerate, fantasize, lie, overstate.

romantic *adj.* amorous, charming, chimerical, colorful, dreamy, exaggerated, exciting, exotic, extravagant, fabulous, fairytale, fanciful, fantastic, fascinating, fictitious, fond, glamorous, high-flown, idealistic, idyllic, imaginary, imaginative, impractical, improbable, legendary, loveydovey, loving, made-up, mushy, mysterious, passionate, picturesque, quixotic, romantical, sentimental, sloppy, soppy, starry-eyed, tender, unrealistic, utopian, visionary, whimsical, wild.

room *n.* allowance, apartment, area, capacity, chamber, chance, compartment, compass, elbow-room, expanse, extent, houseroom, latitude, leeway, margin, occasion, office, opportunity, play, range, salon, saloon, scope, space, territory, volume.

roomy *adj.* ample, broad, capacious, commodious, extensive, generous, large, sizable, spacious, voluminous, wide.

root¹ *n.* base, basis, beginnings, bottom, cause, core, crux, derivation, essence, foundation, fountainhead, fundamental, germ, heart, mainspring, more, nub, nucleus, occasion, origin, radicle, radix, rhizome, seat, seed, source, starting point, stem, tuber. *v.* anchor, embed, entrench, establish, fasten, fix, ground, implant, moor, set, sink, stick.

root² *v.* burrow, delve, dig, ferret, forage, grout, hunt, nose, poke, pry, rummage.

rot *v.* corrode, corrupt, crumble, decay, decline, decompose, degenerate, deteriorate, disintegrate, fester, go bad, languish, molder, perish, putrefy, ret, spoil, taint. *n.* balderdash, blight, bosh, bunk, bunkum, canker, claptrap, collapse, corrosion, corruption, decay, decomposition, deterioration, disintegration, drivel, flapdoodle, guff, hogwash, moonshine, mold, nonsense, poppycock, putrefaction, putrescence, rubbish, tommyrot, twaddle.

rotate *v.* alternate, gyrate, interchange, pirouette, pivot, reel, revolve, spell, spin, switch, swivel, turn, twiddle, wheel.

round *adj.* ample, annular, ball-shaped, blunt, bowed, bulbous, candid, circular, complete, curved, curvilinear, cylindrical, direct, discoid, disc-shaped, entire, fleshy, frank, full, full-fleshed, globular, mellifluous, orbed, orbicular, orby, orotund, outspoken, plain, plump, resonant, rich, ring-shaped, roly-poly, rotund, rotundate, rounded, solid, sonorous, spheral, spheric, spherical, straight-forward, unbroken, undivided, unmodified, whole.

row¹ *n.* bank, colonnade, column, file, line, queue, range, rank, sequence, series, string, tier.

row² *n.* altercation, brawl, castigation, commotion, controversy, dispute, disturbance, donnybrook, dressing-down, falling-out, fracas, fray, fuss, lecture, noise, quarrel, racket, reprimand, reproof, rhubarb, rollicking, rookery, rout, ruckus, ruction, ruffle, rumpus, scrap, shemozzle, shindig, shindy, slanging, match, squabble, talking-to, telling-off, ticking-off, tiff, tongue-lashing, trouble, tumult, uproar.

rude *adj.* abrupt, abusive, artless, barbarous, blunt, boorish, brusque, brutish, cheeky, churlish, coarse, crude, curt, discourteous, disrespectful, graceless, gross, harsh, ignorant, illiterate, ill-mannered, impertinent, impolite, impudent, inartistic, inconsiderate, inelegant, insolent, insulting, loutish, low, makeshift, oafish, obscene, offhand, peremptory, primitive, raw, rough, savage, scurrilous, sharp, short, simple, startling, sudden, uncivil, uncivilized, uncouth, uncultured, uneducated, ungracious, unmannerly, unpleasant, unpolished, unrefined, untutored, violent, vulgar.

ruler *n.* commander, emperor, governor, head of state, king, leader, lord, monarch, potentate, prince, princess, queen, sovereign.

run *v.* abscond, administer, bear, beat it, bleed, bolt, boss, career, carry, cascade, challenge, circulate, clear out, climb, compete, conduct, contend, continue, control, convey, coordinate, course, creep, dart, dash, decamp, depart, direct, discharge, display, dissolve, drive to, escape, extend, feature, flee, flow, function, fuse, gallop, glide, go, gush, hare, hasten, head, hie, hotfoot, hurry, issue jog, ladder, last, lead, leak, lie, liquefy, lope, manage, maneuver, mastermind, melt, mix, move, operate, oversee, own, pass, perform, ply, pour, print, proceed, propel, publish, race, range, reach, regulate, roll, rush, scamper, scarper, scramble, scud, scurry, skedaddle, skim, slide, speed, spill, spout, spread, sprint, stand, stream, stretch, superintend, supervise, tear, tick, trail, transport, unravel, work.

ruse *n.* artifice, blind, deception, device, dodge, hoax, imposture, maneuver, play, sham, stall, stratagem, subterfuge, trick, wile.

rush *v.* accelerate, attack, bolt, capture, career, charge, dart, dash, dispatch, expedite, fly, hasten, hightail it, hotfoot, hurry, hustle, overcome, press, push, quicken, race, run, scour, scramble, scurry, shoot, speed, speed up, sprint, stampede, storm, tear, wallop, w(h)oosh. *n.* assault, charge, dash, dispatch, expedition, flow, haste, hurry, onslaught, push, race, scramble, speed, stampede, storm, streak, surge, swiftness, tear, urgency. *adj.* brisk, careless, cursory, emergency, expeditious, fast, hasty, hurried, prompt, quick, rapid, superficial, swift, urgent.

S

sabotage *v.* cripple, damage, destroy, disable, disrupt, incapacitate, mar, nullify, scupper, subvert, thwart, undermine, vandalize, vitiate, wreck. *n.* damage, destruction, disablement, disruption, impairment, marring, rattening, subversion, treachery, treason, undermining, vandalism, vitiation, wrecking.

sack[1] *v.* axe, discharge, dismiss, fire, lay off, make redundant. *n.* discharge, dismissal, notice, one's books, one's cards, one's marching orders, the ax, the boot, the bum's rush, the chop, the elbow, the push.

sack[2] *v.* demolish, depredate, desecrate, despoil, destroy, devastate, lay waste, level, loot, maraud, pillage, plunder, raid, rape, ravage, raze, rifle, rob, ruin, spoil, strip, waste. *n.* depredation, desecration, despoliation, destruction, devastation, leveling, looting, marauding, pillage, plunder, plundering, rape, rapine, ravage, razing, ruin, waste.

sacred *adj.* blessed, consecrated, dedicated, devotional, divine, ecclesiastical, godly, hallowed, heavenly, holy, inviolable, inviolate, invulnerable, priestly, protected, religious, revered, sacrosanct, saintly, sanctified, secure, solemn, venerable, venerated.

sad *adj.* bad, blue, calamitous, cheerless, chopfallen, crestfallen, crushed, dark, dejected, deplorable, depressed, depressing, desolated, despondent, disastrous, disconsolate, dismal, dispirited, distressed, distressing, doleful, dolesome, doloriferous, dolorific, doughy, dour, downcast, downhearted, drear, dreary, gloomy, glum, grave, grief stricken, grieved, grieving, grievous, heart rending, heavy, heavy-hearted, joyless, lachrymose, lamentable, low, low-spirited, lugubrious, melancholy, miserable, mournful, moving, painful, pathetic, pensive, piteous, pitiable, pitiful, poignant, regrettable, serious, shabby, sober, sober-minded, somber, sorrowful, sorry, sportless, stiff, tearful, touching, tragic, triste, uncheerful, unfortunate, unhappy, unsatisfactory, upsetting, wan, wistful, woebegone, woeful, wretched.

safe *adj.* alive and will, all right, cautious, certain, circumspect, conservative, dependable, discreet, fool-proof, guarded, hale, harmless, immune, impregnable, innocuous, intact, invulnerable, nonpoisonous, nontoxic, OK, out of harm's way, protected, proven, prudent, pure, realistic, reliable, secure, sound, sure, tame, tested, tried, trustworthy, unadventurous, uncontaminated, undamaged, unfailing, unharmed, unhurt, uninjured, unscathed, wholesome.

sage *adj.* astute, canny, discerning, intelligent, judicious, knowing, knowledgeable, learned, perspicacious, politic, prudent, sagacious, sapient, sensible, wise.

saintly *adj.* angelic, beatific, blameless, blessed, blest, celestial, devout, godfearing, godly, holy, immaculate, innocent, pious, pure, religious, righteous, sainted, saintlike, seraphic, sinless, spotless, stainless, upright, virtuous, worthy.

salvage *v.* conserve, glean, preserve, reclaim, recover, recuperate, redeem, repair, rescue, restore, retrieve, salve, save.

sane *adj.* all there, balanced, compos mentis, dependable, judicious, levelheaded, lucid, moderate, normal, rational, reasonable, reliable, right-minded, sensible, sober, sound, stable.

sarcastic *adj.* acerbic, acid, acrimonious, biting, caustic, contemptuous, cutting, cynical, derisive, disparaging, incisive, ironical, mocking, mordant, sardonic, satirical, scathing, sharp, sharp-tongued, sneering, taunting, withering.

satisfactory *adj.* acceptable, adequate, all right, average, competent, fair, fit, OK, passable, proper, sufficient, suitable, tickety-boo, up to the mark.

save v. cache, collect, conserve, cut back, deliver, economize, free, gather, guard, hinder, hoard, hold, husband, keep, lay up, liberate, obviate, preserve, prevent, protect, put aside, put by, reclaim, recover, redeem, rescue, reserve, retain, retrench, safeguard, salt away, salvage, screen, shield, spare, squirrel, stash, store.

saying n. adage, aphorism, apophthegm, axiom, byword, dictum, gnome, maxim, mot, motto, precept, proverb, remnant, saw, slogan.

scald v. blister, burn, sear.

scandal n. abuse, aspersion, backbiting, calumniation, calumny, crime, defamation, detraction, dirt, discredit, disgrace, dishonor, embarrassment, enormity, evil, furor, gossip, gossiping, ignominy, infamy, muckraking, obloquy, odium, offense, opprobrium, outcry, outrage, reproach, rumors, shame, sin, slander, stigma, talk, tattle, traducement, uproar, Watergate, wrongdoing.

scant adj. bare, deficient, hardly any, insufficient, limited, little, little or no, minimal, sparse.

scarce adj. deficient, few, infrequent, insufficient, lacking, rare, scanty, sparse, thin on the ground, uncommon, unusual, wanting.

scare v. affright, alarm, appall, daunt, dismay, frighten, intimidate, panic, shock, startle, terrify, terrorize, unnerve.

scene n. act, arena, backdrop, background, business, chapter, circumstances, commotion, confrontation, display, disturbance, division, drama, environment, episode, exhibition, focus, fuss, incident, landscape, locale, locality, location, melodrama, milieu, mise en scène, outburst, pageant, panorama, part, performance, picture, place, position, prospect, representation, row, set, setting, show, sight, site, situation, spectacle, spot, stage, tableau, tantrum, to-do, upset, view, vista, whereabouts, world.

scent n. aroma, bouquet, fragrance, odor, perfume, smell, spoor, trail, waft, whiff.

scheme n. arrangement, blueprint, chart, codification, configuration, conformation, conspiracy, contrivance, dart, design, device, diagram, disposition, dodge, draft, game, idea, intrigue, layout, machinations, maneuver, method, outline, pattern, plan, plot, ploy, procedure, program, project, proposal, proposition, racket, ruse, schedule, schema, shape, shift, stratagem, strategy,

subterfuge, suggestion, system, tactics, theory. v. collude, conspire, contrive, design, devise, frame, imagine, intrigue, manipulate, maneuver, mastermind, plan, plot, project, pull strings, pull wires, work out.

scholar n. academe, academic, authority, bookworm, egghead, intellectual, pupil, savant, student.

scold v. admonish, bawl out, berate, blame, castigate, censure, chide, find fault with, jaw, lecture, nag, rate, rebuke, remonstrate, reprimand, reproach, reprove, take to task, tell off, tick off, upbraid, vituperate, wig.

scowl v. frown, glare, glower, grimace, lower. n. frown, glare, glower, grimace, moue.

scrap[1] n. atom, bit, bite, crumb, fraction, fragment, grain, iota, junk, mite, modicum, morsel, mouthful, part, particle, piece, portion, remnant, shard, shred, sliver, snap, snatch, snippet, trace, vestige, waste, whit. v. abandon, ax, break up, cancel, chuck, demolish, discard, ditch, drop, jettison, junk, shed, throw out, write off.

scrap[2] n. argument, battle, brawl, disagreement, dispute, dust-up, fight, quarrel, row, ruckus, ruction, rumpus, scuffle, set-to, shindy, squabble, tiff, wrangle.

scream v. bawl, clash, cry, holler, jar, roar, screak, screech, shriek, shrill, squeal, wail, yell, help, yowl. n. howl, outcry, roar, screak, screech, shriek, squeal, wail, yell, yelp, yowl.

script n. book, calligraphy, copy, hand, handwriting, letters, libretto, lines, longhand, manuscript, penmanship, text, words, writing.

search v. check, comb, examine, explore, ferret, frisk, inquire, inspect, investigate, look, probe, pry, quest, ransack, rifle, rummage, scour, scrutinize, sift, test. n. examination, exploration, going-over, hunt, inquiry, inspection, investigation, pursuit, quest, researches, rummage, scrutiny.

secret adj. abstruse, arcane, back door, backstairs, cabalistic(al), camouflaged, clandestine, classified, cloak-and-dagger, close, closet, concealed, conspiratorial, covered, covert, cryptic, deep, discreet, disguised, esoteric, furtive, hidden, hole-and-corner, hush hush, inlay, mysterious, occult, out-of-the-way, private, privy, recondite, reticent, retired, secluded, secretive, sensitive, shrouded, sly, stealthy, tête-à-tête, undercover, underground, underhand, under-the-counter, undisclosed, unfrequented, unknown, unpublished, unrevealed, unseen.

secure *adj.* absolute, assured, certain, conclusive, confident, definite, dependable, easy, fast, fastened, firm, fixed, fortified, immovable, immune, impregnable, on velvet, overconfident, protected, reassured, reliable, safe, sheltered, shielded, solid, stable, steadfast, steady, sure, tight, unassailable, undamaged, unharmed, well-founded.

see *v.* accompany, anticipate, appreciate, ascertain, attend, behold, comprehend, consider, consult, court, date, decide, deem, deliberate, descry, determine, discern, discover, distinguish, divine, encounter, ensure, envisage, escort, espy, experience, fathom, feel, follow, foresee, foretell, get, glimpse, grasp, guarantee, heed, identify, imagine, interview, investigate, judge, know, lead, learn, look, make out, mark, meet, mind, note, notice, observe, perceive, picture, realize, receive, recognize, reflect, regard, show, sight, spot, take, understand, usher, view, visit, visualize, walk, witness.

seek *v.* aim, ask, aspire to, attempt, beg, busk, desire, endeavor, entreat, essay, follow, hunt, inquire, invite, petition, pursue, request, solicit, strive, try, want.

seem *v.* appear, look, look like, pretend, sound like.

select *v.* choose, cull, pick, prefer, single out. *adj.* choice, elite, excellent, exclusive, first-class, first-rate, handpicked, limited, picked, posh, preferable, prime, privileged, rare, selected, special, superior, top, top-notch.

selfish *adj.* egoistic, egotistic, greedy, mercenary, self-centered, self-serving.

sell *v.* barter, cheat, convince, deal in, exchange, handle, hawk, impose on, market, merchandise, peddle, persuade, promote, retail, sell out, stock, surrender, trade, trade in, traffic in, trick, vend.

send *v.* broadcast, cast, charm, communicate, consign, convey, delight, deliver, direct, discharge, dispatch, electrify, emit, enrapture, enthrall, excite, exude, fire, fling, forward, grant, hurl, intoxicate, move, please, propel, radiate, ravish, remit, shoot, stir, thrill, titillate, transmit.

senile *adj.* anile, decrepit, doddering, doting, failing, imbecile, senescent.

sense *n.* appreciation, atmosphere, aura, awareness, brains, clearheadedness, cleverness, consciousness, definition, denotation, direction, discernment, discrimination, drift, faculty, feel, feeling, gist, good, gumption, implication, import, impression, intelligence, interpretation, intuition, judgment, logic, meaning, message, mother wit, perception, point, premonition, presentiment, purport, purpose, quickness, reason, reasonableness, sagacity, sanity, savvy, sensation, sensibility, sentiment, sharpness, significance, signification, substance, tact, understanding, use, value, wisdom, wit(s), worth.

senseless *adj.* absurd, crazy, illogical, inconsistent, ludicrous, pointless, ridiculous, silly, unreasonable, unwise.

sentimental *adj.* corny, dewy-eyed, drippy, emotional, gushing, gushy, gut-bucket, impressionable, lovey-dovey, maudlin, mawkish, mushy, nostalgic, pathetic, romantic, rosewater, schmaltzy, simpering, sloppy, slush, softhearted, tearful, tear-jerking, tender, too-too, touching, treacly, weepy. Wertherian.

separate *v.* abstract, bifurcate, departmentalize, de-tach, disaffiliate, disconnect, disentangle, disjoin, dislink, dispart, dissever, distance, disunite, divaricate, diverge, divide, divorce, eloi(g)n, estrange, exfoliate, isolate, part, part company, rescind, remove, secede, secern, seclude, segregate, sever, shear, split, split up, sunder, uncouple, winnow, withdraw.

serene *adj.* calm, composed, cool, halcyon, imperturbable, peaceful, placid, tranquil, unclouded, undisturbed, unflappable, unruffled, untroubled.

serve *v.* act, aid, answer, arrange, assist, attend, avail, complete, content, dance attendance, deal, deliver, discharge, distribute, do, fulfill, further, handle, help, minister to, oblige, observe, officiate, pass, perform, present, provide, satisfy, succor, suffice, suit, supply, undergo, wait on, work for.

set[1] *v.* adjust, aim, allocate, allot, apply, appoint, arrange, assign, cake, conclude, condense, congeal, coordinate, crystallize, decline, decree, deposit, designate, determine, dip, direct, disappear, embed, establish, fasten, fix, fix up, gelatinize, harden, impose, install, jell, lay, locate, lodge, mount, name, ordain, park, place, plant, plonk, plump, position, prepare, prescribe, propound, put, rectify, regulate, resolve, rest, schedule, seat, settle, sink, situate, solidify, specify, spread, stake, station, stick, stiffen, subside, synchronize, thicken, turn, vanish. *n.* attitude, bearing, carriage, fit, hang, inclination, mise-en-scène, position, posture, scene, scenery, setting, turn. *adj.* agreed, appointed, arranged, artificial, conventional, customary, decided, definite, deliberate, entrenched, established, firm, fixed, formal, hackneyed, immovable, inflexible intentional, prearranged, predetermined, prescribed, regular, rehearsed, rigid, routine, scheduled, settled, standard, stereotyped, stock, strict, stubborn, traditional, unspontaneous, usual.

set² *n.* apparatus, assemblage, assortment, band, batch, circle, class, clique, collection, company, compendium, coterie, covey, crew, crowd, faction, gang, group, kit, outfit, sect, sequence, series.

settle *v.* adjust, agree, alight, appoint, arrange, bed, calm, choose, clear, colonize, compact, complete, compose, conclude, confirm, decide, decree, descend, determine, discharge, dispose, dower, drop, dwell, endow, establish, fall, fix, found, hush, inhabit, land, light, liquidate, live, lower, lull, occupy, ordain, order, pacify, pay, people, pioneer, plant, plump, populate, quell, quiet, quieten, quit, reassure, reconcile, relax, relieve, reside, resolve, sedate, sink, soothe, square, square up, subside, tranquilize.

sever *v.* alienate, bisect, cleave, cut, detach, disconnect, disjoin, dissever, dissociate, dissolve, dissunder, disunite, divide, estrange, part, rend, separate, split, sunder, terminate.

several *adj.* assorted, different, discrete, disparate, distinct, divers, diverse, individual, many, particular, respective, separate, single, some, some few, specific, sundry, various.

sex *n.* coition, coitus, congress, copulation, desire, fornication, gender, intercourse, intimacy, libido, lovemaking, reproduction, screw, sexual intercourse, sexual relations, sexuality, union, venery.

sexual *adj.* carnal, coital, erotic, gamic, genital, intimate, procreative, reproductive, sensual, sex, sex-related, venereal.

shade *n.* amount, apparition, blind, canopy, color, coolness, cover, covering, curtain, darkness, dash, degree, difference, dimness, dusk, eidolon, ghost, gloaming, gloom, gloominess, gradation, hint, hue, manes, murk, nuance, obscurity, phantasm, phantom, screen, semblance, semidarkness, shadiness, shadow, shadows, shelter, shield, shroud, specter, spirit, stain, suggestion, suspicion, tinge, tint, tone, trace, twilight, umbra, umbrage, variation, variety, veil, wraith. *v.* cloud, conceal, cover, darken, dim, hide, mute, obscure, overshadow, protect, screen, shadow, shield, shroud, veil.

shake *n.* agitation, convulsion, disturbance, instant, jar, jerk, jiffy, jolt, jounce, moment, no time, pulsation, quaking, second, shiver, shock, shudder, tick, trembling, tremor, trice, twitch, vellication, vibration. *v.* agitate, brandish, bump, churn, concuss, convulse, discompose, distress, disturb, flourish, fluctuate, frighten, heave, impair, intimidate, jar, joggle, jolt, jounce, move, oscillate, quake, quiver, rattle, rock, rouse, shimmy, shiver, shock, shudder, split, stir, sway, totter, tremble, twitch, undermine, unnerve, unsettle, upset, vellicate, vibrate, wag, waggle, wave, waver, weaken, wobble.

shape *n.* apparition, appearance, aspect, build, condition, configuration, conformation, contours, cut, dimensions, fettle, figure, form, format, frame, gestalt, guise, health, kilter, likeness, lines, make, model, mold, outline, pattern, physique, profile, semblance, silhouette, state, template, trim. *v.* accommodate, adapt, construct, create, define, develop, devise, embody, fashion, forge, form, frame, guide, make, model, modify, mold, plan, prepare, produce, redact, regulate, remodel.

share *v.* allot, apportion, assign, chip in, distribute, divide, divvy, divvy up, go Dutch, go fifty-fifty, go halves, muck in, partake, participate, split, whack. *n.* a piece of the action, allotment, allowance, contribution, cut, dividend, division, divvy, due, finger, lot, part, portion, proportion, quota, ration, snap, snip, stint, whack.

sharp *adj.* abrupt, acerbic, acicular, acid, acidulous, acrid, acrimonious, acute, alert, apt, artful, astute, barbed, biting, bitter, bright, burning, canny, caustic, chic, chiseled, classy, clear, clear-cut, clever, crafty, crisp, cunning, cutting, discerning, dishonest, distinct, dressy, eager, edged, excruciating, extreme, fashionable, fierce, fit, fly, harsh, honed, hot, hurtful, incisive, intense, jagged, keen, knowing, long-headed, marked, natty, nimble-witted, noticing, observant, painful, penetrating, peracute, perceptive, piercing, pointed, pungent, quick, quick-witted, rapid, razor-sharp, ready, sarcastic, sardonic, scathing, serrated, severe, sharpened, shooting, shrewd, sly, smart, snappy, snazzy, sour, spiky, stabbing, stinging, stylish, subtle, sudden, tart, trenchant, trendy, undulled, unscrupulous, vinegary, violent, vitriolic, waspish, wily.

shine *v.* beam, brush, buff, burnish, coruscate, excel, flash, glare, gleam, glimmer, glisten, glitter, glow, luster, polish, radiate, resplend, scintillate, shimmer, sparkle, stand out, star, twinkle. *n.* brightness, burnish, effulgence, glare, glaze, gleam, gloss, glow, lambency, light, luminosity, luster, patina, polish, radiance, sheen, shimmer, sparkle.

shiver *v.* palpitate, quake, quiver, shake, shudder, tremble, vibrate. *n.* flutter, frisson, quiver, shudder, start, thrill, tremble, trembling, tremor, twitch, vibration.

shock *v.* agitate, appall, astound, confound, disgust, dismay, disquiet, horrify, jar, jolt, nauseate, numb, offend, outrage, paralyze, revolt, scandalize, shake, sicken, stagger, stun, stupefy, traumatize, unnerve, unsettle.

short *adj.* abbreviated, abridged, abrupt, blunt, brief, brittle, brusque, compressed, concise, crisp, crumbly, crusty, curt, curtailed, deficient, diminutive, direct, discourteous, dumpy, ephemeral, evanescent, fleeting, friable, gruff, impolite, inadequate, insufficient, lacking, laconic, limited, little, low, meager, momentary, offhand, passing, petite, pithy, poor, sawn-off, scant, scanty, scarce, sententious, sharp, shortened, shorthanded, short-lived, short-term, slender, slim, small, snappish, snappy, sparse, squat, straight, succinct, summarized, summary, tart, terse, tight, tiny, transitory, uncivil, understaffed, unplentiful, wanting, wee.

shout *n.* bay, bellow, belt, call, cheer, cry, roar, scream, shriek, yell. *v.* bawl, bay, bellow, call, cheer, cry, holler, roar, scream, shriek, yell.

show *v.* accompany, accord, assert, attend, attest, bestow, betray, clarify, conduct, confer, demonstrate, disclose, display, divulge, elucidate, escort, evidence, evince, exemplify, exhibit, explain, grant, guide, illustrate, indicate, instruct, lead, manifest, offer, present, prove, register, reveal, teach, usher, witness. *n.* affectation, air, appearance, array, dash, demonstration, display, eclat, elan, entertainment, exhibition, exhibitionism, expo, exposition, extravaganza, façade, fair, flamboyance, gig, illusion, indication, likeness, manifestation, ostentation, pageant, pageantry, panache, parade, performance, pizzazz, plausibility, pose, presentation, pretence, pretext, production, profession, razzle-dazzle, representation, semblance, sight, sign, spectacle, swagger, view.

sick *adj.* ailing, black, blasé, bored, diseased, disgusted, displeased, dog-sick, fed up, feeble, ghoulish, glutted, ill, indisposed, jaded, laid up, morbid, mortified, nauseated, pining, poorly, puking, qualmish, queasy, sated, satiated, sickly, tired, under the weather, unwell, vomiting, weak, weary.

side *n.* airs, angle, arrogance, aspect, bank, border, boundary, brim, brink, camp, cause, department, direction, division, edge, elevation, face, facet, faction, flank, flitch, fringe, gang, hand, insolence, light, limit, margin, opinion, ostentation, page, part, party, perimeter, periphery, position, quarter, region, rim, sect, sector, slant, stand, standpoint, surface, team, twist, verge, view, viewpoint. *adj.* flanking, incidental, indirect, irrelevant, lateral, lesser, marginal, minor, oblique, roundabout, secondary, subordinate, subsidiary.

sight *n.* appearance, apprehension, decko, display, estimation, exhibition, eye, eyes, eyeshot, eyesight, eyesore, field of vision, fright, gander, glance, glimpse, judgment, ken, look, mess, monstrosity, observation, opinion, pageant, perception, range, scene, seeing, show, spectacle, view, viewing, visibility, vision, vista. *v.* behold, discern, distinguish, glimpse, observe, perceive, see, spot.

sign *n.* augury, auspice, badge, beck, betrayal, board, character, cipher, clue, device, emblem, ensign, evidence, figure, foreboding, forewarning, gesture, give-away, hint, indication, insignia, intimation, lexigram, logo, logogram, notice, omen, placard, pointer, portent, presage, proof, reminder, representation, rune, signal, signature, signification, signpost, spoor, suggestion, symbol, symptom, token, trace, trademark, vestige, warning. *v.* autograph, beckon, endorse, gesticulate, gesture, indicate, initial, inscribe, motion, signal, subscribe, wave.

signal *n.* alarm, alert, beacon, beck, cue, flare, flash, gesture, go-ahead, griffin, impulse, indication, indicator, light, mark, OK, password, rocket, sign, tip-off, token, transmitter, waft, warning, watchword. *adj.* conspicuous, distinguished, eminent, exceptional, extraordinary, famous, glorious, impressive, memorable, momentous, notable, noteworthy, outstanding, remarkable, significant, striking. *v.* beckon, communicate, gesticulate, gesture, indicate, motion, nod, sign, telegraph, waft, wave.

silence *n.* calm, numbness, hush, lull, muteness, noiselessness, peace, quiet, speechlessness, stillness, taciturnity, uncommunicativeness.

similar *adj.* alike, analogous, close, comparable, compatible, congruous, corresponding, homogeneous, homogenous, homologous, related, resembling, selflike, uniform.

sin *n.* crime, damnation, debt, error, evil, fault, guilt, hamartia, impiety, iniquity, lapse, misdeed, offense, sinfulness, transgression, trespass, ungodliness, unrighteousness, wickedness, wrong, wrong-doing. *v.* err, fall, fall from grace, go astray, lapse, misbehave, offend, stray, transgress, trespass.

sincere *adj.* artless, bona fide, candid, deep-felt, earnest, frank, genuine, guileless, heartfelt, heart-whole, honest, natural, open, plain-hearted, plainspoken, pure, real, serious, simple, simple-hearted, single-hearted, soulful, straightforward, true, true-hearted, truthful, unadulterated, unaffected unfeigned, unmixed, wholehearted.

single *adj.* celibate, distinct, exclusive, free, individual, lone, man-to-man, one, onefold, one-to-one, only, particular, separate, simple, sincere, single-minded, singular, sole, solitary, unattached, unblended, unbroken, uncombined, uncompounded, undivided, unique, unmarried, unmixed, unshared, unwed, wholehearted.

site *n.* ground, location, lot, place, plot, position, setting, spot, station. *v.* dispose, install, locate, place, position, set, situate, station.

skill *n.* ability, accomplishment, adroitness, aptitude, art, cleverness, competence, dexterity, experience, expertise, expertness, facility, finesse, handiness, ingenuity, intelligence, knack, proficiency, quickness, readiness, savoir faire, savvy, skillfulness, talent, technique, touch.

skinny *adj.* attenuate(d), emaciated, lean, scagged, scraggy, skeletal, skin-and-bone, thin, twiggy, underfed, undernourished, weedy.

slant *v.* angle, bend, bevel, bias, cant, color, distort, incline, lean, list, shelve, skew, slope, tilt, twist, warp, weight. *n.* angle, attitude, bias, camber, declination, diagonal, emphasis, gradient, incline, leaning, obliquity, pitch, prejudice, rake, ramp, slope, tilt, viewpoint.

slavery *n.* bondage, captivity, enslavement, impressment, serfdom, servitude, subjugation, thrall, yoke.

slender *adj.* acicular, faint, feeble, flimsy, fragile, inadequate, inconsiderable, insufficient, lean, little, meager, narrow, poor, remote, scanty, slight, slim, small, spare, svelte, sylphlike, tenuous, thin, thready, waspwaisted, weak, willowish, willowy.

slide *v.* coast, glide, glissade, lapse, skate, skim, slip, slither, toboggan, veer.

slit *v.* cut, gash, knife, lance, pierce, rip, slash, slice, split. *n.* cut, fissure, gash, incision, opening, rent, split, tear, vent. *adj.* cut, pertuse(d), rent, split, torn.

slow *adj.* adagio, backward, behind, behindhand, boring, bovine, conservative, creeping, dawdling, dead, dead-and-alive, delayed, deliberate, dense, dilatory, dim, dull, dumb, easy, gradual, inactive, lackadaisical, laggard, lagging, late, lazy, leaden, leisurely, lingering, loitering, measured, obtuse, one-horse, plodding, ponderous, prolonged, protracted, quiet, retarded, slack, sleepy, slow-moving, slow-witted, sluggardly, sluggish, stupid, tame, tardy, tedious, thick, time-consuming, uneventful, unhasty, unhurried, uninteresting, unproductive, unprogressive, unpunctual, unresponsive, wearisome.

sluggish *adj.* dull, heavy, inactive, indolent, inert, lethargic, lifeless, listless, lymphatic, phlegmatic, slothful, slow, slow-moving, torpid, unresponsive.

slumber *v.* doze, drowse, nap, repose, rest, sleep, snooze.

small *adj.* bantam, base, dilute, diminutive, dwarfish, grudging, humble, illiberal, immature, inadequate, incapacious, inconsiderable, insignificant, insufficient, itsy-bitsy, lesser, limited, little, meager, mean, mignon(ne), mini, miniature, minor, minuscule, minute, modest, narrow, negligible, paltry, petite, petty, pint-size(d), pocket, pocket-sized, puny, pygmean, scanty, selfish, slight, small-scale, tiddl(e)y, tiny, trifling, trivial, undersized, unimportant, unpretentious, wee, young.

smart *adj.* acute, adept, agile, apt, astute, bright, brisk, canny, chic, clever, cracking, dandy, effective, elegant, fashionable, fine, impertinent, ingenious, intelligent, jaunty, keen, lively, modish, natty, neat, nimble, nimble-witted, nobby, pert, pointed, quick, quick-witted, rattling, ready, ready-witted, saucy, sharp, shrewd, smart-alecky, snappy, spanking, spirited, spruce, stylish, swagger, swish, tippy, trim, vigorous, vivacious, wellappointed, witty.

smart[2] *v.* burn, hurt, nip, pain, sting, throb, tingle, twinge. *adj.* hard, keen, nipping, nippy, painful, piercing, resounding, sharp, stinging. *n.* nip, pain, pang, smarting, soreness, sting, twinge.

smell *n.* aroma, bouquet, fragrance, odor, perfume, scent, stench, stink, whiff.

smooth *adj.* agreeable, bland, calm, classy, easy, effortless, elegant, equable, even, facile, fair-spoken, flat, flowing, fluent, flush, frictionless, glassy, glib, glossy, hairless, horizontal, ingratiating, level, levitate, mellow, mild, mirrorlike, peaceful, persuasive, plain, plane, pleasant, polished, regular, rhythmic, serene, shiny, silken, silky, sleek, slick, slippery, smarmy, smug, soft, soothing, steady, suave, tranquil, unbroken, undisturbed, uneventful, uniform, uninterrupted, unpuckered, unruffled, untroubled, unwrinkled, urbane, velvety, well-ordered.

smug *adj.* cocksure, complacent, conceited, holier-than-thou, priggish, self-opinionated, self-righteous, self-satisfied, superior, unctuous.

sneak *v.* cower, cringe, grass on, inform on, lurk, pad, peach, sidle, skulk, slink, slip, smuggle, spirit, steal, tell tales. *n.* informer, snake in the grass, sneaker, telltale. *adj.* clandestine, covert, furtive, quick, secret, stealthy, surprise, surreptitious.

snug *adj.* close, close-fitting, comfortable, comfy, compact, cozy, homely, intimate, neat, sheltered, trim, warm.

sober *adj.* abstemious, abstinent, calm, clearheaded, cold, composed, cool, dark, dispassionate, drab, grave, level-headed, lucid, moderate, peaceful, plain, practical, quiet, rational, realistic, reasonable, restrained, sedate, serene, serious, severe, solemn, somber, sound, staid, steady, subdued, temperate, unexcited, unruffled.

soft *adj.* balmy, bendable, bland, caressing, comfortable, compassionate, cottony, creamy, crumby, cushioned, cushiony, cushy, daft, delicate, diffuse, diffused, dim, dimmed, doughy, downy, ductile, dulcet, easy, easygoing, effeminate, elastic, faint, feathery, feeble-minded, flabby, flaccid, fleecy, flexible, flowing, fluid, foolish, furry, gelatinous, gentle, impressible, indulgent, kind, lash, lax, lenient, liberal light, limp, low, malleable, mellow, melodious, mild, moldable, murmured, muted, namby-pamby, nonalcoholic, overindulgent, pale, pampered, pastel, permissive, pitying, plastic, pleasant, pleasing, pliable, pulpy, quaggy, quiet, restful, sensitive, sentimental, shaded, silky, silly, simple, smooth, soothing, soppy, spineless, spongy, squashy, subdued, supple, swampy, sweet, sympathetic, temperate, tender, tender-hearted, undemanding, understated, unprotected, velvety, weak, whispered, yielding.

sole *adj.* alone, exclusive, individual, one, only, single, singular, solitary, unique.

solemn *adj.* august, awed, awe-inspiring, ceremonial, ceremonious, devotional, dignified, earnest, formal, glum, grand, grave, hallowed, holy, imposing, impressive, majestic, momentous, pompous, portentous, religious, reverential, ritual, sacred, sanctified, sedate, serious, sober, somber, staid, stately, thoughtful, venerable.

solid *adj.* agreed, compact, complete, concrete, constant, continuous, cubic(al), decent, dense, dependable, estimable, firm, genuine, good, hard, law-abiding, level-headed, massed, pure, real, reliable, sensible, serious, sober, sound, square, stable, stocky, strong, sturdy, substantial, trusty, unalloyed, unanimous, unbroken, undivided, uninterrupted, united, unmixed, unshakable, unvaried, upright, upstanding, wealthy, weighty, worthy.

solitude *n.* aloneness, desert, emptiness, isolation, loneliness, privacy, reclusiveness, retirement, seclusion, waste, wasteland, wilderness.

sometimes *adv.* at times, from time to time, now and again, now and then, occasionally, off and on, once in a while, otherwhile.

soothe *v.* allay, alleviate, appease, assuage, calm, coax, comfort, compose, ease, hush, lull, mitigate, mollify, pacify, quiet, relieve, salve, settle, soften, still, tranquilize.

sorry *adj.* abject, apologetic, contrite, distressed, guilt-ridden, penitent, regretful, remorseful, repentant, sorrowful.

sour *adj.* acerb(ic), acetic, acid, acidulated, acrid, acrimonious, bad, bitter, churlish, crabbed, curdled, cynical, disagreeable, discontented, embittered fermented, grouchy, grudging, ill-natured, ill-tempered, inharmonious, jaundiced, off, peevish, pungent, rancid, rank, sharp, tart, turned, ungenerous, unpleasant, unsavory, unsuccessful, unsweet, unwholesome, vinegarish, vinegary, waspish.

special *adj.* appropriate, certain, characteristic, chief, choice, detailed, distinctive, distinguished, especial, exceptional, exclusive, extraordinary, festive, gala, important, individual, intimate, main, major, memorable, momentous, particular, peculiar, precise, primary, red-letter, select, significant, specialized, specific, uncommon, unique, unusual.

speck *n.* atom, bit, blemish, blot, defect, dot, fault, flaw, fleck, grain, iota, jot, macula, mark, mite, modicum, mote, particle, shred, speckle, spot, stain, title, trace, whit.

speed *n.* acceleration, celerity, dispatch, expedition, fleetness, haste, hurry, lick, momentum, pace, precipitation, quickness, rapidity, rush, swiftness, tempo, velocity. *v.* advance, aid, assist, belt, bomb, boost, bowl along, career, dispatch, expedite, facilitate, flash, fleet, further, gallop, hasten, help, hurry, impel, lick, press on, promote, put one's foot down, quicken, race, rush, sprint, step on it, step on the gas, step on the juice, tear, urge, vroom, zap, zoom.

spell *n.* bout, course, innings, interval, patch, period, season, sting, stretch, term, time, turn.

spell *n.* abracadabra, allure, bewitchment, charm, conjuration, enchantment, exorcism, fascination, glamour, hex, incantation, love charm, magic, open sesame, paternoster, philter, rune, sorcery, trance, weird, witchery.

spicy *adj.* aromatic, flavorsome, fragrant, hot, improper, indelicate, off-color, piquant, pointed, pungent, racy, ribald, risque, savory, scandalous, seasoned, sensational, showy, suggestive, tangy, titillating, unseemly. *n.* bland.

spirit *n.* air, animation, apparition, attitude, backbone, character, disposition, energy, feeling, ghost, humor, life, motivation, outlook, phantom, psyche, purport, purpose, python, quality, resolution, resolve, sense, shade, shadow, soul, sparkle, specter, spook, sprite, temper, temperament, tenor, tone, verve, vigor, vision, vivacity, warmth, waterhorse, water nymph, water rixie, water sprite, will, willpower, zeitgeist, zest. *v.* abduct, abstract, capture, carry, convey, kidnap, purloin, remove, seize, snaffle, steal, whisk.

spite *n.* animosity, bitchiness, despite, gall, grudge, hate, hatred, ill nature, malevolence, malice, malignity, pique, rancor, spitefulness, spleen, venom, viciousness.

splinter *n.* chip, flake, fragment, needle, paring, shaving, sliver, spall, spicule. *v.* disintegrate, fracture, fragment, shatter, shiver, smash, split.

split *v.* allocate, allot, apportion, betray, bifurcate, branch, break, burst, cleave, crack, delaminate, disband, distribute, disunite, divaricate, diverge, divide, divulge, fork, gape, grass, halve, inform on, open, parcel out, part, partition, peach, rend, rip, separate, share out, slash, slice up, slit, sliver, snap, spell, splinter, squeal. *n.* breach, break, breakup, cleft, crack, damage, dichotomy, difference, dis-

cord, disruption, dissension, disunion, divergence, division, estrangement, fissure, gap, partition, race, rent, rift, rip, rupture, schism, separation, slash, slit, tear. *adj.* ambivalent, bisected, broken, cleft, cloven, cracked, divided, dual, fractured, ruptured, twofold.

spoil *v.* addle, baby, blemish, curdle, damage, debase, decay, decompose, deface, despoil, destroy, deteriorate, disfigure, go bad, go off, harm, impair, indulge, injure, jigger, louse up, mar, mildew, mollycoddle, pamper, plunder, putrefy, queer, rot, ruin, screw, spoon-feed, turn, upset, wreck.

spontaneous *adj.* extempore, free, impromptu, impulsive, instinctive, natural, ultroneous, unbidden, uncompelled, unconstrained, unforced, unhesitating, unlabored, unpremeditated, unprompted, unstudied, untaught, voluntary, willing.

spray *v.* atomize, diffuse, douse, drench, scatter, shower, sprinkle, wet. *n.* aerosol, atomizer, drizzle, droplets, foam, froth, mist, moisture, spindrift, spoondrift, sprinkler.

spray *n.* bough, branch, corsage, garland, shoot, sprig, wreath.

spry *adj.* active, agile, alert, brisk, energetic, nimble, nippy, peppy, quick, ready, sprightly, supple.

staid *adj.* calm, composed, decorous, demure, grave, quiet, sedate, self-restrained, serious, sober, solemn, steady.

stalk *v.* approach, follow, haunt, hunt, march, pace, pursue, shadow, stride, strut, tail, track.

stalk *n.* bole, branch, shoot, spire, stem, sterigma, trunk.

stall *v.* delay, equivocate, hedge, obstruct, prevaricate.

stamp *v.* bet, brand, bray, categorize, characterize, crush, engrave, exhibit, fix, identify, impress, imprint, inscribe, label, mark, mint, mold, pound, print, pronounce, reveal, strike, trample. *n.* attestation, authorization, brand, breed, cast, character, cut, description, earmark, evidence, fashion, form, hallmark, impression, imprint, kind, mark, mold, sign, signature, sort, stomp, type.

stand *v.* abide, allow, bear, belong, brook, continue, cost, countenance, demur, endure, erect, exist, experience, halt, handle, hold, mount, obtain, pause, place, position, prevail, put, rank, remain, rest, rise, scruple, set, stay, stomach, stop, suffer, support, sustain, take, tolerate, undergo, wear, weather, withstand.

standard[1] *n.* average, benchmark, criterion, guide, measure, specification, touchstone, yardstick.

staple *adj.* basic, chief, essential, fundamental, key, leading, main, major, predominant, primary, principle.

stare *v.* gape, gaze, glare, look, watch.

start *v.* begin, commence, establish, initiate, instigate, launch, originate, pioneer.

startle *v.* affray, agitate, alarm, amaze, astonish, astound, electrify, flush, frighten, scare, shock, spook, start, surprise.

starving *adj.* famished, hungering, hungry, ravenous, undernourished.

state *v.* affirm, articulate, assert, asseverate, aver, declare, enumerate, explain, expound, express, formalize, formulate, present, propound, put, report, say, specify, voice. *n.* attitude, bother, case, category, ceremony, circumstances, condition, dignity, display, flap, glory, grandeur, humor, majesty, mode, mood, panic, pass, phase, plight, pomp, position, pother, predicament, shape, situation, spirits, splendor, stage, station, style, tizzy.

stay *v.* abide, adjourn, allay, arrest, check, continue, curb, defer, delay, detain, discontinue, dwell, endure, halt, hinder, hold out, hover, impede, last, linger, live, lodge, loiter, obstruct, pause, prevent, prorogue, remain, reside, restrain, settle, sojourn, stand, stop, suspend, tarry, visit, wait.

steal *v.* appropriate, filch, heist, misappropriate, pilfer, poach, purloin, sneak, swipe.

steep[1] *adj.* abrupt, bluff, excessive, exorbitant, extortionate, extreme, headlong, high, overpriced, precipitous, sheer, stiff, uncalled-for, unreasonable.

steep[2] *v.* brine, damp, drench, fill, imbrue, imbue, immerse, infuse, macerate, marinate, moisten, permeate, pervade, pickle, saturate, seethe, soak, souse, submerge, suffuse.

steer *v.* conduct, control, direct, govern, guide, pilot.

stem[1] *n.* axis, branch, family, house, line, lineage, peduncle, race, shoot, stalk, stock, trunk.

stem[2] *v.* check, contain, curb, dam, oppose, resist, restrain, stay, stop, tamp.

step *n.* act, action, advance, advancement, deed, degree, demarche, doorstep, expedient, footfall, footprint, footstep, gait, halfpace, impression, level, maneuver, means, measure, move, pace, phase, point, print, procedure, proceeding, process, progression, rank, remove, round, rung, stage, stair, stride, trace, track, tread, walk. *v.* move, pace, stalk, stamp, tread, walk.

sterile *adj.* abortive, antiseptic, aseptic, bare, barren, disinfected, dry, empty, fruitless, germ-free, infecund, pointless, sterilized, unfruitful, unimaginative, unproductive, unprofitable, unprolific.

stick *v.* adhere, affix, attach, bind, bond, bulge, catch, cement, cleave, cling, clog, deposit, dig, drop, endure, extend, fasten, fix, fuse, glue, gore, hold, insert, install, jab, jam, join, jut, lay, linger, lodge, paste, penetrate, persist, pierce, pin, place, plant, plonk, poke, position, prod, project, protrude, puncture, put, put up with, remain, set, show, snag, spear, stab, stand, stay, stop, store, stuff, take, thrust, tolerate, transfix, weld.

stiff *adj.* arduous, arthritic, artificial, austere, awkward, brisk, brittle, buckram, budge, ceremonious, chilly, clumsy, cold, constrained, creaky, crude, cruel, difficult, drastic, exacting, excessive, extreme, fatiguing, firm, forced, formal, formidable, fresh, graceless, great, hard, hardened, harsh, heavy, inelastic, inelegant, inexorable, inflexible, jerky, laborious, labored, mannered, oppressive, pertinacious, pitiless, pompous, powerful, priggish, prim, punctilious, resistant, rigid, rigorous, severe, sharp, solid, solidified, standoffish, starch(y), stark, stilted, strict, stringent, strong, stubborn, taut, tense, tight, toilsome, tough, trying, unbending, uneasy, ungainly, ungraceful, unnatural, unrelaxed, unsupple, unyielding, uphill, vigorous, wooden.

still *adj.* calm, hushed, inert, lifeless, motionless, noiseless, pacific, peaceful, placid, quiet, restful, serene, silent, smooth, stagnant, stationary, stilly, tranquil, undisturbed, unruffled, unstirring.

stingy *adj.* avaricious, cheese-paring, close-fisted, covetous, illiberal, inadequate, insufficient, meager, mean, measly, miserly, near, niggardly, parsimonious, penny-pinching, penurious, save-all, scanty, scrimping, small, tightfisted, ungenerous, ungiving.

stop *v.* arrest, bar, block, break, cease, check, close, conclude, desist, discontinue, end, finish, forestall, frustrate, halt, hinder, impede, intercept, intermit, interrupt, knock off, leave off, lodge, obstruct, pack (it) in, pack up, pause, plug, poop out, prevent, quit, refrain, repress, rest, restrain, scotch, seal, silence, sojourn, stall, staunch, stay, stem, stymie, suspend, tarry, terminate.

story[1] *n.* account, anecdote, article, chronicle, episode, fable, fairy tale, falsehood, feature, fib, fiction, history, legend, lie, myth, narration, narrative, news, novel, plot, recital, record, relation, report, romance, scoop, spiel, tale, untruth, version, yarn.

story[2] *n.* deck, étage, flight, floor, level, stage, stratum, tier.

straight *adj.* accurate, aligned, arranged, authentic, balanced, blunt, bourgeois, candid, consecutive, conservative, continuous, conventional, decent, direct, downright, equitable, erect, even, fair, forthright, frank, honest, honorable, horizontal, just, law-abiding, level, near, neat, nonstop, normal, orderly, organized, orthodox, outright, perpendicular, plain, plumb, point-blank, pure, reliable, respectable, right, running, settled, shipshape, short, smooth, solid, square, straightforward, successive, sustained, thorough, tidy, traditional, true, trustworthy, unadulterated, undeviating, undiluted, uninterrupted, unmixed, unqualified, unrelieved, unswerving, upright, vertical.

strain[1] *v.* compress, distend, drive, embrace, endeavor, exert, express, extend, fatigue, filter, injure, labor, overtax, overwork, percolate, pull, purify, restrain, retch, riddle, screen, seep, separate, sieve, sift, sprain, squeeze, stretch, strive, struggle, tauten, tax, tear, tighten, tire, tug, twist, weaken, wrench, wrest, wrick. *n.* anxiety, burden, effort, exertion, force, height, injury, key, pitch, pressure, pull, sprain, stress, struggle, tautness, tension, wrench.

strain[2] *n.* ancestry, blood, descent, extraction, family, humor, lineage, manner, pedigree, race, spirit, stem, stock, streak, style, suggestion, suspicion, temper, tendency, tone, trace, trait, vein, way.

strange *adj.* abnormal, alien, astonishing, awkward, bewildered, bizarre, curious, disorientated, disoriented, eccentric, eerie, exceptional, exotic, extraordinary, fantastic(al), foreign, funny, irregular, lost, marvelous, mystifying, new, novel, odd, out-of-the-way, peculiar, perplexing, queer, rare, remarkable, remote, singular, sinister, unaccountable, unacquainted, uncanny, unco, uncomfortable, uncommon, unexplained, unexplored, unfamiliar, unheard of, unknown, untired, unversed, weird, wonderful.

street *n.* avenue, boulevard, crescent, drive, expressway, freeway, highway, lane, main drag, parkway, road, roadway, row, terrace, thoroughfare, thruway, turnpike.

strength *n.* advantage, anchor, asset, backbone, brawn, brawniness, cogency, concentration, courage, effectiveness, efficacy, energy, firmness, force, fortitude, health, intensity, lustiness, mainstay, might, muscle, potency, power, resolution, robustness, security, sinew, spirit, stamina, stoutness, sturdiness, toughness, vehemence, vigor, virtue.

stress *n.* accent, accentuation, anxiety, beat, burden, emphasis, emphaticalness, force, hassle, importance, oppression, pressure, significance, strain, tautness, tension, trauma, urgency, weight, worry.

strict *adj.* absolute, accurate, austere, authoritarian, close, complete, exact, faithful, firm, harsh, meticulous, no-nonsense, particular, perfect, precise, religious, restricted, rigid, rigorous, scrupulous, severe, stern, stringent, thoroughgoing, total, true, unsparing, utter, Victorian.

strident *adj.* cacophonous, discordant, grating, harsh, shrill.

strong *adj.* acute, aggressive, athletic, beefy, biting, bold, brave, brawny, bright, brilliant, burly, capable, clear, clear-cut, cogent, compelling, competent, concentrated, convincing, courageous, dazzling, dedicated, deep, deep-rooted, determined, distinct, drastic, durable, eager, effective, efficient, emphasized, excelling, extreme, fast-moving, fervent, fervid, fierce, firm, forceful, forcible, formidable, glaring, great, grievous, gross, hale, hard, hard-nosed, hardwearing, hardy, heady, healthy, hearty, heavy-duty, herculean, highly flavored, highly seasoned, hot, intemperate, intense, intoxicating, keen, loud, lusty, marked, muscular, nappy, numerous, offensive, overpowering, persuasive, piquant, pithy, plucky, potent, powerful, pungent, pure, rank, redoubtable, reinforced, resilient, resolute, resourceful, robust, self-assertive, severe, sharp, sinewy, sound, spicy, stalwart, stark, staunch, steadfast, stout, stouthearted, strapping, stressed, sturdy, substantial, telling, tenacious, tough, trenchant, undiluted, unmistakable, unseemly, unyielding, urgent, vehement, violent, virile, vivid, weighty, well-armed, well-built, well-established, well-founded, well-knit, well-protected, well-set, well-versed, zealous.

struggle *v.* agonize, battle, compete, contend, fight, grapple, labor, scuffle, strain, strive, toil, work, wrestle.

stubborn *adj.* bullheaded, difficult, dogged, headstrong, intractable, obstinate, opinionated, pig-headed, unbending.

stumble *v.* blunder, fall, falter, flounder, fluff, hesitate, lurch, reel, slip, stagger, stutter, trip.

stun *v.* amaze, astonish, astound, bewilder, confound, confuse, daze, deafen, dumbfound, flabbergast, overcome, overpower, shock, stagger, stupefy.

sturdy *adj.* athletic, brawny, determined, durable, firm, flourishing, hardy, hearty, husky, lusty, muscular, obstinate, powerful, resolute, robust, secure, solid, stalwart, stench, steadfast, stout, strong, substantial, vigorous, well-built, well-made.

subject *n.* affair, business, case, chapter, citizen, client, dependant, ground, issue, matter, mind, national, object, participant, patient, point, question, subordinate, substance, theme, topic, vassal, victim.

subordinate *adj.* ancillary, auxiliary, dependent, inferior, junior, lesser, lower, menial, minor, secondary, servient, subject, subservient, subsidiary, supplementary.

subside *v.* abate, collapse, decline, decrease, descend, diminish, drop, dwindle, ease, ebb, fall, lessen, lower, moderate, quieten, recede, settle, sink, slacken, slake, wane.

substitute *v.* change, replace, subrogate, swap, switch. *n.* alternate, equivalent, replacement, surrogate. *adj.* acting, alternative, replacement, temporary.

succeed *v.* arrive, ensue, flourish, follow, make good, make it, prosper, result, supervene, thrive, triumph, work.

success *n.* ascendancy, best-seller, celebrity, eminence, fame, fortune, happiness, hit, luck, prosperity, sensation, somebody, star, triumph, VIP, well-doing, winner.

sudden *adj.* abrupt, hasty, hurried, impulsive, prompt, quick rapid, rash, snap, startling, swift, unexpected, unforeseen, unusual.

suffer *v.* ache, agonize, allow, bear, brook, deteriorate, endure, experience, feel, grieve, hurt, let, permit, sorrow, support, sustain, tolerate, undergo.

sufficient *adj.* adequate, competent, effective, enough, satisfactory, sufficing, well-off, well-to-do.

suffocate *v.* asphyxiate, choke, smother, stifle, strangle, throttle.

suggest *v.* advise, advocate, connote, evoke, hint, imply, indicate, inkle, innuendo, insinuate, intimate, move, propose, recommend.

sum *n.* aggregate, amount, completion, culmination, entirety, height, quantity, reckoning, result, score, substance, sum total, summary, tally, total, totality, whole.

summarize *v.* abbreviate, abridge, condense, encapsulate, epitomize, outline, précis, review, shorten, sum up.

summit *n.* acme, apex, apogee, crown, culmination, head, height, peek, pinnacle, point to, zenith.

superior *adj.* admirable, airy, better, choice, condescending, de luxe, disdainful, distinguished, excellent, exceptional, exclusive, fine, first-class, first-rate, good, grander, greater, haughty, high-class, higher, hoity-toity, lofty, lordly, par excellence, patronizing, predominant, preferred, pretentious, prevailing, respectable, snobbish, snooty, snotty, snouty, stuckup, supercilious, superordinate, surpassing, topflight, topnotch, transcendent, unrivaled, upper, uppish, uppity, upstage, worth.

supervise *v.* administer, conduct, control, direct, general, handle, inspect, manage, oversee, preside over, run, superintend.

supplant *v.* displace, dispossess, oust, overthrow, remove, replace, supersede, topple, undermine, unseat.

suppose *v.* assume, believe, calculate, conceive, conclude, conjecture, consider, expect, fancy, guess, hypothesize, imagine, infer, judge, opine, posit, postulate, presume, presuppose, pretend, surmise, think.

supreme *adj.* cardinal, chief, consummate, crowning, culminating, extreme, final, first, foremost, greatest, head, highest, incomparable, leading, matchless, nonpareil, paramount, peerless, predominant, preeminent, prevailing, prime, principal, second-to-none, sovereign, superlative, surpassing, to, transcendent, ultimate, unbeatable, unbeaten, unsurpassed, utmost, world-beating.

sure *adj.* accurate, assured, bound, certain, clear, confident, convinced, decided, definite, dependable, effective, fast, firm, fixed, foolproof, guaranteed, honest, indisputable, inescapable, inevitable, infallible, irrevocable, persuaded, positive, precise, reliable, safe, satisfied, secure, solid, stable, steadfast, steady, surefire, trustworthy, trusty, undeniable, undoubted, unerring, unfailing, unmistakable, unswerving, unwavering.

surface *n.* covering, façade, face, facet, skin, veneer.

surprise *v.* amaze, astonish, astound, bewilder, confuse, disconcert, dismay, flabbergast, nonplus, stagger, startle, stun. *n.* amazement, astonishment, bewilderment, dismay, eye-opener, incredulity, jolt, revelation, shock, start, stupefaction, wonder.

surrender *v.* abandon, capitulate, cede, concede, give in, give up, quit, renounce, resign, submit, succumb, waive, yield.

surreptitious *adj.* clandestine, covert, furtive, secret, sly, sneaking, stealthy.

survive *v.* endure, exist, last, last out, live, live out, live through, outlast, outlive, ride, stay, subsist, weather, withstand.

suspect *v.* believe, call in question, conclude, conjecture, consider, distrust, doubt, fancy, feel, guess, infer, mistrust, opine, speculate, suppose, surmise. *adj.* debatable, dodgy, doubtful, dubious, fishy, questionable, suspicious, unauthoritative, unreliable.

swamp n. bog, dismal, everglades, fen, marsh, mire, morass, moss, quagmire, quicksands. *v.* beset, besiege, capsize, deluge, drench, engulf, flood, inundate, overload, overwhelm, saturate, sink, submerge, waterlog.

swear[1] *v.* affirm, assert, asseverate, attest, vow, declare, depose, insist, promise, testify, vow, warrant.

swear[2] *v.* blaspheme, blind, curse, cuss, take the Lord's name in vain.

sweet[1] *adj.* affectionate, appealing, aromatic, beloved, cherished, darling, engaging, gentle, lovable, saccharine, sugary, syrupy, wholesome.

sweet[2] *n.* bonbon, candy, comfit, confect, confection, confectionery, sweetie, sweetmeat.

switch *v.* change, change course, change direction, chop and change, deflect, deviate, divert, exchange, interchange, put, rearrange, replace, shift, shunt, substitute, swap, trade, turn, veer. *n.* about-turn, alteration, change, change of direction, exchange, interchange, shift, substitution, swap.

sympathize *v.* agree, commiserate, condole, empathize, feel for, identify with, pity, rap, respond to, side with, understand.

sympathy *n.* affinity, agreement, comfort, commiseration, compassion, condolement, condolence, condolences, empathy, fellow feeling, harmony, pity, rapport, tenderness, thoughtfulness, understanding, warmth.

synopsis *n.* abridgement, abstract, compendium, condensation, digest, epitome, outline, précis, recapitulation, review, sketch, summary, summation.

system *n.* arrangement, classification, coordination, logic, method, methodicalness, methodology, mode, modus operandi, orderliness, organization, plan, practice, procedure, process, regularity, routine, rule, scheme, structure, systematization, tabulation, taxis, taxonomy, technique, theory, usage.

systematic *adj.* businesslike, efficient, habitual, intentional, logical, methodical, ordered, orderly, organized, planned, precise, standardized, systematical, systematized, well-ordered, well-planned.

T

tackle[1] *n.* accouterments, apparatus, equipment, gear, harness, implements, outfit, paraphernalia, rig, rigging, tackling, tools, trappings. *v.* harness.

tackle[2] *n.* attack, block, challenge, interception, intervention, stop. *v.* attempt, begin, block, challenge, clutch, confront, deal with, embark upon, encounter, engage in, essay, face up to, grab, grapple with, grasp, halt, intercept, seize, set about, stop, take on, throw, try, undertake, wade into. *antonyms* avoid, sidestep.

tacky *adj.* adhesive, cheap, gimcrack, gluey, gummy, messy, nasty, scruffy, seedy, shabby, shoddy, sleazy, sticky, tasteless, tatty, tawdry, vulgar, wet.

tact *n.* address, adroitness, consideration, delicacy, diplomacy, discernment, discretion, finesse, grace, judgment, perception, prudence, savoir faire, sensitivity, skill, thoughtfulness, understanding. *antonyms* clumsiness, indiscretion, tactlessness.

tactical *adj.* adroit, artful, calculated, clever, cunning, diplomatic, judicious, politic, prudent, shrewd, skillful, smart, strategic. *antonym* impolitic.

tactics *n.* approach, campaign, game plan, line of attack, maneuvers, moves, plan, plan of campaign, plans, ploys, policy, procedure, shifts, stratagems, strategy.

tag *n.* aglet, aiglet, aiguillette, appellation, dag, designation, docket, epithet, flap, identifications, label, mark, marker, name, note, slip, sticker, tab, tally, ticket. *v.* add, adjoin, affix, annex, append, call, christen, designate, dub, earmark, fasten, identify, label, mark, nickname, style, tack, term, ticket.

tag *n.* dictum, fadaise, gnome, gobbet, maxim, moral, motto, proverb, quotation, quote, remnant, saw, saying.

tail *n.* appendage, backside, behind, bottom, bum, buttocks, conclusion, croup, detective, empennage, end, extremity, file, follower, fud, line, posterior, queue, rear, rear end, retinue, rump, scut, suite, tailback, tailpiece, tailplane, train. *v.* dog, follow, keep with, shadow, spy on, stalk, track, trail.

tailor *n.* clothier, costumer, costumier, couturier, couturière, dressmaker, modiste, outfitter, seamstress, whipcat, whipstitch. *v.* accommodate, adapt, adjust, alter, convert, cut, fashion, fit, modify, mold, shape, style, suit, trim.

taint *v.* adulterate, besmirch, blacken, blemish, blight, blot, brand, contaminate, corrupt, damage, defile, deprave, dirty, disgrace, dishonor, envenom, foul, infect, muddy, poison, pollute, ruin, shame, smear, smirch, soil, spoil, stain, stigmatize, sully, tarnish, vitiate. *n.* blemish, blot, contagion, contamination, corruption, defect, disgrace, dishonor, fault, flaw, infamy, infection, obloquy, odium, opprobrium, pollution, shame, smear, smirch, spot, stain, stigma.

take *v.* abduct, abide, abstract, accept, accommodate, accompany, acquire, adopt, appropriate, arrest, ascertain, assume, attract, bear, believe, betake, bewitch, blight, book, brave, bring, brook, buy, call for, captivate, capture, carry, cart, catch, charm, clutch, conduct, consider, consume, contain, convey, convoy, deduct, deem, delight, demand, derive, detract, do, effect, eliminate, enchant, endure, engage, ensnare, entrap, escort, execute, fascinate, ferry, fetch, filch, gather, glean, grasp, grip, guide, haul, have, have room for, hire, hold, imbibe, ingest, inhale, lead, lease, make, measure, misappropriate, necessitate, need, nick, observe, obtain, operate, perceive, perform, photograph, pick, pinch, please, pocket, portray, presume, purchase, purloin, receive, regard, remove, rent, require, reserve, secure, seize, select, stand, steal, stomach, strike, subtract, succeed, suffer, swallow, swipe, thole, tolerate, tote, transport, undergo, understand, undertake, usher, weather, win, withstand, work. *n.* catch, gate, haul, income, proceeds, profits, receipts, return, revenue, takings, yield.

taking *adj.* alluring, appealing, attractive, beguiling, captivating, catching, charming, compelling, delightful, enchanting, engaging, fascinating, fetching, intriguing, pleasing, prepossessing, winning, winsome. *antonyms* repellent, repulsive, unattractive. *n.* agitation, alarm, coil, commotion, consternation, flap, fuss, panic, passion, pother, state, sweat, tiz-woz, tizzy, turmoil, wax.

tale *n.* account, anecdote, fable, fabrication, falsehood, fib, fiction, legend, lie, märchen, Munchausen, myth, narration, narrative, old wives' tale, relation, report, rigmarole, romance, rumor, saga, spiel, story, superstition, tall story, tradition, untruth, yarn.

talent *n.* ability, aptitude, bent, capacity, endowment, faculty, feel, flair, forte, genius, gift, knack, long suit, nous, parts, power, strength. *antonyms* inability, ineptitude, weakness.

talented *adj.* able, accomplished, adept, adroit, apt, artistic, brilliant, capable, clever, deft, gifted, ingenious, inspired, well-endowed. *antonyms* clumsy, inept, maladroit.

talk *v.* articulate, blab, blather, chat, chatter, chinwag, commune, communicate, confabulate, confer, converse, crack, gab, gossip, grass, inform, jaw, natter, negotiate, palaver, parley, prate, prattle, rap, say, sing, speak, squeak, squeal, utter, verbalize, witter. *n.* address, argot, bavardage, blather, blether, causerie, chat, chatter, chinwag, chitchat, clash, claver, colloquy, conclave, confab, confabulation, conference, consultation, conversation, crack, dialect, dialogue, discourse, discussion, disquisition, dissertation, gab, gossip, harangue, hearsay, jargon, jaw, jawing, language, lecture, lingo, meeting, natter, negotiation, oration, palabra, palaver, parley, patois, rap, rumor, seminar, sermon, slang, speech, spiel, symposium, tittle-tattle, utterance, words.

talkative *adj.* chatty, communicative, conversational, effusive, expansive, forthcoming, gabby, garrulous, gossipy, long-tongued, long-winded, loquacious, rating, prolix, unreserved, verbose, vocal, voluble, wordy. *antonyms* reserved, taciturn.

tall *adj.* absurd, big, dubious, elevated, embellished, exaggerated, far-fetched, giant, grandiloquent, great, high, implausible, improbable, incredible, lanky, leggy, lofty, overblown, preposterous, remarkable, soaring, steep, topless, towering, unbelievable, unlikely. *antonyms* low, reasonable, short, small.

tally *v.* accord, agree, coincide, compute, concur, conform, correspond, figure, fit, harmonize, jibe, mark, match, parallel, reckon, record, register, square, suit, tie in, total. *antonyms* differ, disagree. *n.* account, count, counterfoil, counterpart, credit, duplicate, label, mark, match, mate, notch, reckoning, record, score, stub, tab, tag, tick, total.

tame *adj.* amenable, anemic, biddable, bland, bloodless, boring, broken, compliant, cultivated, disciplined, docile, domesticated, dull, feeble, flat, gentle, humdrum, insipid, lifeless, manageable, meek, obedient, prosaic, spiritless, subdued, submissive, tedious, tractable, unadventurous, unenterprising, unexciting, uninspired, uninspiring, uninteresting, unresisting, vapid, wearisome. *v.* break in, bridle, calm, conquer, curb, discipline, domesticate, enslave, gentle, house-train, humble, master, mellow, mitigate, mute, pacify, quell, repress, soften, subdue, subjugate, suppress, temper, train.

tamper *v.* alter, bribe, cook, corrupt, damage, fiddle, fix, influence, interfere, intrude, juggle, manipulate, meddle, mess, rig, tinker.

tang *n.* aroma, bite, flavor, hint, kick, overtone, piquancy, pungency, reek, savor, scent, smack, smell, suggestion, taste, tinge, touch, trace, whiff.

tangible *adj.* actual, concrete, corporeal, definite, discernible, evident, manifest, material, objective, observable, palpable, perceptible, physical, positive, real, sensible, solid, substantial, tactile, touchable. *antonym* intangible.

tangle *n.* burble, coil, complication, confusion, convolution, embroglio, embroilment, entanglement, fankle, fix, imbroglio, jam, jumble, jungle, know, labyrinth, mass, mat, maze, mesh, mess, mix-up, muddle, raffle, snarl, snarl-up, twist, web. *v.* catch, coil, confuse, convolve, embroil, enmesh, ensnare, entangle, entrap, hamper, implicate, interlace, interlock, intertwine, intertwist, interweave, involve, jam, knot, mat, mesh, muddle, snarl, trap, twist. *antonym* disentangle.

tantrum *n.* bate, fit, flare-up, fury, hysterics, outburst, paddy, paroxysm, rage, scene, storm, temper, wax.

tap^1 *v.* beat, chap, drum, knock, pat, rap, strike, tat, touch. *n.* beat, chap, knock, pat, rap, rat-tat, touch.

tap^2 *n.* bug, bung, faucet, plug, receiver, spigot, spile, spout, stopcock, stopper, valve. *v.* bleed, broach, bug, drain, exploit, milk, mine, open, pierce, quarry, siphon, unplug, use, utilize, wiretap.

tape *n.* band, binding, magnetic tape, riband, ribbon, strip, tape measure. *v.* assess, bind, measure, record, seal, secure, stick, tape-record, video, wrap.

taper^1 *v.* attenuate, decrease, die away, die out, dwindle, fade, lessen, narrow, peter out, reduce, slim, subside, tail off, thin, wane, weaken. *antonyms* increase, swell, widen.

taper^2 *n.* bougie, candle, spill, wax light, wick.

tardy *adj.* backward, behindhand, belated, dawdling, delayed, dilatory, eleventh-hour, lag, last-minute, late, loitering, overdue, procrastinating, retarded, slack, slow, sluggish, unpunctual. *antonyms* prompt, punctual.

target *n.* aim, ambition, bull's-eye, butt, destination, end, goal, intention, jack, mark, object, objective, prey, prick, purpose, quarry, scapegoat, victim.

tarnish *v.* befoul, blacken, blemish, blot, darken, dim, discolor, disluster, dull, mar, rust, soil, spoil, spot, stain, sully, taint. *antonyms* brighten, enhance, polish up. *n.* blackening, blemish, blot, discoloration, film, patina, rust, spot, stain, taint. *antonyms* brightness, polish.

tarry *v.* abide, bide, dally, dawdle, delay, dwell, lag, linger, loiter, pause, remain, rest, sojourn, stay, stop, wait.

tart^1 *n.* pastry, pie, quiche, tartlet.

tart^2 *adj.* acerb, acerbic, acid, acidulous, acrimonious, astringent, barbed, biting, bitter, caustic, cutting, incisive, piquant, pungent, sardonic, scathing, sharp, short, sour, tangy, trenchant, vinegary.

tart^3 *n.* broad, call girl, drab, fallen woman, fille de joie, fille publique, floosie, harlot, hooker, prostitute, slut, streetwalker, strumpet, tramp, trollop, whore.

task *n.* assignment, aufgabe, burden, business, charge, chore, darg, duty, employment, enterprise, exercise, imposition, job, job of work, labor, mission, occupation, pensum, toil, undertaking, work. *v.* burden, charge, commit, encumber, entrust, exhaust, load, lumber, oppress, overload, push, saddle, strain, tax, test, weary.

taste *n.* appetite, appreciation, bent, bit, bite, choice, correctness, cultivation, culture, dash, decorum, delicacy, desire, discernment, discretion, discrimination, drop, elegance, experience, fancy, finesse, flavor, fondness, gout, grace, gustation, inclination, judgment, leaning, liking, morsel, mouthful, nibble, nicety, nip, palate, partiality, penchant, perception, polish, politeness, predilection, preference, propriety, refinement, relish, restraint, sample, sapor, savor, sensitivity, sip, smack, smatch, soupçon, spoonful, style, swallow, tact, tactfulness, tang, tastefulness, tidbit, touch. *v.* assay, degust, degustate, differentiate, discern, distinguish, encounter, experience, feel, know, meet, perceive, relish, sample, savor, sip, smack, test, try, undergo.

tasteful *adj.* aesthetic, artistic, beautiful, charming, comme il faut, correct, cultivated, cultured, delicate, discreet, discriminating, elegant, exquisite, fastidious, graceful, handsome, harmonious, judicious, polished, refined, restrained, smart, stylish, well-judged. *antonym* tasteless.

tasteless *adj.* barbaric, bland, boring, cheap, coarse, crass, crude, dilute, dull, flashy, flat, flavorless, garish, gaudy, graceless, gross, improper, inartistic, indecorous, indelicate, indiscreet, inelegant, inharmonious, insipid, low, mild, rude, stale, tacky, tactless, tame, tatty, tawdry, thin, uncouth, undiscriminating, uninspired, uninteresting, unseemly, untasteful, vapid, vulgar, watered-down, watery, weak, wearish. *antonym* tasteful.

tasty *adj.* appetizing, delectable, delicious, flavorful, flavorous, flavorsome, gusty, luscious, mouthwatering, palatable, piquant, sapid, saporous, savory, scrumptious, succulent, toothsome, yummy. *antonyms* disgusting, insipid, tasteless.

tattered *adj.* duddie, frayed, in shreds, lacerated, ragged, raggy, rent, ripped, tatty, threadbare, torn. *antonyms* neat, trim.

tattle *v.* babble, blab, blather, blether, chat, chatter, clash, claver, gab, gash, gossip, jabber, natter, prate, prattle, talk, tittle-tattle, yak, yap. *n.* babble, blather, blether, chat, chatter, chitchat, clash, claver, gossip, hearsay, jabber, prattle, rumor, talk, tittle-tattle, yak, yap.

taunt *v.* bait, chiack, deride, fleer, flout, flyte, gibe, insult, jeer, mock, provoke, reproach, revile, rib, ridicule, sneer, tease, torment, twit. *n.* barb, catcall, censure, cut, derision, dig, fling, gibe, insult, jeer, poke, provocation, reproach, ridicule, sarcasm, sneer, teasing.

taut *adj.* contracted, rigid, strained, stressed, stretched, tense, tensed, tight, tightened, unrelaxed. *antonyms* loose, relaxed, slack.

tautology *n.* duplication, iteration, otioseness, perissology, pleonasm, redundancy, repetition, repetitiousness, repetitiveness, superfluity. *antonyms* economy, succinctness.

tawdry *adj.* cheap, cheap-jack, flashy, garish, gaudy, gimcrack, gingerbread, glittering, meretricious, pinchbeck, plastic, raffish, showy, tacky, tasteless, tatty, tinsel, tinsely, vulgar. *antonyms* excellent, fine, superior.

tax *n.* agistment, assessment, burden, charge, contribution, customs, demand, drain, duty, excise, geld, imposition, impost, levy, load, octroi, pressure, rate, scat, scot, strain, tariff, tithe, toll, tribute, weight. *v.* accuse, arraign, assess, blame, burden, censure, charge, demand, drain, enervate, exact, exhaust, extract, geld, impeach, impose, impugn, incriminate, load, overburden, overtax, push, rate, reproach, sap, strain, stretch, task, tithe, try, weaken, weary.

taxi *n.* cab, fiacre, hack, hansom cab, taxicab.

teach *v.* accustom, advise, coach, counsel, demonstrate, direct, discipline, drill, edify, educate, enlighten, ground, guide, impart, implant, inculcate, inform, instill, instruct, school, show, train, tutor, verse.

teacher *n.* abecedarian, coach, dominie, don, educator, guide, guru, instructor, khodja, kindergartener, kindergartner, lecturer, luminary, maharishi, master, mentor, mistress, pedagogue, professor, pundit, schoolmarm, schoolmaster, schoolmistress, schoolteacher, trainer, tutor, usher.

team *n.* band, body, bunch, company, crew, écurie, équipe, gang, group, lineup, pair, set, shift, side, span, squad, stable, troupe, yoke.

teamwork *n.* collaboration, cooperation, coordination, esprit de corps, fellowship, joint effort, team spirit. *antonyms* disharmony, disunity.

tear *v.* belt, bolt, career, charge, claw, dart, dash, dilacerate, divide, drag, fly, gallop, gash, grab, hurry, lacerate, mangle, mutilate, pluck, pull, race, rend, rip, rive, run, rupture, rush, scratch, seize, sever, shoot, shred, snag, snatch, speed, split, sprint, sunder, wrench, wrest, yank, zoom. *n.* hole, laceration, rent, rip, run, rupture, scratch, snag, split.

tearful *adj.* blubbering, crying, distressing, dolorous, emotional, lachrymose, lamentable, maudlin, mournful, pathetic, pitiable, pitiful, poignant, sad, sobbing, sorrowful, upsetting, weeping, weepy, whimpering, woeful.

tease *v.* aggravate, annoy, badger, bait, banter, bedevil, chaff, chip, gibe, goad, grig, guy, irritate, josh, mock, needle, pester, plague, provoke, rag, rib, ridicule, take a rise out of, tantalize, taunt, torment, twit, vex, worry.

technique *n.* address, adroitness, approach, art, artistry, course, craft, craftsmanship, delivery, executancy, execution, expertise, facility, fashion, knack, know-how, manner, means, method, mode, modus operandi, performance, procedure, proficiency, skill, style, system, touch, way.

tedious *adj.* annoying, banal, boring, deadly, drab, dreary, dreich, dull, fatiguing, humdrum, irksome, laborious, lifeless, long-drawn-out, longsome, longspun, monotonous, prosaic, prosy, soporific, tiring, unexciting, uninteresting, vapid, wearisome.

tedium *n.* banality, boredom, drabness, dreariness, dullness, ennui, lifelessness, monotony, prosiness, routing, sameness, tediousness, vapidity.

teem *v.* abound, bear, brim, bristle, burst, increase, multiply, overflow, overspill, produce, proliferate, pullulate, swarm. *antonyms* lack, want.

teeming *adj.* abundant, alive, brimful, brimming, bristling, bursting, chock-a-block, chock-full, crawling, fruitful, full, numerous, overflowing, packed, pregnant, proliferating, pullulating, replete, swarming, thick. *antonyms* lacking, rare, sparse.

teeter *v.* balance, lurch, pitch, pivot, rock, seesaw, stagger, sway, titubate, totter, tremble, waver, wobble.

teetotaller *n.* abstainer, nephalist, nondrinker, Rechabite, water drinker.

telephone *n.* blower, handset, line, phone. *v.* buzz, call, call up, contact, dial, get in touch, get on the blower, give someone a tinkle, phone ring (up).

telescope *v.* abbreviate, abridge, compress, concertina, condense, contract, crush, curtail, cut, reduce, shorten, shrink, squash, trim, truncate.

television *n.* boob tube, goggle box, idiot box, receiver, set, small screen, the box, the tube, TV, TV set.

tell *v.* acquaint, announce, apprize, authorize, bid, calculate, chronicle, command, communicate, comprehend, compute, confess, count, depict, describe, differentiate, direct, discern, disclose, discover, discriminate, distinguish, divulge, enjoin, enumerate, express, foresee, identify, impart, inform, instruct, mention, militate, narrate, notify, number, order, portray, predict, proclaim, reckon, recount, register, rehearse, relate, report, require, reveal, say, see, speak, state, summon, tally, understand, utter, weigh.

temerity *n.* assurance, audacity, boldness, brass neck, chutzpah, daring, effrontery, forwardness, gall, heedlessness, impudence, impulsiveness, intrepidity, nerve, pluck, rashness, recklessness. *antonym* caution.

temper *n.* anger, annoyance, attitude, bate, calm, calmness, character, composure, constitution, cool, coolness, disposition, equanimity, fury, heat, humor, ill-humor, irascibility, irritability, irritation, mind, moderation, mood, nature, paddy, passion, peevishness, pet, petulance, rage, resentment, sangfroid, self-control, taking, tantrum, temperament, tenor, tranquillity, vein, wax, wrath. *v.* abate, admix, allay, anneal, assuage, calm, harden, indurate, lessen, mitigate, moderate, modify, mollify, palliate, restrain, soften, soothe, strengthen, toughen.

temperament *n.* anger, bent, character, complexion, constitution, crasis, disposition, excitability, explosiveness, hotheadedness, humor, impatience, makeup, mettle, moodiness, moods, nature, outlook, personality, petulance, quality, soul, spirit, stamp, temper, tendencies, tendency, volatility.

temperamental *adj.* capricious, congenital, constitutional, emotional, erratic, excitable, explosive, fiery, highlystrung, hotheaded, hypersensitive, impatient, inborn, inconsistent, ingrained, inherent, innate, irritable, mercurial, moody, natural, neurotic, over-emotional, passionate, petulant, sensitive, touchy, undependable, unpredictable, unreliable, volatile, volcanic. *antonyms* calm, serene, steady.

temperate *adj.* abstemious, abstinent, agreeable, balanced, balmy, calm, clement, composed, continent, controlled, cool, dispassionate, equable, even-tempered, fair, gentle, mild, moderate, pleasant, reasonable, restrained, sensible, sober, soft, stable. *antonyms* excessive, extreme, intemperate.

tempest *n.* bourasque, commotion, cyclone, disturbance, ferment, furore, gale, hurricane, squall, storm, tornado, tumult, typhoon, upheaval, uproar.

tempo *n.* beat, cadence, measure, meter, pace, pulse, rate, rhythm, speed, time, velocity.

temporal *adj.* carnal, civil, earthly, evanescent, fleeting, fleshly, fugacious, fugitive, impermanent, lay, material, momentary, mortal, mundane, passing, profane, secular, short-lived, sublunary, temporary, terrestrial, transient, transitory, unspiritual, worldly. *antonym* spiritual.

temporary *adj.* brief, ephemeral, evanescent, fleeting, fugacious, fugitive, impermanent, interim, makeshift, momentary, passing, pro tem, pro tempore, provisional, short-lived, stopgap, transient, transitory. *antonyms* everlasting, permanent.

tempt *v.* allure, attract, bait, coax, dare, decoy, draw, enamor, entice, incite, inveigle, invite, lure, provoke, risk, seduce, tantalize, test, try, woo. *antonyms* discourage, dissuade.

tenacious *adj.* adamant, adhesive, clinging, coherent, cohesive, determined, dogged, fast, firm, forceful, gluey, glutinous, inflexible, intransigent, mucilaginous, obdurate, obstinate, persistent, pertinacious, resolute, retentive, single-minded, solid, staunch, steadfast, sticky, strong, strong-willed, stubborn, sure, tight, tough, unshakable, unswerving, unwavering, unyielding, viscous. *antonyms* loose, slack, weak.

tenant *n.* gavelman, inhabitant, landholder, leaseholder, lessee, occupant, occupier, renter, resident.

tend[1] *v.* affect, aim, bear, bend, conduce, contribute, go, gravitate, head, incline, influence, lead, lean, move, point, trend, verge.

tend[2] *v.* attend, comfort, control, cultivate, feed, guard, handle, keep, maintain, manage, minister to, nurse, nurture, protect, serve, succor. *antonym* neglect.

tendency *n.* bearing, bent, bias, conatus, course, direction, disposition, drift, drive, heading, inclination, leaning, liability, movement, partiality, penchant, predilection, predisposition, proclivity, proneness, propensity, purport, readiness, susceptibility, tenor, thrust, trend, turning.

tender[1] *adj.* aching, acute, affectionate, affettuoso, amoroso, amorous, benevolent, breakable, bruised, callow, caring, chary, compassionate, complicated, considerate, dangerous, delicate, difficult, emotional, evocative, feeble, fond, fragile, frail, gentle, green, humane, immature, impressionable, inexperienced, inflamed, irritated, kind, loving, merciful, moving, new, painful, pathetic, pitiful, poignant, raw, risky, romantic, scrupulous, sensitive, sentimental, smarting, soft, softhearted, sore, sympathetic, tenderhearted, ticklish, touching, touchy, tricky, vulnerable, warm, warmhearted, weak, young, youthful. *antonyms* callous, chewy, hard, harsh, rough, severe, tough.

tender[2] *v.* advance, extend, give, offer, present, proffer, propose, submit, suggest, volunteer. *n.* bid, currency, estimate, medium, money, offer, payment, proffer, proposal, proposition, submissions, suggestion.

tenderness *n.* ache, aching, affection, amorousness, attachment, benevolence, bruising, callowness, care, compassion, consideration, delicateness, devotion, discomfort, feebleness, fondness, fragility, frailness, gentleness, greenness, humaneness, humanity, immaturity, impressionableness, inexperience, inflammation, irritation, kindness, liking, love, loving-kindness, mercy, newness, pain, painfulness, pity, rawness, sensitiveness, sensitivity, sentimentality, softheartedness, softness, soreness, sweetness, sympathy, tenderheartedness, vulnerability, warmheartedness, warmth, weakness, youth, youthfulness. *antonyms* cruelty, hardness, harshness.

tenet *n.* article of faith, belief, canon, conviction, credo, creed, doctrine, dogma, maxim, opinion, precept, presumption, principle, rule, teaching, thesis, view.

tense *adj.* anxious, apprehensive, edgy, electric, exciting, fidgety, jittery, jumpy, moving, nerve-racking, nervous, overwrought, restless, rigid, strained, stressful, stretched, strung up, taut, tight, uneasy, uptight, worrying. *antonyms* calm, lax, loose, relaxed. *v.* brace, contract, strain, stretch, tauten, tighten. *antonyms* loosen, relax.

tension *n.* anxiety, apprehension, edginess, hostility, nervousness, pressure, restlessness, rigidity, stiffness, strain, straining, stress, stretching, suspense, tautness, tightness, tone, unease, worry. *antonyms* calm(ness), laxness, looseness, relaxation.

tentative *adj.* cautious, conjectural, diffident, doubtful, experimental, faltering, hesitant, indefinite, peirastic, provisional, speculative, timid, uncertain, unconfirmed, undecided, unformulated, unsettled, unsure. *antonyms* conclusive, decisive, definite, final.

tenure *n.* habitation, holding, incumbency, occupancy, occupation, possession, proprietorship, residence, tenancy, term, time.

tepid *adj.* apathetic, cool, halfhearted, indifferent, lew, lukewarm, unenthusiastic, warmish. *antonyms* animated, cold, hot, passionate.

term[1] *n.* appellation, denomination, designation, epithet, epitheton, expression, locution, name, phrase, title, word. *v.* call, denominate, designate, dub, entitle, label, name, style, tag, title.

term² *n.* bound, boundary, close, conclusion, confine, course, culmination, duration, end, finish, fruition, half, interval, limit, period, season, semester, session, space, span, spell, terminus, time, while.

terminal *adj.* bounding, concluding, deadly, desinent, desinential, extreme, fatal, final, incurable, killing, last, lethal, limiting, mortal, ultimate, utmost. *n.* boundary, depot, end, extremity, limit, termination, terminus.

terminate *v.* abort, cease, close, complete, conclude, cut off, discontinue, drop, end, expire, finish, issue, lapse, result, stop, wind up. *antonyms* begin, initiate, start.

terminology *n.* argot, cant, jargon, language, lingo, nomenclature, patois, phraseology, terms, vocabulary, words.

terms *n.* agreement, charges, compromise, conditions, fees, footing, language, particulars, payment, phraseology, position, premises, price, provisions, provisos, qualifications, rates, relations, relationship, specifications, standing, status, stipulations, terminology, understanding.

terrible *adj.* abhorrent, appalling, awful, bad, beastly, dangerous, desperate, dire, disgusting, distressing, dread, dreaded, dreadful, extreme, fearful, foul, frightful, god-awful, gruesome, harrowing, hateful, hideous, horrendous, horrible, horrid, horrific, horrifying, loathsome, monstrous, obnoxious, odious, offensive, outrageous, poor, repulsive, revolting, rotten, serious, severe, shocking, unpleasant, vile.

terrific *adj.* ace, amazing, awesome, awful, breathtaking, brilliant, dreadful, enormous, excellent, excessive, extreme, fabulous, fantastic, fearful, fierce, fine, gigantic, great, harsh, horrific, huge, intense, magnificent, marvelous, monstrous, outstanding, prodigious, sensational, severe, smashing, stupendous, super, superb, terrible, tremendous, wonderful.

terrify *v.* affright, alarm, appall, awe, dismay, frighten, horrify, intimidate, petrify, scare, shock, terrorize.

territory *n.* area, bailiwick, country, dependency, district, domain, jurisdiction, land, park, preserve, province, region, sector, state, terrain, tract, zone.

terror *n.* affright, alarm, anxiety, awe, blue funk, bogeyman, bugbear, consternation, devil, dismay, dread, fear, fiend, fright, horror, intimidation, monster, panic, rascal, rogue, scourge, shock, tearaway.

terse *adj.* abrupt, aphoristic, brief, brusque, clipped, compact, concise, condensed, crisp, curt, economical, elliptical, epigrammatic, gnomic, incisive, laconic, neat, pithy, sententious, short, snappy, succinct. *antonyms* long-winded, prolix, repetitious.

test *v.* analyze, assay, assess, check, examine, experiment, investigate, prove, screen, try, verify. *n.* analysis, assessment, attempt, catechism, check, evaluation, examination, hurdle, investigation, moment of truth, ordeal, pons asinorum, probation, proof, shibboleth, trial, tryout.

testify *v.* affirm, assert, asseverate, attest, avow, certify, corroborate, declare, depone, depose, evince, show, state, swear, vouch, witness.

testimony *n.* affidavit, affirmation, asseveration, attestation, avowal, confirmation, corroboration, declaration, demonstration, deposition, evidence, indication, information, manifestation, profession, proof, statement, submission, support, verification, witness.

tether *n.* bond, chain, cord, fastening, fetter, halter, lead, leash, line, restraint, rope, shackle. *v.* bind, chain, fasten, fetter, lash, leash, manacle, picket, restrain, rope, secure, shackle, tie.

text *n.* argument, body, contents, lection, libretto, matter, motif, paragraph, passage, reader, reading, script, sentence, source, subject, textbook, theme, topic, verse, wordage, wording, words.

texture *n.* character, composition, consistency, constitution, fabric, feel, grain, quality, structure, surface, tissue, weave, weftage, woof.

thankful *adj.* appreciative, beholden, contented, grateful, indebted, obliged, pleased, relieved.

thaw *v.* defreeze, defrost, dissolve, liquefy, melt, soften, unbend, uncongeal, unfreeze, unthaw, warm. *antonym* freeze.

theater *n.* amphitheater, auditorium, hall, lyceum, odeon, opera house, playhouse.

theatrical *adj.* affected, artificial, ceremonious, dramatic, dramaturgic, exaggerated, extravagant, hammy, histrionic, mannered, melodramatic, ostentatious, overdone, pompous, scenic, showy, stagy, stilted, theatric, thespian, unreal.

theft *n.* abstraction, embezzlement, fraud, heist, kleptomania, larceny, pilfering, plunderage, purloining, rip-off, robbery, stealing, thieving.

theme *n.* argument, burden, composition, dissertation, essay, exercise, idea, keynote, leitmotiv, lemma, matter, motif, mythos, paper, subject, subject matter, text, thesis, topic, topos.

theoretical *adj.* abstract, academic, conjectural, doctrinaire, doctrinal, hypothetical, ideal, impractical, on paper, pure, speculative. *antonyms* applied, concrete, practical.

theory *n.* abstraction, assumption, conjecture, guess, hypothesis, ism, philosophy, plan, postulation, resumption, proposal, scheme, speculation, supposition, surmise, system, thesis. *antonyms* certainty, practice.

therefore *adv.* accordingly, as a result, consequently, ergo, for that reason, hence, so, then, thence, thus.

thick *adj.* abundant, brainless, brimming, bristling, broad, bulky, bursting, chock-a-block, chock-full, chummy, close, clotted, coagulated, compact, concentrated, condensed, confidential, covered, crass, crawling, crowded, decided, deep, dense, devoted, dim-witted, distinct, distorted, dopey, dull, excessive, familiar, fat, foggy, frequent, friendly, full, gross, guttural, heavy, hoarse, husky, impenetrable, inarticulate, indistinct, insensitive, inseparable, intimate, marked, matey, moronic, muffled, numerous, obtuse, opaque, packed, pally, pronounced, replete, rich, slow, slow-witted, solid, soupy, squabbish, strong, stupid, substantial, swarming, teeming, thickheaded, throaty, turbid, wide. *antonyms* brainy, clever, slender, slight, slim, thin, watery. *n.* center, focus, heart, hub, middle, midst.

thief *n.* abactor, Autolycus, bandit, burglar, cheat, cracksman, crook, cutpurse, embezzler, filcher, housebreaker, kleptomaniac, ladrone, land rat, larcener, larcenist, latron, mugger, pickpocket, pilferer, plunderer, prigger, purloiner, robber, shoplifter, snatchpurse, St. Nicholas's clerk, stealer, swindler.

thin *adj.* attenuate, attenuated, bony, deficient, delicate, diaphanous, dilute, diluted, emaciated, feeble, filmy, fine, fine-drawn, flimsy, gaunt, gossamer, inadequate, insubstantial, insufficient, lanky, lean, light, meager, narrow, poor, rarefied, runny, scant, scanty, scarce, scattered, scragged, scraggy, scrawny, see-through, shallow, sheer, skeletal, skimpy, skinny, slender, slight, slim, spare, sparse, spindly, superficial, tenuous, translucent, transparent, unconvincing, undernourished, underweight, unsubstantial, washy, watery, weak, wishy-washy, wispy.

antonyms broad, dense, fat, solid, strong, thick. *v.* attenuate, decrassify, dilute, diminish, emaciate, prune, rarefy, reduce, refine, trim, water down, weaken, weed out.

think *v.* anticipate, be under the impression, believe, brood, calculate, cerebrate, cogitate, conceive, conclude, consider, contemplate, deem, deliberate, design, determine, envisage, esteem, estimate, expect, foresee, hold, ideate, imagine, intellectualize, judge, meditate, mull over, muse, ponder, presume, purpose, ratiocinate, reason, recall, reckon, recollect, reflect, regard, remember, revolve, ruminate, suppose, surmise. *n.* assessment, cogitation, consideration, contemplation, deliberation, meditation, reflection.

thirst *n.* appetite, craving, desire, drought, drouth, drouthiness, dryness, eagerness, hankering, hunger, hydromania, keenness, longing, lust, passion, yearning, yen.

thirsty *adj.* adry, appetitive, arid, athirst, avid, burning, craving, dehydrated, desirous, drouthy, dry, dying, eager, greedy, hankering, hungry, hydropic, itching, longing, lusting, parched, thirsting, yearning.

thorough *adj.* absolute, all-embracing, all-inclusive, arrant, assiduous, careful, complete, comprehensive, conscientious, deep-seated, downright, efficient, entire, exhausted, full, in-depth, intensive, meticulous, out-and-out, painstaking, perfect, pure, root-and-branch, scrupulous, sheer, sweeping, thoroughgoing, total, unmitigated, unqualified, utter. *antonyms* careless, haphazard, partial.

though *conj.* albeit, allowing, although, even if, granted, howbeit, notwithstanding, while. *adv.* all the same, even so, for all that, however, in spite of that, nevertheless, nonetheless, notwithstanding, still, yet.

thought *n.* aim, anticipation, anxiety, aspiration, assessment, attention, attentiveness, belief, brainwork, care, cerebration, cogitation, compassion, concept, conception, concern, conclusion, conjecture, considerateness, consideration, contemplation, conviction, dash, deliberation, design, dream, estimation, excogitation, expectation, heed, hope, idea, intention, introspection, jot, judgment, kindness, little, meditation, mentation, muse, musing, notion, object, opinion, plan, prospect, purpose, reflection, regard, resolution, rumination, scrutiny, solicitude, study, sympathy, thinking, thoughtfulness, touch, trifle, view, whisker.

thoughtful *adj.* absorbed, abstracted, astute, attentive, canny, careful, caring, cautious, circumspect, considerate, contemplative, deliberate, deliberative, discreet, heedful, helpful, introspective, kind, kindly, meditative, mindful, musing, pensieroso, pensive, prudent, rapt, reflective, ruminative, serious, solicitous, studious, thinking, unselfish, wary, wistful. *antonym* thoughtless.

thoughtless *adj.* absentminded, careless, étourdi(e), foolish, heedless, ill-considered, impolite, imprudent, inadvertent, inattentive, inconsiderate, indiscreet, injudicious, insensitive, mindless, neglectful, negligent, rash, reckless, regardless, remiss, rude, selfish, silly, stupid, tactless, uncaring, undiplomatic, unkind, unmindful, unobservant, unreflecting, unthinking. *antonym* thoughtful.

thrash *v.* beat, belt, bethump, bethwack, birch, cane, chastise, clobber, crush, defeat, drub, flagellate, flair, flog, hammer, heave, horsewhip, jerk, lam, lambaste, larrup, lather, lay into, leather, maul, overwhelm, paste, plunge, punish, quilt, rout, scourge, slaughter, spank, squirm, swish, tan, thresh, toss, towel, trim, trounce, wallop, whale, whap, whip, writhe.

thread *n.* cotton, course, direction, drift, fiber, filament, film, fimbria, line, motif, plot, storyline, strain, strand, string, tenor, theme, yarn. *v.* ease, inch, meander, pass, string, weave, wind.

threadbare *adj.* clichéd, cliché-ridden, commonplace, conventional, corny, down-at-heel, frayed, hackneyed, motheaten, old, overused, overworn, ragged, scruffy, shabby, stale, stereotyped, stock, tattered, tatty, tired, trite, used, well-worn, worn, worn-out. *antonyms* fresh, luxurious, new, plush.

threat *n.* commination, danger, foreboding, foreshadowing, frighteners, hazard, menace, omen, peril, portent, presage, risk, saber rattling, warning.

threaten *v.* browbeat, bully, comminate, cow, endanger, forebode, foreshadow, impend, imperil, intimidate, jeopardize, menace, portend, presage, pressurize, terrorize, warn.

threatening *adj.* baleful, bullying, cautionary, comminatory, Damoclean, grim, inauspicious, intimidatory, menacing, minacious, minatory, ominous, sinister, terrorizing, warning.

threshold *n.* beginning, brink, dawn, door, doorsill, doorstead, doorstep, doorway, entrance, inception, minimum, opening, outset, sill, start, starting point, verge.

thrift *n.* carefulness, conservation, economy, frugality, husbandry, parsimony, prudence, saving, thriftiness.

thrifty *adj.* careful, conserving, economical, frugal, parsimonious, provident, prudent, saving, sparing. *antonyms* prodigal, profligate, thriftless, wasteful.

thrill *n.* adventure, buzz, charge, flutter, fluttering, frisson, glow, kick, pleasure, quiver, sensation, shudder, stimulation, throb, tingle, titillation, tremble, tremor, vibration. *v.* arouse, electrify, excite, flush, flutter, glow, move, quake, quiver, send, shake, shudder, stimulate, stir, throb, tingle, titillate, tremble, vibrate, wow.

thrive *v.* advance, bloom, blossom, boom, burgeon, develop, flourish, gain, grow, increase, profit, prosper, succeed, wax. *antonyms* die, fail, languish, stagnate.

throb *v.* beat, palpitate, pound, pulsate, pulse, thump, vibrate. *n.* beat, palpitation, pounding, pulsating, pulsation, pulse, thump, thumping, vibration, vibrato.

throe *n.* convulsion, fit, pain, pang, paroxysm, seizure, spasm, stab.

throng *n.* assemblage, bevy, concourse, congregation, crowd, crush, flock, herd, horde, host, jam, mass, mob, multitude, pack, press, swarm. *v.* bunch, congregate, converge, cram, crowd, fill, flock, herd, jam, mill around, pack, press, swarm.

through *prep.* as a result of, because of, between, by, by means of, by reason of, by virtue of, by way of, during, in, in and out, in consequence of, in the middle of, past, thanks to, throughout, using, via. *adj.* completed, direct, done, ended, express, finished, nonstop, terminated.

throughout *adv.* everywhere, extensively, ubiquitously, widely.

throw *v.* astonish, baffle, bemuse, bring down, cast, chuck, confound, confuse, defeat, discomfit, disconcert, dislodge, dumbfound, elance, execute, fell, fling, floor, heave, hurl, jaculate, launch, lob, overturn, perform, perplex, pitch, produce, project, propel, put, send, shy, sling, slug, toss, unhorse, unsaddle, unseat, upset, whang. *n.* attempt, cast, chance, essay, fling, gamble, hazard, heave, lob, pitch, projection, put, shy, sling, spill, toss, try, venture, wager.

thrust v. bear, butt, drive, force, impel, intrude, jab, jam, lunge, pierce, plunge, poke, press, prod, propel, push, ram, shove, stab, stick, urge, wedge. n. drive, flanconade, impetus, lunge, momentum, poke, prod, prog, push, shove, stab, stoccado.

thug n. animal, assassin, bandit, bangster, bruiser, bullyboy, cutthroat, gangster, goon, gorilla, heavy, highbinder, hood, hoodlum, hooligan, killer, mugger, murderer, robber, ruffian, tough.

thus adv. accordingly, as follows, consequently, ergo, hence, in this way, like so, like this, so, then, therefore, thuswise.

thwart v. baffle, balk, check, defeat, foil, frustrate, hinder, impede, obstruct, oppose, outwit, prevent, spite, stonker, stop, stymie, transverse, traverse. antonyms abet, aid, assist.

ticket n. card, certificate, coupon, docket, label, marker, pass, slip, sticker, tab, tag, tessera, token, voucher.

tickle v. amuse, cheer, delight, divert, enchant, entertain, excite, gratify, please, thrill, titillate.

ticklish adj. awkward, critical, delicate, difficult, dodgy, hazardous, nice, precarious, risky, sensitive, thorny, touchy, tricky, uncertain, unstable, unsteady. antonyms easy, straightforward.

tidings n. advice, bulletin, communication, dope, gen, greetings, information, intelligence, message, news, report, word.

tidy adj. ample, businesslike, clean, cleanly, considerable, fair, generous, good, goodly, handsome, healthy, large, largish, methodical, neat, ordered, orderly, respectable, shipshape, sizable, spick, spick-and-span, spruce, substantial, systematic, trim, uncluttered, well-groomed, well-kept. antonyms disorganized, untidy. v. arrange, clean, fettle, groom, neaten, order, spruce up, straighten.

tie v. attach, bind, confine, connect, draw, equal, fasten, hamper, hinder, hold, interlace, join, knot, lash, ligature, limit, link, match, moor, oblige, restrain, restrict, rope, secure, strap, tether, truss, unite. n. affiliation, allegiance, band, bond, commitment, connection, contest, copula, cord, dead heat, deadlock, draw, duty, encumbrance, fastening, fetter, fixture, game, hindrance, joint, kinship, knot, liaison, ligature, limitation, link, match, obligation, relationship, restraint, restriction, rope, stalemate, string.

tier n. band, belt, echelon, floor, gradin(e), layer, level, line, rank, row, stage, story, stratification, stratum, zone.

tight[1] adj. close, close-fitting, compact, competent, constricted, cramped, dangerous, difficult, even, evenly balanced, fast, firm, fixed, grasping, harsh, hazardous, hermetic, impervious, inflexible, mean, miserly, narrow, near, niggardly, parsimonious, penurious, perilous, precarious, precise, proof, rigid, rigorous, sealed, secure, severe, snug, sound, sparing, stern, sticky, stiff, stingy, stretched, strict, stringent, taut, tense, ticklish, tightfisted, tough, tricky, trig, troublesome, uncompromising, unyielding, well-matched, worrisome. antonyms lax, loose, slack.

tight[2] adj. blotto, drunk, half cut, half-seas-over, in one's cups, inebriated, intoxicated, pickled, pie-eyed, pissed, plastered, smashed, sozzled, stewed, stoned, three sheets in the wind, tiddly, tipsy, under the influence. antonym sober.

till v. cultivate, dig, dress, plow, work.

tilt v. attack, cant, clash, contend, duel, encounter, fight, heel, incline, joust, lean, list, overthrow, pitch, slant, slope, spar, tip. n. angle, cant, clash, combat, duel, encounter, fight, inclination, incline, joust, list, lists, pitch, set-to, slant, slope, thrust, tournament, tourney.

timber n. beams, boarding, boards, forest, logs, planking, planks, trees, wood.

time n. age, beat, chronology, date, day, duration, epoch, era, generation, heyday, hour, instance, interval, juncture, life, lifespan, lifetime, measure, meter, occasion, peak, period, point, rhythm, season, space, span, spell, stage, stretch, tempo, term, tide, while. v. clock, control, count, judge, measure, meter, regulate, schedule, set.

timeless adj. abiding, ageless, amaranthine, ceaseless, changeless, deathless, endless, enduring, eternal, everlasting, immortal, immutable, imperishable, indestructible, lasting, permanent, perpetual, persistent, undying.

timely adj. appropriate, convenient, judicious, opportune, prompt, propitious, punctual, seasonable, suitable, tempestive, well-timed. antonyms ill-timed, inappropriate, unfavorable.

timetable n. agenda, calendar, curriculum, diary, list, listing, program, roster, rota, schedule.

timid *adj.* afraid, apprehensive, bashful, cowardly, coy, diffident, fainthearted, fearful, henhearted, irresolute, modest, mousy, nervous, pavid, pusillanimous, retiring, shrinking, shy, spineless, timorous. *antonyms* audacious, bold, brave.

tinge *n.* bit, cast, color, dash, drop, dye, flavor, pinch, shade, smack, smatch, smattering, sprinkling, stain, suggestion, tinct, tincture, tinge, tone, touch, trace, wash. *v.* affect, color, dye, influence, rinse, stain, streak, taint, tincture, tinge.

tiny *adj.* diminutive, dwarfish, infinitesimal, insignificant, itsy-bitsy, Lilliputian, little, microscopic, mini, miniature, minute, negligible, petite, pint-size(d), pocket, puny, pygmy, slight, small, teensy, teentsy, teeny, teeny-weeny, tiddl(e)y, tottie, totty, trifling, wee, weeny. *antonyms* big, immense.

tip¹ *n.* acme, apex, cap, crown, end, extremity, ferrule, head, nib, peak, pinnacle, point, summit, top. *v.* cap, crown, finish, pinnacle, poll, pollard, prune, surmount, top.

tip² *v.* cant, capsize, ditch, dump, empty, heel, incline, lean, list, overturn, pour out, slant, spill, tilt, topple over, unload, upend, upset. *n.* bing, coup, dump, midden, refuse heap, rubbish-heap, slag-heap.

tip³ *n.* baksheesh, clue, forecast, gen, gift, gratuity, hint, information, inside information, lagniappe, perquisite, pointer, pourboire, refresher, suggestion, tip-off, warning, word, word of advice, wrinkle. *v.* advise, caution, forewarn, inform, remunerate, reward, suggest, tell, warn.

tipsy *adj.* a peg too low, a pip out, cockeyed, corny, drunk, elevated, fuddled, happy, mellow, merry, moony, moppy, mops and brooms, nappy, pixil(l)ated, rocky, screwed, screwy, slewed, sprung, squiff(y), tiddled, tiddley, tiddly, tight, totty, wet, woozy.

tire *v.* annoy, betoil, bore, cook, drain, droop, enervate, exasperate, exhaust, fag, fail, fatigue, flag, harass, irk, irritate, jade, knacker, sink, weary. *antonyms* energize, enliven, exhilarate, invigorate, refresh.

tired *adj.* all in, awearied, aweary, beat, bone-weary, bushed, clapped-out, clichéd, conventional, corny, deadbeat, disjaskit, dog-tired, drained, drooping, drowsy, enervated, épuisé(e), exhausted, fagged, familiar, fatigued, flagging, forfairn, forfough(t)en, forjeskit, hackneyed, jaded, knackered, old, outworn, shagged, shattered, sleepy, spent, stale, stock, threadbare, trite, weary, well-worn, whacked, worn out. *antonyms* active, energetic, fresh, lively, rested.

tireless *adj.* determined, diligent, energetic, indefatigable, industrious, resolute, sedulous, unflagging, untiring, unwearied, vigorous. *antonyms* tired, unenthusiastic, weak.

tiresome *adj.* annoying, boring, bothersome, dull, exasperating, fatiguing, flat, irksome, irritating, laborious, monotonous, pesky, tedious, troublesome, trying, uninteresting, vexatious, wearing, wearisome. *antonyms* easy, interesting, stimulating.

tiring *adj.* arduous, demanding, draining, enervating, enervative, exacting, exhausting, fagging, fatiguing, laborious, strenuous, tough, wearing, wearying.

titan *n.* Atlas, colossus, giant, Hercules, leviathan, superman.

title *n.* appellation, caption, championship, claim, crown, denomination, designation, entitlement, epithet, handle, heading, inscription, label, laurels, legend, letterhead, moniker, name, nickname, nom de plume, ownership, prerogative, privilege, pseudonym, right, sobriquet, style, term. *v.* call, christen, designate, dub, entitle, label, name, style, term.

toast¹ *v.* broil, brown, grill, heat, roast, warm.

toast² *n.* compliment, darling, drink, favorite, grace cup, health, hero, heroine, pledge, salutation, salute, tribute, wassail.

together *adv.* all at once, arranged, as one, as one man, at the same time, cheek by jowl, closely, collectively, concurrently, consecutively, contemporaneously, continuously, en masse, fixed, hand in glove, hand in hand, in a body, in a row, in concert, in cooperation, in fere, in mass, in succession, in unison, jointly, mutually, on end, ordered, organized, pari passu, settled, shoulder to shoulder, side by side, simultaneously, sorted out, straight, successively. *antonym* separately. *adj.* calm, commonsensical, composed, cool, down-to-earth, levelheaded, sensible, stable, well-adjusted, well-balanced, well-organized.

toil *n.* application, donkey-work, drudgery, effort, elbow grease, exertion, graft, industry, labor, labor improbus, pains, slog, sweat, travail. *v.* drudge, graft, grind, grub, labor, persevere, plug away, slave, slog, strive, struggle, sweat, tew, work.

token *n.* badge, clue, demonstration, earnest, evidence, expression, index, indication, keepsake, manifestation, mark, memento, memorial, note, proof, remembrance, reminder, representation, sign, souvenir, symbol, tessera, testimony, voucher, warning. *adj.* emblematic, hollow, inconsiderable, minimal, nominal, perfunctory, superficial, symbolic.

tolerant *adj.* biddable, broad-minded, catholic, charitable, complaisant, compliant, easygoing, fair, forbearing, indulgent, kindhearted, latitudinarian, lax, lenient, liberal, long-suffering, magnanimous, openminded, patient, permissive, soft, sympathetic, understanding, unprejudiced. *antonyms* biased, bigoted, intolerant, prejudiced, unsympathetic.

tolerate *v.* abear, abide, accept, admit, allow, bear, brook, condone, connive at, countenance, endure, indulge, permit, pocket, put up with, receive, sanction, stand, stomach, suffer, swallow, take, thole, turn a blind eye to, undergo, wear, wink at.

toll[1] *v.* announce, call, chime, clang, knell, peal, ring, send, signal, sound, strike, summon, warn.

toll[2] *n.* assessment, charge, cost, customs, damage, demand, duty, fee, impost, inroad, levy, loss, payment, penalty, rate, tariff, tax, tithe, tribute.

tomb *n.* burial place, catacomb, cenotaph, crypt, dolmen, grave, mastaba, mausoleum, sepulcher, sepulture, speos, vault.

tone *n.* accent, air, approach, aspect, attitude, cast, character, color, drift, effect, emphasis, feel, force, frame, grain, harmony, hue, inflection, intonation, klang, manner, modulation, mood, note, pitch, quality, shade, spirit, strength, stress, style, temper, tenor, timbre, tinge, tint, tonality, vein, volume. *v.* blend, harmonize, intone, match, sound, suit.

tongue *n.* argot, articulation, clack, clapper, dialect, discourse, idiom, language, languet(te), lath, lingo, parlance, patois, red rag, speech, talk, utterance, vernacular, voice.

too[1] *adv.* also, as well, besides, further, in addition to, into the bargain, likewise, moreover, to boot, what's more.

too[2] *adv.* excessively, exorbitantly, extremely, immoderately, inordinately, over, overly, ridiculously, to excess, to extremes, unduly, unreasonably, very.

tool *n.* agency, agent, apparatus, appliance, cat's-paw, contraption , contrivance, creature, device, dupe, flunkey, front, gadget, hireling, implement, instrument, intermedi-

ary, jackal, lackey, machine, means, medium, minion, pawn, puppet, stooge, toady, utensil, vehicle, weapon, widget. *v.* chase, cut, decorate, fashion, machine, ornament, shape, work.

top *n.* acme, apex, apogee, cacumen, cap, cop, cork, cover, crest, crown, culmen, culmination, head, height, high point, hood, lead, lid, meridian, peak, pinnacle, roof, stopper, summit, upside, vertex, zenith. *antonyms* base, bottom, nadir. *adj.* best, chief, crack, crowning, culminating, dominant, elite, finest, first, foremost, greatest, head, highest, lead, leading, preeminent, prime, principal, ruling, sovereign, superior, topmost, upmost, upper, uppermost. *v.* ascend, beat, best, better, cap, climb, command, cover, crest, crown, decorate, eclipse, exceed, excel, finish, finish off, garnish, head, lead, outdo, outshine, outstrip, roof, rule, scale, surmount, surpass, tip, transcend.

topic *n.* issue, lemma, matter, motif, point, question, subject, subject matter, talking point, text, theme, thesis.

topical *adj.* contemporary, current, familiar, newsworthy, popular, relevant, up-to-date, up-to-the-minute.

topple *v.* capsize, collapse, oust, overbalance, overthrow, overturn, totter, tumble, unseat, upset.

torment *v.* afflict, agitate, agonize, annoy, bedevil, bother, chivvy, crucify, devil, distort, distress, excruciate, harass, harrow, harry, hound, irritate, nag, pain, persecute, pester, plague, provoke, rack, tease, torture, trouble, vex, worry, wrack. *n.* affliction, agony, angst, anguish, annoyance, bane, bother, distress, harassment, hassle, hell, irritation, misery, nag, nagging, nuisance, pain, persecution, pest, plague, provocation, scourge, suffering, torture, trouble, vexation, worry.

torpid *adj.* apathetic, benumbed, dormant, drowsy, dull, fainéant, inactive, indolent, inert, lackadaisical, languid, languorous, lazy, lethargic, listless, lymphatic, motionless, numb, passive, slothful, slow, slow-moving, sluggish, somnolent, stagnant, supine. *antonyms* active, lively, vigorous.

torrent *n.* barrage, cascade, deluge, downpour, effusion, flood, flow, gush, outburst, rush, spate, stream, tide, volley.

torrid *adj.* ardent, arid, blistering, boiling, broiling, burning, dried, dry, emotional, erotic, fervent, fiery, hot, intense, parched, parching, passionate, scorched, scorching, sexy, sizzling, steamy, stifling, sultry, sweltering, tropical. *antonym* arctic.

tortuous *adj.* ambagious, ambiguous, bent, Byzantine, circuitous, complicated, convoluted, crooked, cunning, curved, deceptive, devious, indirect, involved, mazy, meandering, misleading, roundabout, serpentine, sinuous, tricky, twisted, twisting, winding, zigzag. *antonyms* straight, straightforward.

torture *v.* afflict, agonize, crucify, distress, excruciate, harrow, lacerate, martyr, martyrize, pain, persecute, rack, torment, wrack. *n.* affliction, agony, anguish, distress, gyp, hell, laceration, martyrdom, misery, pain, pang(s), persecution, rack, suffering, torment.

toss *v.* agitate, cant, cast, chuck, disturb, fling, flip, heave, hurl, jiggle, joggle, jolt, labor, launch, lob, lurch, pitch, project, propel, rock, roll, shake, shy, sling, thrash, throw, tumble, wallow, welter, wriggle, writhe. *n.* cast, chuck, fling, lob, pitch, shy, sling, throw.

total *n.* aggregate, all, amount, ensemble, entirety, lot, mass, sum, totality, whole. *adj.* absolute, all-out, complete, comprehensive, consummate, downright, entire, full, gross, integral, out-and-out, outright, perfect, root-and-branch, sheer, sweeping, thorough, thoroughgoing, unconditional, undisputed, undivided, unmitigated, unqualified, utter, whole, whole-hog. *antonyms* limited, partial, restricted. *v.* add (up), amount to, come to, count (up), reach, reckon, sum (up), tot up.

totalitarian *adj.* authoritarian, despotic, dictatorial, monocratic, monolithic, omnipotent, one-party, oppressive, tyrannous, undemocratic. *antonym* democratic.

touch *n.* ability, acquaintance, adroitness, approach, art, artistry, awareness, bit, blow, brush, caress, characteristic, command, communication, contact, correspondence, dash, deftness, detail, direction, drop, effect, facility, familiarity, feel, feeling, flair, fondling, hand, handiwork, handling, hint, hit, influence, intimation, jot, knack, manner, mastery, method, palpation, pat, pinch, push, skill, smack, smattering, soupçon, speck, spot, stroke, style, suggestion, suspicion, tactility, tap, taste, technique, tig, tincture, tinge, trace, trademark, understanding, virtuosity, way, whiff. *v.* abut, adjoin, affect, attain, border, brush, caress, cheat, compare with, concern, consume, contact, converge, disturb, drink, eat, equal, feel, finger, fondle, graze,

handle, hit, hold a candle to, impress, influence, inspire, interest, mark, match, meet, melt, move, palp, palpate, parallel, pat, pertain to, push, reach, regard, rival, soften, stir, strike, stroke, tap, tat, tinge, upset, use, utilize.

touching *adj.* affecting, emotional, emotive, haptic, heartbreaking, libant, melting, moving, pathetic, piteous, pitiable, pitiful, poignant, sad, stirring, tender.

touchy *adj.* bad-tempered, captious, crabbed, cross, feisty, grouchy, grumpy, huffy, irascible, irritable, miffy, peevish, pettish, petulant, querulous, quick-tempered, snippety, snuffy, sore, splenetic, surly, testy, tetchy, thin-skinned. *antonyms* calm, imperturbable, serene, unflappable.

tough *adj.* adamant, arduous, bad, baffling, brawny, butch, callous, cohesive, difficult, durable, exacting, exhausting, firm, fit, had, hard-bitten, hard-boiled, hardened, hard-nosed, hardy, herculean, inflexible, intractable, irksome, knotty, laborious, lamentable, leathery, merciless, obdurate, obstinate, perplexing, pugnacious, puzzling, refractory, regrettable, resilient, resistant, resolute, rigid, rough, ruffianly, rugged, ruthless, seasoned, sever, solid, stalwart, stern, stiff, stout, strapping, strenuous, strict, strong, stubborn, sturdy, tenacious, thorny, trouble-some, unbending, unforgiving, unfortunate, unlucky, unyielding, uphill, vicious, vigorous, violent. *antonyms* brittle, delicate, fragile, liberal, soft, tender, vulnerable, weak. *n.* bravo, bruiser, brute, bully, bully-boy, bully-rook, gorilla, hooligan, rough, roughneck, rowdy, ruffian, thug, yob, yobbo.

toughness *n.* arduousness, callousness, difficulty, durability, firmness, fitness, grit, hardiness, hardness, inflexibility, intractability, laboriousness, obduracy, obstinacy, pugnacity, resilience, resistance, rigidity, roughness, ruggedness, ruthlessness, severity, solidity, sternness, stiffness, strength, strenuousness, strictness, sturdiness, tenacity, viciousness. *antonyms* fragility, liberality, softness, vulnerability, weakness.

tour *n.* circuit, course, drive, excursion, expedition, jaunt, journey, outing, peregrination, progress, ride, round, trip. *v.* drive, explore, journey, ride, sightsee, travel, visit.

tourist *n.* excursionist, globe-trotter, holidaymaker, journeyer, rubberneck, sightseer, sojourner, traveler.

tow *v.* drag, draw, haul, lug, pull, tote, trail, transport, trawl, tug, yank.

towering *adj.* burning, colossal, elevated, excessive, extraordinary, extreme, fiery, gigantic, great, high, immoderate, imposing, impressive, inordinate, intemperate, intense, lofty, magnificent, mighty, monumental, outstanding, overpowering, paramount, passionate, prodigious, soaring, sublime, superior, supreme, surpassing, tall, transcendent, vehement, violent. *antonyms* minor, small, trivial.

town *n.* borough, bourg, burg, burgh, city, metropolis, municipality, settlement, township. *antonym* country.

toxic *adj.* baneful, deadly, harmful, lethal, morbific, noxious, pernicious, pestilential, poisonous, septic, unhealthy. *antonym* harmless.

toy *n.* bauble, doll, game, gewgaw, kickshaw(s), knickknack, plaything, trifle, trinket. *v.* dally, fiddle, flirt, play, potter, putter, sport, tinker, trifle, wanton.

trace *n.* bit, dash, drop, evidence, footmark, footprint, footstep, hint, indication, iota, jot, mark, path, record, relic, remains, remnant, scintilla, shadow, sign, smack, soupçon, spoor, spot, suggestion, survival, suspicion, tincture, tinge, token, touch, track, trail, trifle, vestige, whiff. *v.* ascertain, chart, copy, delineate, depict, detect, determine, discover, draw, find, follow, map, mark, outline, pursue, record, seek, shadow, show, sketch, stalk, track, trail, traverse, unearth, write.

track *n.* course, drift, footmark, footprint, footstep, line, mark, orbit, pat, pathway, piste, rail, rails, ridgeway, road, scent, sequence, slot, spoor, tack, trace, trail, train, trajectory, wake, wavelength, way. *v.* chase, dog, follow, hunt, pursue, shadow, spoor, stalk, tail, trace, trail, travel, traverse.

tract[1] *n.* area, district, estate, expanse, extent, lot, plot, quarter, region, section, stretch, territory, zone.

tract[2] *n.* booklet, brochure, discourse, disquisition, dissertation, essay, homily, leaflet, monograph, pamphlet, sermon, tractate, treatise.

tractable *adj.* amenable, biddable, complaisant, compliant, controllable, docile, ductile, fictile, governable, malleable, manageable, obedient, persuadable, plastic, pliable, pliant, submissive, tame, tractile, willing, workable, yielding. *antonyms* headstrong, intractable, obstinate, refractory, stubborn, unruly, willful.

trade *n.* avocation, barter, business, calling, clientele, commerce, commodities, craft, custom, customers, deal, dealing, employment, exchange, interchange, job, line, market, métier, occupation, patrons, profession, public, pursuit, shopkeeping, skill, swap, traffic, transactions, truck. *v.* bargain, barter, commerce, deal, do business, exchange, peddle, swap, switch, traffic, transact, truck.

trademark *n.* badge, brand, crest, emblem, hallmark, identification, ideograph, insignia, label, logo, logotype, name, sign, symbol.

tradition *n.* convention, custom, customs, folklore, habit, institution, lore, praxis, ritual, usage, usance, way, wony.

traduce *v.* abuse, asperse, blacken, calumniate, decry, defame, denigrate, deprecate, depreciate, detract, disparage, knock, malign, misrepresent, revile, run down, slag, slander, smear, vilify.

tragedy *n.* adversity, affliction, blow, calamity, catastrophe, disaster, misfortune, unhappiness. *antonyms* prosperity, success, triumph.

tragic *adj.* anguished, appalling, awful, calamitous, catastrophic, deadly, dire, disastrous, doleful, dreadful, fatal, grievous, heartbreaking, heartrending, ill-fated, ill-starred, lamentable, miserable, mournful, pathetic, pitiable, ruinous, sad, shocking, sorrowful, thespian, unfortunate, unhappy, woeful, wretched. *antonyms* comic, successful, triumphant.

trail *v.* chase, dangle, dawdle, drag, draw, droop, extend, follow, hang, haul, hunt, lag, linger, loiter, pull, pursue, shadow, stalk, straggle, stream, sweep, tail, tow, trace, track, traipse. *n.* abature, appendage, drag, footpath, footprints, footsteps, mark, marks, path, road, route, scent, spoor, stream, tail, trace, track, train, wake, way.

train *v.* aim, coach, direct, discipline, drill, educate, exercise, focus, guide, improve, instruct, lesson, level, point, prepare, rear, rehearse, school, teach, tutor. *n.* appendage, attendants, caravan, chain, choo-choo, column, concatenation, convoy, cortege, course, court, entourage, file, followers, following, household, lure, order, process, procession, progression, retinue, sequence, series, set, staff, string, succession, suite, tail, trail.

trait *n.* attribute, characteristic, feature, idiosyncrasy, lineament, mannerism, peculiarity, quality, quirk, thew.

traitor *n.* apostate, back-stabber, betrayer, deceiver, defector, deserter, double-crosser, fifth columnist, informer, Judas, miscreant, nithing, proditor, quisling, rebel, renegade, turncoat.

trajectory *n.* course, flight, line, path, route, track, trail.

tramp *v.* crush, footslog, hike, march, plod, ramble, range, roam, rove, slog, stamp, stomp, stump, toil, traipse, trample, tread, trek, trudge, walk, yomp. *n.* call girl, clochard, derelict, dosser, down-and-out, drifter, drummer, footfall, footstep, hike, hobo, hooker, march, piker, plod, ramble, slog, stamp, streetwalker, toe-rag(ger), tread, trek, vagabond, vagrant, weary willie.

trample *v.* crush, flatten, hurt, infringe, insult, squash, stamp, tread, violate.

tranquil *adj.* at peace, calm, composed, cool, disimpassioned, dispassionate, pacific, peaceful, placid, quiet, reposeful, restful, sedate, serene, still, undisturbed, unexcited, unperturbed, unruffled, untroubled. *antonyms* agitated, disturbed, noisy, troubled.

tranquillity *n.* ataraxia, ataraxy, calm, calmness, composure, coolness, equanimity, hush, imperturbability, peace, peacefulness, placidity, quiet, quietness, quietude, repose, rest, restfulness, sedateness, serenity, silence, stillness. *antonyms* agitation, disturbance, noise.

transact *v.* accomplish, carry on, carry out, conclude, conduct, discharge, dispatch, do, enact, execute, handle, manage, negotiate, perform, prosecute, settle.

transaction *n.* action, affair, arrangement, bargain, business, coup, deal, deed, enterprise, event, execution, matter, negotiation, occurrence, proceeding, undertaking.

transcend *v.* eclipse, exceed, excel, outdo, outrival, outshine, outstrip, overleap, overstep, overtop, surmount, surpass.

transcribe *v.* copy, engross, exemplify, interpret, note, record, render, reproduce, rewrite, take down, tape, tape-record, transfer, translate, transliterate.

transfer *v.* carry, cede, change, consign, convey, decal, decant, demise, displace, grant, hand over, move, relocate, remove, second, shift, translate, transmit, transplant, transport, transpose. *n.* change, changeover, crossover, decantation, displacement, handover, move, relocation, removal, shift, switch, switch-over, transference, translation, transmission, transposition, virement.

transform *v.* alter, change, convert, metamorphose, reconstruct, remodel, renew, revolutionize, transfigure, translate, transmogrify, transmute, transverse. *antonym* preserve.

transgression *n.* breach, contravention, crime, debt, encroachment, error, fault, infraction, infringement, iniquity, lapse, misbehavior, misdeed, misdemeanor, offense, peccadillo, peccancy, sin, trespass, violation, wrong, wrongdoing.

transient *adj.* brief, caducous, deciduous, ephemeral, evanescent, fleeting, flying, fugacious, fugitive, impermanent, momentary, passing, short, short-lived, short-term, temporary, transitory. *antonym* permanent.

transition *n.* alteration, change, changeover, conversion, development, evolution, flux, metabasis, metamorphosis, metastasis, passage, passing, progress, progression, sift, transformation, transit, transmutation, upheaval. *antonyms* beginning, end.

translate *v.* alter, carry, change, construe, convert, convey, decipher, decode, do, do up, elucidate, enrapture, explain, improve, interpret, metamorphose, move, paraphrase, remove, render, renovate, send, simplify, spell out, transcribe, transfer, transfigure, transform, transliterate, transmogrify, transmute, transplant, transport, transpose, turn.

transmit *v.* bear, broadcast, carry, communicate, convey, diffuse, dispatch, disseminate, forward, impart, network, radio, relay, remit, send, spread, traject, transfer, transport. *antonym* receive.

transparent *adj.* apparent, candid, clear, crystalline, diaphanous, dioptric, direct, distinct, easy, evident, explicit, filmy, forthright, frank, gauzy, hyaline, hyaloid, ingenuous, limpid, lucent, lucid, manifest, obvious, open, patent, pellucid, perspicuous, plain, plainspoken, recognizable, see-through, sheer, straight, straightforward, translucent, transpicuous, unambiguous, understandable, undisguised, unequivocal, visible. *antonyms* ambiguous, opaque, unclear.

transpire *v.* appear, arise, befall, betide, chance, come out, come to light, emerge, happen, leak out, occur, take place, turn up.

transport *v.* banish, bear, bring, captivate, carry, carry away, convey, delight, deport, ecstasize, electrify, enchant, enrapture, entrance, exile, fetch, haul, move, ravish, remove, run, ship, spellbind, take, transfer, waft. *antonyms* bore, leave. *n.* bliss, carriage, cartage, carting, conveyance, delight, ecstasy, enchantment, euphoria, happiness, haulage, heaven, rapture, ravishment, removal, shipment, shipping, transference, transportation, vehicle, waterage. *antonym* boredom.

transpose *v.* alter, change, exchange, interchange, metathesize, move, rearrange, relocate, reorder, shift, substitute, swap, switch, transfer. *antonym* leave.

trap *n.* ambush, artifice, bunker, danger, deception, device, gin, hazard, net, noose, pitfall, ruse, snare, spring, springe, springle, stratagem, subterfuge, toils, trapdoor, trepan, trick, trickery, wile. *v.* ambush, beguile, benet, catch, corner, deceive, dupe, enmesh, ensnare, entrap, illaqueate, inveigle, lime, snare, take, tangle, trepan, trick.

trash *n.* balderdash, draff, dregs, drivel, dross, garbage, hogwash, inanity, junk, kitsch, litter, nonsense, offscourings, offscum, refuse, riddlings, rot, rubbish, scoria, sullage, sweepings, trashery, tripe, trumpery, twaddle, waste. *antonym* sense.

trashy *adj.* catchpenny, cheap, cheapjack, flimsy, grotty, inferior, kitschy, meretricious, pinchbeck, rubbishy, shabby, shoddy, tawdry, third-rate, tinsel, worthless. *antonym* first-rate.

trauma *n.* agony, anguish, damage, disturbance, hurt, injury, jolt, lesion, ordeal, pain, scar, shock, strain, suffering, torture, upheaval, upset, wound. *antonyms* healing, relaxation.

travail *n.* birth pangs, childbirth, distress, drudgery, effort, exertion, grind, hardship, labor, labor pains, pain, slavery, slog, strain, stress, suffering, sweat, tears, throes, toil, tribulation. *antonym* rest.

travel *v.* carry, commute, cross, excursionize, go, journey, locomote, move, peregrinate, proceed, progress, ramble, roam, rove, tour, traverse, trek, voyage, walk, wander, wayfare, wend. *antonym* stay.

travesty *n.* apology, botch, burlesque, caricature, distortion, lampoon, mockery, parody, perversion, send-up, sham, takeoff. *v.* burlesque, caricature, deride, distort, lampoon, mock, parody, pervert, pillory, ridicule, send up, sham, spoof, takeoff.

treachery *n.* betrayal, disloyalty, doublecross, double-dealing, duplicity, faithlessness, falseness, infidelity, Judas kiss, laesa majestas, Medism, perfidiousness, perfidy, Punic faith, Punica fides, treason. *antonyms* dependability, loyalty.

treason *n.* disaffection, disloyalty, duplicity, laesa majestas, lese majesty, mutiny, perfidy, sedition, subversion, trahison, traitorousness, treachery. *antonym* loyalty.

treasure *n.* cash, darling, ewe lamb, flower, fortune, funds, gem, gold, jewel, jewels, money, nonpareil, paragon, pearl, precious, pride and joy, prize, riches, valuables, wealth. *v.* adore, cherish, esteem, idolize, love, preserve, prize, revere, value, venerate, worship. *antonym* disparage.

treat *n.* banquet, celebration, delight, enjoyment, entertainment, excursion, feast, fun, gift, ratification, joy, outing, party, pleasure, refreshment, satisfaction, surprise, thrill, wayzgoose. *antonym* drag. *v.* attend to, bargain, care for, confer, consider, contain, deal with, discourse upon, discuss, doctor, entertain, feast, give, handle, manage, medicament, medicate, medicine, negotiate, nurse, parley, provide, regale, regard, stand, use.

treaty *n.* agreement, alliance, bargain, bond, compact, concordat, contract, convention, covenant, entente, negotiation, pact.

tremble *v.* heave, oscillate, quake, quiver, rock, shake, shiver, shudder, teeter, totter, vibrate, wobble. *n.* heartquake, oscillation, quake, quiver, shake, shiver, shudder, tremblement, tremor, vibration. *antonym* steadiness.

trembling *n.* heartquake, oscillation, quaking, quavering, quivering, rocking, shakes, shaking, shivering, shuddering, tremblement, trepidation, vibration. *antonym* steadiness.

tremendous *adj.* ace, amazing, appalling, awe-inspiring, awesome, awful, colossal, deafening, dreadful, enormous, excellent, exceptional, extraordinary, fabulous, fantastic, fearful, formidable, frightful, gargantuan, gigantic, great, herculean, huge, immense, incredible, mammoth, marvelous, monstrous, prodigious, sensational, spectacular, stupendous, super, terrible, terrific, titanic, towering, vast, whopping, wonderful. *antonyms* boring, dreadful, run-of-the-mill, tiny.

tremor *n.* agitation, earthquake, quake, quaking, quaver, quavering, quiver, quivering, shake, shaking, shiver, shock, thrill, tremble, trembling, trepidation, trillo, vibration, wobble. *antonym* steadiness.

tremulous *adj.* afraid, agitated, agog, anxious, aspen, excited, fearful, frightened, jittery, jumpy, nervous, quavering, quivering, quivery, scared, shaking, shivering, timid, trembling, trembly, tremulant, trepid, trepidant, vibrating, wavering. *antonyms* calm, firm.

trenchant *adj.* acerbic, acid, acidulous, acute, astringent, biting, caustic, clear, clearcut, cogent, crisp, cutting, distinct, driving, effective, effectual, emphatic, energetic, explicit, forceful, forthright, hurtful, incisive, keen, mordant, penetrating, piquant, pointed, potent, powerful, pungent, sarcastic, scratching, severe, sharp, strong, tart, unequivocal, vigorous. *antonym* woolly.

trend *n.* bias, course, crazed, current, dernier cri, direction, fad, fashion, flow, inclination, leaning, look, mode, rage, style, tendency, thing, vogue.

trepidation *n.* agitation, alarm, anxiety, apprehension, butterflies, cold sweat, consternation, dismay, disquiet, disturbance, dread, emotion, excitement, fear, fright, jitters, misgivings, nervousness, palpitation, perturbation, qualms, quivering, shaking, trembling, tremor, unease, uneasiness, worry. *antonym* calm.

trespass *v.* encroach, err, infringe, injure, intrude, invade, obtrude, offend, poach, sin, transgress, violate, wrong. *antonyms* keep to, obey. *n.* breach, contravention, crime, debt, delinquency, encroachment, error, evildoing, fault, infraction, infringement, iniquity, injury, intrusion, invasion, misbehavior, misconduct, misdeed, misdemeanor, offense, poaching, sin, transgression, wrongdoing.

trespasser *n.* criminal, debtor, delinquent, evildoer, infringer, interloper, intruder, invader, malefactor, offender, poacher, sinner, transgressor, wrongdoer.

tribe *n.* blood, branch, caste, clan, class, division, dynasty, family, gens, group, house, ilk, nation, people, phratry, race, seed, sept, stock.

tribulation *n.* adversity, affliction, blow, burden, care, curse, distress, grief, heartache, misery, misfortune, ordeal, pain, reverse, sorrow, suffering, travail, trial, trouble, unhappiness, vexation, woe, worry, wretchedness. *antonyms* happiness, rest.

tribunal *n.* bar, bench, court, examination, hearing, inquisition, trial.

tribute *n.* accolade, acknowledgment, annates, applause, charge, commendation, compliment, contribution, cornage, credit, customs, duty, encomium, esteem, eulogy, excise, firstfruits, gavel, gift, gratitude, homage, honor, horngeld, impost, laudation, offering, panegyric, payment, praise, ransom, recognition, respect, subsidy, tax, testimonial, testimony, toll. *antonym* blame.

trick *n.* antic, art, artifice, cantrip, caper, characteristic, chicane, command, con, craft, deceit, deception, device, dodge, dog-trick, expedient, expertise, feat, feint, foible, fraud, frolic, gag, gambol, gift, gimmick, habit, hang, hoax, idiosyncrasy, imposition, imposture, jape, joke, josh, knack, know-how, legerdemain, leg-pull, maneuver, mannerism, peculiarity, ploy, practical joke, practice, prank, put-on, quirk, quiz, rig, ruse, secret, shot, skill, sleight, spell, stall, stratagem, stunt, subterfuge, swindle, technique, toy, trait, trap, trinket, turn, wile. *adj.* artificial, bogus, counterfeit, ersatz, fake, false, feigned, forged, imitation, mock, pretend, sham. *antonym* genuine. *v.* bamboozle, beguile, cheat, con, cozen, deceive, defraud, delude, diddle, dupe, fool, gull, hoax, hocuspocus, hoodwink, hornswoggle, illude, lead on, mislead, outwit, pull a fast one on, pull someone's leg, sell, swindle, trap.

trickle *v.* dribble, drip, drop, exude, filter, gutter, leak, ooze, percolate, run, seep. *antonyms* gush, stream. *n.* drib, dribble, driblet, dribs and drabs, drip, seepage. *antonyms* gush, stream.

tricky *adj.* artful, complicated, crafty, cunning, deceitful, deceptive, delicate, devious, difficult, foxy, Gordian, knotty, legerdemain, problematic, risky, scheming, slippery, sly, sticky, subtle, thorny, ticklish, touch-and-go, trickish, tricksome, tricksy, wily. *antonyms* easy, honest.

trigger *v.* activate, actuate, cause, elicit, generate, initiate, produce, prompt, provoke, set off, spark off, start. *n.* catch, goad, lever, release, spur, stimulus, switch.

trim *adj.* clean-limbed, compact, dapper, natty, neat, orderly, shipshape, slender, slim, smart, smirk, soigné, spick-and-span, spruce, streamlined, svelte, trig, well-dressed, well-groomed, willowy. *antonym* scruffy. *v.* adjust, adorn, arrange, array, balance, barb, barber, beautify, bedeck, clip, crop, curtail, cut, decorate, distribute, dock, dress, dub, embellish, embroider, garnish, lop, order, ornament, pare, prepare, prune, settle, shave, shear, tidy, trick. *n.* adornment, array, attire, border, clipping, condition, crop, cut, decoration, disposition, dress, edging, embellishment, equipment, fettle, fitness, fittings, form, frill, fringe, garnish, gear, health, humor, nick, order, ornament, ornamentation, piping, pruning, repair, shape, shave, shearing, situation, state, temper, trappings, trimming.

trimmings *n.* accessories, accompaniments, additions, appurtenances, clippings, cuttings, ends, extras, frills, garnish, ornaments, paraphernalia, parings, remnants, shavings, trappings.

trinket *n.* bagatelle, bauble, bibelot, bijou, doodad, fairing, gewgaw, gimcrack, kickshaws, knickknack, nothing, ornament, toy, trifle, trinkum-trankum, whig-maleerie, whim-wham.

trio *n.* terzetto, threesome, triad, trilogy, trine, trinity, triple, triplet, triptych, triumvirate, triune.

trip *n.* blunder, boob, errand, error, excursion, expedition, fall, faux pas, foray, indiscretion, jaunt, journey, lapse, misstep, outing, ramble, run, skip, slip, step, stumble, tour, travel, voyage. *v.* activate, blunder, boob, caper, confuse, dance, disconcert, engage, err, fall, flip, flit, frisk, gambol, go, hop, lapse, miscalculate, misstep, pull, ramble, release, set off, skip, slip, slip up, spring, stumble, stitch on, throw, tilt up, tip up, tour, trap, travel, tumble, unsettle, voyage.

trite *adj.* banal, bromidic, clichéd, common, commonplace, corny, dull, hack, hackneyed, Mickey Mouse, ordinary, overworn, pedestrian, routing, run-of-the-mill, stale, stereotyped, stock, threadbare, tired, uninspired, unoriginal, well-trodden, well-worn, worn, worn-out. *antonym* original.

triumph *n.* accomplishment, achievement, ascendancy, attainment, conquest, coup, elation, exultation, feat, happiness, hit, joy, jubilation, masterstroke, mastery, pride, rejoicing, sensation, smash, smash hit, success, tour de force, victory, walkaway, walkover, win. *antonym* disaster. *v.* best, celebrate, crow, defeat, dominate, exult, gloat, glory, have the last laugh, humble, humiliate, jubilate, overcome, overwhelm, prevail, prosper, rejoice, revel, subdue, succeed, swagger, vanquish, win. *antonym* fail.

triumphant *adj.* boastful, celebratory, cock-a-hoop, conquering, dominant, elated, epinikian, exultant, gloating, glorious, joyful, jubilant, proud, rejoicing, successful, swaggering, undefeated, victorious, winning. *antonyms* defeated, humble.

trivial *adj.* commonplace, dinky, everyday, frivolous, incidental, inconsequential, inconsiderable, insignificant, little, meaningless, Mickey Mouse, minor, negligible, nugatory, paltry, pettifogging, petty, piddling, piffling, puny, slight, small, snippety, trifling, trite, unimportant, valueless, worthless. *antonym* significant.

troops *n.* army, forces, men, military, servicemen, soldiers, soldiery.

trophy *n.* award, booty, cup, laurels, memento, memorial, prize, souvenir, spoils.

tropical *adj.* equatorial, hot, humid, lush, luxuriant, steamy, stifling, sultry, sweltering, torrid. *antonyms* arctic, cold, cool, temperate.

trouble *n.* affliction, agitation, ailment, annoyance, anxiety, attention, bother, care, commotion, complaint, concern, danger, defect, difficulty, dilemma, disability, discontent, discord, disease, disorder, disquiet, dissatisfaction, distress, disturbance, effort, exertion, failure, grief, heartache, illness, inconvenience, irritation, labor, malfunction, mess, misfortune, nuisance, pain, pains, pest, pickle, predicament, problem, row, scrape, solicitude, sorrow, spot, strife, struggle, suffering, thought, torment, travail, trial, tribulation, tumult, uneasiness, unrest, upheaval, upset, vexation, woe, work, worry. *antonyms* calm, peace. *v.* afflict, agitate, annoy, bother, burden, discomfort, discommode, discompose, disconcert, disquiet, distress, disturb, fash, fret, grieve, harass, incommode, inconvenience, molest, muddy, pain, perplex, perturb, pester, plague, sadden, torment, upset, vex, worry. *antonyms* help, reassure.

troublemaker *n.* agent provocateur, agitator, bellwether, bolshevik, firebrand, heller, incendiary, instigator, meddler, mischief maker, rabblerouser, ring-leader, stirrer, tub-thumper. *antonym* peacemaker.

troublesome *adj.* annoying, arduous, bothersome, burdensome, demanding, difficult, disorderly, fashious, harassing, hard, importunate, inconvenient, insubordinate, irksome, irritating, laborious, oppressive, pestilential, plaguesome, plaguey, rebellious, recalcitrant, refractory, rowdy, spiny, taxing, thorn, tiresome, tricky, trying, turbulent, uncooperative, undisciplined, unruly, upsetting, vexatious, violent, wearisome, worrisome, worrying. *antonyms* easy, helpful, polite.

trounce *v.* beat, best, censure, clobber, crush, drub, hammer, lick, overwhelm, paste, punish, rebuke, rout, slaughter, thrash, whale, whitewash.

truant *n.* absentee, deserter, dodger, hookey, malingerer, runaway, shirker, skiver, wab. *adj.* absent, malingering, miss-

truce n. armistice, break, cease-fire, cessation, intermission, interval, letup, lull, moratorium, peace, respite, rest, stay, suspension, treaty. *antonym* hostilities.

truculent adj. aggressive, antagonistic, bad-tempered, bellicose, belligerent, combative, contentious, cross, defiant, fierce, hostile, ill-tempered, obstreperous, pugnacious, quarrelsome, savage, scrappy, sullen, violent. *antonyms* cooperative, good-natured.

trudge v. clump, footslog, hike, labor, lumber, march, mush, plod, slog, stump, traipse, tramp, trek, walk. n. footslog, haul, hike, march, mush, slog, traipse, tramp, trek, walk.

true adj. absolute, accurate, actual, apod(e)ictic, authentic, bona fide, confirmed, conformable, constant, correct, corrected, dedicated, devoted, dutiful, exact, factual, faithful, fast, firm, genuine, honest, honorable, legitimate, loyal, natural, perfect, precise, proper, pure, real, right, rightful, sincere, sooth, spot-on, square, staunch, steady, true-blue, true-born, truehearted, trustworthy, trusty, truthful, typical, unerring, unswerving, upright, valid, veracious, veridical, veritable. *antonyms* faithless, false, inaccurate. adv. accurately, correctly, exactly, faithfully, honestly, perfectly, precisely, properly, rightly, truly, truthfully, unerringly, veraciously, veritably. *antonyms* falsely, inaccurately.

truly adv. accurately, authentically, constantly, correctly, devotedly, dutifully, en vérité, exactly, exceptionally, extremely, factually, faithfully, firmly, genuinely, greatly, honestly, honorably, in good sooth, in reality, in truth, indeed, indubitably, legitimately, loyally, precisely, properly, really, rightly, sincerely, soothly, staunchly, steadfastly, steadily, truthfully, undeniably, veraciously, verily, veritably, very. *antonyms* faithlessly, falsely, incorrectly, slightly.

truncate v. abbreviate, clip, crop, curtail, cut, cut short, lop, maim, pare, prune, shorten, trim. *antonym* lengthen.

trust n. affiance, assurance, belief, care, certainty, certitude, charge, confidence, conviction, credence, credit, custody, duty, expectation, faith, fidelity, guard, guardianship, hope, obligation, protection, reliance, responsiblity, safekeeping, trusteeship, uberrima feids. *antonym* mistrust. v. assign, assume, bank on, believe, command, commit, confide, consign, count on, credit, delegate, depend on, entrust, expect, give, hope, imagine, presume, rely on, suppose, surmise, swear by. *antonym* mistrust.

trusting adj. confiding, credulous, gullible, innocent, naive, optimistic, simple, trustful, unguarded, unquestioning, unsuspecting, unsuspicious, unwary. *antonyms* cautious, distrustful.

trustworthy adj. authentic, dependable, ethical, foursquare, honest, honorable, level-headed, mature, principled, reliable, responsible, righteous, sensible, steadfast, true, trusty, truthful, upright. *antonym* unreliable.

truth n. accuracy, actuality, axiom, candor, certainty, constance, dedication, devotion, dutifulness, exactness, fact, facts, factuality, factualness, faith, faithfulness, fidelity, frankness, genuineness, historicity, honesty, integrity, law, legitimacy, loyalty, maxim, naturalism, precision, realism, reality, sooth, truism, truthfulness, uprightness, validity, veracity, veridicality, verity. *antonym* falsehood.

truthful adj. accurate, candid, correct, exact, faithful, forthright, frank, honest, literal, naturalistic, plainspoken, precise, realistic, reliable, sincere, sooth, soothfast, soothful, straight, straightforward, true, trustworthy, veracious, veridicous, verist, veristic, veritable. *antonym* untruthful.

try v. adjudge, adjudicate, afflict, aim, annoy, appraise, attempt, catechize, endeavor, essay, evaluate, examine, experiment, hear, inconvenience, inspect, investigate, irk, irritate, pain, plague, prove, sample, seek, strain, stress, strive, struggle, sate, tax, test, tire, trouble, undertake, upset, venture, vex, wear out, weary. n. appraisal, attempt, bash, crack, effort, endeavor, essay, evaluation, experiment, fling, go, inspection, sample, shot, stab, taste, taster, test, trial, whack.

trying adj. aggravating, annoying, arduous, bothersome, difficult, distressing, exasperating, fatiguing, hard, irksome, irritating, searching, severe, stressful, taxing, testing, tiresome, tough, troublesome, upsetting, vexing, wearisome. *antonym* calming.

tub n. back, barrel, basin, bath, bathtub, bucket, butt, cask, hogshead, keeve, keg, kid, kit, pail, puncheon, stand, tun, vat.

tube n. channel, conduit, cylinder, duct, hose, inlet, main, outlet, pipe, shaft, spout, trunk, valve, vas.

tubular adj. pipelike, pipy, tubate, tubelike, tubiform, tubulate, tubulous, vasiform.

tuck[1] _v._ cram, crease, fold, gather, insert, push, stuff. _n._ crease, fold, gather, pinch, pleat, pucker.

tuck[2] _n._ comestibles, eats, food, grub, nosh, prog, scoff, victuals, vittles.

tuft _n._ beard, bunch, clump, cluster, collection, crest, dag, daglock, dollop, floccule, flocculus, floccus, flock, knot, shock, tassle, topknot, truss, tussock.

tug _v._ drag, draw, haul, heave, jerk, jigger, lug, pluck, pull, tow, wrench, yank. _n._ drag, haul, heave, jerk, pluck, pull, tow, traction, wrench, yank.

tuition _n._ education, instruction, lessons, pedagogics, pedagogy, schooling, teaching, training, tutelage, tutoring.

tumble _v._ disorder, drop, fall, flop, jumble, overthrow, pitch, plummet, roll, rumple, stumble, topple, toss, trip up. _n._ collapse, drop, fall, flop, plunge, roll, spill, stumble, toss, trip.

tumult _n._ ado, affray, agitation, altercation, bedlam, brattle, brawl, brouhaha, bustle, clamor, coil, commotion, deray, din, disorder, disturbance, donnybrook, émeute, excitement, fracas, hubbub, hullabaloo, outbreak, pandemonium, quarrel, racket, riot, rookery, rout, row, ruction, ruffle, stir, stramash, strife, turmoil, unrest, upheaval, uproar. _antonym_ calm.

tune _n._ agreement, air, attitude, concert, concord, consonance, demeanor, disposition, euphony, frame of mind, harmony, melisma, melody, mood, motif, pitch, song, strain, sympathy, temper, theme, unison. _v._ adapt, adjust, attune, harmonize, pitch, regulate, set, synchronize, temper.

tunnel _n._ burrow, channel, chimney, drift, flue, gallery, hole, passage, passageway, sap, shaft, subway, underpass. _v._ burrow, dig, excavate, mine, penetrate, sap, undermine.

turbid _adj._ clouded, cloudy, confused, dense, dim, disordered, feculent, foggy, foul, fuzzy, hazy, impure, incoherent, muddled, muddy, murky, opaque, roily, thick, unclear, unsettled. _antonym_ clear.

turbulent _adj._ agitated, anarchic, blustery, boiling, boisterous, choppy, confused, disordered, disorderly, foaming, furious, insubordinate, lawless, mutinous, obstreperous, raging, rebellious, refractory, riotous, rough, rowdy, seditious, stormy, tempestuous, tumultuous, unbridled, undisciplined, ungovernable, unruly, unsettled, unstable, uproarious, violent, wild. _antonym_ calm.

turf _n._ clod, divot, glebe, grass, green, sod, sward.

turmoil _n._ agitation, bedlam, brouhaha, bustle, chaos, combustion, commotion, confusion, disorder, disquiet, disturbance, donnybrook, dust, émeute, ferment, flurry, hubbub, hubbuboo, noise, pandemonium, pother, pudder, rookery, rout, row, ruffle, stir, stour, stramash, strife, tracasserie, trouble, tumult, turbulence, uproar, violence, welter. _antonym_ calm.

turn _v._ adapt, alter, apostatize, appeal, apply, approach, become, caracol, change, circle, construct, convert, corner, curdle, defect, deliver, depend, desert, divert, double, execute, fashion, fit, form, frame, go, gyrate, hang, hinge, infatuate, influence, issue, look, make, metamorphose, mold, move, mutate, nauseate, negotiate, pass, perform, persuade, pivot, prejudice, remodel, renege, resort, retract, return, reverse, revolve, roll, rotate, shape, shift, sicken, sour, spin, spoil, swerve, switch, swivel, taint, transfigure, transform, translate, transmute, twirl, twist, upset, veer, wheel, whirl, write. _n._ act, action, airing, aptitude, bend, bent, bias, bout, caracol, cast, chance, change, circle, circuit, constitutional, crack, crankle, crisis, culmination, curve, cycle, deed, departure, deviation, direction, distortion, drift, drive, excursion, exigency, fashion, favor, fling, form, format, fright, gesture, go, guise, gyration, heading, innings, jaunt, makeup, manner, mode, mold, occasion, opportunity, outing, performance, performer, period, pivot, promenade, reversal, revolution, ride, rotation, round, saunter, scare, service, shape, shift, shock, shot, spell, spin, start, stint, stroll, style, succession, surprise, swing, tendency, time, trend, trick, try, turning, twist, uey, U-turn, vicissitude, walk, warp, way, whack, whirl.

turncoat _n._ apostate, backslider, blackleg, defector, deserter, fink, rat, recreant, renegade, renegate, scab, seceder, tergiversator, traitor.

turning _n._ bend, crossroads, curve, flexure, fork, junction, turn, turnoff.

turnover _n._ business, change, flow, income, movement, output, outturn, production, productivity, profits, replacement, volume, yield.

tutor _n._ coach, director of studies, educator, governor, guardian, guide, guru, instructor, lecturer, master, mentor, preceptor, répétiteur, supervisor, teacher. _v._ coach, control, direct, discipline, drill, edify, educate, guide, instruct, lecture, school, supervise, teach, train.

tweak *v., n.* jerk, nip, pull, punch, snatch, squeeze, tug, twist, twitch.

twig *n.* branch, offshoot, ramulus, shoot, spray, spring, stick, wattle, whip, withe, withy.

twig *v.* catch on, comprehend, cotton on, fathom, get, grasp, rumble, savvy, see, tumble to, understand.

twilight *n.* crepuscle, crepuscule, decline, demi-jour, dimness, dusk, ebb, evening, eventide, gloaming, half-light, sundown, sunset. *adj.* crepuscular, darkening, declining, dim, dying, ebbing, evening, final, last, shadowy.

twin *n.* clone, corollary, counterpart, doppelgänger, double, duplicate, fellow, gemel, likeness, lookalike, match, mate, ringer. *adj.* balancing, corresponding, didymous, double, dual, duplicate, geminate, geminous, identical, matched, matching, paired, parallel, symmetrical, twofold. *v.* combine, couple, join, link, match, pair, yoke.

twine *n.* cord, string, twist, yarn. *v.* bend, braid, coil, curl, encircle, entwine, interlace, interweave, knit, loop, meander, plait, snake, spiral, splice, surround, tie, twist, weave, wind, wrap, wreathe, wriggle, zigzag.

twinkle *v.* blink, coruscate, flash, flicker, gleam, glint, glisten, glitter, scintillate, shimmer, shine, sparkle, vibrate, wink. *n.* amusement, blink, coruscation, flash, flicker, gleam, glimmer, glistening, glitter, glittering, light, quiver, scintillation, shimmer, shine, spark, sparkle, wink.

twirl *v.* birl, coil, gyrate, gyre, pirouette, pivot, revolve, rotate, spin, swivel, turn, twiddle, twist, wheel, whirl, wind. *n.* coil, convolution, gyration, gyre, helix, pirouette, revolution, rotation, spin, spiral, turn, twiddle, twist, wheel, whirl, whorl.

twist *v.* alter, change, coil, contort, corkscrew, crankle, crinkle, crisp, curl, distort, encircle, entangle, entwine, garble, intertwine, misquote, misrepresent, pervert, pivot, revolve, rick, screw, spin, sprain, squirm, strain, swivel, turn, tweak, twine, warp, weave, wigwag, wind, wrap, wreathe, wrench, wrest, wreck, wriggle, wring, writhe. *n.* aberration, arc, bend, bent, braid, break, change, characteristic, coil, confusion, contortion, convolution, crankle, curl, curlicue, curve, defect, deformation, development, distortion, eccentricity, entangle-

ment, fault, flaw, foible, hank, idiosyncrasy, imperfection, intortion, jerk, kink, know, meander, mess, mix-up, nuance, oddity, peculiarity, plug, proclivity, pull, quid, quirk, revelation, roll, screw, slant, snarl, spin, sprain, squiggle, surprise, swivel, tangle, tortion, trait, turn, twine, undulation, variation, warp, wind, wrench, wrest, zigzag.

twitch *v.* blink, flutter, jerk, jump, pinch, pluck, pull, spasmytic, subsultus, tremor, tweak, twinge, vellication.

tycoon *n.* baron, big cheese, big noise, big shot, capitalist, captain of industry, Croesus, Dives, entrepreneur, fat cat, financier, goldbug, industrialist, magnate, mogul, nabob, plutocrat, potentate, supremo.

type^1 *n.* archetype, breed, category, class, classification, description, designation, emblem, embodiment, epitome, essence, example, exemplar, form, genre, group, ilk, insignia, kidney, kind, mark, model, order, original, paradigm, pattern, personification, prototype, quintessence, sort, species, specimen, stamp, standard, strain, subdivision, variety.

type^2 *n.* case, characters, face, font, fount, lettering, print, printing.

typhoon *n.* baguio, cordonazo, cyclone, hurricane, squall, storm, tempest, tornado, twister, whirlwind, willy-willy.

typical *adj.* archetypal, average, characteristic, classic, conventional, distinctive, essential, illustrative, indicative, model, normal, orthodox, quintessential, representative, standard, stock, symptomatic, usual, vintage. *antonyms* atypical, untypical.

typify *v.* characterize, embody, encapsulate, epitomize, exemplify, illustrate, incarnate, personify, represent, symbolize.

tyrannical *adj.* absolute, arbitrary, authoritarian, autocratic, coercive, despotic, dictatorial, domineering, high-handed, imperious, inexorable, iron-handed, magisterial, Neronian, oppressive, overbearing, overpowering, overweening, peremptory, ruthless, severe, tyrannous, unjust, unreasonable. *antonyms* liberal, tolerant.

tyrannize *v.* browbeat, bully, coerce, crush, dictate, domineer, enslave, intimidate, lord it, oppress, subjugate, terrorize.

U

ubiquitous *adj.* all-over, common, commonly encountered, ever-present, everywhere, frequent, global, omnipresent, pervasive, universal. *antonym* rare.

ugly *adj.* angry, bad-tempered, dangerous, dark, disagreeable, disgusting, distasteful, evil, evil-favored, forbidding, frightful, hagged, haggish, hard-favored, hard-featured, hideous, homely, horrid, ill-faced, ill-favored, ill-looking, malevolent, menacing, misshapen, monstrous, nasty, objectionable, offensive, ominous, plain, repugnant, repulsive, revolting, shocking, sinister, spiteful, sullen, surly, terrible, threatening, truculent, unattractive, unlovely, unpleasant, unprepossessing, unsightly, vile. *antonyms* beautiful, charming, good, pretty.

ultimate *adj.* basic, conclusive, consummate, decisive, elemental, end, eventual, extreme, final, fundamental, furthest, greatest, highest, last, maximum, paramount, perfect, primary, radical, remotest, superlative, supreme, terminal, topmost, utmost. *n.* consummation, culmination, daddy of them all, dinger, epitome, extreme, granddaddy, greatest, height, peak, perfection, summit.

umpire *n.* adjudicator, arbiter, arbitrator, daysman, judge, linesman, mediator, moderator, ref, referee. *v.* adjudicate, arbitrate, call, control, judge, moderate, ref, referee.

unabashed *adj.* blatant, bold, brazen, composed, confident, unawed, unblushing, unconcerned, undaunted, undismayed, unembarrassed. *antonyms* abashed, sheepish.

unaccountable *adj.* astonishing, baffling, extraordinary, impenetrable, incomprehensible, inexplicable, inscrutable, mysterious, odd, peculiar, puzzling, singular, strange, uncommon, unexplainable, unfathomable, unheard-of, unintelligible, unusual, unwonted. *antonyms* accountable, explicable.

unaffected[1] *adj.* aloof, impervious, naïf, natural, proof, spontaneous, unaltered, unchanged, unimpressed, unmoved, unresponsive, untouched. *antonyms* affected, unnatural.

unaffected[2] *adj.* artless, blasé, genuine, honest, indifferent, ingenuous, naive, plain, simple, sincere, straightforward, unassuming, unconcerned, unpretentious, unsophisticated, unspoiled, unstudied. *antonyms* affected, impressed, moved.

unalterable *adj.* final, fixed, immutable, inflexible, invariable, permanent, rigid, steadfast, unchangeable, unchanging, unyielding. *antonyms* alterable, flexible.

unanimous *adj.* agreed, common, concerted, concordant, harmonious, in accord, in agreement, joint, united. *antonyms* disunited, split.

unapproachable *adj.* aloof, distant, forbidding, formidable, frigid, godforsaken, inaccessible, remote, reserved, standoffish, unbending, unfriendly, unreachable, unsociable, withdrawn. *antonym* approachable.

unassailable *adj.* absolute, conclusive, impregnable, incontestable, incontrovertible, indisputable, invincible, inviolable, invulnerable, irrefutable, positive, proven, sacrosanct, secure, sound, undeniable, well-armed, well-fortified. *antonym* assailable.

unassuming *adj.* diffident, humble, meek, modest, natural, quiet, restrained, retiring, self-effacing, simple, unassertive, unobtrusive, unostentatious, unpresuming, unpretentious. *antonyms* assuming, presumptuous, pretentious.

unattached *adj.* autonomous, available, fancy-free, footloose, free, independent, nonaligned, single, unaffiliated, uncommitted, unengaged, unmarried, unspoken for. *antonyms* attached, committed, engaged.

unavailing *adj.* abortive, barren, bootless, fruitless, futile, idle, ineffective, ineffectual, inefficacious, pointless, unproductive, unprofitable, unsuccessful, useless, vain. *antonyms* productive, successful.

unavoidable *adj.* certain, compulsory, fated, ineluctable, inescapable, inevitable, inexorable, mandatory, necessary, obligatory. *antonym* avoidable.

unawares *adv.* aback, abruptly, accidentally, by surprise, imperceptibly, inadvertently, insidiously, mistakenly, off guard, on the hop, suddenly, unconsciously, unexpectedly, unintentionally, unknowingly, unprepared, unthinkingly, unwittingly.

unbalanced *adj.* asymmetrical, biased, crazy, demented, deranged, disturbed, disharmonic, eccentric, erratic, inequitable, insane, irrational, irregular, lopsided, lunatic, mad, off-balance, one-sided, partial, partisan, prejudiced, shaky, touched, unequal, uneven, unfair, unhinged, unjust, unsound, unstable, unsteady, wobbly. *antonym* balanced.

unbearable *adj.* insufferable, insupportable, intolerable, outrageous, unacceptable, unendurable, unspeakable. *antonyms* acceptable, bearable.

unbecoming *adj.* discreditable, dishonorable ill-suited, improper, inappropriate, incongruous, indecorous, indelicate, offensive, tasteless, unattractive, unbefitting, unfit, unflattering, unmaidenly, unmeet, unseemly, unsightly, unsuitable, unsuited. *antonyms* becoming, seemly.

unbelievable *adj.* astonishing, far-fetched, implausible, impossible, improbably, inconceivable, incredible, outlandish, prepos-terous, questionable, staggering, unconvincing, unimaginable, unlikely, unthinkable. *antonyms* believable, credible.

unbending *adj.* aloof, distant, firm, forbidding, formal, formidable, hard-line, inflexible, intransigent, reserved, resolute, Rhadamanthine, rigid, severe, stiff, strict, stubborn, tough, uncompromising, unyielding. *antonyms* approachable, friendly, relaxed.

unbiased *adj.* disinterested, dispassionate, equitable, evenhanded, fair, fair-minded, impartial, independent, just, neutral, objective, open-minded, uncolored, uninfluenced, unprejudiced. *antonym* biased.

unbidden *adj.* free, spontaneous, unasked, unforced, uninvited, unprompted, unsolicited, unwanted, unwelcome, voluntary, willing. *antonyms* invited, solicited.

unblemished *adj.* clear, flawless, immaculate, irreproachable, perfect, pure, spotless, unflawed, unimpeachable, unspotted, unstained, unsullied, untarnished. *antonyms* blemished, flawed, imperfect.

unbosom *v.* admit, bare, confess, confide, disburden, disclose, divulge, lay bare, let out, pour out, reveal, tell, unburden, uncover. *antonyms* conceal, suppress.

unbridled *adj.* excessive, immoderate, intemperate, licentious, profligate, rampant, riotous, unchecked, unconstrained, uncontrolled, uncurbed, ungovernable, ungoverned, unrestrained, unruly, violent, wanton.

unbroken *adj.* ceaseless, complete, constant, continuous, endless, entire, incessant, intact, integral, perpetual, progressive, serried, solid, successive, total, unbowed, unceasing, undivided, unimpaired, uninterrupted, unremitting, unsubdued, untamed, whole. *antonyms* cowed, fitful, intermittent.

unburden *v.* confess, confide, disburden, discharge, disclose, discumber, disencumber, empty, lay bare, lighten, off-load, pour out, relieve, reveal, tell all, unbosom, unload. *antonyms* conceal, hide, suppress.

uncanny *adj.* astonishing, astounding, bizarre, creepy, eerie, eldritch, exceptional, extraordinary, fantastic, incredible, inspired, miraculous, mysterious, preternatural, prodigious, queer, remarkable, scary, singular, spooky, strange, supernatural, unaccountable, unco, unearthly, unerring, unheard-of, unnatural, unusual, weird.

uncertain *adj.* ambiguous, ambivalent, chancy, changeable, conjectural, dicky, doubtful, dubious, erratic, fitful, hazardous, hazy, hesitant, iffy, in the lap of the gods, incalculable, inconstant, indefinite, indeterminate, indistinct, insecure, irregular, irresolute, on the knees of the gods, precarious, problematic, questionable, risky, shaky, slippy, speculative, unclear, unconfirmed, undecided, undetermined, unfixed, unforeseeable, unpredictable, unreliable, unresolved, unsettled, unsure, vacillating, vague, variable, wavering. *antonym* certain.

uncertainty *n.* ambiguity, bewilderment, confusion, diffidence, dilemma, doubt, dubiety, hesitancy, hesitation, incalculability, inconclusiveness, indecision, insecurity, irresolution, misgiving, peradventure, perplexity, puzzlement, qualm, quandary, risk, skepticism, unpredictability, vagueness. *antonym* certainty.

uncharitable *adj.* callous, captious, cruel, hard-hearted, hypercritical, inhumane, insensitive, mean, merciless, pitiless, stingy, unchristian, unfeeling, unforgiving, unfriendly, ungenerous, unkind, unsympathetic. *antonym* charitable.

uncharted *adj.* foreign, mysterious, new, novel, strange, undiscovered, unexplored, unfamiliar, unknown, unplumbed, virgin. *antonyms* familiar, well-known.

uncivil *adj.* abrupt, bad-mannered, bearish, boorish, brusque, churlish, curt, discourteous, disrespectful, gruff, ill-bred, ill-mannered, impolite, rude, surly, uncouth, ungracious, unmannerly. *antonym* civil.

uncivilized *adj.* antisocial, barbarian, barbaric, barbarous, boorish, brutish, churlish, coarse, gross, heathenish, ill-bred, illiterate, philistine, primitive, savage, tramontane, uncouth, uncultivated, uncultured, uneducated, unpolished, unsophisticated, untamed, vulgar, wild. *antonym* civilized.

unclean *adj.* contaminated, corrupt, defiled, dirty, evil, filthy, foul, impure, insalubrious, nasty, polluted, soiled, spotted, stained, sullied, tainted, unhygienic, unwholesome. *antonym* clean.

uncomfortable *adj.* awkward, bleak, confused, conscience-stricken, cramped, disagreeable, discomfited, discomfortable, discomposed, disquieted, distressed, disturbed, embarrassed, hard, ill-fitting, incommodious, irritating, painful, poky, self-conscious, sheepish, troubled, troublesome, uneasy. *antonyms* comfortable, easy.

uncommon *adj.* abnormal, atypical, bizarre, curious, distinctive, exceptional, extraordinary, incomparable, infrequent, inimitable, notable, noteworthy, novel, odd, outstanding, peculiar, queer, rare, remarkable, scarce, singular, special, strange, superior, unfamiliar, unparalleled, unprecedented, unusual, unwonted. *antonym* common.

uncompromising *adj.* decided, diehard, firm, hard-core, hard-line, hardshell, inexorable, inflexible, intransigent, obdurate, obstinate, rigid, steadfast, strict, stubborn, tough, unaccommodating, unbending, unyielding. *antonyms* flexible, open-minded.

unconcerned *adj.* aloof, apathetic, blithe, callous, carefree, careless, complacent, composed, cool, detached, dispassionate, distant, easy, incurious, indifferent, insouciant, jock, nonchalant, oblivious, pococurante, relaxed, serene, uncaring, uninterested, uninvolved, unmoved, unperturbed, unruffled, unsympathetic, untroubled, unworried. *antonym* concerned.

unconditional *adj.* absolute, categorical, complete, downright, entire, full, implicit, out-and-out, outright, plenary, positive, thoroughgoing, total, unequivocal, unlimited, unqualified, unreserved, unrestricted, utter, wholehearted. *antonym* conditional.

unconscious *adj.* accidental, automatic, blind to, comatose, concussed, deaf to, heedless, ignorant, inadvertent, innate, insensible, instinctive, involuntary, knocked out, latent, oblivious, out, out cold, out for the count, reflex, repressed, senseless, stunned, subconscious, subliminal, suppressed, unaware, unintended, unintentional, unknowing, unmindful, unsuspecting, unwitting. *antonym* conscious.

unconventional *adj.* abnormal, alternative, atypical, bizarre, bohemian, different, eccentric, freakish, idiosyncratic, individual, individualistic, informal, irregular, nonconforming, odd, offbeat, original, spacy, uncomfortable, unorthodox, unusual, way-out, wayward. *antonym* conventional.

uncouth *adj.* awkward, barbarian, barbaric, boorish, clownish, clumsy, coarse, crude, gauche, gawky, graceless, gross, ill-

mannered, loutish, lubberly, oafish, rough, rude, rustic, uncivilized, uncultivated, ungainly, unrefined, unseemly, vulgar. *antonyms* polished, polite, refined, urbane.

uncover *v.* bare, detect, disclose, discover, dismask, disrobe, divulge, exhume, expose, leak, lift the lid off, open, reveal, show, strip, unearth, unmask, unveil, unwrap. *antonyms* conceal, cover, suppress.

undaunted *adj.* bold, brave, courageous, dauntless, fearless, gallant, indomitable, intrepid, resolute, steadfast, unbowed, undeterred, undiscouraged, undismayed, unfaltering, unflinching, unperturbed, unshrinking. *antonyms* cowed, timorous.

undefined *adj.* formless, hazy, ill-defined, imprecise, indefinite, indeterminate, indistinct, inexact, nebulous, shadowy, tenuous, unclear, unexplained, unspecified, vague, woolly. *antonyms* definite, precise.

undependable *adj.* capricious, changeable, erratic, fair-weather, fickle, inconsistent, inconstant, irresponsible, mercurial, treach-erous, uncertain, unpredictable, unreliable, unstable, untrustworthy, variable, *antonyms* dependable, reliable.

under *prep.* belonging to, below, beneath, governed by, included in, inferior to, junior to, led by, less than, lower than, secondary to, subject to, subordinate to, subservient to, underneath. *adv.* below, beneath, down, downward, less, lower.

undercover *adj.* clandestine, concealed, confidential, covert, furtive, hidden, hush-hush, intelligence, private, secret, spy, stealthy, surreptitious, underground. *antonyms* open, unconcealed.

undercurrent *n.* atmosphere, aura, crosscurrent, drift, eddy, feeling, flavor, hint, movement, murmur, overtone, rip, riptide, sense, suggestion, tendency, tenor, tide, tinge, trend, underflow, undertone, undertow, vibes, vibrations.

undergo *v.* bear, brook, endure, experience, run the gauntlet, stand, submit to, suffer, sustain, weather, withstand.

underhand *adj.* clandestine, crafty, crooked, deceitful, deceptive, devious, dishonest, dishonorable, fraudulent, furtive, immoral, improper, shady, shifty, sly, sneaky, stealthy, surreptitious, treacherous, underhanded, unethical, unscrupulous. *antonym* aboveboard.

undermine *v.* debilitate, disable, erode, excavate, impair, mar, mine, sabotage, sap, subvert, threaten, tunnel, undercut, vitiate, weaken, wear away. *antonyms* fortify, strengthen.

underprivileged *adj.* deprived, destitute, disadvantaged, impecunious, impoverished, needy, poor, poverty-stricken. *antonyms* affluent, fortunate, privileged.

understand *v.* accept, appreciate, apprehend, assume, believe, commiserate, comprehend, conceive, conclude, cotton on, discern, fathom, follow, gather, get, get the message, get the picture, grasp, hear, know, learn, penetrate, perceive, presume, realize, recognize, savvy, see, see daylight, suppose, sympathize, think, tolerate, tumble, twig. *antonym* misunderstand.

understanding *n.* accord, agreement, appreciation, awareness, belief, comprehension, conclusion, discernment, estimation, grasp, idea, impression, insight, intellect, intellection, intelligence, interpretation, judgment, knowledge, opinion, pact, penetration, perception, reading, sense, view, viewpoint, wisdom. *adj.* accepting, compassionate, considerate, discerning, forbearing, forgiving, kind, kindly, loving, patient, perceptive, responsive, sensitive, sympathetic, tender, tolerant. *antonyms* impatient, insensitive, intolerant, unsympathetic.

understudy *n.* alternate, deputy, double, fill-in, replacement, reserve, stand-in, substitute.

undertake *v.* accept, agree, assume, attempt, bargain, begin, commence, contract, covenant, embark on, endeavor, engage, guarantee, pledge, promise, shoulder, stipulate, tackle, try.

undertaking *n.* adventure, affair, assurance, attempt, business, commitment, effort, emprise, endeavor, enterprise, game, operation, pledge, project, promise, task, venture, vow, word.

undervalue *v.* depreciate, discount, dismiss, disparage, disprize, minimize, misjudge, misprice, misprize, underestimate, underrate. *antonyms* exaggerate, overrate.

underwrite *v.* approve, authorize, back, consent, countenance, countersign, endorse, finance, fund, guarantee, initial, insure, okay, sanction, sign, sponsor, subscribe, subsidize, validate.

undesirable *adj.* disagreeable, disliked, disreputable, distasteful, dreaded, objectionable, obnoxious, offensive, repugnant, unacceptable, unattractive, unpleasant, unpopular, unsavory, unsuitable, unwanted, unwelcome, unwished-for. *antonym* desirable.

undignified *adj.* foolish, improper, inappropriate, indecorous, inelegant, infra dig, petty, unbecoming, ungentlemanly, unladylike, unrefined, unseemly, unsuitable. *antonym* dignified.

undisciplined *adj.* disobedient, disorganized, obstreperous, uncontrolled, unpredictable, unreliable, unrestrained, unruly, unschooled, unsteady, unsystematic, untrained, wayward, wild, willful. *antonym* disciplined.

undivided *adj.* combined, complete, concentrated, concerted, entire, exclusive, full, individuated, solid, thorough, tight-knit, unanimous, unbroken, united, whole, wholehearted.

undoing *n.* besetting sin, blight, collapse, curse, defeat, destruction, disgrace, downfall, hamartia, humiliation, misfortune, overthrow, overturn, reversal, ruin, ruination, shame, tragic fault, trouble, weakness.

undoubtedly *adv.* assuredly, certainly, definitely, doubtless, indubitably, of course, surely, undeniably, unmistakably, unquestionably.

undulating *adj.* billowing, flexuose, flexuous, rippling, rolling, sinuous, undated, undulant, wavy. *antonym* flat.

unduly *adv.* disproportionately, excessively, extravagantly, immoderately, inordinately, over, overly, overmuch, too, unjustifiably, unnecessarily, unreasonably. *antonym* reasonably.

undying *adj.* abiding, constant, continuing, deathless, eternal, everlasting, immortal, imperishable, indestructible, inextinguishable, infinite, lasting, perennial, permanent, perpetual, sempiternal, undiminished, unending, unfading. *antonyms* impermanent, inconstant.

unearthly *adj.* abnormal, eerie, eldritch, ethereal, extraordinary, ghostly, haunted, heavenly, nightmarish, otherworldly, phantom, preternatural, spectral, spine-chilling, strange, sublime, supernatural, uncanny, ungodly, unreasonable, weird.

uneasy *adj.* agitated, anxious, apprehensive, awkward, constrained, discomposed, disquieting, disturbed, disturbing, edgy, impatient, insecure, jittery, nervous, niggling, on edge, perturbed, precarious, restive, restless, shaky, strained, tense, troubled, troubling, uncomfortable, unquiet, unsettled, unstable, upset, upsetting, worried, worrying. *antonyms* calm, composed.

unemotional *adj.* apathetic, cold, cool, dispassionate, impassive, indifferent, laid-back, low-key, objective, passionless, phlegmatic, reserved, undemonstrative, passionless, phlegmatic, reserved, undemonstrative, unexcitable, unfeeling, unimpassioned, unresponsive. *antonyms* emotional, excitable.

unemployed *adj.* idle, jobless, out of employ, out of work, redundant, resting, unoccupied, workless. *antonym* employed.

unenviable *adj.* disagreeable, painful, thankless, uncomfortable, uncongenial, undesirable, unpalatable, unpleasant, unsavory. *antonyms* desirable, enviable.

unequal *adj.* asymmetrical, different, differing, disparate, disproportionate, dissimilar, ill-equipped, ill-matched, inadequate, incapable, incompetent, insufficient, irregular, unbalanced, uneven, unlike, unmatched, variable, varying. *antonym* equal.

unequivocal *adj.* absolute, certain, clear, clear-cut, crystal-clear, decisive, definite, direct, distinct, evident, explicit, express, incontrovertible, indubitable, manifest, plain, positive, straight, unambiguous, uncontestable, unmistakable. *antonyms* ambiguous, vague.

unerring *adj.* accurate, certain, dead, exact, faultless, impeccable, infallible, perfect, sure, uncanny, unfailing. *antonym* fallible.

unethical *adj.* dirty, discreditable, dishonest, dishonorable, disreputable, illegal, illicit, immoral, improper, shady, underhand, unfair, unprincipled, unprofessional, unscrupulous, wrong. *antonym* ethical.

uneven *adj.* accidented, asymmetrical, broken, bumpy, changeable, desultory, disparate, erratic, fitful, fluctuating, ill-matched, inconsistent, intermittent, irregular, jerky, lopsided, odd, one-sided, patchy, rough, spasmodic, unbalanced, unequal, unfair, unsteady, variable. *antonym* even.

unexceptional *adj.* average, commonplace, conventional, indifferent, insignificant, mediocre, normal, ordinary, pedestrian, run-of-the-mill, typical, undistinguished, unimpressive, unmemorable, unremarkable, usual. *antonyms* exceptional, impressive.

unexpected *adj.* abrupt, accidental, amazing, astonishing, chance, fortuitous, startling, sudden, surprising, unaccustomed, unanticipated, unforeseen, unlooked-for, unpredictable, unusual, unwonted. *antonyms* expected, normal, predictable.

unfair *adj.* arbitrary, biased, bigoted, crooked, discriminatory, dishonest, dishonorable, inequitable, one-sided, partial, partisan, prejudiced, uncalled-for, undeserved, unethical, unjust, unmerited, unprincipled, unscrupulous, unsporting, unwarranted, wrongful. *antonym* fair.

unfaithful *adj.* adulterous, deceitful, dishonest, disloyal, faithless, false, false-hearted, fickle, godless, inconstant, perfidious, recreant, traitorous, treacherous, treasonable, two-timing, unbelieving, unchaste, unreliable, untrue, untrustworthy. *antonyms* faithful, loyal.

unfamiliar *adj.* alien, curious, different, foreign, new, novel, out-of-the-way, strange, unaccustomed, unacquainted, uncharted, uncommon, unconversant, unexplored, unknown, unpracticed, unskilled, unusual, unversed. *antonyms* customary, familiar.

unfasten *v.* detach, disconnect, loosen, open, separate, uncouple, undo, unlace, unlock, unloose, unloosen, untie. *antonym* fasten.

unfavorable *adj.* adverse, bad, contrary, critical, disadvantageous, discouraging, hostile, ill-suited, inauspicious, infelicitous, inimical, inopportune, low, negative, ominous, poor, threatening, uncomplimentary, unfortunate, unfriendly, unlucky, unpromising, unpropitious, unseasonable, unsuited, untimely, untoward. *antonym* favorable.

unfeeling *adj.* apathetic, callous, cold, cruel, hard, hardened, hard-hearted, harsh, heartless, inhuman, insensitive, pitiless, soulless, stony, uncaring, unsympathetic. *antonym* concerned.

unfeigned *adj.* frank, genuine, heartfelt, natural, pure, real, sincere, spontaneous, unaffected, unforced, wholehearted. *antonyms* feigned, insincere, pretended.

unfit *adj.* debilitated, decrepit, feeble, flabby, flaccid, hypotonic, ill-adapted, ill-equipped, inadequate, inappropriate, incapable, incompetent, ineffective, ineligible, unequal, unhealthy, unprepared, unqualified, unsuitable, unsuited, untrained, useless. *antonyms* competent, fit, suitable.

unfold *v.* clarify, describe, develop, disclose, disentangle, divulge, elaborate, evolve, expand, explain, flatten, grow, illustrate, mature, open, present, reveal, show, spread, straighten, stretch out, uncoil, uncover, undo, unfurl, unravel, unroll, unwrap. *antonyms* fold, suppress, withhold, wrap.

unforeseen *adj.* abrupt, accidental, fortuitous, startling, sudden, surprise, surprising, unanticipated, unavoidable, unexpected, unheralded, unlooked-for, unpredicted. *antonyms* expected, predictable.

unfortunate *adj.* adverse, calamitous, cursed, deplorable, disadventurous, disastrous, doomed, hapless, hopeless, ill-advised, ill-fated, ill-starred, ill-timed, inappropriate, infelicitous, inopportune, lamentable, luckless, poor, regrettable, ruinous, star-crossed, tactless, unbecoming, unfavorable, unhappy, unlucky, unprosperous, unsuccessful, unsuitable, untimely, untoward, wretched. *antonym* fortunate.

unfriendly *adj.* alien, aloof, antagonistic, chilly, cold, critical, disagreeable, distant, hostile, ill-disposed, inauspicious, inhospitable, inimical, quarrelsome, sour, standoffish, surly, unapproachable, unbending, uncongenial, unfavorable, unneighborly, unsociable, unwelcoming. *antonyms* agreeable, amiable, friendly.

ungainly *adj.* awkward, clumsy, gangling, gauche, gawky, inelegant, loutish, lubberly, lumbering, slouching, uncoordinated, uncouth, unwieldy. *antonyms* elegant, graceful.

ungodly *adj.* blasphemous, corrupt, depraved, dreadful, godless, horrendous, immoral, impious, intolerable, irreligious, outrageous, profane, sinful, unearthly, unreasonable, unseasonable, unseemly, unsocial, vile, wicked.

ungrateful *adj.* heedless, ill-mannered, ingrate, selfish, thankless, unappreciative, ungracious, unmindful. *antonym* grateful.

unguarded[1] *adj.* careless, foolhardy, foolish, heedless, ill-considered, impolitic, imprudent, incautious, indiscreet, rash, thoughtless, uncircumspect, undiplomatic, unheeding, unthinking, unwary. *antonyms* cautious, guarded.

unguarded[2] *adj.* defenseless, exposed, pregnable, undefended, unpatrolled, unprotected, vulnerable. *antonyms* guarded, protected.

unhappy *adj.* awkward, blue, clumsy, contentless, crestfallen, cursed, dejected, depressed, despondent, disconsolate, dismal, dispirited, down, downcast, gauche, gloomy, hapless, ill-advised, ill-chosen, ill-fated, ill-omened, ill-timed, inappropriate, inapt, inept, infelicitous, injudicious, long-

faced, luckless, lugubrious, malapropos, melancholy, miserable, mournful, sad, sorrowful, sorry, tactless, uneasy, unfortunate, unlucky, unsuitable, wretched. *antonyms* fortunate, happy.

unhealthy *adj.* ailing, bad, baneful, corrupt, corrupting, degrading, deleterious, delicate, demoralizing, detrimental, epinosic, feeble, frail, harmful, infirm, insalubrious, insalutary, insanitary, invalid, morbid, noisome, noxious, polluted, poorly, sick, sickly, undesirable, unhygienic, unsound, unwell, unwholesome, weak. *antonyms* healthy, hygienic, robust, salubrious.

unheard-of *adj.* disgraceful, extreme, inconceivable, new, novel, obscure, offensive, out of the question, outrageous, preposterous, shocking, singular, unacceptable, unbelievable, undiscovered, undreamed-of, unexampled, unfamiliar, unimaginable, unique, unknown, unprecedented, unregarded, unremarked, unsung, unthinkable, unthought-of, unusual. *antonyms* famous, normal, usual.

unhurried *adj.* calm, deliberate, easy, easy-going, laid-back, leisurely, relaxed, sedate, slow. *antonyms* hasty, hurried.

uniform *antonyms* costume, dress, garb, gear, habit, insignia, livery, outfit, regalia, regimentals, rig, robes, suit. *adj.* alike, consistent, constant, equable, equal, even, homochromous, homogeneous, homomorphic, homomorphus, identical, like, monochrome, monotonous, of a piece, regular, same, selfsame, similar, smooth, unbroken, unchanging, undeviating, unvarying. *antonyms* changing, colorful, varied.

unify *v.* amalgamate, bind, combine, confederate, consolidate, federate, fuse, join, marry, merge, unite, weld. *antonyms* separate, split.

unimaginable *adj.* fantastic, impossible, inconceivable, incredible, indescribable, ineffable, mind-boggling, unbelievable, undreamed-of, unheard-of, unhoped-for, unknowable, unthinkable.

unimportant *adj.* immaterial, inconsequential, insignificant, irrelevant, low-ranking, Mickey Mouse, minor, minuscule, negligible, nugatory, off the map, paltry, paravail, petty, slight, small-time, trifling, trivial, worthless. *antonyms* important.

unimpressive *adj.* average, commonplace, dull, indifferent, mediocre, undistinguished, unexceptional, uninteresting, unremarkable, unspectacular. *antonyms* impressive, memorable, notable.

uninhibited *adj.* abandoned, candid, emancipated, frank, free, informal, instinctive, liberated, natural, open, relaxed, spontaneous, unbridled, unchecked, unconstrained, uncontrolled, uncurbed, unrepressed, unreserved, unrestrained, unrestricted, unselfconscious. *antonyms* constrained, inhibited, repressed.

uninspired *adj.* boring, commonplace, dull, humdrum, indifferent, ordinary, pedestrian, prosaic, stale, stock, trite, undistinguished, unexciting, unimaginative, uninspiring, uninteresting, unoriginal. *antonyms* inspired, original.

unintelligent *adj.* brainless, dense, dull, dumb, empty-headed, fatuous, foolish, gormless, half-witted, obtuse, silly, slow, stupid, thick, unreasoning, unthinking. *antonym* intelligent.

unintelligible *adj.* double Dutch, garbled, illegible, inapprehensible, inarticulate, incoherent, incomprehensible, indecipherable, indistinct, jumbled, meaningless, muddled, unfathomable. *antonym* intelligible.

unintentional *adj.* accidental, fortuitous, inadvertent, involuntary, unconscious, undeliberate, unintended, unpremeditated, unthinking, unwitting. *antonyms* deliberate, intentional.

uninviting *adj.* disagreeable, distasteful, offensive, off-putting, repellent, repulsive, unappealing, unappetizing, unattractive, undesirable, unpleasant, unsavory, unwelcoming. *antonyms* inviting, welcome.

union *n.* accord, agreement, alliance, amalgam, amalgamation, association, blend, Bund, coalition, coition, coitus, combination, compact, concord, concrescence, concurrence, confederacy, confederation, conjugation, conjunction, copulation, couplement, coupling, enosis, federation, fusion, harmony, intercourse, junction, juncture, league, marriage, matrimony, mixture, symphysis, synthesis, unanimity, unison, uniting, unity, wedlock. *antonyms* alienation, disunity, estrangement, separation.

unique *adj.* incomparable, inimitable, lone, matchless, nonpareil, one-off, only, peerless, single, sole, solitary, sui generis, unequaled, unexampled, unmatched, unparalleled, unprecedented, unrivaled. *antonym* commonplace.

unison *n.* accord, accordance, agreement, concert, concord, cooperation, harmony, ho-

mophony, monophony, unanimity, unity. *antonyms* disharmony, polyphony.

unit *n.* ace, assembly, component, constituent, detachment, element, entity, gestalt, group, item, measure, measurement, member, module, monad, monas, one, part, piece, portion, quantity, section, segment, system, whole.

unite *v.* accrete, ally, amalgamate, associate, band, blend, coadunate, coalesce, combine, confederate, conglutinate, conjoin, conjugate, consolidate, cooperate, couple, fay, fuse, incorporate, join, join forces, league, link, marry, merge, pool, splice, unify, wed. *antonyms* separate, sever.

universal *adj.* across-the-board, all-embracing, all-inclusive, all-round, catholic, common, ecumenic, ecumenical, entire, general, global, omnipresent, total, ubiquitous, unlimited, whole, widespread, worldwide.

unjustifiable *adj.* excessive, immoderate, indefensible, inexcusable, outrageous, steep, unacceptable, unforgivable, unjust, unpardonable, unreasonable, unwarrantable, wrong. *antonym* justifiable.

unkind *adj.* callous, cruel, disobliging, hard-hearted, harsh, inconsiderate, inhuman, inhumane, insensitive, malevolent, malicious, mean, nasty, spiteful, thoughtless, unamiable, uncaring, uncharitable, unchristian, unfeeling, unfriendly, unsympathetic. *antonyms* considerate, kind.

unknown *adj.* alien, anonymous, concealed, dark, foreign, hidden, humble, incognito, mysterious, nameless, new, obscure, secret, strange, uncharted, undisclosed, undiscovered, undistinguished, unexplored, unfamiliar, unheard-of, unidentified, unnamed, unrecognized, unsung, untold. *antonyms* familiar, known.

unlawful *adj.* actionable, banned, criminal, forbidden, illegal, illegitimate, illicit, outlawed, prohibited, unauthorized, unconstitutional, unlicensed, unsanctioned. *antonym* lawful.

unlike *adj.* contrasted, different, difform, disparate, dissimilar, distinct, divergent, diverse, ill-matched, incompatible, opposed, opposite, unequal, unrelated. *antonyms* related, similar.

unlimited *adj.* absolute, all-encompassing, boundless, complete, countless, endless, extensive, full, great, illimitable, immeasurable, immense, incalculable, infinite, limitless, total, unbounded, uncircumscribed, unconditional, unconstrained, unfettered, un-hampered, unqualified, unrestricted, vast. *antonyms* circumscribed, limited.

unlucky *adj.* cursed, disastrous, doomed, hapless, ill-fated, ill-omened, ill-starred, in-auspicious, infaust, jinxed, left-handed, luckless, mischanceful, miserable, ominous, unfavorable, unfortunate, unhappy, unsuc-cessful, untimely, wretched. *antonym* lucky.

unmanageable *adj.* awkward, bulky, cumbersome, difficult, disorderly, fractious, inconvenient, intractable, obstreperous, re-calcitrant, refractory, stroppy, uncon-trollable, uncooperative, unhandy, unruly, unwieldy, wild. *antonyms* docile, manage-able.

unmannerly *adj.* badly behaved, bad-mannered, boorish, discourteous, disre-spectful, graceless, ill-bred, ill-mannered, impolite, lowbred, rude, uncivil, uncouth, ungracious. *antonym* polite.

unmerciful *adj.* brutal, callous, cruel, hard, heartless, implacable, merciless, piti-less, relentless, remorseless, ruthless, sadis-tic, uncaring, unfeeling, unrelenting, unspar-ing. *antonym* merciful.

unmistakable *adj.* certain, clear, con-spicuous, crystal-clear, decided, distinct, evident, explicit, glaring, indisputable, manifest, obvious, palpable, patent, plain, positive, pronounced, sure, unambiguous, undeniable, undisputed, unequivocal, un-questionable. *antonyms* ambiguous, un-clear.

unmitigated *adj.* absolute, arrant, com-plete, consummate, downright, grim, harsh, intense, oppressive, out-and-out, outright, perfect, persistent, pure, rank, relentless, sheer, thorough, thoroughgoing, unabated, unalleviated, unbroken, undiminished, un-modified, unqualified, unredeemed, unre-lenting, unrelieved, unremitting, utter.

unnatural *adj.* aberrant, abnormal, abso-nant, affected, anomalous, artificial, as-sumed, bizarre, brutal, callous, cataphysical, cold-blooded, contrived, cruel, disnatured, evil, extraordinary, factitious, false, feigned, fiendish, forced, freakish, heartless, inhu-man, insincere, irregular, labored, mannered, monstrous, odd, outlandish, perverse, per-verted, phony, queer, ruthless, sadistic, sav-age, self-conscious, stagy, stiff, stilted, strained, strange, studied, supernatural, the-atrical, unaccountable, uncanny, unfeeling, unspontaneous, unusual, wicked. *antonyms* acceptable, natural, normal.

unnecessary *adj.* dispensable, expend-able, inessential, needless, nonessential, oti-ose, pleonastic, redundant, supererogatory, superfluous, supernumerary, tautological, uncalled-for, unjustified, unneeded, useless. *antonyms* indispensable, necessary.

unobtrusive *adj.* humble, inconspicuous, low-key, meek, modest, quiet, restrained, re-tiring, self-effacing, subdued, unassertive, unassuming, unemphatic, unnoticeable, un-ostentatious, unpretentious. *antonyms* ob-trusive, ostentatious.

unoccupied *adj.* disengaged, empty, free, idle, inactive, jobless, unemployed, unin-habited, untenanted, vacant, workless. *anto-nyms* busy, occupied.

unofficial *adj.* confidential, illegal, infor-mal, personal, private, ulterior, unauthor-ized, unconfirmed, undeclared, wildcat. *an-tonym* official.

unorthodox *adj.* abnormal, alternative, fringe, heterodox, irregular, nonconformist, unconventional, unusual, unwonted. *anto-nyms* conventional, orthodox.

unparalleled *adj.* consummate, excep-tional, incomparable, matchless, peerless, rare, singular, superlative, supreme, surpass-ing, unequaled, unexampled, unique, un-matched, unprecedented, unrivaled, unsur-passed.

unpleasant *adj.* abhorrent, bad, disagree-able, displeasing, distasteful, god-awful, ill-natured, irksome, nasty, objectionable, ob-noxious, repulsive, rocky, sticky, traumatic, troublesome, unattractive, unpalatable. *an-tonym* pleasant.

unpopular *adj.* avoided, detested, dis-liked, hated, neglected, rejected, shunned, undesirable, unfashionable, unloved, un-sought-after, unwanted, unwelcome. *anto-nyms* fashionable, popular.

unprecedented *adj.* abnormal, excep-tional, extraordinary, freakish, new, novel, original, remarkable, revolutionary, singu-lar, unexampled, unheard-of, unknown, un-paralleled, unrivaled, unusual.

unpredictable *adj.* chance, changeable, doubtful, erratic, fickle, fluky, iffy, in the lap of the gods, inconstant, on the knees of the gods, random, scatty, unforeseeable, unreli-able, unstable, variable, *antonym* predict-able.

unprejudiced *adj.* balanced, detached, dispassionate, enlightened, evenhanded, fair, fair-minded, impartial, just, nonpartisan, objective, open-minded, unbiased, un-colored. *antonyms* narrow-minded, preju-diced.

unpremeditated *adj.* extempore, fortui-tous, impromptu, impulsive, offhand, off-the-cuff, spontaneous, spur-of-the-moment, unintentional, unplanned, unprepared, unre-hearsed. *antonym* premeditated.

unprincipled *adj.* amoral, corrupt, crooked, deceitful, devious, discreditable, dishonest, dishonorable, immoral, under-hand, unethical, unprofessional, unscrupu-lous. *antonym* ethical.

unprofessional *adj.* amateur, amateur-ish, improper, inadmissible, incompetent, in-efficient, inexperienced, inexpert, lax, neg-ligent, unacceptable, unbecoming, unethical, unfitting, unprincipled, unseemly, unskilled, untrained, unworthy. *antonyms* professional, skillful.

unprotected *adj.* defenseless, exposed, helpless, inert, liable, naked, open, pregna-ble, unarmed, unattended, undefended, un-fortified, unguarded, unsheltered, un-shielded, unvaccinated, vulnerable. *antonyms* immune, protected, safe.

unqualified *adj.* absolute, categorical, complete, consummate, ill-equipped, inca-pable, incompetent, ineligible, out-and-out, outright, thorough, thoroughgoing, total, un-certificated, unconditional, unfit, unmiti-gated, unmixed, unprepared, unreserved, unrestricted, untrained, utter, wholehearted. *antonyms* conditional, tentative.

unreal *adj.* academic, artificial, chimerical, fabulous, fairy-tale, fake, false, fanciful, fan-tastic, fictitious, hypothetical, illusory, imaginary, immaterial, impalpable, insin-cere, insubstantial, intangible, made-up, make-believe, mock, moonshiny, mythical, nebulous, ostensible, phantasmagorical, pretended, seeming, sham, storybook, syn-thetic, vaporous, visionary. *antonyms* genu-ine, real.

unrealistic *adj.* half-baked, idealistic, im-practicable, impractical, improbable, quix-otic, romantic, starry-eyed, theoretical, un-workable. *antonyms* pragmatic, realistic.

unreasonable *adj.* absurd, arbitrary, bi-ased, blindered, capricious, cussed, erratic, excessive, exorbitant, extortionate, extrava-gant, far-fetched, foolish, froward, head-strong, illogical, immoderate, inconsistent, irrational, mad, nonsensical, opinionated, perverse, preposterous, quirky, senseless, silly, steep, stupid, thrawn, uncalled-for, un-

due, unfair, unjust, unjustifiable, unjustified, unwarranted. *antonyms* moderate, rational, reasonable.

unrelenting *adj.* ceaseless, constant, con-tinual, continuous, cruel, endless, implaca-ble, incessant, inexorable, insistent, intransi-gent, merciless, perpetual, pitiless, relentless, remorseless, ruthless, steady, stern, tough, unabated, unalleviated, unbro-ken, unceasing, uncompromising, unmerci-ful, unremitting, unsparing. *antonyms* inter-mittent, spasmodic.

unreliable *adj.* deceptive, delusive, dis-reputable, erroneous, fair-weather, fallible, false, implausible, inaccurate, inauthentic, irresponsible, mistaken, specious, uncertain, unconvincing, undependable, unsound, un-stable, untrustworthy. *antonym* reliable.

unrepentant *adj.* callous, hardened, im-penitent, incorrigible, obdurate, shameless, unabashed, unashamed, unregenerate, unre-morseful, unrepenting. *antonyms* penitent, repentant.

unresponsive *adj.* aloof, apathetic, cool, echoless, indifferent, unaffected, uninter-ested, unmoved, unsympathetic. *antonyms* responsive, sympathetic.

unrest *n.* agitation, anxiety, apprehension, disaffection, discontent, discord, disquiet, dissatisfaction, dissension, distress, pertur-bation, protest, rebellion, restlessness, sedi-tion, strife, tumult, turmoil, unease, uneasi-ness, worry. *antonyms* calm, peace.

unrestrained *adj.* abandoned, boister-ous, free, immoderate, inordinate, intemper-ate, irrepressible, natural, rampant, un-bounded, unbridled, unchecked, unconstrained, uncontrolled, unhindered, uninhibited, unrepressed, unreserved, up-roarious. *antonym* inhibited.

unruffled *adj.* calm, collected, composed, cool, even, imperturbable, level, peaceful, placid, serene, smooth, tranquil, unbroken, undisturbed, unflustered, unmoved, unper-turbed, untroubled. *antonyms* anxious, trou-bled.

unruly *adj.* camstairy, disobedient, disor-derly, fractious, headstrong, insubordinate, intractable, lawless, mutinous, obstreperous, rebellious, refractory, riotous, rowdy, ruleless, turbulent, uncontrollable, ungov-ernable, unmanageable, wayward, wild, willful. *antonym* manageable.

unsafe *adj.* dangerous, exposed, hazard-ous, insecure, parlous, perilous, precarious, risky, threatening, treacherous, uncertain, unreliable, unsound, unstable, vulnerable. *antonyms* safe, secure.

unsatisfactory *adj.* deficient, disappointing, displeasing, dissatisfying, frustrating, inadequate, inferior, insufficient, leaving a lot to be desired, mediocre, poor, rocky, thwarting, unacceptable, unsatisfying, unsuitable, unworthy, weak. *antonym* satisfactory.

unscrupulous *adj.* corrupt, crooked, cynical, discreditable, dishonest, dishonorable, immoral, improper, ruthless, shameless, unethical, unprincipled. *antonym* scrupulous.

unseemly *adj.* discreditable, disreputable, improper, inappropriate, indecorous, indelicate, shocking, unbecoming, unbefitting, undignified, undue, ungentlemanly, unladylike, unrefined, unsuitable. *antonyms* decorous, seemly.

unselfish *adj.* altruistic, charitable, dedicated, devoted, disinterested, generous, humanitarian, kind, liberal, magnanimous, noble, philanthropic, self-denying, selfless, self-sacrificing, single-eyed, ungrudging, unstinting. *antonym* selfish.

unsentimental *adj.* cynical, hard as nails, hardheaded, levelheaded, practical, pragmatic, realistic, shrewd, tough. *antonyms* sentimental, soft.

unsettled *adj.* agitated, anxious, changeable, changing, confused, debatable, disorderly, disoriented, disturbed, doubtful, due, edgy, flustered, iffy, inconstant, insecure, moot, open, outstanding, overdue, owing, payable, pending, perturbed, problematical, restive, restless, shaken, shaky, tense, troubled, uncertain, undecided, undetermined, uneasy, unnerved, unpredictable, unresolved, unstable, unsteady, upset, variable. *antonyms* certain, composed, settled.

unsightly *adj.* disagreeable, displeasing, hideous, horrid, off-putting, repellent, repugnant, repulsive, revolting, ugly, unattractive, unpleasant, unprepossessing. *antonym* pleasing.

unsolicited *adj.* gratuitous, spontaneous, unasked, uncalled-for, unforced, uninvited, unrequested, unsought, unwanted, unwelcome, voluntary. *antonyms* invited, solicited.

unsophisticated *adj.* artless, childlike, funky, guileless, hick, homespun, inexperienced, ingenuous, innocent, naïve, natural, plain, simple, straightforward, unaffected, uncomplicated, uninvolved, unpretentious,

unrefined, unspecialized, unspoiled, untutored, unworldly. *antonyms* complex, pretentious, sophisticated.

unsound *adj.* ailing, defective, delicate, deranged, dicky, diseased, erroneous, fallacious, fallible, false, faulty, flawed, frail, ill, ill-founded, illogical, insecure, invalid, shaky, specious, unbalanced, unhealthy, unhinged, unreliable, unsafe, unstable, unsteady, unwell, weak, wobbly. *antonyms* safe, sound.

unspeakable *adj.* abhorrent, abominable, appalling, dreadful, evil, execrable, frightful, heinous, horrible, inconceivable, indescribable, ineffable, inexpressible, loathsome, monstrous, nefandous, odious, overwhelming, repellent, shocking, unbelievable, unimaginable, unutterable, wonderful.

unstable *adj.* astable, capricious, changeable, erratic, fitful, fluctuating, inconsistent, inconstant, insecure, irrational, labile, precarious, rickety, risky, shaky, shoogly, slippy, ticklish, tottering, unpredictable, unsettled, unsteady, untrustworthy, vacillating, variable, volatile, wobbly. *antonyms* stable, steady.

unsteady *adj.* changeable, dicky, erratic, flickering, flighty, fluctuating, frail, inconstant, infirm, insecure, irregular, precarious, reeling, rickety, shaky, shoogly, skittish, tittupy, tottering, totty, treacherous, tremulous, unreliable, unsafe, unstable, unsteeled, vacillating, variable, volatile, wavering, wobbly. *antonyms* firm, steady.

unsubstantiated *adj.* debatable, dubious, questionable, unattested, unconfirmed, uncorroborated, unestablished, unproved, unproven, unsupported, unverified. *antonyms* proved, proven.

unsuccessful *adj.* abortive, bootless, failed, foiled, fruitless, frustrated, futile, ill-fated, inadequate, ineffective, ineffectual, losing, luckless, manqué, otiose, sterile, thwarted, unavailing, unfortunate, unlucky, unproductive, unsatisfactory, useless, vain. *antonyms* effective, successful.

unsuitable *adj.* improper, inapposite, inappropriate, inapt, incompatible, incongruous, inconsistent, indecorous, ineligible, infelicitous, malapropos, unacceptable, unbecoming, unbefitting, unfitting, unlikely, unseasonable, unseemly, unsuited. *antonyms* seemly, suitable.

unsuspecting *adj.* childlike, confiding, credulous, green, gullible, inexperienced, ingenuous, innocent, naive, trustful, trusting, unconscious, unsuspicious, unwary, unwitting. *antonyms* conscious, knowing.

unswerving *adj.* constant, dedicated, devoted, direct, firm, fixed, immovable, resolute, single-minded, staunch, steadfast, steady, sure, true, undeviating, unfaltering, unflagging, untiring, unwavering. *antonyms* irresolute, tentative.

unsympathetic *adj.* antagonistic, antipathetic, apathetic, callous, cold, compassionless, cruel, hard, hard as nails, hard-hearted, harsh, heartless, indifferent, inhuman, insensitive, soulless, stony, uncharitable, uncompassionate, unconcerned, unfeeling, unkind, unmoved, unpitying, unresponsive. *antonyms* compassionate, sympathetic.

untamed *adj.* barbarous, ferae naturae, feral, fierce, haggard, savage, unbroken, undomesticated, unmellowed, untameable, wild. *antonyms* domesticated, tame.

untenable *adj.* fallacious, flawed, illogical, indefensible, insupportable, rocky, shaky, unmaintainable, unreasonable, unsound, unsustainable. *antonyms* sound, tenable.

untidy *adj.* bedraggled, chaotic, cluttered, disheveled, disorderly, higgledy-piggledy, jumbled, littered, messy, muddled, ratty, raunchy, rumpled, scruffy, shambolic, slatternly, slipshod, sloppy, slovenly, sluttish, topsy-turvy, unkempt, unsystematic. *antonyms* systematic, tidy.

untimely *adj.* awkward, early, ill-timed, inappropriate, inauspicious, inconvenient, inopportune, intempestive, malapropos, mistimed, premature, unfortunate, unseasonable, unsuitable. *antonyms* opportune, timely.

untold *adj.* boundless, countless, hidden, incalculable, indescribable, inexhaustible, inexpressible, infinite, innumerable, measureless, myriad, numberless, private, secret, uncountable, uncounted, undisclosed, undreamed-of, unimaginable, unknown, unnumbered, unpublished, unreckoned, unrecounted, unrelated, unrevealed, unthinkable, unutterable.

untoward *adj.* adverse, annoying, awkward, contrary, disastrous, ill-timed, improper, inappropriate, inauspicious, inconvenient, indecorous, inimical, inopportune, irritating, ominous, troublesome, unbecoming, unexpected, unfavorable, unfitting, unfortunate, unlucky, unpropitious, unseemly, unsuitable, untimely, vexatious, worrying. *antonyms* auspicious, suitable.

untrustworthy *adj.* capricious, deceitful, devious, dishonest, disloyal, dubious, duplicitous, fair-weather, faithless, false, fickle, fly-by-night, shady, slippery, treacherous, tricky, two-faced, undependable, unfaithful, unreliable, unsafe, untrue, untrusty. *antonyms* reliable, trustworthy.

untruthful *adj.* crooked, deceitful, deceptive, dishonest, dissembling, false, hypocritical, lying, mendacious, untrustworthy, unveracious. *antonym* truthful.

untutored *adj.* artless, ignorant, illiterate, inexperienced, inexpert, simple, uneducated, unlearned, unlessoned, unpracticed, unrefined, unschooled, unsophisticated, untrained, unversed. *antonyms* educated, trained.

unusual *adj.* abnormal, anomalous, atypical, bizarre, curious, different, eccentric, exceptional, extraordinary, odd, phenomenal, queer, rare, remarkable, singular, strange, surprising, uncommon, unconventional, unexpected, unfamiliar, unwonted. *antonyms* normal, usual.

unutterable *adj.* egregious, extreme, indescribable, ineffable, nefandous, overwhelming, unimaginable, unspeakable.

unwarranted *adj.* baseless, gratuitous, groundless, indefensible, inexcusable, uncalled-for, unjust, unjustified, unprovoked, unreasonable, vain, wrong. *antonyms* justifiable, warranted.

unwary *adj.* careless, credulous, hasty, heedless, imprudent, incautious, indiscreet, rash, reckless, thoughtless, unchary, uncircumspect, unguarded, unthinking, unwatchful. *antonyms* cautious, wary.

unwieldy *adj.* awkward, bulky, burdensome, clumsy, cumbersome, cumbrous, gangling, hefty, hulking, inconvenient, massive, ponderous, ungainly, unhandy, unmanageable, weighty. *antonyms* dainty, neat, petite.

unwilling *adj.* averse, disinclined, grudging, indisposed, laggard, loath, loathful, opposed, reluctant, resistant, slow, unenthusiastic. *antonyms* enthusiastic, willing.

unwise *adj.* foolhardy, foolish, ill-advised, ill-considered, ill-judged, impolitic, improvident, imprudent, inadvisable, indiscreet, inexpedient, injudicious, irresponsible, rash, reckless, senseless, shortsighted, silly, stupid, thoughtless, unintelligent. *antonyms* prudent, wise.

unwitting *adj.* accidental, chance, ignorant, inadvertent, innocent, involuntary, unaware, unconscious, unintended, unintentional, unknowing, unmeant, unplanned, unsuspecting, unthinking. *antonyms* conscious, deliberate, knowing, witting.

unwonted *adj.* atypical, exceptional, extraordinary, infrequent, peculiar, rare, singular, strange, unaccustomed, uncommon, uncustomary, unexpected, unfamiliar, unheard-of, unusual. *antonyms* usual, wonted.

unyielding *adj.* adamant, determined, firm, hardline, immovable, implacable, inexorable, inflexible, intractable, intransigent, obdurate, obstinate, relentless, resolute, rigid, solid, staunch, steadfast, stubborn, tough, unbending, uncompromising, unrelenting, unwavering. *antonyms* flexible, yielding.

upbeat *adj.* bright, bullish, buoyant, cheerful, cheery, encouraging, favorable, forward-looking, heartening, hopeful, optimistic, positive, promising, rosy. *antonyms* down-beat, gloomy.

upbraid *v.* admonish, berate, blame, carpet, castigate, censure, chide, condemn, criticize, dress down, jaw, lecture, rate, rebuke, reprimand, reproach, reprove, scold, take to task, tell off, tick off. *antonyms* commend, praise.

upbringing *n.* breeding, bringing-up, care, cultivation, education, instruction, nurture, parenting, raising, rearing, tending, training.

upgrade *v.* advance, ameliorate, better, elevate, embourgeoise, enhance, gentilize, gentrify, improve, promote, raise. *antonyms* degrade, downgrade.

uphold *v.* advocate, aid, back, champion, countenance, defend, encourage, endorse, fortify, hold to, justify, maintain, promote, stand by, strength, support, sustain, vindicate.

upkeep *n.* care, conservation, expenditure, expenses, keep, maintenance, oncosts, operating costs, outgoing, outlay, overheads, preservation, repair, running, running costs, subsistence, support, sustenance. *antonym* neglect.

uppish *adj.* affected, arrogant, assuming, bigheaded, bumptious, cocky, conceited, hoity-toity, impertinent, overweening, presumptuous, self-important, snobbish, stuckup, supercilious, swanky, toffee-nosed, uppity. *antonyms* diffident, unassertive.

upright *adj.* arrect, bluff, conscientious, erect, ethical, faithful, foursquare, good,

high-minded, honest, honorable, incorruptible, just, noble, perpendicular, principled, righteous, straight, straightforward, true, trustworthy, unimpeachable, upstanding, vertical, virtuous. *antonyms* dishonest, flat, horizontal, prone, supine.

uprising *n.* insurgence, insurgency, insurrection, mutiny, putsch, rebellion, revolt, revolution, rising, sedition, upheaval.

uproar *n.* brawl, brouhaha, clamor, commotion, confusion, din, disorder, furore, hubbub, hullabaloo, hurly-burly, katzenjammer, noise, outcry, pandemonium, racket, rammy, randan, riot, ruckus, ruction, rumpus, stramash, tumult, turbulence, turmoil.

uproarious *adj.* boisterous, clamorous, confused, convulsive, deafening, disorderly, gleeful, hilarious, hysterical, killing, loud, noisy, rib-tickling, riotous, rip-roaring, roistering, rollicking, rowdy, rowdy-dowdy, sidesplitting, tempestuous, tumultuous, turbulent, unrestrained, wild. *antonym* sedate.

upset *v.* agitate, bother, capsize, change, conquer, defeat, destabilize, discombobulate, discompose, disconcert, dismay, disorder, disorganize, disquiet, distress, disturb, fluster, grieve, hop, overcome, overset, overthrow, overturn, perturb, ruffle, shake, spill, spoil, tip, topple, trouble, unnerve, unsteady. *n.* agitation, bother, bug, complaint, defeat, disorder, disruption, disturbance, illness, indisposition, malady, purl, reverse, shake-up, shock, sickness, surprise, trouble, upheaval, worry. *adj.* agitate, bothered, capsized, chaotic, choked, confused, disconcerted, dismayed, disordered, disquieted, distressed, disturbed, frantic, gippy, grieved, hurt, ill, messed up, muddled, overturned, overwrought, pained, poorly, qualmish, queasy, ruffled, shattered, sick, spilled, toppled, topsy-turvy, troubled, tumbled, worried.

upshot *n.* conclusion, consequence, culmination, end, event, finale, finish, issue, outcome, payoff, result.

urbane *adj.* bland, civil, civilized, cosmopolitan, courteous, cultivated, cultured, debonair, easy, elegant, mannerly, polished, refined, smooth, sophisticated, suave, well-bred, well-mannered. *antonyms* gauche, uncouth.

urge *v.* advise, advocate, beg, beseech, champion, compel, constrain, counsel, drive, emphasize, encourage, entreat, exhort, force, goad, hasten, hist, impel, implore, incite, induce, instigate, nag, plead, press, propel, push, recommend, solicit, spur, stimulate, support, underline, underscore. *antonyms* deter, dissuade. *n.* compulsion, desire, drive, eagerness, fancy, impulse, inclination, itch, libido, longing, wish, yearning, yen. *antonym* disinclination.

urgency *n.* exigence, exigency, extremity, gravity, hurry, imperativeness, importance, importunity, instancy, necessity, need, pressure, seriousness, stress.

urgent *adj.* clamorous, cogent, compelling, critical, crucial, eager, earnest, emergent, exigent, immediate, imperative, important, importunate, insistent, instant, intense, persistent, persuasive, pressing, top-priority.

usage *n.* application, control, convention, custom, employment, etiquette, form, habit, handling, management, method, mode, operation, practice, procedure, protocol, régime, regulation, routing, rule, running, tradition, treatment, use, wont.

use *v.* apply, bring, consume, employ, enjoy, exercise, exhaust, expend, exploit, handle, manipulate, misuse, operate, ply, practice, spend, treat, usufruct, utilize, waste, wield, work. *n.* advantage, application, avail, benefit, call, cause, custom, employment, end, enjoyment, exercise, good, habit, handling, help, meaning, mileage, necessity, need, object, occasion, operation, point, practice, profit, purpose, reason, service, treatment, usage, usefulness, usufruct, utility, value, way, wont, worth.

useful *adj.* advantageous, all-purpose, beneficial, convenient, effective, fruitful, general-purpose, handy, helpful, practical, productive, profitable, salutary, serviceable, valuable, worthwhile. *antonym* useless.

useless *adj.* bootless, clapped-out, disadvantageous, effectless, feckless, fruitless, futile, hopeless, idle, impractical, incompetent, ineffective, ineffectual, inefficient, inept, of no use, pointless, profitless, shiftless, stupid, unavailing, unproductive, unworkable, vain, valueless, weak, worthless. *antonym* useful.

usher *n.* attendant, doorkeeper, escort, guide, huissier, usherette. *v.* conduct, direct, escort, guide, lead, pilot, shepherd, steer.

usual *adj.* accepted, accustomed, common, constant, conventional, customary, everyday, expected, familiar, fixed, general, habitual, nomic, normal, ordinary, recognized, regular, routine, standard, stock, typical, unexceptional, wonted. *antonyms* unheard-of, unusual.

usually *adv.* as a rule, by and large, chiefly, commonly, customarily, generally, generally speaking, habitually, in the main, mainly, mostly, normally, on the whole, ordinarily, regularly, routinely, traditionally, typically. *antonym* exceptionally.

utensil *n.* apparatus, contrivance, device, gadget, gismo, implement, instrument, tool.

utility *n.* advantage, advantageousness, avail, benefit, convenience, efficacy, expedience, fitness, point, practicality, profit, satisfactoriness, service, serviceableness, use, usefulness, value. *antonym* inutility.

utilize *v.* adapt, appropriate, employ, exploit, make use of, put to use, resort to, take advantage of, turn to account, use.

utopian *adj.* airy, chimerical, dream, elysian, fanciful, fantastic, ideal, idealistic, illusory, imaginary, impractical, perfect, romantic, unworkable, visionary, wishful.

utter[1] *adj.* absolute, arrant, complete, consummate, dead, downright, entire, out-and-out, perfect, sheer, stark, thorough, thoroughgoing, total, unalleviated, unmitigated, unqualified.

utter[2] *v.* articulate, declare, deliver, divulge, enounce, enunciate, express, proclaim, promulgate, pronounce, publish, reveal, say, sound, speak, state, tell, tongue, verbalize, vocalize, voice.

V

vacancy *n.* accommodation, emptiness, gap, job, opening, opportunity, place, position, post, room, situation, space, vacuity, vacuousness, vacuum, void.

vacant *adj.* absent, absentminded, abstracted, available, blank, disengaged, dreaming, dreamy, empty, expressionless, free, idle, inane, inattentive, incurious, thoughtless, to let, unemployed, unengaged, unfilled, unoccupied, unthinking, vacuous, void. *antonyms* engaged, occupied.

vacate *v.* abandon, depart, evacuate, leave, quit, withdraw.

vacillate *v.* fluctuate, haver, hesitate, oscillate, shilly-shally, shuffle, sway, swither, temporize, tergiversate, waver.

vacuity *n.* apathy, blankness, emptiness, inanity, incognizance, incomprehension, incuriosity, nothingness, space, vacuousness, vacuum, void.

vacuum *n.* chasm, emptiness, gap, nothingness, space, vacuity, void.

vagabond *n.* beggar, bo, bum, down-and-out, hobo, itinerant, knight of the road, migrant, nomad, outcast, rascal, rover, runabout, runagate, tramp, vagrant, wanderer, wayfarer.

vagary *n.* caprice, crotchet, fancy, fegary, humor, megrim, notion, prank, quirk, whim, whimsy.

vagrant *n.* beggar, bum, gangrel, hobo, itinerant, rolling stone, stroller, tramp, wanderer. *adj.* footloose, homeless, itinerant, nomadic, roaming, rootless, roving, shiftless, traveling, vagabond, wandering.

vague *adj.* amorphous, blurred, dim, doubtful, evasive, fuzzy, generalized, hazy, ill-defined, imprecise, indefinite, indeterminate, indistinct, inexact, lax, loose, misty, nebulous, obscure, shadowy, uncertain, unclear, undefined, undetermined, unknown, unspecific, unspecified, woolly. *antonyms* certain, clear, definite.

vain *adj.* abortive, affected, arrogant, baseless, bigheaded, conceited, egotistical, empty, fruitless, futile, groundless, hollow, idle, inflated, mindless, narcissistic, nugatory, ostentatious, overweening, peacockish, pointless, pretentious, proud, purposeless, self-important, self-satisfied, senseless, stuck-up, swaggering, swanky, swollenheaded, time-wasting, trifling, trivial, unavailing, unimportant, unproductive, unprofitable, unsubstantial, useless, vainglorious, vaporous, worthless. *antonyms* modest, self-effacing.

valet *n.* body servant, gentleman's gentleman, man, manservant, valet de chambre.

valiant *adj.* bold, brave, courageous, dauntless, doughty, fearless, gallant, heroic, indomitable, intrepid, plucky, redoubtable, stalwart, staunch, stout, stouthearted, valorous, worthy. *antonym* cowardly.

valid *adj.* approved, authentic, binding, bona fide, cogent, conclusive, convincing, efficacious, efficient, genuine, good, just, lawful, legal, legitimate, logical, official, potent, powerful, proper, rational, reliable, sound, substantial, telling, weighty, wellfounded, well-grounded. *antonym* invalid.

validate *v.* attest, authenticate, authorize, certify, confirm, corroborate, endorse, legalize, ratify, substantiate, underwrite.

validity *n.* authority, cogency, force, foundation, grounds, justifiability, lawfulness, legality, legitimacy, logic, point, power, soundness, strength, substance, weight. *antonym* invalidity.

valley *n.* arroyo, canyon, cwm, dale, dell, depression, dingle, draw, glen, gorge, gulch, hollow, hope, slade, strath, vale.

valor *n.* boldness, bravery, courage, derring-do, doughtiness, fearlessness, fortitude, gallantry, hardiness, heroism, intrepidity, lion-heartedness, mettle, spirit. *antonyms* cowardice, weakness.

valuable *adj.* advantageous, beneficial, blue-chip, cherished, costly, dear, esteemed, estimable, expensive, fruitful, handy, helpful, high-priced, important, invaluable, precious, prizable, prized, productive, profitable, serviceable, treasured, useful, valued, worthwhile, worthy. *antonyms* useless, valueless.

value *n.* account, advantage, avail, benefit, cost, desirability, equivalent, good, help, importance, merit, price, profit, rate, significance, use, usefulness, utility, worth. *v.* account, appraise, appreciate, apprize, assess, cherish, compute, esteem, estimate, evaluate, hold dear, price, prize, rate, regard, respect, survey, treasure. *antonyms* disregard, neglect, undervalue.

vanish *v.* dematerialize, depart, die out, disappear, disperse, dissolve, evanesce, evaporate, exit, fade, fizzle out, melt, peter out. *antonyms* appear, materialize.

vanity *n.* affectation, airs, arrogance, bigheadedness, conceit, conceitedness, egotism, emptiness, frivolity, fruitlessness, fume, futility, hollowness, idleness, inanity, narcissism, ostentation, peacockery, pointlessness, pretension, pride, self-admiration, self-conceit, self-love, self-satisfaction, swollen-headedness, triviality, unreality, unsubstantiality, uselessness, vainglory, worthlessness. *antonyms* modesty, worth.

vanquish *v.* beat, confound, conquer, crush, defeat, humble, master, overcome, overpower, overwhelm, quell, reduce, repress, rout, subdue, subjugate, triumph over.

vapid *adj.* banal, bland, bloodless, boring, colorless, dead, dull, flat, flavorless, insipid, jejune, lifeless, limp, stale, tame, tasteless, tedious, tiresome, trite, uninspiring, uninteresting, watery, weak, wishy-washy. *antonyms* interesting, vigorous.

vapor *n.* breath, brume, damp, dampness, exhalation, fog, fumes, halitus, haze, miasm, miasma, mist, reek, roke, smoke, steam.

variable *adj.* capricious, chameleonic, changeable, fickle, fitful, flexible, fluctuating, inconstant, mercurial, moonish, mutable, protean, shifting, temperamental, unpredictable, unstable, unsteady, vacillating, varying, versiform, wagering. *antonym* invariable. *n.* factor, parameter.

variant *adj.* alternative, derived, deviant, different, divergent, exceptional, modified. *antonyms* normal, standard, usual. *n.* alternative, development, deviant, modification, rogue, sport, variation.

variation *n.* alteration, change, departure, deviation, difference, discrepancy, diversification, diversity, elaboration, inflection, innovation, modification, modulation, novelty, variety. *antonyms* monotony, similitude, uniformity.

variety *n.* array, assortment, brand, breed, category, change, class, collection, difference, discrepancy, diversification, diversity, intermixture, kind, make, manifoldness, many-sidedness, medley, miscellany, mixture, multifariousness, multiplicity, olio, olla podrida, order, potpourri, range, sort, species, strain, type, variation. *antonyms* monotony, similitude, uniformity.

various *adj.* assorted, different, differing, disparate, distinct, divers, diverse, diversified, heterogeneous, many, many-sided, miscellaneous, multifarious, omnifarious, several, sundry, varied, variegated, varying.

vary *v.* alter, alternate, change, depart, differ, disagree, diverge, diversify, fluctuate, inflect, intermix, modify, modulate, permutate, reorder, transform.

vassalage *n.* bondage, dependence, serfdom, servitude, slavery, subjection, subjugation, thralldom, villeinage.

vast *adj.* astronomical, boundless, capacious, colossal, cyclopean, enormous, extensive, far-flung, fathomless, gigantic, great, huge, illimitable, immeasurable, immense, limitless, mammoth, massive, measureless, monstrous, monumental, never-ending, prodigious, stupendous, sweeping, tremendous, unbounded, unlimited, vasty, voluminous, wide.

vault[1] *v.* bound, clear, hurdle, jump, leap, leapfrog, spring.

vault[2] *n.* arch, camera, cavern, cellar, concave, crypt, depository, mausoleum, repository, roof, span, strong room, tomb, undercroft, wine cellar.

veer *v.* change, sheer, shift, swerve, tack, turn, wheel.

vehement *adj.* animated, ardent eager, earnest, emphatic, enthusiastic, fervent, fervid, fierce, forceful, forcible, heated, impassioned, impetuous, intense, passionate, powerful, strong, urgent, violent, zealous. *antonyms* apathetic, indifferent.

veil *v.* cloak, conceal, cover, dim, disguise, dissemble, dissimulate, hide, mantle, mask, obscure, screen, shade, shadow, shield. *antonyms* expose, uncover. *n.* blind, cloak, cover, curtain, disguise, film, humeral, integument, mask, screen, shade, shroud, velum.

venal *adj.* bent, bribable, buyable, corrupt, corruptible, grafting, mercenary, purchasable, simoniacal. *antonym* incorruptible.

venerable *adj.* aged, august, dignified, esteemed, grave, honored, respected, revered, reverenced, reverend, sage, sedate, venerated, wise, worshipful.

venerate *v.* adore, esteem, hallow, honor, respect, revere, reverence, worship. *antonyms* anathematize, disregard, execrate.

vengeance *n.* avengement, lex talionis, reprisal, requital, retaliation, retribution, revanche, revenge, talion, tit for tat. *antonym* forgiveness.

venom *n.* acrimony, bane, bitterness, gall, grudge, hat, hatred, ill will, malevolence, malice, maliciousness, malignity, poison, rancor, spite, spitefulness, spleen, toxin, venin, vindictiveness, virus, vitrio.

vent *n.* aperture, blowhole, duct, hole, opening, orifice, outlet, passage, spiracle, split. *v.* air, discharge, emit, express, let fly, release, unloose, utter, voice.

venture *v.* advance, adventure, chance, dare, endanger, hazard, imperil, jeopardize, make bold, presume, put forward, risk, speculate, stake, suggest, take the liberty, volunteer, wager. *n.* adventure, chance, endeavor, enterprise, fling, gamble, hazard, operation, project, risk, speculation, undertaking.

verbal *adj.* lexical, oral, spoken, unwritten, verbatim, word-of-mouth.

verbatim *adv.* exactly, literally, precisely, to the letter, (verbatim et) literatim, word for word.

verbose *adj.* ambagious, circumlocutory, diffuse, garrulous, long-winded, loquacious, multiloquent, periphrastic, phrasy, pleonastic, prolix, windy, wordy. *antonyms* economical, laconic, succinct.

verbosity *n.* garrulity, logorrhea, long-windedness, loquaciousness, loquacity, multiloquy, prolixity, verbiage, verboseness, windiness, wordiness. *antonyms* economy, succinctness.

verdict *n.* adjudication, assessment, conclusion, decision, finding, judgment, opinion, sentence.

verge *n.* border, boundary, brim, brink, edge, edging, extreme, limit, lip, margin, roadside, threshold.

verification *n.* attestation, authentication, checking, confirmation, corroboration, proof, substantiation, validation.

verify *v.* attest, authenticate, check, confirm, corroborate, prove, substantiate, support, testify, validate. *antonyms* discredit, invalidate.

vernacular *adj.* colloquial, common, endemic, indigenous, informal, local, mother, native, popular, vulgar. *n.* argot, cant, dialect, idiom, jargon, language, lingo, parlance, patois, speech, tongue.

versatile *adj.* adaptable, adjustable, all-round, flexible, functional, general-purpose, handy, many-sided, multifaceted, multipurpose, protean, renaissance, resourceful, variable. *antonym* inflexible.

versed *adj.* accomplished, acquainted, au fait, competent, conversant, experienced, familiar, knowledgeable, learned, practiced, proficient, qualified, seasoned, skilled.

version *n.* account, adaptation, design, form, interpretation, kind, model, paraphrase, portrayal, reading, rendering, rendition, style, translation, type, variant.

vertical *adj.* erect, on end, perpendicular, upright, upstanding. *antonym* horizontal.

verve *n.* animation, brio, dash, élan, energy, enthusiasm, force, gusto, life, liveliness, pizzazz, punch, relish, sparkle, spirit, vigor, vim, vitality, zeal, zip. *antonym* apathy.

very *adv.* absolutely, acutely, awfully, decidedly, deeply, dogged, dooms, eminently, exceeding(ly), excessively, extremely, fell, gey, greatly, highly, jolly, noticeably, particularly, passing, rattling, really, remarkably, superlatively, surpassingly, terribly, truly, uncommonly, unusually, wonderfully. *antonyms* hardly, scarcely, slightly. *adj.* actual, appropriate, bare, exact, express, identical, mere, perfect, plain, precise, pure, real, same, selfsame, sheer, simple, unqualified, utter.

vestige *n.* evidence, glimmer, hint, indication, print, relic, remainder, remains, remnant, residue, scrap, sign, suspicion, token, trace, track, whiff.

veto *v.* ban, blackball, disallow, forbid, interdict, kill, negative, prohibit, reject, rule out, turn down. *antonyms* approve, sanction. *n.* ban, embargo, prohibition, rejection, thumbs-down. *antonyms* approval, assent.

vex *v.* afflict, aggravate, agitate, annoy, bother, bug, chagrin, deave, displease, distress, disturb, exasperate, fret, gall, get (to), harass, hump, irritate, molest, needle, nettle, offend, peeve, perplex, pester, pique, plague, provoke, rile, spite, tease, torment, trouble, upset, worry. *antonym* soothe.

vexation *n.* aggravation, anger, annoyance, bore, bother, chagrin, difficulty, displeasure, dissatisfaction, exasperation, frustration, fury, headache, irritant, misfortune, nuisance, pique, problem, trouble, upset, worry.

viable *adj.* achievable, applicable, feasible, operable, possible, practicable, usable, workable. *antonyms* impossible, unworkable.

vibrate *v.* fluctuate, judder, oscillate, pendulate, pulsate, pulse, quiver, resonate, reverberate, shake, shimmy, shiver, shudder, sway, swing, throb, tremble, undulate.

vice *n.* bad habit, besetting sin, blemish, corruption, defect, degeneracy, depravity, evil, evildoing, failing, fault, hamartia, immorality, imperfection, iniquity, profligacy, shortcoming, sin, venality, weakness, wickedness. *antonym* virtue.

vicinity *n.* area, circumjacency, district, environs, locality, neighborhood, precincts, propinquity, proximity, purlieus, vicinage.

vicious *adj.* abhorrent, atrocious, backbiting, bad, barbarous, bitchy, brutal, catty, corrupt, cruel, dangerous, debased, defamatory, depraved, diabolical, fiendish, foul, heinous, immoral, infamous, malicious, mean, monstrous, nasty, perverted, profligate, rancorous, savage, sinful, slanderous, spiteful, unprincipled, venomous, vile, vindictive, violent, virulent, vitriolic, wicked, worthless, wrong. *antonyms* gentle, good, virtuous.

victimize *v.* bully, cheat, deceive, defraud, discriminate against, dupe, exploit, fool, gull, hoodwink, oppress, persecute, pick on, prey on, swindle, use.

victor *n.* champ, champion, conqueror, first, prizewinner, subjugator, top dog, vanquisher, victor ludorum, victrix, winner. *antonyms* loser, vanquished.

victory *n.* conquest, laurels, mastery, palm, prize, subjugation, success, superiority, triumph, win. *antonyms* defeat, loss.

view *n.* aspect, attitude, belief, contemplation, conviction, display, estimation, examination, feeling, glimpse, impression, inspection, judgment, landscape, look, notion, opinion, outlook, panorama, perception, perspective, picture, prospect, scan, scene, scrutiny, sentiment, sight, spectacle, survey, viewing, vision, vista. *v.* behold, consider, contemplate, deem, examine, explore, eye, inspect, judge, observe, perceive, read, regard, scan, speculate, survey, watch.

viewpoint *n.* angle, attitude, feeling, opinion, perspective, position, slant, stance, standpoint.

vigilant *adj.* alert, *adj.* Argus-eyed, attentive, careful, cautious, circumspect, guarded, on one's guard, on one's toes, on the alert, on the lookout, on the qui vive, sleepless, unsleeping, wakeful, watchful, wideawake. *antonyms* careless, forgetful, lax, negligent.

vigor *n.* activity, animation, dash, dynamism, energy, force, forcefulness, gusto, health, liveliness, might, oomph, pep, potency, power, punch, robustness, snap, soundness, spirit, stamina, strength, verve, vim, virility, vitality, zip. *antonyms* impotence, sluggishness, weakness.

vigorous *adj.* active, brisk, dynamic, effective, efficient, energetic, enterprising, flourishing, forceful, forcible, full-blooded, hale, heady, healthy, hearty, intense, lively, lusty, mettlesome, powerful, red-blooded, robust, sound, spanking, spirited, stout, strenuous, strong, virile, vital, zippy. *antonyms* feeble, lethargic, weak.

vile *adj.* abandoned, abject, appalling, bad, base, coarse, contemptible, corrupt, debased, degenerate, degrading, depraved, de-spicable, disgraceful, disgusting, earthly, evil, foul, horrid, humiliating, ignoble, impure, loathsome, low, mean, miserable, nasty, nauseating, nefarious, noxious, offensive, perverted, repellent, repugnant, repulsive, revolting, scabbed, scabby, scandalous, scurvy, shocking, sickening, sinful, ugly, vicious, vulgar, wicked, worthless, wretched.

vilify *v.* abuse, asperse, bad-mouth, berate, calumniate, criticize, debase, decry, defame, denigrate, denounce, disparage, malign, revile, slander, smear, stigmatize, traduce, vilipend, vituperate. *antonyms* adore, compliment, eulogize, glorify.

village *n.* clachan, community, district, dorp, hamlet, kraal, pueblo, settlement, township.

villain *n.* antihero, baddy, blackguard, bravo, caitiff, criminal, devil, evildoer, heavy, knave, libertine, malefactor, miscreant, profligate, rapscallion, rascal, reprobate,

rogue, scoundrel, wretch. *antonyms* angel, goody, hero, heroine.

villainous *adj.* atrocious, bad, base, blackguardly, criminal, cruel, debased, degenerate, depraved, detestable, diabolical, disgraceful, evil, fiendish, hateful, heinous, ignoble, infamous, inhuman, malevolent, mean, nefarious, opprobrious, outrageous, ruffianly, scoundrelly, sinful, terrible, thievish, vicious, vile, wicked. *antonyms* angelic, good, heroic.

vindication *n.* apology, assertion, defense, exculpation, excuse, exoneration, extenuation, justification, maintenance, plea, rehabilitation, support, verification. *antonyms* accusation, conviction.

violate *v.* abuse, assault, befoul, break, contravene, debauch, defile, desecrate, dishonor, disobey, disregard, flout, infract, infringe, invade, outrage, pollute, profane, rape, ravish, transgress. *antonyms* obey, observe, uphold.

violence *n.* abandon, acuteness, bestiality, bloodshed, bloodthirstiness, boisterousness, brutality, conflict, cruelty, destructiveness, ferocity, fervor, fierceness, fighting, force, frenzy, fury, harshness, hostilities, intensity, murderousness, passion, power, roughness, savagery, severity, sharpness, storminess, terrorism, thuggery, tumult, turbulence, vehemence, wildness. *antonyms* passivity, peacefulness.

violent *adj.* acute, agonizing, berserk, biting, bloodthirsty, blustery, boisterous, brutal, cruel, destructive, devastating, excruciating, extreme, fiery, forceful, forcible, furious, harsh, headstrong, homicidal, hotheaded, impetuous, intemperate, intense, maddened, maniacal, murderous, outrageous, painful, passionate, peracute, powerful, raging, riotous, rough, ruinous, savage, severe, sharp, strong, tempestuous, tumultuous, turbulent, uncontrollable, ungovernable, unrestrained, vehement, vicious, wild. *antonyms* calm, gentle, moderate, passive, peaceful.

virgin *n.* bachelor, celibate, damsel, girl, maid, maiden, spinster, vestal, virgo intacta. *adj.* chaste, fresh, immaculate, intact, maidenly, modest, new, pristine, pure, snowy, spotless, stainless, uncorrupted, undefiled, unsullied, untouched, unused, vestal, virginal.

virile *adj.* forceful, husky, lusty, macho, male, manlike, manly, masculine, potent, red-blooded, robust, rugged, strong, vigorous. *antonyms* effeminate, impotent, weak.

virtue *n.* advantage, asset, attribute, chastity, credit, excellence, goodness, high-mindedness, honor, incorruptibility, innocence, integrity, justice, merit, morality, plus, probity, purity, quality, rectitude, redeeming feature, righteousness, strength, uprightness, virginity, worth, worthiness. *antonym* vice.

virtuous *adj.* blameless, celibate, chaste, clean-living, continent, ethical, excellent, exemplary, good, high-principled, hones, honorable, incorruptible, innocent, irreproachable, moral, praiseworthy, pure, righteous, spotless, unimpeachable, upright, virginal, worthy. *antonyms* bad, dishonest, immoral, vicious, wicked.

virulent *adj.* acrimonious, baneful, bitter, deadly, envenomed, hostile, infective, injurious, lethal, malevolent, malicious, malignant, noxious, pernicious, poisonous, rancorous, resentful, septic, spiteful, splenetic, toxic, venomous, vicious, vindictive, vitriolic.

vision *n.* apparition, chimera, concept, conception, construct, daydream, delusion, discernment, dream, eyes, eyesight, fantasy, farsightedness, foresight, ghost, hallucination, idea, ideal, illusion, image, imagination, insight, intuition, mirage, penetration, perception, phantasm, phantasma, phantom, picture, prescience, revelation, seeing, sight, spectacle, specter, view, wraith.

visionary *adj.* chimerical, delusory, dreaming, dreamy, fanciful, fantastic, ideal, idealized, idealistic, illusory, imaginary, impractical, moonshiny, prophetic, quixotic, romantic, speculative, starry-eyed, unreal, unrealistic, unworkable, utopian. *n.* daydreamer, Don Quixote, dreamer, enthusiast, fantasist, idealist, mystic, prophet, rainbow-chaser, romantic, seer, theorist, utopian, zealot. *antonym* pragmatist.

visit *v.* afflict, assail, attack, befall, call in, call on, drop in on, haunt, inspect, look in, look up, pop in, punish, see, smite, stay at, stay with, stop by, take in, trouble. *n.* call, excursion, sojourn, stay, stop.

visitor *n.* caller, company, guest, holidaymaker, tourist, visitant.

vista *n.* enfilade, panorama, perspective, prospect, view.

vital *adj.* alive, animate, animated, animating, basic, cardinal, critical, crucial, decisive, dynamic, energetic, essential, forceful, fundamental, generative, imperative, important, indispensable, invigorating, key, life-giving, life-or-death, live, lively, living, necessary, quickening, requisite, significant, spirited, urgent, vibrant, vigorous, vivacious, zestful. *antonyms* inessential, peripheral, unimportant.

vitality *n.* animation, energy, exuberance, foison, go, life, liveliness, lustiness, oomph, pep, robustness, sparkle, stamina, strength, vigor, vim, vivaciousness, vivacity.

vitiate *v.* blemish, blight, contaminate, corrupt, debase, defile, deprave, deteriorate, devalue, harm, impair, injure, invalidate, mar, nullify, pervert, pollute, ruin, spoil, sully, taint, undermine. *antonym* purify.

vivacious *adj.* animated, bubbling, bubbly, cheerful, chipper, ebullient, effervescent, frisky, frolicsome, gay, high-spirited, jolly, lighthearted, lively, merry, scintillating, sparkling, spirited, sportive, sprightly, vital. *antonym* languid.

vivid *adj.* active, animated, bright, brilliant, clear, colorful, distinct, dramatic, dynamic, eidetic, energetic, expressive, flamboyant, glowing, graphic, highly colored, intense, lifelike, lively, memorable, powerful, quick, realistic, rich, sharp, spirited, stirring, striking, strong, telling, vibrant, vigorous. *antonyms* dull, lifeless.

vocal *adj.* articulate, clamorous, eloquent, expressive, forthright, frank, free-spoken, noisy, oral, outspoken, plainspoken, said, shrill, spoken, strident, uttered, vociferous, voiced. *antonyms* inarticulate, quiet.

vocation *n.* bag, business, calling, career, employment, job, métier, mission, niche, office, post, profession, pursuit, role, trade, work.

void *adj.* bare, blank, canceled, clear, dead, drained, emptied, empty, free, inane, ineffective, ineffectual, inoperative, invalid, nugatory, null, tenantless, unenforceable, unfilled, unoccupied, useless, vacant, vain, worthless. *antonyms* full, valid. *n.* blank, blankness, cavity, chasm, emptiness, gap, hiatus, hollow, lack, opening, space, vacuity, vacuum, want. *v.* abnegate, annul, cancel, defecate, discharge, drain, eject, eliminate, emit, empty, evacuate, invalidate, nullify, rescind. *antonyms* fill, validate.

volatile *adj.* airy, changeable, erratic, explosive, fickle, flighty, gay, giddy, hotheaded, hot-tempered, inconstant, lively, mercurial, sprightly, temperamental, unsettled, unstable, unsteady, variable, volcanic. *antonyms* constant, steady.

volition n. choice, choosing, determination, discretion, election, option, preference, purpose, resolution, taste, velleity, will.

voluble adj. articulate, fluent, forthcoming, garrulous, glib, loquacious, talkative.

volume n. aggregate, amount, amplitude, bigness, body, book, bulk, capacity, compass, dimensions, fascic(u)le, heft, mass, part, publication, quantity, tome, total, treatise.

voluminous adj. abounding, ample, big, billowing, bulky, capacious, cavernous, commodious, copious, full, large, massive, prolific, roomy, vast. antonyms scanty, slight.

voluntary adj. conscious, deliberate, discretional, free, gratuitous, honorary, intended, intentional, optional, purposeful, purposive, spontaneous, unconstrained, unforced, unpaid, volunteer, willful, willing. antonyms compulsory, forced, involuntary, unwilling.

voluptuous adj. ample, buxom, curvaceous, effeminate, enticing, epicurean, erotic, goluptious, hedonistic, licentious, luscious, luxurious, pleasure-loving, provocative, seductive, self-indulgent, sensual, shapely, sybaritic. antonym ascetic.

voracious adj. acquisitive, avid, devouring, edacious, gluttonous, greedy, hungry, insatiable, omnivorous, pantophagous, prodigious, rapacious, ravening, ravenous, uncontrolled, unquenchable.

vouch for v. affirm, assert, asseverate, attest to, avouch, back, certify, confirm, endorse, guarantee, support, swear to, uphold.

vouchsafe v. accord, bestow, cede, confer, deign, grant, impart, yield.

vow v. affirm, avouch, bename, consecrate, dedicate, devote, maintain, pledge, profess, promise, swear. n. avouchment, oath, pledge, promise, troth.

voyage n. crossing, cruise, expedition, journey, passage, peregrination, travels, trip.

vulgar adj. banausic, blue, boorish, cheap and nasty, coarse, common, crude, dirty, flashy, gaudy, general, gross, ill-bred, impolite, improper, indecent, indecorous, indelicate, low, low-life, low-lived, low-minded, low-thoughted, nasty, native, naughty, ordinary, pandemian, plebby, plebeian, ribald, risqué, rude, suggestive, tacky, tasteless, tawdry, uncouth, unmannerly, unrefined, vernacular. antonyms correct, decent, elegant, noble, polite, refined.

vulnerable adj. accessible, assailable, defenseless, exposed, expugnable, pregnable, sensitive, susceptible, tender, thin-skinned, unprotected, weak, wide open. antonyms protected, strong.

W

wacky adj. crazy, daft, eccentric, erratic, goofy, irrational, loony, loopy, nutty, odd, screwy, silly, unpredictable, wild, zany. antonym sensible.

wad n. ball, block, bundle, chunk, hump, hunk, mass, pledget, plug, roll.

waffle v. blather, fudge, jabber, prate, prattle, prevaricate, rabbit on, spout, witter on. n. blather, gobbledygook, guff, jabber, nonsense, padding, prating, prattle, prolixity, verbiage, verbosity, wordiness.

waft v. bear, carry, convey, drift, float, ride, transmit, transport, whiffle, winnow. n. breath, breeze, current, draft, puff, scent, whiff.

wage n. allowance, compensation, earnings, emolument, fee, guerdon, hire, pay, payment, penny-fee, recompense, remuneration, reward, salary, screw, stipend, wage packet, wages. v. carry on, conduct, engage in, practice, prosecute, pursue, undertake.

wager n. bet, flutter, gage, gamble, hazard, pledge, punt, speculation, stake, venture. v. bet, chance, gamble, hazard, lay, lay odds, pledge, punt, risk, speculate, stake, venture.

waggish adj. amusing, arch, bantering, comical, droll, espiègle, facetious, frolicsome, funny, humorous, impish, jesting, jocose, jocular, merry, mischievous, playful, puckish, risible, roguish, sportive, witty. antonyms grave, serious, staid.

wagon n. buggy, carriage, cart, float, pushcart, train, truck, wain.

waif n. foundling, orphan, stray, wastrel.

wail v. bemoan, bewail, complain, cry, deplore, grieve, howl, keen, lament, mewl, moan, ululate, weep, yammer, yowl. n. caterwaul, complaint, cry, grief, howl, keen, lament, lamentation, moan, ululation, weeping, yowl.

wait v. abide, dally, delay, hang fire, hesitate, hold back, hover, linger, loiter, mark time, pause, remain, rest, stay, tarry. antonyms depart, go, leave. n. delay, halt, hesitation, hiatus, holdup, interval, pause, rest, stay.

waive[1] v. abandon, defer, disclaim, forgo, postpone, relinquish, remit, renounce, resign, surrender. antonyms claim, maintain.

wake² *v.* activate, animate, arise, arouse, awake, awaken, bestir, enliven, excite, fire, galvanize, get up, kindle, provoke, quicken, rise, rouse, stimulate, stir, unbed. *antonyms* relax, sleep. *n.* deathwatch, funeral, pernoctation, vigil, watch.

wake³ *n.* aftermath, backwash, path, rear, tract, trail, train, wash, waves.

waken *v.* activate; animate, arouse, awake, awaken, enliven, fire, galvanize, get up, ignite, kindle, quicken, rouse, stimulate, stir, whet.

walk *v.* accompany, advance, able, convoy, escort, go by Shanks's pony, hike, hoof it, march, move, pace, pedestrianize, perambulate, plod, promenade, saunter, step, stride, stroll, take, traipse, tramp, tread, trek, trog, trudge. *n.* aisle, alley, ambulatory, avenue, carriage, constitutional, esplanade, footpath, frescade, gait, hike, lane, mall, march, pace, path, pathway, pavement, pawn, perambulation, promenade, ramble, saunter, sidewalk, step, stride, stroll, trail, traipse, tramp, trek, trudge, turn.

wall *n.* bailey, barricade, barrier, block, breastwork, bulkhead, bulwark, dike, divider, dyke, embankment, enclosure, fence, fortification, hedge, impediment, membrane, obstacle, obstruction, palisade, panel, parapet, partition, rampart, screen, septum, stockade.

wallow *v.* bask, delight, enjoy, flounder, glory, indulge, lie, lurch, luxuriate, relish, revel, roll, splash, stagger, stumble, tumble, wade, welter.

wan *adj.* anemic, ashen, bleak, bloodless, cadaverous, colorless, dim, discolored, faint, feeble, ghastly, livid, lurid, mournful, pale, pallid, pasty, sickly, waxen, weak, weary, whey-faced, white.

wander *v.* aberrate, babble, cruise, depart, deviate, digress, divagate, diverge, drift, err, hump the bluey, lapse, meander, mill around, peregrinate, ramble, range, rave, roam, rove, saunter, squander, straggle, stravaig, stray, stroll, swerve, traipse, veer, wilder. *n.* cruise, excursion, meander, peregrination, ramble, saunter, stroll, traipse.

wane *v.* abate, atrophy, contract, decline, decrease, dim, diminish, droop, drop, dwindle, ebb, fade, fail, lessen, shrink, sink, subside, taper off, weaken, wither. *antonyms* increase, wax. *n.* abatement, atrophy, contraction, decay, decline, diminution, drop, dwindling, ebb, fading, failure, fall, lessening, sinking, subsidence, tapering off, weakening. *antonym* increase.

want *v.* call for, covet, crave, demand, desiderate, desire, fancy, hanker after, hunger for, lack, long for, miss, need, pine for, require, thirst for, wish, yearn for, yen. *n.* absence, appetite, besoin, craving, dearth, default, deficiency, demand, desideratum, desire, destitution, famine, fancy, hankering, hunger, indigence, insufficiency, lack, longing, necessity, need, neediness, paucity, pauperism, penury, poverty, privation, requirement, scantiness, scarcity, shortage, thirst, wish, yearning, yen. *antonyms* abundance, plenty, riches.

wanton *adj.* abandoned, arbitrary, careless, coltish, cruel, dissipated, dissolute, evil, extravagant, fast, gratuitous, groundless, heedless, immoderate, immoral, intemperate, lavish, lecherous, lewd, libertine, libidinous, licentious, loose, lubricious, lustful, malevolent, malicious, motiveless, needless, outrageous, promiscuous, rakish, rash, reckless, senseless, shameless, spiteful, uncalledfor, unchaste, unjustifiable, unjustified, unprovoked, unrestrained, vicious, wicked, wild, willful. *n.* baggage, Casanova, debauchee, Don Juan, floozy, harlot, hussy, lecher, libertine, loose woman, profligate, prostitute, rake, roué, slut, strumpet, tart, trollop, voluptuary, wench, whore.

war *n.* battle, bloodshed, combat, conflict, contention, contest, enmity, fighting, hostilities, hostility, jihad, strife, struggle, ultima ratio regum, warfare. *antonym* peace. *v.* battle, clash, combat, contend, contest, fight, skirmish, strive, struggle, take up arms, wage war.

ward *n.* apartment, area, care, charge, cubicle, custody, dependent, district, division, guardianship, keeping, minor, precinct, protection, protégé, pupil, quarter, room, safekeeping, vigil, watch, zone.

warden *n.* administrator, captain, caretaker, castellan, châtelaine, concierge, curator, custodian, guardian, janitor, keeper, ranger, steward, superintendent, warder, watchman.

wardrobe *n.* apparel, attire, closet, clothes, cupboard, garderobe, outfit.

warehouse *n.* depository, depot, entrepot, freightshed, godown, hong, repository, stockroom, store, storehouse.

wares *n.* commodities, goods, lines, manufactures, merchandise, produce, products, stock, stuff, vendibles.

wariness *n.* alertness, apprehension, attention, caginess, care, carefulness, caution, circumspection, discretion, distrust, foresight, heedfulness, hesitancy, mindfulness, prudence, suspicion, unease, vigilance, watchfulness. *antonyms* heedlessness, recklessness, thoughtlessness.

warlike *adj.* aggressive, antagonistic, bellicose, belligerent, bloodthirsty, combative, hawkish, hostile, inimical, jingoistic, martial, militaristic, military, pugnacious, saber-rattling, truculent, unfriendly. *antonym* peaceable.

warm *adj.* affable, affectionate, amiable, amorous, animated, ardent, balmy, calid, cheerful, cordial, dangerous, disagreeable, earnest, effusive, emotional, enthusiastic, excited, fervent, friendly, genial, glowing, happy, hazardous, hearty, heated, hospitable, impassioned, incalescent, intense, irascible, irritable, keen, kindly, lively, loving, lukewarm, passionate, perilous, pleasant, quick, sensitive, short, spirited, stormy, sunny, tender, tepid, thermal, touchy, tricky, uncomfortable, unpleasant, vehement, vigorous, violent, zealous. *antonyms* cool, indifferent, unfriendly. *v.* animate, awaken, excite, heat, heat up, interest, melt, mull, put some life into, reheat, rouse, stimulate, stir, thaw, turn on. *antonym* cool.

warmhearted *adj.* affectionate, ardent, compassionate, cordial, generous, genial, kindhearted, kindly, loving, sympathetic, tender, tenderhearted. *antonyms* cold, unsympathetic.

warmth *n.* affability, affection, amorousness, animation, ardor, calidity, cheerfulness, cordiality, eagerness, earnestness, effusiveness, empressement, enthusiasm, excitement, fervency, fervor, fire, happiness, heartiness, heat, hospitableness, hotness, intensity, kindliness, love, passion, spirit, tenderness, transport, vehemence, vigor, violence, warmness, zeal, zest. *antonyms* coldness, coolness, unfriendliness.

warn *v.* admonish, advise, alert, apprize, caution, counsel, forewarn, inform, notify, put on one's guard, tip off.

warning *n.* admonishment, admonition, advance notice, advice, alarm, alert, augury, caution, caveat, forenotice, foretoken, forewarning, griffin, hint, larum, larum bell, lesson, monition, notice, notification, omen, premonition, presage, prodrome, sign, signal, siren, threat, tip, tip-off, token, vigia, word, word to the wise. *adj.* admonitory,

aposematic, cautionary, in terrorem, monitive, monitory, ominous, premonitory, prodromal, prodromic, threatening.

warp *v.* bend, contort, deform, deviate, distort, kink, misshape, pervert, twist. *antonym* straighten. *n.* bend, bent, bias, contortion, deformation, deviation, distortion, irregularity, kink, perversion, quirk, turn, twist.

warranty *n.* assurance, authorization, bond, certificate, contract, covenant, guarantee, justification, pledge.

warrior *n.* champion, combatant, fighter, fighting man, knight, man-at-arms, soldier, wardog, warhorse.

wary *adj.* alert, apprehensive, attentive, cagey, careful, cautious, chary, circumspect, distrustful, guarded, hawkeyed, heedful, leery, on one's guard, on the lookout, on the qui vive, prudent, suspicious, vigilant, watchful, wideawake. *antonyms* careless, foolhardy, heedless, reckless, unwary.

wash[1] *v.* bath, bathe, clean, cleanse, launder, moisten, rinse, scrub, shampoo, shower, sluice, swill, wet. *n.* a lick and a promise, ablution, bath, bathe, cleaning, cleansing, coat, coating, ebb and flow, film, flow, laundering, layer, overlay, rinse, roll, screen, scrub, shampoo, shower, souse, stain, suffusion, surge, sweep, swell, washing, wave.

wash[2] *v.* bear examination, bear scrutiny, carry weight, hold up, hold water, pass muster, stand up, stick.

washed-out *adj.* all in, blanched, bleached, colorless, dead on one's feet, dog-tired, drained, drawn, etiolated, exhausted, faded, fatigued, flat, haggard, knackered, lackluster, mat, pale, pallid, peelie-wally, spent, tired-out, wan, weary, worn-out.

waspish *adj.* bad-tempered, bitchy, cantankerous, captious, crabbed, crabby, cross, crotchety, fretful, grouchy, grumpy, ill-tempered, irascible, irritable, peevish, peppery, pettish, petulant, prickly, snappish, splenetic, testy, touchy, waxy.

waste *v.* atrophy, blow, consume, corrode, crumble, debilitate, decay, decline, deplete, despoil, destroy, devastate, disable, dissipate, drain, dwindle, eat away, ebb, emaciate, enfeeble, exhaust, fade, fritter away, gnaw, lavish, lay waste, misspend, misuse, perish, pillage, prodigalize, rape, ravage, raze, rig, ruin, sack, sink, spend, spoil, squander, tabefy, throw away, undermine, wane, wanton, wear out, wither. *n.* debris, desert, desolation, destruction, devastation, dissipation, dregs, dross, effluent, expenditure, extravagance, garbage, havoc, leavings, leftovers, litter, loss, misapplication, misuse, mullock, offal, offscouring(s), prodigality, ravage, recrement, refuse, rubbish, ruin, scrap, slops, solitude, spoilage, squandering, sweepings, trash, void, wastefulness, wasteland, wild, wilderness. *adj.* bare, barren, desolate, devastate, dismal, dreary, empty, extra, leftover, superfluous, supernumerary, uncultivated, uninhabited, unproductive, unprofitable, unused, unwanted, useless, wild, worthless.

wasteful *adj.* dissipative, extravagant, improvident, lavish, prodigal, profligate, ruinous, spendthrift, thriftless, uneconomical, unthrifty. *antonyms* economical, frugal, thrifty.

watch[1] *v.* attend, contemplate, eye, gaze at, guard, keep, keep an eye open, look, look after, look at, look on, look out, mark, mind, note, observe, ogle, pay attention, peer at, protect, regard, see, spectate, stare at, superintend, take care of, take heed, tend, view, wait. *n.* alertness, attention, eye, heed, inspection, lookout, notice, observation, pernoctation, supervision, surveillance, vigil, vigilance, wake, watchfulness.

watch[2] *n.* chronometer, clock, ticker, ticktick, tick-tock, timepiece, wristwatch.

watchful *adj.* alert, attentive, cautious, circumspect, guarded, heedful, observant, on one's guard, on the lookout, on the qui vive, on the watch, suspicious, unmistaking, vigilant, wary, wideawake. *antonym* inattentive.

water *n.* Adam's ale, Adam's wine, aqua, lake, ocean, rain, river, saliva, sea, stream, sweat, tears, urine. *v.* adulterate, damp, dampen, dilute, douse, drench, drink, flood, hose, irrigate, moisten, soak, souse, spray, sprinkle, thin, water down, weaken. *antonyms* dry out, purify, strengthen.

waterfall *n.* cascade, cataract, chute, fall, force, lash, lin(n), torrent.

watery *adj.* adulterated, aqueous, damp, dilute, diluted, flavorless, fluid, humid, hydatoid, insipid, liquid, marshy, moist, poor, rheumy, runny, soggy, squelchy, tasteless, tear-filled, tearful, thin, washy, watered-down, waterish, weak, weepy, wet, wishy-washy. *antonyms* solid, strong.

wave[1] *v.* beckon, brandish, direct, flap, flourish, flutter, gesticulate, gesture, indicate, oscillate, quiver, ripple, shake, sign, signal, stir, sway, swing, undulate, waft, wag, waver, weave, wield.

wave[2] *n.* billow, breaker, comber, current, drift, flood, groundswell, movement, out-break, rash, ripple, roller, rush, stream, surge, sweep, swell, tendency, tidal wave, trend, tsunami, undulation, unevenness, upsurge, water wave, wavelet, white horse.

waver *v.* blow hot and cold, dither, falter, flicker, fluctuate, haver, hesitate, hem and haw, quiver, reel, rock, seesaw, shake, shilly-shally, sway, swither, totter, tremble, undulate, vacillate, vary, waffle, wave, weave, wobble. *antonyms* decide, stand.

wavering *adj.* dithering, dithery, doubtful, doubting, havering, hesitant, in two minds, shilly-shallying. *antonym* determined.

wavy *adj.* curly, curvy, flamboyant, ridged, ridgy, rippled, ripply, sinuate(d), sinuous, undate, undulate, undulated, winding, wrinkled, zigzag. *antonyms* flat, smooth.

wax *v.* become, develop, dilate, enlarge, expand, fill out, grow, increase, magnify, mount, rise, swell. *antonym* wane.

way *n.* access, advance, aim, ambition, approach, aspect, avenue, channel, characteristic, choice, circumstance, condition, conduct, course, custom, demand, desire, detail, direction, distance, elbowroom, fashion, feature, fettle, gate, goal, habit, headway, highway, idiosyncrasy, journey, lane, length, manner, march, means, method, mode, movement, nature, opening, particular, passage, path, pathway, personality, plan, pleasure, point, practice, procedure, process, progress, respect, road, room, route, scheme, sense, shape, situation, space, state, status, street, stretch, style, system, technique, thoroughfare, tract, trail, trait, usage, will, wish, wont.

waylay *v.* accost, ambush, attack, buttonhole, catch, hold up, intercept, lie in wait for, seize, set upon, surprise.

way-out *adj.* advanced, amazing, avantgarde, bizarre, crazy, eccentric, excellent, experimental, fantastic, far-out, freaky, great, marvelous, offbeat, outlandish, progressive, satisfying, tremendous, unconventional, unorthodox, unusual, weird, wild, wonderful. *antonym* ordinary.

wayward *adj.* capricious, changeable, contrary, contumacious, cross-grained, disobedient, erratic, fickle, flighty, froward, headstrong, inconstant, incorrigible, insubordinate, intractable, mulish, obdurate, obstinate, perverse, rebellious, refractory, self-willed, stubborn, undependable, ungovernable, unmanageable, unpredictable, unruly, uppity, willful. *antonyms* complaisant, good-natured.

weak *adj.* anemic, asthenic, atonic, cowardly, debile, debilitated, decrepit, defenseless, deficient, delicate, diluted, disturbant, dull, effete, enervated, exhausted, exposed, faint, faulty, feeble, fiberless, flimsy, fragile, frail, helpless, hollow, imperceptible, impotent, inadequate, inconclusive, indecisive, ineffective, ineffectual, infirm, insipid, invalid, irresolute, lacking, lame, languid, low, milk-and-water, muffled, namby-pamby, pathetic, poor, powerless, puny, quiet, runny, shaky, shallow, sickly, slight, small, soft, spent, spineless, substandard, tasteless, tender, thin, timorous, toothless, unconvincing, under-strength, unguarded, unprotected, unresisting, unsafe, unsatisfactory, unsound, unsteady, unstressed, untenable, vulnerable, wanting, wasted, watery, weakhearted, weak-kneed, weakly, weak-minded, weak-spirited, wishy-washy. *antonym* strong.

weaken *v.* abate, adulterate, craze, cut, debase, debilitate, depress, dilute, diminish, disinvigorate, droop, dwindle, ease up, effeminate, effeminize, emasculate, enervate, enfeeble, fade, fail, flag, give way, impair, invalidate, lessen, lower, mitigate, moderate, reduce, sap, soften up, temper, thin, tire, undermine, wane, water down. *antonym* strengthen.

weakling *n.* coward, doormat, drip, milksop, mouse, namby-pamby, puff, pushover, sissy, softling, underdog, underling, wally, weed, wet, wimp, wraith. *antonyms* hero, stalwart.

weakness *n.* Achilles' heel, asthenia, atonicity, atony, blemish, debility, decrepitude, defect, deficiency, enervation, enfeeblement, foible, failing, faintness, fault, feebleness, flaw, foible, fondness, fragility, frailty, imperfection, impotence, inclination, infirmity, irresolution, lack, liking, passion, penchant, powerlessness, predilection, proclivity, proneness, shortcoming, soft spot, soft underbelly, underbelly, vulnerability, weak point, weediness. *antonyms* dislike, strength.

wealth *n.* abundance, affluence, assets, bounty, capital, cash, copiousness, cornucopia, estate, fortune, fullness, funds, golden calf, goods, klondike, lucre, mammon, means, money, opulence, pelf, plenitude, plenty, possessions, profusion, property, prosperity, resources, riches, richness, store, substance. *antonym* poverty.

wealthy *adj.* affluent, comfortable, easy, filthy rich, flush, living in clover, loaded, moneyed, opulent, prosperous, rich, rolling in it, well-heeled, well-off, well-to-do. *antonym* poor.

wear *v.* abrade, accept, allow, annoy, bear, bear up, believe, brook, carry, consume, corrode, countenance, deteriorate, display, don, drain, dress in, endure, enervate, erode, exasperate, exhibit, fall for, fatigue, fly, fray, grind, harass, have on, hold up, irk, last, permit, pester, put on, put up with, rub, show, sport, stand for, stand up, stomach, swallow, take, tax, tolerate, undermine, use, vex, waste, weaken, weary. *n.* abrasion, apparel, attire, attrition, clothes, corrosion, costume, damage, depreciation, deterioration, dress, durability, employment, erosion, friction, garb, garments, gear, habit, mileage, outfit, service, things, use, usefulness, utility, wear and tear.

weariness *n.* drowsiness, enervation, ennui, exhaustion, fatigue, languor, lassitude, lethargy, listlessness, prostration, sleepiness, tiredness. *antonym* freshness.

wearisome *adj.* annoying, boring, bothersome, burdensome, dreary, dull, exasperating, exhausting, fatiguing, humdrum, irksome, monotonous, oppressive, pestilential, prolix, prosaic, protracted, tedious, troublesome, trying, vexatious, weariful, wearing. *antonym* refreshing.

weary *adj.* all in, arduous, awearied, aweary, beat, bored, browned-off, dead beat, dead on one's feet, discontented, dog-tired, drained, drooping, drowsy, enervated, enervative, ennuied, ennuyé, exhausted, fagged, fatigued, fed up, flagging, impatient, indifferent, irksome, jaded, knackered, laborious, sick, sick and tired, sleepy, spent, taxing, tired, tiresome, tiring, wayworn, wearied, wearing, wearisome, whacked, worn-out. *antonyms* excited, fresh, lively. *v.* annoy, betoil, bore, bug, burden, debilitate, drain, droop, enervate, exasperate, fade, fag, fail, fatigue, irk, irritate, jade, plague, sap, sicken, tax, tire, tire out, wear out.

weather *n.* climate, conditions, rainfall, temperature. *v.* brave, come through, endure, expose, harden, live through, overcome, pull through, resist, ride out, rise above, season, stand, stick out, suffer, surmount, survive, toughen, weather out, withstand. *antonym* succumb.

weave *v.* blend, braid, build, construct, contrive, create, crisscross, entwine, fabricate, fuse, incorporate, intercross, interdigitate, interlace, intermingle, intertwine, introduce, knit, make, mat, merge, plait, put together, spin, twist, unite, wind, zigzag.

web *n.* interlacing, lattice, mesh, meshwork, net, netting, network, palama, screen, snare, tangle, tela, texture, toils, trap, weave, webbing, weft.

wed *v.* ally, blend, coalesce, combine, commingle, dedicate, espouse, fuse, get hitched, interweave, join, jump the broomstick, link, marry, merge, splice, tie the knot, unify, unite, wive, yoke. *antonym* divorce.

wedlock *n.* holy matrimony, marriage, matrimony, union.

wee *adj.* diminutive, insignificant, itsybitsy, lilliputian, little, microscopic, midget, miniature, minuscule, minute, negligible, small, teeny, teeny-weeny, tiny, weeny. *antonym* large.

weep *v.* bemoan, bewail, blub, blubber, boohoo, bubble, complain, cry, drip, exude, greet, keen, lament, leak, moan, mourn, ooze, pipe, pipe one's eye, pour forth, pour out, rain, snivel, sob, tune one's pipes, ululate, whimper, whine. *antonym* rejoice. *n.* blub, bubble, cry, greet, lament, moan, snivel, sob.

weigh *v.* bear down, burden, carry weight, consider, contemplate, count, deliberate, evaluate, examine, give thought to, impress, matter, mediate on, mull over, oppress, ponder, ponderate, prey, reflect on, study, tell, think over. *antonyms* cut no ice, hearten.

weight *n.* authority, avoirdupois, ballast, burden, clout, consequence, consideration, efficacy, emphasis, force, gravity, heaviness, heft, impact, import, importance, impressiveness, influence, load, mass, millstone, moment, onus, oppression, persuasiveness, ponderance, ponderancy, poundage, power, preponderance, pressure, significance, strain, substance, tonnage, value. *antonym* lightness. *v.* ballast, bias, burden, charge, encumber, freight, handicap, hold down, impede, keep down, load, oppress, overburden, slant, unbalance, weigh down. *antonym* lighten.

weird *adj.* bizarre, creepy, eerie, eldritch, freakish, ghostly, grotesque, mysterious, odd, outlandish, preternatural, queer, spooky, strange, superlunar, supernatural, uncanny, unco, unearthly, unnatural, witching. *antonym* normal.

welcome *adj.* able, acceptable, accepted, agreeable, allowed, appreciated, delightful, desirable, entitled, free, gratifying, permitted, pleasant, pleasing, refreshing. *antonym* unwelcome. *n.* acceptance, greeting, hospitality, reception, red carpet, salaam, salutation. *v.* accept, approve of, embrace, greet, hail, meet, receive, roll out the red carpet for. *antonyms* reject, snub.

weld *v.* bind, bond, cement, connect, fuse, join, link, seal, solder, unite. *antonym* separate. *n.* bond, joint, seal, seam.

welfare *n.* advantage, benefit, good, happiness, heal, health, interest, profit, prosperity, success, weal, well-being. *antonym* harm.

well[1] *n.* bore, cavity, fount, fountain, hole, lift-shaft, mine, pit, pool, repository, shaft, source, spring, water hole, wellspring. *v.* brim over, flood, flow, gush, jet, ooze, pour, rise, run, seep, spout, spring, spurt, stream, surge, swell, trickle.

well[2] *adv.* ably, abundantly, accurately, adeptly, adequately, admirably, agreeably, amply, approvingly, attentively, capitally, carefully, clearly, closely, comfortably, completely, conscientiously, considerably, correctly, deeply, easily, effectively, efficiently, expertly, fairly, famously, favorably, fittingly, flourishingly, fully, glowingly, graciously, greatly, happily, heartily, highly, intimately, justly, kindly, nicely, personally, pleasantly, possibly, proficiently, profoundly, properly, prosperously, readily, rightly, satisfactorily, skillfully, smoothly, splendidly, substantially, successfully, sufficiently, suitably, thoroughly, warmly. *antonym* badly. *adj.* A1, able-bodied, advisable, agreeable, bright, fine, fit, fitting, flourishing, fortunate, good, great, hale, happy, healthy, hearty, in fine fettle, in good health, lucky, on the top of the world, pleasing, profitable, proper, prudent, right, robust, satisfactory, sound, strong, thriving, up to par, useful. *antonyms* bad, ill.

well-being *n.* comfort, contentment, good, happiness, prosperity, weal, welfare. *antonyms* discomfort, harm.

well-bred *adj.* aristocratic, blue-blooded, civil, courteous, courtly, cultivated, cultured, gallant, genteel, gentle, gentlemanly, highborn, ladylike, mannerly, noble, patrician, polished, polite, refined, titled, uppercrust, urbane, well-born, well-brought-up, well-mannered. *antonym* ill-bred.

well-known *adj.* celebrated, famed, familiar, famous, illustrious, notable, noted, popular, renowned. *antonym* unknown.

well-off *adj.* affluent, comfortable, flourishing, flush, fortunate, in the money, loaded, lucky, moneyed, prosperous, rich, successful, thriving, warm, wealthy, well-heeled, well-to-do. *antonym* poor.

well-thought-of *adj.* admired, esteemed, highly regarded, honored, reputable, respected, revered, venerated, weighty. *antonym.* despised.

well-to-to *adj.* affluent, comfortable, flush, loaded, moneyed, prosperous, rich, warm, wealthy, well-heeled, well-off. *antonym* poor.

welsh *v.* cheat, defraud, diddle, do, swindle, welch.

wet *adj.* boggy, clammy, damp, dank, drenched, dripping, drizzling, effete, feeble, foolish, humid, ineffectual, irresolute, misty, moist, moistened, namby-pamby, pouring, raining, rainy, saturated, showery, silly, sloppy, soaked, soaking, sodden, soft, soggy, sopping, soppy, soused, spineless, spongy, teeming, timorous, waterlogged, watery, weak, weedy. *antonyms* dry, resolute, strong. *n.* clamminess, condensation, damp, dampness, drip, drizzle, humidity, liquid, milksop, moisture, rain, rains, sap, water, weakling, weed, wetness, wimp. *antonym* dryness. *v.* bedabble, bedew, bedrench, damp, dampen, dip, douse, drench, humidify, imbue, irrigate, moisten, saturate, sluice, soak, splash, spray, sprinkle, steep, water. *antonym* dry.

wharf *n.* dock, dockyard, jetty, landing stage, marina, pier, quay, quayside.

wheedle *v.* cajole, charm, coax, court, draw, entice, flatter, importune, inveigle, persuade, whilly, whillywha(w). *antonym* force.

whereabouts *n.* location, place, position, site, situation, vicinity.

wherewithal *n.* capital, cash, funds, means, money, necessary, readies, resources, supplies.

whim *n.* caprice, chimera, conceit, concetto, crank, craze, crotchet, fad, fancy, fizgig, flam, freak, humor, impulse, maggot, notion, quirk, sport, urge, vagary, whims(e)y.

whimper *v.* blub, blubber, cry, girn, grizzle, mewl, moan, pule, snivel, sob, weep, whine, whinge. *n.* girn, moan, snivel, sob, whine.

whimsical *adj.* capricious, chimeric(al), crotchety, curious, dotty, droll, eccentric, fanciful, fantastic(al), freakish, funny, maggoty, mischievous, odd, peculiar, playful,

quaint, queer, singular, unusual, waggish, weird, whimmy. *antonym* sensible.

whine *n.* beef, bellyache, complaint, cry, girn, gripe, grouch, grouse, grumble, moan, sob, wail, whimper. *v.* beef, bellyache, complain, cry, girn, gripe, grizzle, grouch, grouse, grumble, kvetch, moan, sob, wail, whimper, whine.

whip *v.* agitate, beat, best, birch, cane, castigate, clobber, compel, conquer, dart, dash, defeat, dive, drive, drub, flagellate, flash, flit, flog, flounce, fly, foment, goad, hammer, hound, incite, instigate, jambok, jerk, knout, lash, leather, lick, outdo, overcome, overpower, overwhelm, paddle, prick, prod, produce, provoke, pull, punish, push, quirt, remove, rout, rush, scourge, shoot, sjambok, snatch, spank, spur, stir, strap, switch, tan, tear, thrash, trounce, urge, whale, whisk, whop, worst. *n.* birch, bullwhip, cane, cat, cat-o'-nine-tails, crop, flagellum, horsewhip, jambok, knout lash, paddle, quirt, rawhide, riding crop, scourge, sjambok, switch, thong.

whirl *v.* birl, circle, gyrate, tyre, pirouette, pivot, reel, revolve, roll, rotate, spin, swirl, swivel, turn, twirl, twist, wheel. *n.* agitation, birl, bustle, circle, commotion, confusion, daze, dither, flurry, giddiness, gyration, tyre, hubbub, hubbuboo, hurly-burly, merry-go-round, pirouette, reel, revolution, roll, rotation, round, series, spin, stir, succession, swirl, tumult, turn, twirl, twist, uproar, vortex, wheel, whorl. *antonym* calm.

whisk *v.* beat, brush, dart, dash, flick, fly, grab, hasten, hurry, race, rush, scoot, shoot, speed, sweep, swipe, tear, twitch, whip, wipe. *n.* beater, brush, swizzle stick.

whisper *v.* breathe, buzz, divulge, gossip, hint, hiss, insinuate, intimate, murmur, rustle, sigh, sough, susurrate, tittle. *antonym* shout. *n.* breath, buzz, gossip, hint, hiss, innuendo, insinuation, murmur, report, rumor, rustle, shadow, sigh, sighing, soughing, soupçon, suggestion, suspicion, susurration, susurrus, swish, tinge, trace, underbreath, undertone, whiff, word. *antonym* roar.

whistle *n.* call, cheep, chirp, hooter, siren, song, warble. *v.* call, cheep, chirp, pipe, siffle, sing, warble, wheeze, whiss.

whole *adj.* better, complete, cured, entire, faultless, fit, flawless, full, good, hale, healed, healthy, in one piece, intact, integral, integrated, inviolate, mint, perfect, recovered, robust, sound, strong, total, unabbreviated, unabridged, unbroken, uncut, undamaged, undivided, unedited, unexpurgated, unharmed, unhurt, unimpaired, uninjured, unmutilated, unscathed, untouched, well. *antonyms* damaged, ill, partial. *n.* aggregate, all, ensemble, entirety, entity, everything, fullness, gestalt, lot, piece, total, totality, unit, unity. *antonym* part.

wholesome *adj.* advantageous, beneficial, clean, decent, edifying, exemplary, good, healthful, health-giving, healthy, helpful, honorable, hygienic, improving, innocent, invigorating, moral, nice, nourishing, nutritious, propitious, pure, respectable, righteous, salubrious, salutary, sanitary, uplifting, virtuous, worthy. *antonym* unwholesome.

wholly *adv.* absolutely, all, altogether, completely, comprehensively, entirely, exclusively, fully, in toto, only, perfectly, solely, thoroughly, through and through, totally, utterly. *antonym* partly.

wicked *adj.* abandoned, abominable, acute, agonizing, amoral, arch, atrocious, awful, bad, black-hearted, bothersome, corrupt, debased, depraved, destructive, devilish, difficult, dissolute, distressing, dreadful, egregious, evil, facinorous, fearful, fiendish, fierce, flagitious, foul, galling, guilty, harmful, heinous, immoral, impious, impish, incorrigible, inexpiable, iniquitous, injurious, intense, irreligious, mighty, mischievous, nasty, naughty, nefarious, nefast, offensive, painful, piacular, rascal-like, rascally, roguish, scandalous, severe, shameful, sinful, spiteful, terrible, troublesome, trying, ungodly, unpleasant, unprincipled, unrighteous, vicious, vile, villainous, worthless. *antonyms* good, harmless, modest, upright.

wide *adj.* ample, away, baggy, broad, capacious, catholic, commodious, comprehensive, diffuse, dilated, distant, distended, encyclopedic, expanded, expansive, extensive, far-reaching, full, general, immense, inclusive, large, latitudinous, loose, off, off-course, off-target, outspread, outstretched, remote, roomy, spacious, sweeping, vast. *antonyms* limited, narrow. *adv.* aside, astray, off course, off target, off the mark, out. *antonym* on target.

wide-awake *adj.* alert, astute, aware, conscious, fully awake, heedful, keen, observant, on one's toes, on the alert, on the ball, on the qui vive, quick-witted, roused, sharp, vigilant, wakened, wary, watchful. *antonym* asleep.

width *n.* amplitude, beam, breadth, compass, diameter, extent, girth, measure, range, reach, scope, span, thickness, wideness.

wield *v.* apply, brandish, command, control, employ, exercise, exert, flourish, handle, have, hold, maintain, manage, manipulate, ply, possess, swing, use, utilize, wave, weave.

wild *adj.* agrest(i)al, barbaric, barbarous, berserk, blustery, boisterous, brutish, chaotic, chimeric(al), choppy, crazed, crazy, daft, delirious, demented, desert, deserted, desolate, disheveled, disordered, disorderly, eager, empty, enthusiastic, excited, extravagant, fantastic, ferae naturae, feral, feralized, ferine, ferocious, fierce, flighty, foolhardy, foolish, frantic, free, frenzied, furious, giddy, godforsaken, howling, hysterical, ill-considered, impetuous, impracticable, imprudent, inaccurate, indigenous, intense, irrational, lawless, mad, madcap, maniacal, native, natural, noisy, nuts, outrageous, potty, preposterous, primitive, rabid, raging, rash, raving, reckless, riotous, rough, rowdy, rude, savage, self-willed, tempestuous, tousled, trackless, turbulent, unbridled, unbroken, uncheated, uncivilized, uncontrollable, uncontrolled, uncultivated, undisciplined, undomesticated, unfettered, ungovernable, uninhabited, unjustified, unkempt, unmanageable, unpopulated, unpruned, unrestrained, unruly, unsubstantiated, untamed, untidy, uproarious, violent, virgin, wayward, woolly. *antonyms* civilized, peaceful, sane, sensible, tame, unenthusiastic.

wilderness *n.* clutter, confusion, congeries, desert, jumble, jungle, mass, maze, muddle, tangle, waste, wasteland, welter, wild, wild-land.

wile *n.* artfulness, artifice, cheating, chicanery, contrivance, craft, craftiness, cunning, deceit, device, dodge, expedient, fraud, guile, hanky-panky, imposition, lure, maneuver, ploy, ruse, slyness, stratagem, subterfuge, trick, trickery. *antonym* guilelessness.

will *n.* aim, attitude, choice, command, decision, declaration, decree, desire, determination, discretion, disposition, fancy, feeling, inclination, intention, mind, option, pleasure, preference, prerogative, purpose, resolution, resolve, testament, velleity, volition, willpower, wish, wishes. *v.* bequeath, bid, cause, choose, command, confer, decree, desire, determine, devise, direct, dispose of, elect, give, leave, opt, ordain, order, pass on, resolve, transfer, want, wish.

willful *adj.* adamant, bloody-minded, bull-headed, conscious, deliberate, determined, dogged, froward, headstrong, inflexible, intended, intentional, intractable, intransigent, mulish, obdurate, obstinate, persistent, perverse, pigheaded, purposeful, refractory, self-willed, stubborn, thrawn, uncompromising, unyielding, volitional, voluntary. *antonyms* complaisant, good-natured.

willing *adj.* agreeable, amenable, biddable, compliant, consenting, content, desirous, disposed, eager, enthusiastic, favorable, game, happy, inclined, nothing lo(a)th, pleased, prepared, ready, so-minded, volitient, willing-hearted. *antonym* unwilling.

wilt *v.* atrophy, diminish, droop, dwindle, ebb, fade, fail, flag, flop, languish, melt away, sag, shrivel, sink, wane, weaken, wither. *antonym* perk up.

wily *adj.* arch, artful, astute, cagey, crafty, crooked, cunning, deceitful, deceptive, designing, fly, foxy, guileful, intriguing, longheaded, Machiavellian, scheming, sharp, shifty, shrewd, sly, tricky, underhand, versute, wileful. *antonym* guileless.

win *v.* accomplish, achieve, acquire, attain, bag, capture, catch, collect, come away with, conquer, earn, gain, get, net, obtain, overcome, pick up, prevail, procure, receive, secure, succeed, sweep the board, triumph. *antonym* lose. *n.* conquest, mastery, success, triumph, victory. *antonym* defeat.

wind[1] *n.* air, air current, babble, blast, blather, bluster, boasting, breath, breeze, clue, current, cyclone, draft, flatulence, flatus, gab, gale, gas, gust, hint, hot air, humbug, hurricane, idle talk, inkling, intimation, northeaster, notice, puff, report, respiration, rumor, sirocco, southwester, suggestion, talk, tidings, tornado, twister, typhoon, warning, whisper, williwaw, windiness, zephyr.

wind[2] *v.* bend, coil, curl, curve, deviate, encircle, furl, loop, meander, ramble, reel, roll, serpent, serpentine, serpentinize, snake, spiral, turn, twine, twist, wreath, zigzag. *n.* bend, curve, meander, turn, twist, zigzag.

windfall *n.* bonanza, find, godsend, jackpot, manna, pennies from heaven, stroke of luck, treasure trove.

windy *adj.* afraid, blowy, blustering, blustery, boastful, boisterous, bombastic, breezy, changeable, chicken, conceited, cowardly, diffuse, empty, fearful, flatulent, flatuous, frightened, garrulous, gusty, long-winded, loquacious, meandering, nervous, pompous, prolix, rambling, scared, squally, stormy, tempestuous, thrasonic, timid, turgid, ventose, verbose, wild, windswept, wordy. *antonyms* calm, fearless, modest.

wing *n.* adjunct, annex, arm, branch, circle, clique, coterie, extension, faction, fender, flank, group, grouping, pinion, protection, section, segment, set, side. *v.* clip, fleet, flit, fly, glide, hasten, hit, hurry, move, nick, pass, race, soar, speed, travel, wound, zoom.

wink *v.* bat, blink, flash, flicker, flutter, gleam, glimmer, glint, nictate, nictitate, pink, sparkly, twinkle. *n.* blink, flash, flutter, gleam, glimmering, glint, hint, instant, jiffy, moment, nictation, nictitation, second, sparkly, split second, twinkle, twinkling.

winnow *v.* comb, cull, diffuse, divide, fan, part, screen, select, separate, sift, waft.

winsome *adj.* agreeable, alluring, amiable, attractive, bewitching, captivating, charming, cheerful, comely, delectable, disarming, enchanting, endearing, engaging, fair, fascinating, fetching, graceful, pleasant, pleasing, prepossessing, pretty, sweet, taking, winning. *antonym* unattractive.

wire-pulling *n.* clout, conspiring, influence, intrigue, Machiavellianism, manipulation, plotting, pull, scheming.

wisdom *n.* anthroposophy, astuteness, circumspection, comprehension, discernment, enlightenment, erudition, foresight, gnosis, intelligence, judgment, judiciousness, knowledge, learning, penetration, prudence, reason, sagacity, sapience, sense, sophia, understanding. *antonym* folly.

wise *adj.* aware, clever, discerning, enlightened, erudite, informed, intelligent, judicious, knowing, longheaded, long-sighted, perceptive, politic, prudent, rational, reasonable, sagacious, sage, sapient, sensible, shrewd, sound, understanding, well-advised, well-informed. *antonym* foolish.

wish *v.* ask, aspire, bid, command, covet, crave, desiderate, desire, direct, greet, hanker, hope, hunger, instruct, long, need, order, require, thirst, want, whim, yearn, yen. *antonyms* dislike, fear. *n.* aspiration, bidding, command, desire, hankering, hope, hunger, inclination, intention, liking, order, request, thirst, urge, velleity, voice, want, whim, will, yearning, yen. *antonyms* dislike, fear.

wispy *adj.* attenuate, attenuated, delicate, diaphanous, ethereal, faint, fine, flimsy, flyaway, fragile, frail, gossamer, insubstantial. *antonym* substantial.

wistful *adj.* contemplative, disconsolate, dreaming, dreamy, forlorn, longing, meditative, melancholy, mournful, musing, pensive, reflective, sad, soulful, thoughtful, wishful, yearning.

wit *n.* acumen, badinage, banter, brains, card, cleverness, comedian, common sense, comprehension, conceit, discernment, drollery, epigrammatist, eutrapelia, facetiousness, farceur, fun, homme d'esprit, humor, humorist, ingenuity, insight, intellect, intelligence, jocularity, joker, judgment, levity, merum sal, mind, nous, perception, pleasantry, punster, quipster, raillery, reason, repartee, sense, smeddum, understanding, wag, wisdom, wit-cracker, wordplay. *antonyms* seriousness, stupidity.

witch *n.* enchantress, hag, hex, lamia, magician, necromancer, occultist, pythoness, sorceress, sortileger, weird, wise- woman, witch-wife.

witchcraft *n.* black magic, conjuration, divination, enchantment, glamour, goety, incantation, invultuation, magic, myalism, necromancy, occultism, pishogue, sorcery, sortilege, sortilegy, spell, the black art, the occult, voodoo, witchery, witching, wizardry.

withdraw *v.* abjure, absent oneself, back out, depart, disavow, disclaim, disengage, disenroll, disinvest, draw back, draw out, drop out, extract, fall back, go, go away, hive off, leave, pull back, pull out, recall, recant, remove, repair, rescind, retire, retract, retreat, revoke, secede, subduct, subtract, take away, take back, take off, unsay, waive. *antonyms* advance, deposit, persist.

wither *v.* abash, blast, blight, decay, decline, desiccate, disintegrate, droop, dry, fade, humiliate, languish, miff, mortify, perish, put down, shame, shrink, shrivel, snub, wane, waste, welt, wilt. *antonyms* boost, thrive.

withhold *v.* check, conceal, deduct, detain, hide, keen, keep back, refuse, repress, reserve, resist, restrain, retain, sit on, suppress, suspend. *antonyms* accord, give.

withstand *v.* bear, brave, combat, confront, cope with, defy, endure, face, grapple with, hold off, hold one's ground, hold out, last out, oppose, put up with, resist, stand, stand fast, stand one's ground, stand up to, survive, take, take on, thwart, tolerate, weather. *antonyms* collapse, yield.

witness *n.* attestant, beholder, bystander, corroborator, deponent, eyewitness, looker-on, observer, onlooker, spectator, testifier, viewer, vouchee, voucher, watcher, witnesser. *v.* attend, attest, bear out, bear witness,

confirm, corroborate, countersign, depone, depose, endorse, look on, mark, note, notice, observe, perceive, see, sign, testify, view, watch.

wits *n.* acumen, astuteness, brains, cleverness, comprehension, faculties, gumption, ingenuity, intelligence, judgment, marbles, mother wit, nous, reason, sense, understanding. *antonym* stupidity.

witty *adj.* amusing, brilliant, clever, comic, droll, epigrammatic, facetious, fanciful, funny, humorous, sparkling, waggish, whimsical. *antonyms* dull, unamusing.

wizard[1] *n.* conjurer, enchanter, mage, magician, magus, necromancer, occultist, shaman, sorcerer, sortileger, thaumaturge, warlock, witch.

wizard[2] *n.* ace, adept, dabster, deacon, expert, genius, hotshot, maestro, master, prodigy, star, virtuoso, whiz. *antonym* duffer. *adj.* ace, brilliant, enjoyable, fab, fantastic, good, great, marvelous, sensational, smashing, super, superb, terrif, terrific, tiptop, topping, tremendous, wonderful. *antonym* rotten.

wizardry *n.* black magic, conjuration, divination, enchantment, glamour, goety, incantation, invultuation, magic, myalism, necromancy, occultism, pishogue, sorcery, sortilege, sortilegy, the black art, the occult, voodoo, warlockry, witchcraft, witchery, witching.

woe *n.* adversity, affliction, agony, anguish, burden, curse, dejection, depression, disaster, distress, dole, dolor, dule, gloom, grief, hardship, heartache, heartbreak, melancholy, misery, misfortune, pain, sadness, sorrow, suffering, tears, trial, tribulation, trouble, unhappiness, wretchedness. *antonym* joy.

woebegone *adj.* blue, crestfallen, dejected, disconsolate, dispirited, doleful, down in the mouth, downcast, downhearted, forlorn, gloomy, grief-stricken, hangdog, long-faced, lugubrious, miserable, mournful, sad, sorrowful, tearful, tear-stained, troubled, wretched. *antonym* joyful.

woman *n.* bride, broad, chambermaid, char, charwoman, chick, dame, daughter, domestic, fair, female, feme, femme, frau, girl, girlfriend, handmaiden, housekeeper, kept woman, lady, lady-in-waiting, ladylove, lass, lassie, maid, maiden, maidservant, mate, miss, mistress, old lady, partner, piece, she, sheila, spouse, sweetheart, wife, woman body. *antonym* man.

womanly *adj.* female, feminine, ladylike, matronly, motherly, weak, womanish. *antonym* manly.

wonder *n.* admiration, amaze, amazement, astonishment, awe, bewilderment, curiosity, fascination, marvel, miracle, nonpareil, phenomenon, portent, prodigy, rarity, sight, spectacle, stupefaction, surprise, wonderment, wunderkind. *antonyms* disinterest, ordinariness. *v.* ask oneself, boggle, conjecture, doubt, gape, gaup, gawk, inquire, marvel, meditate, ponder, puzzle, query, question, speculate, stare, think.

wonderful *adj.* ace, admirable, amazing, astonishing, astounding, awe-inspiring, awesome, brilliant, épatant, excellent, extraordinary, fab, fabulous, fantastic, great, incredible, magnificent, marvelous, mirac-ulous, mirific(al), odd, outstanding, peculiar, phenomenal, remarkable, sensational, smashing, staggering, startling, strange, stupendous, super, superb, surprising, terrif, terrific, tip-top, top-hole, topping, tremendous, unheard-of, wizard, wondrous. *antonyms* ordinary, rotten.

wooden *adj.* awkward, blank, clumsy, colorless, deadpan, dense, dim, dim-witted, dull, dull-witted, emotionless, empty, expressionless, gauche, gawky, glassy, graceless, inelegant, inflexible, lifeless, ligneous, maladroit, muffled, oaken, obstinate, obtuse, rigid, slow, spiritless, stiff, stupid, thick, timber, treen, unbending, unemotional, ungainly, unresponsive, unyielding, vacant, woody, xyloid. *antonyms* bright, lively.

word *n.* account, advice, affirmation, assertion, assurance, bidding, bulletin, chat, colloquy, command, commandment, comment, communication, communiqué, confab, confabulation, consultation, conversation, countersign, declaration, decree, discussion, dispatch, edict, expression, firman, go-ahead, green light, guarantee, hint, information, intelligence, interlocution, intimation, lexigram, locution, mandate, message, news, notice, oath, order, palabra, parole, password, pledge, promise, remark, report, rescript, rumor, sign, signal, slogan, talk, term, tête-à-tête, tidings, ukase, undertaking, utterance, vocable, vow, warcry, watchword, will. *v.* couch, explain, express, phrase, put, say, write.

wordy *adj.* diffuse, discursive, garrulous, longiloquent, long-winded, loquacious, phrasy, pleonastic, prolix, rambling, verbose, windy. *antonyms* concise, laconic.

work *n.* achievement, art, assignment, book, business, calling, chore, commission, composition, craft, creation, darg, deed, doings, drudgery, duty, effort, elbow grease, employ, employment, exertion, graft, grind, handiwork, industry, job, labor, line, livelihood, métier, occupation, oeuvre, office, opus, performance, piece, play, poem, production, profession, pursuit, service, skill, slog, stint, sweat, task, toil, trade, travail, undertaking, workload, workmanship. *antonyms* hobby, play, rest. *v.* accomplish, achieve, act, arrange, beaver, bring about, cause, contrive, control, convulse, create, cultivate, dig, direct, drive, drudge, effect, encompass, execute, exploit, farm, fashion, fiddle, fix, force, form, function, go, graft, handle, implement, knead, labor, make, manager, maneuver, manipulate, mold, move, operate, peg away, perform, ply, process, progress, pull off, run, shape, slave, slog, sweat, swing, till, toil, twitch, use, wield, writhe. *antonyms* fail, play, rest.

workable *adj.* doable, effectible, feasible, possible, practicable, practical, realistic, viable. *antonym* unworkable.

working *n.* action, functioning, manner, method, operation, routing, running. *adj.* active, employed, functioning, going, laboring, operational, operative, running. *antonyms* idle, inoperative, retired, unemployed.

workmanlike *adj.* adept, careful, efficient, expert, masterly, painstaking, professional, proficient, satisfactory, skilled, skillful, thorough, workmanly. *antonym* amateurish.

workmanship *n.* art, artistry, craft, craftsmanship, execution, expertise, facture, finish, handicraft, handiwork, manufacture, skill, technique, work.

world *n.* age, area, class, creation, days, division, domain, earth, environment, epoch, era, existence, field, globe, human race, humanity, humankind, kingdom, life, man, mankind, men, nature, people, period, planet, province, public, realm, society, sphere, star, system, terrene, times, universe.

wordly *adj.* ambitious, avaricious, blasé, carnal, cosmopolitan, covetous, earthly, experienced, fleshly, grasping, greedy, knowing, lay, materialistic, mundane, physical, politic, profane, secular, selfish, sophisticated, sublunary, temporal, terrene, terrestrial, unspiritual, urbane, worldly-minded, worldly-wise. *antonym* unworldly.

worn *adj.* attrite, bromidic, careworn, clichéd, drawn, exhausted, fatigued, frayed, hackneyed, haggard, jaded, lined, pinched, played-out, ragged, shabby, shiny, spent, tattered, tatty, threadbare, tired, trite, wearied, weary, wizened, woe-wearied, woe-worn, worn-out. *antonyms* fresh, new.

worried *adj.* afraid, agonized, anxious, apprehensive, bothered, concerned, distracted, distraught, distressed, disturbed, fearful, frabbit, fretful, frightened, ill at ease, nervous, on edge, overwrought, perturbed, strained, tense, tormented, troubled, uneasy, unquiet, upset. *antonyms* calm, unconcerned, unworried.

worry *v.* agonize, annoy, attack, badger, bite, bother, brood, disquiet, distress, disturb, faze, fret, get one's knickers in a twist, gnaw at, go for, harass, harry, hassle, hector, importune, irritate, kill, lacerate, nag, perturb, pester, plague, savage, tantalize, tear, tease, torment, trouble, unsettle, upset, vex. *antonyms* comfort, reassure. *n.* agitation, annoyance, anxiety, apprehension, care, concern, disturbance, fear, irritation, misery, misgiving, perplexity, pest, plague, problem, stew, tew, tizz, tizzy, torment, trial, trouble, unease, vexation, woe, worriment. *antonyms* comfort, reassurance.

worsen *v.* aggravate, damage, decay, decline, degenerate, deteriorate, disimprove, exacerbate, go downhill, pejorate, retrogress, sink, take a turn for the worse. *antonym* improve.

worship *v.* adore, adulate, deify, exalt, glorify, honor, idolatrize, idolize, kanticoy, laud, love, misworship, praise, pray to, respect, revere, reverence, venerate. *antonym* despise. *n.* adoration, adulation, deification, devotion(s), dulia, exaltation, glorification, glory, homage, honor, hyperdulia, image worship, knee drill, latria, latry, laudation, love, misdevotion, misworship, monolatry, praise, prayer(s), regard, respect, reverence, will worship. *antonym* vilification.

worth *n.* aid, assistance, avail, benefit, cost, credit, desert(s), excellence, goodness, help, importance, merit, price, quality, rate, significance, use, usefulness, utility, value, virtue, worthiness. *antonym* worthlessness.

worthless *adj.* abandoned, abject, base, beggarly, contemptible, depraved, despicable, draffish, draffy, futile, good-for-nothing, grotty, ignoble, ineffectual, insignificant, littleworth, meaningless, miserable, no use, no-account, nugatory, paltry, pointless, poor, rubbishy, scabbed, scabby, screwy, stramineous, trashy, trifling, trivial, unavailing, unimportant, unusable, useless, valueless, vile, wretched. *antonym* valuable.

worthy *adj.* admirable, appropriate, commendable, creditable, decent, dependable, deserving, estimable, excellent, fit, good, honest, honorable, laudable, meritorious, praiseworthy, reliable, reputable, respectable, righteous, suitable, upright, valuable, virtuous, worthwhile. *antonyms* disreputable, unworthy. *n.* big cheese, big noise, big pot, big shot, bigwig, dignitary, luminary, name, notable, personage.

wound *n.* anguish, cut, damage, distress, gash, grief, harm, heartbreak, hurt, injury, insult, laceration, lesion, offense, pain, pang, scar, shock, slash, slight, torment, torture, trauma. *v.* annoy, bless, cut, cut to the quick, damage, distress, gash, grieve, harm, hit, hurt, injure, irritate, lacerate, mortify, offend, pain, pierce, pip, shock, slash, sting, traumatize, wing, wring someone's withers.

wrangle *n.* altercation, argument, argybargy, barney, bickering, brawl, clash, contest, controversy, dispute, quarrel, row, set-to, slanging match, squabble, tiff, tussle. *antonym* agreement. *v.* altercate, argue, argufy, bicker, brawl, contend, digladiate, disagree, dispute, ergotize, fall out, fight, quarrel, row, scrap, squabble. *antonym* agree.

wrap *v.* absorb, bind, bundle up, cloak, cocoon, cover, encase, enclose, enfold, envelop, fold, hap, immerse, muffle, pack, package, roll up, sheathe, shroud, surround, swathe, wind. *antonym* unwrap. *n.* cape, cloak, mantle, pelisse, robe, shawl, stole.

wrath *n.* anger, bitterness, choler, displeasure, exasperation, fury, indignation, ire, irritation, passion, rage, resentment, spleen, temper. *antonyms* calm, pleasure.

wreck *v.* break, crab, demolish, destroy, devastate, mar, play havoc with, ravage, ruin, shatter, smash, spoil, torpedo, write off. *antonyms* repair, save. *n.* derelict, desolation, destruction, devastation, disruption, hulk, mess, overthrow, ruin, ruination, shipwreck, undoing, write-off.

wrench *v.* distort, force, jerk, pull, rax, rick, rip, sprain, strain, tear, tug, twist, upheaval, uprooting.

wrestle *v.* battle, combat, contend, contest, fight, grapple, scuffle, strive, struggle, tussle, vie.

wretch *n.* blackguard, cad, caitiff, cullion, cut, good-for-nothing, insect, miscreant, outcast, profligate, rapscallion, rascal, rascal lion, rat, rogue, rotter, ruffian, scoundrel, swine, vagabond, villain, wight, worm.

wretched *adj.* abject, base, brokenhearted, caitiff, calamitous, cheerless, comfortless, contemptible, crestfallen, dejected, deplo-rable, depressed, despicable, disconsolate, distressed, doggone, doleful, downcast, forlorn, gloomy, grotty, hapless, hopeless, inferior, low, low-down, mean, melancholy, miserable, paltry, pathetic, pesky, pitiable, pitiful, poor, ratty, scurvy, shabby, shameful, sorry, unfortunate, unhappy, vile, woebegone, woeful, worthless. *antonyms* excellent, happy.

write *v.* compose, copy, correspond, create, draft, draw up, indite, inscribe, jot down, pen, record, screeve, scribble, scribe, set down, take down, tell, transcribe.

writer *n.* amanuensis, author, authoress, clerk, columnist, copyist, crime writer, detectivist, dialogist, diarist, diatribist, dramatist, dramaturg, dramaturgist, elegiast, elegist, encomiast, epigrammatist, epistler, epistolarian, epistoler, epistolist, epitapher, epitaphist, epitomist, essayist, farceur, fictionist, hack, librettist, littérateur, man of letters, memoirist, novelist, panegyrist, paper-stainer, pen, penman, penny-a-liner, penpusher, penwoman, periodicalist, playwright, prosaist, proseman, proser, prose writer, quill-driver, scribbler, scribe, secretary, wordsmith, writeress.

writhe *v.* coil, contort, jerk, squirm, struggle, thrash, thresh, toss, twist, wiggle, wreathe, wriggle.

wrong *adj.* abusive, amiss, askew, awry, bad, blameworthy, criminal, crooked, defective, dishonest, dishonorable, erroneous, evil, fallacious, false, faulty, felonious, funny, illegal, illicit, immoral, improper, in error, in the wrong, inaccurate, inappropriate, inapt, incongruous, incorrect, indecorous, infelicitous, iniquitous, inner, inside, inverse, malapropos, misinformed, mistaken, off-beam, off-target, off-base, opposite, out, out of commission, out of order, reprehensible, reverse, sinful, unacceptable, unbecoming, unconventional, under, undesirable, unethical, unfair, unfitting, unhappy, unjust, unlawful, unseemly, unsound, unsuitable, untrue, wicked, wide of the mark, wrongful. *adv.* amiss, askew, astray, awry, badly, erroneously, faultily, improperly, inaccurately, incorrectly, mistakenly, wrongly. *n.* abuse, crime, error, grievance, immorality, inequity, infraction, infringement, iniquity, injury, injustice, misdeed, offense, sin, sinfulness, transgression, trespass, unfairness, wicked-

ness, wrongdoing. *v.* abuse, cheat, discredit, dishonor, harm, hurt, ill-treat, ill-use, impose on, injure, malign, maltreat, misrepresent, mistreat, oppress, traduce.

wry *adj.* askew, aslant, awry, contorted, crooked, deformed, distorted, droll, dry, ironic, mocking, pawky, perverse, sarcastic, sardonic, thrawn, twisted, uneven, warped. *antonym* straight.

Y

yank *v.* haul, heave, jerk, pull, snatch, tug, wrench.

yap *v.* babble, blather, chatter, go on, gossip, jabber, jaw, prattle, talk, tattle, twattle, ya(c)k, yammer, yatter, yelp, yip.

yard *n.* court, courtyard, garden, garth, hypaethron, quad, quadrangle.

yarn¹ *n.* abb, fiber, fingering, gimp, lisle, thread.

yarn² *n.* anecdote, cock-and-bull story, fable, fabrication, story, tale, tall story.

yawn *v.* gape, ga(u)nt, open, split.

yearly *adj.* annual, per annum, per year. *adv.* annually, every year, once a year.

yearn for *v.* ache for, covet, crave, desire, hanker for, hunger for, itch for, languish for, long for, lust for, pant for, pine for, want, wish for, yen for. *antonym* dislike.

yell *v.* bawl, bellow, holler, hollo, howl, roar, scream, screech, shout, shriek, squawl, squeal, whoop, yelp, yowl. *n.* bellow, cry, holler, hollo, howl, roar, scream, screech, shriek, squawl, whoop, yelp. *antonym* whisper.

yellow *adj.* flavescent, flaxen, fulvid, fulvous, gold, golden, lemon, primrose, saffron, vitellary, vitelline, xanthic, xanthochromic, xanthomelanous, xanthous.

yelp *v.* bark, bay, cry, yap, yell, yip, yowl. *n.* bark, cry, yap, yell, yip, yowl.

yen *n.* craving, desire, hankering, hunger, itch, longing, lust, passion, thing, yearning. *antonym* dislike.

yield¹ *v.* abandon, abdicate, accede, acquiesce, admit defeat, agree, allow, bow, capitulate, cave in, cede, comply, concede, consent, cry quits, give, give in, give way, go along with, grant, knuckle under, part with, permit, relinquish, resign, resign oneself, submit, succumb, surrender, throw in the towel. *antonym* withstand.

yield² *v.* afford, bear, bring forth, bring in, earn, fructify, fructuate, fruit, furnish, generate, give, net, pay, produce, provide, return, supply. *n.* crop, earning, harvest, income, output, proceeds, produce, product, profit, return, revenue, takings.

yielding *adj.* accommodating, acquiescent, amenable, biddable, complaisant, compliant, docile, easy, elastic, flexible, obedient, obliging, pliable, pliant, quaggy, resilient, soft, spongy, springy, submissive, supple, tractable, unresisting. *antonyms* obstinate, solid.

yoke *n.* bond, bondage, burden, chain, coupling, enslavement, helotry, ligament, link, oppression, serfdom, service, servility, servitude, slavery, subjugation, thralldom, tie, vassalage. *v.* bracket, connect, couple, enslave, harness, hitch, inspan, join, link, tie, unite. *antonym* unhitch.

yokel *n.* boor, bucolic, bumpkin, clodhopper, cornball, country cousin, hick, hillbilly, jake, peasant, rustic.

young *adj.* adolescent, baby, callow, cub, early, fledgling, green, growing, immature, infant, junior, juvenile, little, new, recent, unblown, unfledged, youthful. *antonym* old. *n.* babies, brood, chicks, cubs, family, fledglings, issue, litter, little ones, offspring, progeny, quiverful. *antonym* parents.

youngster *n.* boy, girl, juvenile, kid, lad, laddie, lass, lassie, nipper, shaver, teenybopper, urchin, young pup, youth.

youthful *adj.* active, boyish, childish, ephebic, fresh, girlish, immature, inexperienced, juvenescent, juvenile, lively, pubescent, puerile, sprightly, spry, vigorous, vivacious, well-preserved, young. *antonyms* aged, languorous.

youthfulness *n.* freshness, juvenileness, juvenility, liveliness, sprightliness, spryness, vigor, vivaciousness, vivacity. *antonyms* agedness, languor.

yowl *v.* bay, caterwaul, cry, howl, screech, squall, ululate, wail, yell, yelp. *n.* cry, howl, screech, wail, yell, yelp.

Z

zany *adj.* amusing, clownish, comical, crazy, daft, droll, eccentric, funny, goofy, kooky, loony, madcap, nutty, screwy, wacky. *antonym* serious. *n.* buffoon, card, clown, comedian, cure, droll, fool, jester, joker, kook, laugh, merry-andrew, nut, nutcase, nutter, screwball, wag.

zeal *n.* ardor, dedication, devotion, eagerness, earnestness, enthusiasm, fanaticism, fervency, fervor, fire, gusto, keenness, militancy, passion, spirit, verve, warmth, zelotypia, zest. *antonym* apathy.

zealot *n.* bigot, devotee, enthusiast, extremist, fanatic, fiend, freak, maniac, militant.

zealous *adj.* ardent, burning, devoted, eager, earnest, enthusiastic, fanatical, fervent, fervid, fired, gung ho, impassioned, keen, militant, passionate, rabid, spirited. *antonym* apathetic.

zenith *n.* acme, apex, apogee, climax, culmination, height, high point, meridian, peak, pinnacle, summit, top, vertex. *antonym* nadir.

zero *n.* bottom, cipher, duck, goose egg, love, nadir, naught, nil, nothing, nought.

zest *n.* appetite, charm, delectation, élan, enjoyment, flavor, gusto, interest, joie de vivre, keenness, kick, peel, piquancy, pungency, relish, rind, savor, smack, spice, tang, taste, zeal, zing. *antonym* apathy.

zip *n.* brio, drive, élan, energy, enthusiasm, get-up-and-go, go, gusto, life, liveliness, oomph, pep, pizzazz, punch, sparkle, spirit, verve, vigor, vim, vitality, zest, zing. *antonym* listlessness. *v.* dash, flash, fly, gallop, hurry, race, rush, scoot, shoot, speed, tear, whiz, whoosh, zoom.

zone *n.* area, belt, district, region, section, sector, sphere, stratum, territory, tract, zona, zonule, zonulet.

zoo *n.* animal park, aquarium, aviary, menagerie, safari park, zoological gardens.